By the same Author

MEDIÆVAL LATIN LYRICS
(Fourth Edition)

◆

PETER ABELARD
A Novel
(16th Impression)

THE WANDERING S

THE WANDERING SCHOLARS

by

HELEN WADDELL

Seventh Edition

LONDON
CONSTABLE & CO LTD

PUBLISHED BY
Constable and Company Ltd.
LONDON
•
Oxford University Press
BOMBAY CALCUTTA MADRAS
•
The Macmillan Company
of Canada, Limited
TORONTO

First Published, April 1927.
Second Edition, August 1927.
Third Edition, December 1927.
Fourth Edition, January 1929.
Fifth Edition, January 1930.
Sixth Edition (revised and enlarged), October 1932.
Seventh Edition (revised), February 1934.

PRINTED IN GREAT BRITAIN BY ROBERT MACLEHOSE AND CO. LTD.
THE UNIVERSITY PRESS, GLASGOW

PREFACE

THIS study of the *Vagantes* is little more than the scaffolding of its subject. It was begun as an introduction to a book of translations from mediaeval Latin lyric, soon to be published, and outgrew the original intention, without outgrowing its limitations. The historical interest of the *Vagantes* as one of the earliest disintegrating forces in the mediaeval church has been left on one side; with it, their place in literary history, in the development of satire and the secularising of the stage. They have been studied only as the inheritors of the pagan learning, the classic tradition that came to its wild flowering in the rhyming Latin lyric of the twelfth and thirteenth centuries.

To Professor Saintsbury, in whom that lyric finds its last and greatest lover, the book owes more than actual accomplishment may warrant; and his running commentary on manuscript and proof has sometimes found its way into footnotes that hardly need his initials for identification. To Professor Gregory Smith for unwearying suggestion and criticism, again both in manuscript and proof, I have to acknowledge what is only the most recently incurred of many debts. Mr. Robin Flower has been good enough to read in proof the chapter on the Irish scholars, and to give me the use of his delightful version of *Pangur Bán*.

My last debt is to two colleges in Oxford: to Lady Margaret Hall, which made me Susette Taylor Fellow for the two years in Paris in which the research for the book was completed, and pursued me with many kindnesses during the third in which it was written; and to Somerville College, whose hospitality to a *vagans* six years ago saw it first begun.

HELEN WADDELL.

LONDON,
December, 1926.

NOTE TO THE SIXTH EDITION

THAT this edition is less imperfect than its predecessors is a good deal due to the kindness of several readers, especially of Professor C. H. Haskins, Professor E. F. Jacob, Miss E. M. Jamison, Mr. Henry Broadbent, and Mr. A. L. Poole. The text has been revised, a table of biographical dates added, and since much has been written on the medieval Latin lyric since 1926, when this book went to press, a new list of authorities has been compiled.

The five years which have passed since its first publication have only deepened the note of apology of the original preface. For in spite of its title, this is far from being an adequate history of the Vagantes, *tamquam folium a vento rapitur, et quasi scintilla in arundinete,* leaves caught by the wind, sparks in the brushwood, of medieval literature and history. It is the record, as they appeared to one reader, of the visitations of lyric beauty as fugitive and swift as they, in medieval verse: not among the vernaculars, which have all men's praise, but in the Low Latin which seemed for long enough no better than the discoloured stubble of harvests long since gathered.

This deprecation of the title raises another question. The trend of modern scholarship is to abandon the old romantic name of *Vagantenlieder*, goliard poetry, and to call the whole corpus of this kind of verse, "secular clerical lyric." [1] Wilhelm Meyer came even to speak of the *Vagantenmythus*, and (though one remembers that Andrew Lang once disposed of Mr. Gladstone as a solar myth) there was reason for his exasperation. Golias, richly gifted and ubiquitous though he was, did not write all the lyrics of the great age; and before crediting him, as even the cautious Schumann does, with the Bacchanalian verse, it is sobering to reflect that the greatest drinking song in English,

"Back and sides go bare, go bare."

is laid to the charge of a Prebendar of Durham.

The truth is that, with very few exceptions, there is no pigeon-holing possible. We cannot often say that this was written by a vagabond and this by an archdeacon: one tremendous indictment of the Curia that suggests the embittered *vagans* was in fact the work of the Chancellor of Notre Dame. And apart from the inveterate romanticism of the

[1] I have myself preferred to call it, as in Chapter IX., "The Scholars' Lyric," for this covers both religious and profane, and the Archpoet, like Sedulius Scotus before him, Villon and Dunbar after him, was capable of both.

human mind, there was some justification for the instinct that grouped these lyrics of satire and love and wine as *Vagantenlieder* or goliardic verse, just as Herrick, a Devonshire rector, is liable to be called a Cavalier lyrist. The name of Golias, ancestor of Pantagruel and Panurge alike, is mighty yet. The *Carmina Burana* may be, as its latest editor suggests, an anthology commissioned by a wealthy amateur, bishop or abbot, and not, in the old romantic hypothesis, the copy of a goliard's song-book. Yet it cannot be too often remembered that lyrics in the Middle Ages were made to be sung, not to be read ; and that some of these at any rate were sung for bread. The Archpoet at the beginning of the tradition, and Villon at the end, have stamped their image on this ancient coinage.

The date and place of the actual compilation of the *Carmina Burana* have been brought in question by its latest editors.[1] Wilhelm Meyer, to whose years of patient and inspired work on the text they give affectionate recognition, held that the manuscript was written about 1225, and in the Moselle valley. Otto Schumann is convinced, from the dialect of the German poems scattered through it, that it was written in Bavaria, possibly in Benedictbeuern itself : he holds, moreover, that it must be dated in the last years of the thirteenth century. He admits that the handwriting of one of the three copyists at work upon it suggests the earlier date, as well as the use of the old-fashioned neums instead of choral notation : but this he explains by the remoteness of the region of its origin. The " Stilcharacter " of the German lyrics belongs, he says, to late minnesong ; and in the form of a section of the Latin poems, lovesongs and springsongs, he detects the signs of the decay of the art. " Confronted with such clear internal evidence as we have here, the arguments from palæography must retire into the background." The doctrine may seem heretical ; but the application of it is an admirable piece of reasoning. The actual " deutlich inhaltliche Kriterien " will be found in his article, " Die deutsche Lieder der Carmina Burana," *Germanisch-Romanische Monatsschrift*, 1926, and are summarised in the masterly if controversial preface to the critical text. His conclusion is that by setting it in the closing years of the thirteenth century, the *Carmina* finds its place among its kindred, the great MSS. of Middle High German lovesong. " For medieval Latin, as for Middle High German poetry, the burst of bloom was over : and men were fain to gather the harvest into barns." It is a lovely metaphor : dangerous only if it suggests that their ingathering was autumn fruit already touched with frost, and not this miracle of bud and blossom.

H. W.

PRIMROSE HILL,
September, 1932.

[1] *Carmina Burana :* mit Benutzung der Vorarbeiten Wilhelm Meyers Kritisch herausgegeben von Alfons Hilka und Otto Schumann. Bd. i. II. Heidelberg, 1930.

CONTENTS

APPENDICES

INTRODUCTION

THERE is no beginning, this side the classics, to a history of mediaeval Latin ; its roots take hold too firmly on the kingdoms of the dead. The scholar's lyric of the twelfth century seems as new a miracle as the first crocus ; but its earth is the leafdrift of centuries of forgotten scholarship. His emotional background is of his own time ; his literary background is pagan, and such furniture as his mind contains is classical or pseudo-classical. The great Age of the Augustans is to us a thing set in amber, a civilisation distinct and remote like the Chinese : there is a whole world of literature, created in another language, between us and them. To the mediaeval scholar, with no sense of perspective, but a strong sense of continuity, Virgil and Cicero are but upper reaches of the river that still flows past his door. The language in which they wrote is still the medium of the artist, even the creative artist : it was so, even in the seventeenth century, to Milton, still more to Bacon. Gautier de Châtillon wrote an epic on Alexander, and the scholars of the next generation compare him with Virgil just as naturally as Macaulay compares Jane Austen with Shakespeare. Another scholar, lecturing on the two kinds of poetry, metrical and rhythmic, says that Virgil is the best example of the first, Primas of the second, just as naturally as a lecturer on blank verse and the heroic couplet would instance Milton and Pope.[1] The gulf between the god of Renaissance idolatry and the disreputable canon of Orleans does not exist for him : they simply used the same medium

[1] Thomas of Capua. See Thurot, *Notices et Extraits*, xxii. 2. 418.

in different ways. Moreover, the sacred canon of classical Latin is not yet closed: a thirteenth century text book ranges from Ovid and Cicero to Gautier de Châtillon and Matthew of Vendôme, as our own range from Chaucer to William Morris and Swinburne.[1] Peter of Blois, archdeacon of Bath, thinks it was very good for his style that he once had to learn by heart the letters of Hildebert; those letters had been written only a generation before, but were already models of prose composition:[2] and as for his own works, Peter modestly concludes that they will outlast ruin and flood and fire and the manifold procession of the centuries.[3] Latin in the twelfth century was a study of as much practical importance as English composition in the twentieth. It was not only the language of literature, of the Church, of the law-courts, of all educated men, but of ordinary correspondence: the language in which a student will write home for a pair of boots,[4] or suggest that it is the part of a discreet sister to inflame the affection of the relations, nay, even the brother-in-law, of a deserving scholar, who at the moment has neither sheets to his bed, nor shirt to his back, and in which she will reply that she is sending him two pairs of sheets and 100 sol., but not a word to my husband, or "I shall be dead and destroyed [*mortua essem penitus et destructa*]. I think he means to send you something himself";[5] or, a more delicate matter, to a sweetheart, that he sees a fellow-student ruffling it in the girdle he had given her, and fears her favours have gone with it. "I could stand the loss of the belt," says he magnificently.[6] Clearly, an even livelier language than the Latin of Erasmus or More.

[1] *Laborintus.* Text in Faral, *Les Arts poétiques du XIIe et du XIIIe Siècle.*

[2] *Chart. Univ. Paris*, i. 27.

[3] Peter of Blois, *Epist.* 77. Migne, *P.L.* 207, c. 238.

[4] *Bibl. Ec. Ch.* 1855, p. 454. Cf. B.N. MS. Lat. 1093 f. 82 *v.*

[5] *Ib.* 8653, f. 13.

[6] *Ib.* 1093, f. 67 *v.*

THE PAGAN LEARNING

Petrarch has too long been taken at his own valuation, the first to whom the ancient world was solid, more than a flat decorated surface ; to whom Virgil and Cicero were brother and father, rather than a book of Sibylline magic and an impersonal fountain of rhetoric. "What says our Arbiter," says John of Salisbury affectionately every few pages ; it is as though the archdeacon has the Arbiter of Elegance by the arm. Those who come to John for information on contemporary manners do so warily ; he may so easily be thinking of the court of Augustus, not of Henry II. Not many knew the classics as John did ; but such as they do know they treat with friendliness, as distinguished contemporaries. Homer was a clerk marvellous, says Benoît de Sainte-More; there was not much that Homer did not know. Sallust, too, Sallust was a clerk marvellous, and Sallust had a nephew, Cornelius Nepos, who was also a great clerk, and lectured at Athens. And one day when he went to look in an *armoire* for a book on grammar, before his lecture, he found instead a diary written by a Trojan called Dares, who was shut up in Troy all through the siege, who also was a great clerk but a fighter too. And of course it is better to believe Dares than Homer, who was born by his own showing a hundred years after Troy was burnt, and had his facts only by hearsay : but all the same Homer was a great clerk.[1] Then there is the thirteenth century story of the two clerks who went to the tomb of Ovid to ask what in his opinion was the best line he ever wrote : to whom a sonorous voice made answer,

"Virtue it is to abstain even from that which is lawful."

And the worst line ? ventured the second student.

"Whatsoever delights is accounted by Jove to be righteous."

Much edified, and moved by the chastening of so great a talent, the two fell to prayer, Paternosters and Aves, for

[1] *Roman de Troie*, i. ll. 45 *et seq.*

the redemption of the enlightened spirit, but a third time the great voice boomed upon them,

"I like not Paternosters: travellers, go your way."[1]

To the scholars who invented that story, Ovid was something more than one of the "auctores"; in the old phrase of divinity, they had recognised his person.

Moreover, to return to Benoît de Sainte-More, this interest in the right way of it at Troy is not merely academic. Not one of the barbarian races but believed they had ancestors in the Great Dispersion; to have fought on the right side at Troy was to have come over with the Conqueror. The tendency had been noticed very early. Cicero sneered in the House at the pretensions of the half-baked barbarians shouldering themselves into the mellow radiance of the Roman orbit.[2] Cassiodorus the undefeated discovered an ancestor in Troy for his enormous client, Theodoric himself;[3] and the Normans sat more firmly on the English throne when Geoffrey of Monmouth and Wace traced out their common Trojan ancestry with Arthur and the Britons, with an industry worthy of the College of Arms. Western Europe was an immense family party; and Trojan, unlike Greek, remains an adjective of unequivocal praise. Dares, the Trojan diarist, was much more popular in Western libraries than Dictys, the equally impudent forgery on the side of the Greeks; while Dictys was much tasted in the Eastern Empire.

This liveliness is not the popular impression of mediaeval scholarship; but this is a good deal due to the diabolic and immortal parody of the sixteenth century, of Erasmus, of Rabelais, of the *Epistolae Obscurorum Virorum*. "*Ista est via qua debemus studere in poetria* . . . Sallust and such like poets."[4] It was true enough for the fifteenth

[1] B.M. MS. Harl. 219 f. 12. Wright, *Latin Stories*, p. 43.

[2] Joly, *Benoît de Sainte-More*, p. 117.

[3] Hodgkin, iii. 294.

[4] *Epist. Obscurorum Virorum*, i. 7; i. 28.

century outside Italy, and for the fourteenth, when theology and law and the commercial spirit among them had killed the study of classics at the Universities. Already in the thirteenth century John of Garland complained that the grass was withering in the ancient fields,

> " withers the Latin tongue,
> The springtime fields of the old poets are bare.
> Across the flowering fields the North wind blows,
> And they are winter-starved."

He would have had the poets restored by law if he could.[1] Yet only a quarter century before a good Puritan grammarian had complained that the old gods were worshipped again at Orleans, that Faunus and Bacchus had their altars and their feasts,

> " Sacrificare deis nos edocet Aurelianis
> Indicens festum Fauni, Iovis atque Liei." [2]

Professorial commentary on the classics, from the days of Virgilius Maro of Toulouse to Brother Conrad Dollenkopf[3] was sapless enough: it is not often, perhaps, intoxicating. But the effect of the actual reading of the classics is evident on the minds that they took captive, in the splendid melancholy prose of St. Peter Damian and John of Salisbury; in the unbroken chain of lyric from Paul the Deacon's sonnet in praise of Lake Garda to the crystalline enchantment of

> " Dum Dianae vitrea
> Sero lampas oritur ";

above all, in the persisting dread of the Church. " We are in danger, we who read the writings of the pagan

1
> " emarcet lingua latina
> Auctorum vernans exaruit area, pratum
> Florigerum boreas flatu livente perussit."

Quoted by Delisle, *Les Écoles d'Orléans*, p. 8. See Paetow, *The Arts Course at Mediaeval Universities*, pp. 16, 18, 42.

2 Alexandre de Ville-Dieu, *Ecclesiale*, Thurot, *ib.* 115.

3 *Epist. Obsc. Vir.* I. 28.

poets," was said, not by Jerome in the fourth century face to face with a paganism dying indeed, yet dying dangerously, but by Nicholas, Chancellor of the University of Paris in 1285.[1] "Not by burning incense, but by a too ardent reading of the poets," says Jacques de Vitry, "do we worship the gods."[2] The opposition is not the natural antagonism of the illiterate to a knowledge too high for it, the crassness of the Philistines. There are instances of that. Gregory the Great was not an imaginative man; and when the report reached him "which we cannot mention without a blush," that the Bishop of Vienne was expounding grammar to his friends, his scolding is precisely Jack Cade's complaint to Lord Say: "It will be proved to thy face that thou hast men about thee that usually talk of a noun and a verb and such abominable words as no Christian ear can endure to hear."[3] But for the most part the opposition came from men who had found in pagan literature a place unholy but enchanted, the shore of the lotus, the coast of the Sirens. "And not only pagan literature," says Paulinus of Nola, "but the whole sensible appearance of things (*omnes rerum temporalium species*) is the lotus flower; so men forget their own land, which is God, the country of us all."[4] "The whole sensible appearance of things,"—it is the mystic's dread, Buddhist or Christian, of the Great Illusion, and in a single sentence Paulinus has pierced to the secret antagonism, deeper than any occasional wantonness or cult of the gods, between the old poets and the new faith, has revealed unconsciously that which is at once the weakness and the strength of Latin literature, its absorp-

[1] Hauréau, *Notices et Extraits*, iv. p. 155.

[2] Thurot, *op. cit.* p. 202. Jacques is quoting Isidore of Seville, *De Sum. Bon.* c. 13.

[3] Greg. *Epist.* ix. 54. The jest is Hauréau's. See Poole, *Illustrations of Mediaeval Thought*, p. 7. Yet in justice to Gregory, Gratian explains that he rebuked the bishop not because he taught grammar, but because he taught it in place of the Evangel. (*Decret.* i. Dist. 37, c. 8.)

[4] Migne, *P.L.* lxi. Epist. 16.

tion in the actual. For with what else but "the sensible appearance of things" is that literature concerned: at its greatest in Lucretius' "austerity of rapture," denying all that lies beyond the flaming ramparts of the world; at its loveliest in lines from the Georgics, the blue smoke mounting at evening from the little farms, and the shadow of the hills on the plain. "How shall I be rid of these things?" says the novice in Cassian's Dialogues, "At mass, in the very act of contrition, the old stories flaunt before my mind, the shameless loves, the sight of the old heroes going into battle."[1] They accused Jerome of breaking his vow never again to read the poets, when reminiscences of them crowded every page, and he made answer that he must needs drink of the water of Lethe if he is to forget. "Dye your wool once purple, and what water will cleanse it of that stain?"[2] There is a poet in Jerome buried in the theologian, and his metaphor is absolute for mediaeval literature.

Remains, that the Church continued to teach the classics; that only for the Church, the memory of them would have vanished from Europe. It is true that scholarship took long to recover from Gregory's aversion: like his own story of the horse that was lent to Bishop Boniface, and was never the same again "after the session of so great a pontiff," *post sessionem tanti pontificis*.[3] But Gregory himself had a hearty belief in education: and education for the sixth century meant the Roman training for the Forum.[4] The Church inherited the Roman respect for eloquence. "The holy writings do not teach the art of eloquence," said Socrates the Historian, "and by eloquence a man defends the truth."[5] St. Jerome confesses that for long enough the uncouth style of the Prophets grated upon him; even after a night of

[1] *Ib.* xlix. 74. [2] Migne, *P.L.* xxiii. "Apol. ad Lib. Ruf." 30.

[3] Greg. *Dial.* iii. 2.

[4] See Boissier, *La Fin du Paganisme*, i. 171-304.

[5] *Soc. Hist. Eccles.* iii. 16.

contrition and agony one sees him reaching for Plautus as a man reaches for his pipe.[1] St. Peter Damian owns to the same distaste.[2] It is to be remembered that the Vulgate, with all its greatness, is not the masterpiece of Latin prose that the Authorised version is of English; and the mediaeval scholar had more critical sense than he has credit for.[3] "To forbid wholly the reading of the pagan authors," says Gratian, "is to cloud and weaken the intellect."[4] Augustine is strong for rhetoric as a liberal discipline, and would have you spoil the pagans of their grace of style as the Israelites spoiled the Egyptians.[5] "Better grammarians than heretics," says Abelard briefly, therein quoting Isidore:[6] and Clement I insists that secular learning is necessary to the right understanding of Holy Writ.[7] Gregory himself in a passage so extraordinary that its genuineness has been questioned, comments on the Israelites going down to the Philistines to sharpen their knives, and explains it by the Christian use of the pagan learning. Christian simplicity is in the heights; pagan learning is in the plain; we go down to the Philistines to make subtle our wits. Moses was learned in the wisdom of the Egyptians: Isaiah, the greatest of the prophets, was *urbanus et instructus*, a gentleman and a scholar; St. Paul, the Apostle par excellence, as versed in secular letters as afterwards in spiritual.[8] And so, in

[1] Jerome, *Epist.* xxii. Migne, *P.L.* xxii. c. 416.

[2] Migne, *P.L.* 144, c. 852.

[3] See John of Salisbury's account of the teaching of Classics at Chartres, *Metal.* i. 24, and his own appreciation of the style of *Ecclesiastes* (iv. 35.) Also Peter of Blois, *Ep.* 76, rebuking his poetic namesake, who had declared the speech of the Gospels "*durum, insipidum, infantilem.*"

[4] Gratian, *Decret.* i. 37, c. 8.

[5] Augustine, *De Doct. Christ.* ii. 37; ii. 17; ii. 40.

[6] Migne, *P.L.* 178, c. 1043. The whole question is argued by Abelard in the *Introductio ad Theologiam*, ii. cap. 1, 2, and again less favourably, in *Theol. Christ.* ii. (Migne, 178, c. 1206-1211).

[7] Clement I, *Epist.* 4, quoted by Gratian, *Decret.* i. 37, c. 14.

[8] Migne, *P.L.* 79, c. 356.

spite of Gregory's defence of his own bad grammar, which one gathers was partly due to indigestion as well as to holy zeal,[1] the divine oracles continued to be subject to the rules of Donatus, and Priscian continued to illustrate for generations of schoolboys the nominative absolute and the deterrent paradigm by lines and half-lines of pagan poetry, sometimes incendiary enough. Alexandre de Ville-Dieu at the beginning of the thirteenth century fell foul of the old grammars and wrote a new one, illustrating as far as possible from Christian poets.[2] Gone the great names of Hector and Achilles and Agamemnon: he exercises his faculty and the quantitative rules on Melchisedech and Noah and Abimelech. His grammar, the *Doctrinale*, had an immense success. "The old apostate" fell into obscurity: and one consequence of it is the trough into which Latin scholarship descended in the prose of the fourteenth century.[3]

Ermenrich of Ellwangen was no humanist, even for the ninth century, unless his anxious disclaimer of any regard for Virgil leaves him a little suspect; but he is sound on the function of the classics in education. Writing a grammatical treatise to the Abbot of St. Gall, he suddenly becomes conscious that he has quoted an inordinate number of times from the pagan Virgil, and hastens to clear himself. "Not that I have any wish to see him, whom I believe to be in a Very Bad Place, and besides the sight of him terrifies me. Often indeed when I have been reading him, and after reading put him under my head, in that first sleep which should be sweetest after toil, comes to me a dark monster carrying a codex with a pen behind its ear as one about to write, and mocks at me . . . but I waking sign the cross and hurling the book far

[1] Migne, *P.L.* 75, *Praef. Moral.* c. 516.

[2] Alexandre de Ville-Dieu, *Doctrinale*, ed. D. Reichling (Kehrbach, *Monumenta Germaniae Paedagogica*, Bd. xii. 1893).

[3] See the mocking praises of the *Doctrinale* in the *Epist. Obsc. Vir.* i. 6, 7, 9, 18; ii. 46.

from me again give my limbs to sleep. . . . Let us leave him, my father, let us leave him, liar that he is, sunk with Apollo and the Muses in the foulest swamp of the Styx. There let him hug Proserpine and listen to Orpheus fiddling for his Eurydice from the infernal gods. . . . The King of Heaven sets his curse on suchlike leasings. Why then do I harp upon them? . . . Since even as dung spread upon the field enriches it to good harvest, so the filthy writings of the pagan poets are a mighty aid to divine eloquence."[1] It is not a handsome metaphor, but it is very near being absolute.

How to manure the right seed, without turning it into the degenerate plant of a strange vine, was the problem of mediaeval scholarship. "The songs of the poets are the food of demons," says Jerome, "the pagan learning, the pomps of rhetoric; their suavity is a delight to all men. . . . The very priests of God are reading comedies, singing the love songs of the Bucolics, turning over Virgil: and that which was a necessity in boyhood, they make the guilty pleasure of their maturity."[2] The better the Ciceronian, the worse, as a rule, the Christian.[3] The language of the Missal was the language of Virgil and Ovid; and Virgil and Ovid are the great enchanters. Now, it was Dr. Opimian's view that a bald head in women is a wise precaution against solicitation: that Venus, hairless, has no power against the heart. With something of the same conviction St. Jerome lighted on the text in Deuteronomy setting forth the conditions on which an Israelite might take unto himself a captive maid, and applied it to pagan poetry. "Whatsoever is in her of love, of wantonness, of idolatry, I shave; and having made of her an Israelite indeed, I beget sons unto the Lord."[4] That text is the most popular quotation of orthodox scholarship for the next eight centuries. Yet by some

[1] E. Dümmler, *Epist. Ermenric. ad Grim.* p. 29.

[2] Jerome, *Epist.* xxi. Migne, *P.L.* 22, c. 385-6.

[3] *Ib.*, *Epist.* xxii. [4] *Ib.*, *Epist.* lxx. *P.L.* 22, c. 666.

miracle the goddess escapes disfiguring; even as the statue of Venus which Magister Gregorius saw in Rome escaped the holy zeal, *multo sudore*, of the Blessed Gregory. It was a statue of the goddess as she showed herself to Paris in the fatal judgment: "and that image was fashioned of Parian marble with so marvellous and inexplicable art that rather did she seem a living creature than a statue. Blushing she stood . . . and it seemed to the beholder that the blood mantled in that snow-white face. And because of her amazing beauty and I know not what magical persuasion I was drawn three times to visit her, though she was distant two miles from my lodging."[1] "*Nescio quam magicam persuasionem*": the history of it is the history of mediaeval lyric.

II

But "to come to a more ordinary opening of him," as Sir Philip Sidney would say, what was the *fonds classique* of the average twelfth century scholar? Here again it is dangerous to go for evidence to John of Salisbury's library: he would be a scholar in any age, and was head and shoulders above his own. Even two smaller men, Alexander Neckam and Eberhard the German, who both drew up courses in Arts, perhaps a little exaggerated their reading: it is the eternal temptation of bibliographers. But they were both practical schoolmasters. Not much is known of Eberhard, except that he had starved as a student in Paris and in Orleans, but found the Muses there, and that he was a schoolmaster with no illusions about his profession.[2] His book, the *Labo-*

[1] Magister Gregorius, *de Mirabilibus Urbis Romae*, *Journal of Roman Studies*, ix. 51.

[2] Text edited by Faral, *Les Arts Poétiques du XIIe et du XIIIe Siècle*. 1923. Vide ll. 944-950.

"Afflixit corpus Parisiana fames. . . .
. . . Aurilianis, alumna
Auctorum, Musae fons, Heliconis apex."

rinthus, written before 1280, comes at the very end of the great age of mediaeval scholarship. But Neckam[1] was an English scholar of some distinction, taught in Paris in the last quarter of the twelfth century ("he knew the city, even to its stenches"[2]), then in Dunstable, and died Abbot of Cirencester in 1217; an honest man, with a hearty faith in the power of the decent mind to select.

Given the rudiments, Donatus is his threshold of knowledge, and with Donatus one studies "that useful compendium of morality which is vulgarly ascribed to Cato:" Cato is the father of the copy-book headline, and very valuable to students writing home[3], even more so to the less scholarly parent making suitable reply. From Theodulus let him pass to the "Egglogas" of the Bucolics, the satirists and the historians, for Alexander believed that boys are apt to imitate the heroic. Statius he finds jocund, the Aeneid divine, and he would have you read Lucan, and know the horror of civil war; Juvenal is to be treasured in the heart, and he would have one read all Horace, Satires, Epistles, Odes, Epodes, and the Art of Poetry; Ovid's Elegies, and the Metamorphoses also, but above all let you be familiar with the *De Remedio Amoris*. The Art of Love he does not mention, but no mediaeval clerk who had Latin enough to spell his way through Cato was likely to omit that book, which even Sir John Paston owned, and lent, and earnestly desired again. Some men of weight would withdraw the amatorious poems and the satires from the hands of young men, but Alexander thinks it enough to leave them with Virgil's warning,

> "You gather flowers and fresh-grown strawberries,
> Fly hence, O youths, a cold snake lurks in the grass."

Some would have it that the *Fasti* should not be read, and here one catches an echo of the outcry against Orleans

[1] Haskins, *Mediaeval Science*, p. 356 *et seq.*

[2] *Ib.* p. 364.

[3] B.N. MS. 1093, f. 82 *v.*

where Satan had his seat, and where Arnulf the Redheaded lectured on the *Fasti* with a knowledge of the intimacies of paganism that scandalised less erudite rivals.[1] Similarly, though Sallust and Tully, *De Oratore,* and the Tusculan Disputations and *De Fato, De Amicitia, De Senectute* are very commendable, and the *Paradoxa,* the book *De Multitudine Deorum* is disapproved by some. Tully, *De Officiis,* is exceeding useful. Martial and Petronius contain much that is profitable, but much that is unfit for any ear. The brevity of Symmachus begets admiration. He commends Solinus on the Marvels of the World, and Sidonius and Suetonius and Quintus Curtius and Trogus Pompeius [Justin] and Titus Livius and Chrysippus, and you may find it profitable to read Seneca, *Ad Lucillum* and *De Quaestionibus Physicis* and *De Beneficiis,* nor are his Tragedies and Declamations unprofitable. The student of Grammar should attend lectures on the *Barbarismus* of Donatus, and the Major Priscian and the book of Constructions ; also Rémy and Priscian on metre and quantity, and Priscian on accent, although some deny his authorship. There follows a further list for rhetoric (Cicero and Quintilian) and logic, music, mathematics, medicine, civil and canon law, and finally, for the "mature scholar," theology, but the literary texts suffice. Add to this from the gloss and from the still richer list of Eberhard, Persius, Claudian, Plautus, Terence, a few writers of the Silver Age, Arator, Prudentius, Sedulius, Boethius' *Consolation of Philosophy,* Martianus Capella, and half a dozen contemporaries, some of them making their reputations when Neckam was a student in Paris, but standard authors to Eberhard, fifty years later. The list is at least respectable.

There are gaps, notably Catullus, Propertius, Tibullus, and the great name of Lucretius, though the Byronic glamour about the first three was well known, for to a Love's Assize of the twelfth century Catullus comes

[1] *Hist. Litt.* xxix. 576.

with Lesbia, Propertius with Cynthia, Tibullus with Delia.[1] The general impression is of an almost unfamiliar richness. The truth is that the Middle Ages profited imaginatively, if not in technique, by their use of the Classical Apocrypha. The limitation of the classical canon has left the average reader with the impression of a literature composed wholly in the eighteenth century. Because Cicero wrote as a senator should, and too many of Virgil's lines begin *At pius Aeneas*, and Juvenal's best translator is Dr. Johnson, and Horace's wildest dissipations tinkle like the teacups at Strawberry Hill, we have forgotten that Apuleius wrote as strange a novel of adventure as exists in European literature ; that Petronius created the only figure on whom Falstaff's belt would even slackly have hung ; that Claudian, though something of a crustacean, achieved in the "Old Man of Verona" a grey autumnal peace all but comparable with the *Leech-Gatherer* ; that the *Pumpkinification of the Divine Claudius* is funnier than Byron's *Vision of Judgment* ; that the *Copa Syrisca* has the sensuous cynicism of the eighteen-nineties, and a virility that they had not ; that the *Pervigilium Veneris* remained alone in literature till Keats wrote the *Ode to a Nightingale* and the *Hymn to Pan* ; forgotten, above all, a score of lovely lyrics buried in the anthologies of the sixth and ninth and tenth centuries :

> "Lady Venus, what's to do,
> If the loved loves not again ?
> Beauty passes, youth's undone,
> Violets wither, spite of dew,
> Roses shrivel in the sun,
> Lilies all their whiteness stain.
> Lady, take these home to you,
> And who loves thee, love again." [2]

[1] *Metamorphosis Goliae*, Wright. *Latin Poems attributed to Walter Mapes*, 27.

[2] *Anthologia Latina*, i. 24.

or, their first lines only :

> " Dreams, dreams that mock us with their flitting shadows,"[1]
>
> " Canst thou paint a maid of such a whiteness
> As Love himself hath made ? "[2]
>
> " Not fair enough is she that's only fair."[3]
>
> " Laid on my bed in silence of the night."[4]
>
> " Sister art to Phoebus, Lady Moon ? "[5]
>
> " By day mine eyes, by night my soul desires thee."[6]

ending with the sheer Shakespearean splendour of

> " Still let me love, though I may not possess."[7]

" Classical Latin poetry," says Rémy de Gourmont, " died of the Virgilian perfection " ; and there is truth in it, though not as he devised.

Virgil himself they read as we do not, thanks partly to a glut of inferior and more accessible romances. Dido, Queen of Carthage, was the romantic heroine of the Middle Ages. They could not read the lines in Homer where the old men on the wall hushed their swallows' chattering as Helen passed by ; they knew her only in Dictys, sweet-natured, long-limbed and golden-haired, or in the amazing flashlight vision of Virgil, crouching on the steps of the Temple of Vesta in the light of the fires, " Erynnis to her father's house and Troy." She is Absolute Beauty, even as *Venus generosa.* But Dido they took to their hearts, wrote lament after lament for her, cried over her as the young men of the eighteenth century cried over Manon Lescaut. St. Augustine broke his heart for her ;[8] and the schoolboy Alcuin, waking at night and watching the devils nip the toes of the other monks in the dormitory, called anxiously to mind that he had scamped the Psalms to read the Aeneid.[9] Nor in this do they show their simplicity.

[1] *Ib.* ii. 651. [2] *Ib.* i. 23. [3] *Ib.* i. 479.
[4] *Ib.* ii. 697. [5] *Ib.* ii. 693. [6] *Ib.* ii. 702.
[7] *Ib.* ii. 712. [8] Conf. i. 13.
[9] Jaffé, *Mon. Alcuin*, p. 7.

To come back to Dido after much novel reading is to recognise a great heroine in the hands of a great novelist. From the first scene to the last—the gracious welcome, self-possessed and royal, of the sea-tossed wanderers, the empty banquet hall with the lights out and the household asleep, and the queen stealing down in the light of the dying stars to lie huddled on the couch where Aeneas that night had lain, the surrender in the cave in the blackness of the thunderstorm, the night when the owl cries with its note of doom, the pitiful sorrowful dreaming in Virgil's loveliest lines of herself always alone, always abandoned, wandering on long roads companionless, seeking her people far from her own land, the last murmur, her cheek crushed against the couch that had been their bed—"At least I die"—they saw for the first time "the ambiguous face of woman as she is." It is the romantic quality in Latin that captured the imagination of the Middle Ages, as well as of the Elizabethans; the mystery of the untrodden wood in Lucan,

> "Lucus erat longo nunquam violatus ab aevo,"

quoted by the seventh century monk who wrote the life of St. Sequanus, the wood of Statius and of Spenser,

> "Not perceable with power of anie starre,"

the headland where the clouds rest, and the wearied stars,

> "ubi prona dies longos super aequora fines
> exigit atque ingens medio natat umbra profundo."

that is also the mount of Purgatory. They found there too the sense of pity. The passages chosen for the eleventh-century anthology that once belonged to St. Augustine's in Canterbury, were not the fights, but the laments, the dream of Aeneas seeing the bloodstained corpse of Hector with the poignant amazing cry

> "O lux Dardaniae!"

the lament of the mother in the Thebaid for the child left

in the wood with its wide baby's smile and small noises of delight, of the young wife for the husband slain by her brother—a situation like enough the Edda.[1] Anatole France was haunted all his life long by the vision of Dido in the Fields of Sorrow, half-guessed, half-seen,

> " Like him who sees the light of the new moon
> Rising, or thinks he sees, faint through the clouds " ;

at seventeen he found in the forest of myrtles some surcease of his own unrest. But the path was beaten long before him,

> " With footing worne, and leading inward farre."

Yet, granted Virgil and Ovid, it is in the last three centuries of the Empire, the centuries of which the classical scholar is rightly impatient, seeing only mere glimmerings and decays, that the spiritual foundations of the Middle Ages were laid. It is hardly possible to exaggerate their importance ; the centuries of Augustine and Jerome and Ambrose ; of the Confessions, the *De Civitate Dei*, the Vulgate translation of the Bible, the first of the Latin hymns ; the massive strategic common-sense of Gregory the Great ; the moulding of the Liturgy ; the *Te Deum* ; the founding of the Benedictine order that kept the gates of knowledge for Europe ; the codifying of Roman law ; the inspiration of Cassiodorus to " utilise the vast leisure of the convent " in copying manuscripts, and thereby opening a window in the Middle Ages on a prospect like his own Scyllace, " a city set above the bosom of the Adriatic, clinging like a bunch of grapes to the hillside, and gazing at its pleasure over green fields and the blue backs of the waves. It sees the sun at his rising, . . . the light is clear and fair, . . . men go lightly there, *sensu liberior.*"[2] And in the smaller things, the every-day business of the schools, they are the centuries of Donatus and Priscian, the

[1] *The Cambridge Songs*, edited by K. Breul, 1915, pp. 19, 18, 17.

[2] Cass, *Variae*, xii. 15.

schoolmasters of Europe for a thousand years; of Martianus Capella, sometimes the only text book, whose *Marriage of Mercury and Philology* was famous even on the Elizabethan stage; and though it bound on the Middle Ages a grievous burden of allegory, yet after all was the only wedding to which a clerk might legitimately go, and had some sense of roses and precious stones and even the spring meadows where the lambs go wagging their tails; of Boethius' translation of Euclid, his treatise on Arithmetic and Music, his translation and comment on Aristotle, the "builder-oak" of scholastic philosophy; above all his *Consolation of Philosophy*, written in prison, the book of most serene and kindly wisdom that the Middle Ages knew. Not Augustine himself breaks his mind upon eternity as Boethius did.

"There is in GOD, some say
A deep but dazzling darkness . . .
O for that night, that I in Him
Might live invisible and dim."

That is Augustine's mood, at his height of abnegation; but Boethius sees not so much infinite darkness, as a multitude of quiet stars.

"If Light can thus conceal, wherefore not Life?"

No verse, not even Milton's, is so haunted with the austere and sonorous music of their names; and in Theodoric's dungeon, in presence of torture and imminence of death, the ex-senator steadies his soul on their unchanging way,

"Look to the highest of the heights of heaven,
See where the stars still keep their ancient peace." [1]

He is both mystic and stoic, but without the contempts of either; a lover of life and unafraid of death, but neither its shadow nor the light of the world to come has

[1] *De Cons. Phil.* iv. 6.

taken from the greenness of the grass. It was fortunate for the sanity of the Middle Ages that the man who taught them so much of their philosophy, whose book was "for the youngest in our schools," [1] was of a temperament so humane and so serene; that the *maxime scrutator magnarum rerum,*[2] "mightiest observer of mighty things," who defined eternity with an exulting plenitude that no man has approached before or since, had gone to gather violets in a spring wood, and watched with a sore heart a bird in a cage that had caught a glimpse of waving trees and now grieved its heart out, scattering its seed with small impotent claws.[3] Two men wrote what might serve for his epitaph, and revealed themselves in doing it:

> "So by the Gothic Bacchanalian sword
> Died Roman freedom . . .
> . . . consul and exile, thou
> Laid greatness down to win it in thy death.
> . . . that intellect divine
> Compels for thee the world's *imperium.*" [4]

Thus far Gerbert, perhaps the most astute scholar and statesman of the mediaeval popes. It is the Brutus in Boethius that he reveres, the *mens divina*; it is for Dante to recognise the diviner wisdom of the heart.

> "Nessun maggior dolore
> Che ricordarsi del tempo felice
> Nella miseria," [5]

is a memory of "in omne adversitate fortunae infelicissimum est genus infortunii fuisse felicem," [6] and his, too, the ineffable sunrise at the end of the *Paradiso*,

> "The love that sways the sun and the other stars." [7]

[1] Ser Lappo Mazzei, Florentine notary, xiv. cent., quoted by Ker, *The Dark Ages*, 106.

[2] Maximian, *Eleg.* iii.

[3] *De Cons. Phil.* v. 6; i. 6; iii. 2.

[4] Migne, *P.L.* 139, 287.

[5] *Inferno*, v. 121.

[6] *Cons. Phil.* ii. iv.

[7] *Cons. Phil.* ii. 8. *Paradiso*, xxxiii. 145.

Dante saw him among the twelve "living and victorious splendours,"

> " Here in the vision of all good rejoices
> That sainted soul . . .
> The body, whence that soul was reft, now lies
> Down in Cieldaro, but the soul from exile
> And martyr's pain hath come unto this peace." [1]

Yet the real achievement is that the soul had come unto this peace before it left the body; had endured its travail,

> " This discord in the pact of things,
> This endless war 'twixt truth and truth," [2]

and found its reconciliation in what is perhaps the deepest word of mediaeval philosophy or religion, "simplicitas Dei," the simplicity of God.

[1] *Paradiso,* x. 124. J. Sandys' translation.

[2] *Cons. Phil.* v. 3.

CHAPTER I

THE BREAK WITH THE PAGAN TRADITION

St. Augustine and Boethius brought the sense of infinity into Latin prose: Latin verse began with it, in Lucretius, and lost it again for centuries. And even in Lucretius, it is rather the infinite of negation; a space that the swiftest lightning leaves still in darkness; immortal Death to ease our mortal life. After him, eternity becomes a sort of superlative of time; an adjective for Rome, a compliment to an Emperor, in the mood of Statius watching the stars already crowding up to make room for Domitian; a lover's cry, holding his mistress, that for this the envious gods deny us immortality; the long night for sleeping, *una nox dormienda*, like Herrick's

> " All love, all liking, all delight
> Lie drowned with us in endless night."

But the sense that besieges every gate and inlet of the poetry of Donne, that leaves St. Paul beating about for words of length and breadth and depth and height, stumbling on the threshold of the fourth dimension, the *tanto oltraggio,* the mighty outrage on the experience of the human mind of Dante's final ecstasy, of this it is empty. By the middle of the fourth century the Vulgate translation was not yet begun: Latin had a Virgilian cento of the Life of our Lord written by a Spanish priest; a shrill Apocalypse from the African Commodianus: in Milan, the new and haunting cadence of the Ambrosian chant, that melted the heart of Augustine but left him questioning whether religion might safely ally itself with delight so exquisite of the senses. But the main current of Latin verse went its way as peacefully as Ausonius' own Moselle. Like him, it dallies in its old age not always with the innocence of love : with anagram and compliment, enamelled fragments of philosophy, the fading of roses, the flavour of oysters. And suddenly, in the midst of this lacquered correspondence, this pleasant Chinese game of painted ivories, of flowers and characters and dragons and seasons, the great wind blows. It broke upon Paulinus, a middle-aged scholarly senator of some distinction in letters and some service to the State, of immense wealth and married to a wife of rank and fortune equal to his own, drove him into exile in Spain, to sell estates that were themselves a little kingdom, and to end his days in Nola, serving the altar of a village saint.

It was not a spectacular conversion. Even the sale of the great estates, the *regna Paulini*,[1] was done gradually, without drama : there was no halt, dazzled with excess of light, on the Damascus road. Paulinus wakened under the countenance of eternity as a man might waken sleeping out of doors at sunrise. But the finality of the experience is absolute. His old friend Ausonius wanders round it, bewildered and estranged, fumbling for the key to it—solitude, romantic scenery, that Spanish wife of his—wringing impotent hands. But for all his vast gentleness, Paulinus goes his way with a kind of instinctive fatality, the terrible simplicity of a man walking in his sleep. There is no agony of repentance, no great regret for the past; "As a dream when one awaketh, so shalt thou despise their image" ; no railing on mortality. It is hardly substantial enough for that : "a shadow at sunset," he calls it, *occidui temporis umbra*. "Cry not to Apollo and the Muses to bring me back ; you call to deaf things and vain, *sine numine nomina*. . . . No more do I seek the word from woods and hill-tops, but from the Word . . .

[1] Ausonius, *Epist.* 27. 116.

God the source, God the kindling fire, . . . Flower of God.[1]

It is hardly fantastic to take the parting of these two as the parting of the ways in literature. *Ceci tuera cela.* Ausonius is the last of the untroubled age, the last to whom Roman eloquence was as invincible as Roman arms; he died before the legend of both was broken at the sack of Rome in 410. He had reason to believe in eloquence: it had brought him from the chair of rhetoric at Bordeaux to the consulate. Yet there is nothing of the politician in Ausonius; he is very near Pliny's definition of the *scholasticus*, "nihil aut est simplicius, aut sincerius aut melius,"[2] and his amazing honours were due to nothing but an old pupil's gratitude. Ausonius and Sulpicius Severus, barrister and biographer before Anatole France of the Desert Fathers, the father of French prose although he writes in Latin,[3] are the first representatives in literature of the French *haute bourgeoisie*, perhaps the most intellectual in Europe. In his old age Ausonius wrote his Memoirs, the *vie intime* of a professional family, in a French university town: the father a doctor, better read in Greek than in Latin (Ausonius' ancestry is Gallic, not Roman):[4] the grandmother sunburnt and strict, but kindly, the mother *bonne ménagère*, the merry aunt Aemilia who was something of a garçon, with a profound contempt for her own sex and for matrimony, who studied medicine and died, still a bachelor, at the age of sixty-three: Aemilia the Dryad, tender and young, whose marriage torches lighted her to death: the dis-

[1] Ausonius, *Epist.* xxxi. 19-30, 110-115, 45-50.

[2] Pliny I. *Epist.* 3.

[3] Sulpicius Severus, *c.* 363-410; born at Toulouse; lost his young wife and renounced the world, but not its humours. *Vide* Dialogus I, on the five men in the desert, and one of them a Gaul, confronted by half a loaf. "Facis inhumane qui nos Gallos homines cogis exemplo angelorum vivere:—and anyhow I am convinced that for the sheer pleasure of eating the angels eat themselves." Migne, *P.L.* xx. c. 187.

[4] Ausonius, *Epicedion in Patrem*, 9.

tinguished uncle, the pride of the connection, barrister of Toulouse and professor at Constantinople.[1] Ausonius went to college at Toulouse, but to literature rather than to law. At twenty-five he is in the chair of rhetoric at Bordeaux, and collecting material for yet another book of reminiscences,[2] kindly common-room gossip, without a spark of malice to cheer it : at fifty-five, so famous that he is summoned by the Emperor to take charge of his only son. Valentinian was a violent man and kept bears, who were believed to dine on those whom he disliked : but his own cub was as gentle as the schoolmaster chosen to instruct him, and when Gratian succeeded his father, there was no honour in the empire too great for his old tutor. In the four years between 376 and 380, Ausonius saw his father, at ninety, honorary prefect of Illyricum, his son and son-in-law proconsuls of Africa, his nephew prefect of Rome : himself praetorian prefect of Gaul, including Spain, Africa, and Southern Britain as well as France, and in the next year consul, an eminence at which he never ceased to regard himself with awe. In 383 the Emperor was assassinated : Ausonius comes back from the noise of the captains, not unwillingly, to Bordeaux, to settle down on his *parvum herediolum*[3]—not so very little, for in tilth and vineyard[4] and wood there were a thousand acres—" the nest of my old age "—to superintend the education of his little grandson, grow Paestum roses, write his memoirs, and engage in that kind of correspondence which is circulated in manuscript among our private friends.

There is something Chinese about Ausonius. He reminds one of half-a-dozen provincial governors in the *Dictionary of Chinese Biography* : of Han Yü, whose friends washed their hands in rose water before opening

[1] *Parentalia*, 5. 2. 6. 25. 3.

[2] *Commemoratio Professorum Burdigalensium.*

[3] *De Herediolo.*

[4] " To this day it boasts itself as *Château-Ausone*, one of the two best of the St. Emilion clarets." G. S.

the manuscript of his poems, and who rid his province of a large and pestiferous crocodile by addressing to it a written censure, committed to the river along with a pig and a goat, a censure still regarded as a model of Chinese prose composition: of Po Chu-i, sitting on the terrace under the peach trees in blossom.

> "Sometimes I sweep the flagstones of the terrace;
> Sometimes in the wind I raise my cup and drink. . . .
> Alone drinking, alone singing my songs.
> I do not notice that the moon is level with the steps . . .
> . . . The people of Pa do not care for flowers . . .
> But their Governor General, alone with his cup of wine,
> Sits till evening and will not stir from the place." [1]

Ausonius walks in his formal garden before sunrise, and watches the frost sharp on the blades of long grass and sitting in fat globes on the cabbage leaves, and the Paestum roses laugh at him.

> "Tell me now, did dawn come first, or roses?
> Or did the Cyprian stain them from one shell?"

and so to the thought of their brief passing,

> "So long as a day is long, so short is the life of a rose,"

and thence to the "Gather ye rosebuds" motif, which Ronsard caught from him after twelve hundred years and made exquisite, and the Cavalier lyrists more exquisite still.[2] He is a Roman citizen, but at heart a countryman of the Gironde.

> "What colour are they now, thy quiet waters?
> The evening star has brought the evening light,
> And filled the river with the green hill-side.

[1] *A Hundred and Seventy Chinese Poems*; translated by Arthur Waley, p. 152.

[2] *De Rosis Nascentibus*, 9:

"... caulibus et patulis teretes conludere guttas.

15. "Ambigeres, raperetne rosis Aurora ruborem,
an dant et flores tingeret orta dies . . . .
communis Paphie dea sideris et dea floris
praecipit unius muricis esse habitum. . . .
quam longa una dies, aetas tam longa rosarum. . . .
collige, virgo, rosas, dum flos novus et nova pubes."

The hill-tops waver in the rippling water,
Trembles the absent vine and swells the grape
In thy clear crystal." [1]

Cupido Cruciatur is the new romantic imagination working upon Virgil, himself romantic enough, and in one passage he has set himself in direct concurrence with his master, and surpassed him, even as Keats surpassed his master Spenser. It is the Fields of the Sorrowful Lovers—

" They wander in deep woods, in mournful light,
Amid long reeds and drowsy-headed poppies,
And lakes where no wave laps, and voiceless streams,
Along whose banks in the dim light grow old
Flowers that were once bewailèd names of Kings." [2]

This is that strangeness, without which beauty is not made perfect.

For his religion, Christian and pagan are words too absolute : he will write of Easter or a Vigil of Venus with the same temperate pleasure. Like Milton, he has an exquisite self-regard. " Let me not be to myself a cause of shame," says he in his morning prayer. " Take from me the power of doing ill : give me the tranquil power of doing good." [3] His paganism is purely romantic : great conservative that he is, he would no doubt have joined with Symmachus in his appeal that the Altar of Victory should be restored to the Senate House, but he

[1] *Mosella*, 192-5 :
" Quis color ille vadis, seras cum propulit umbras
Hesperus et viridi perfudit monte Mosellam.
tota natant crispis iuga motibus et tremit absens
pampinus et vitreis vindemia turget in undis."

[2] *Cupido Cruciatur*, 5-9 :
" Errantes silva in magna et sub luce maligna
inter harundineasque comas gravidumque papaver,
et tacitos sine labe lacus, sine murmure rivos :
quorum per ripas nebuloso lumine marcent
fleti, olim regum et puerorum nomina, flores."

[3] *Ephemeris, Oratio*, 60-65 :
" nec causa pudoris
sim mihi . . . male posse facultas
nulla sit et bene posse adsit tranquilla potestas."

would never have conceived the sentence in which that appeal comes to its close—" Not by one path alone may men come at so great a mystery." [1] The wife of his youth died after a few years: he had written her a lyric in life exquisite and tender; [2] another after thirty-six years, tenderer still. Lights o' love,

> " Saucy, fair, and hard to please,
> Strike her, she takes flight to kisses," [3]

had beguiled his leisure, but not the emptiness of his heart, and it cries out to her still. But her children are with him, and his prayer is that in the last dark his ashes may cry to hers that they yet live.[4] It is his only immortality.

But, in this again Chinese, it was friendship and not love that broke his heart, and wrung from him his greatest elegy. There is a vast and pleasant correspondence: to Theon, commending the excellence and lamenting the fewness of his oysters: to Theon, who will not come to see him because he owes Ausonius 14 philips, witness the I.O.U. written with reluctance; dear philips, if they are to cost him his society; so pay up, or pay in kind with your good company: to Theon, complaining of the badness of his verses, over against the goodness of his apples; who would think they were chips of the same block? But it is not for you to go to school, nor for a royal tutor like me to teach the art of scribbling to a country bumpkin like you.[5] To Symmachus, verses, after a night of wine and flutes, " But do you read them also a little flown and "—the incomparable word for that state of solution and relaxation—" *dilutior*; for it is

[1] Symmachus, *Epist.* x. 3:
" uno itinere non potest pervenire ad tam grande secretum."

[2] *Epigrammata*, 40:
" nec ferat ulla dies ut commutemur in aevo,
quin tibi sim iuvenis tuque puella mihi."

[3] *Epigrammata*, 89, " caesaque ad oscula confugiat."

[4] *Parentalia*, ix.

[5] Ausonius, *Epist.* 15. 16. 14. 17.

outrageous that a strictly abstemious reader should sit in judgment on a poet a little drunk." [1] But to one man the tone changes ; still light-hearted, yet with an immense respect for a talent that he believes greater than his own. Paulinus, governor of a province and consul before he was thirty, was the pupil of whom a Roman master dreamed : Ausonius is never weary of recalling that in the consulship the pupil had preceded his master. Now with political honours behind him, he had come to settle down on the Aquitaine estate, and follow the laurel of Apollo which no less surely awaited him. One notes that Rome is no longer the goal of poets, and the Midi with its tradition of Greek culture will be the nucleus of light for centuries. It was to Desiderius at Vienne that the Blessed Gregory wrote in wrath and grief, for that he sang the songs of Apollo, and the grammarians of Toulouse argue over the vocative of *ego* amid the crash of empires.[2] There are four letters to Paulinus, casual and gay, thanks for a new savoury, a harassed bailiff, an exchange of verses, affectionate chiding of the younger man's reluctance to create.[3] Then, suddenly, emptiness and silence. Paulinus had taken a sudden journey into Spain, presumably on some business connected with his wife's estates, but no man certainly knew the reason. He gave no explanation, took leave of no one, not even so much as the *salve* of courteous enemies for which Ausonius pleaded. No message came from him. Lover and friend he had put far from him, and his acquaintance into darkness. There followed four years of impenetrable and cruel silence.

Four years is a long time at seventy, and Ausonius loved him. Letter follows letter, of affectionate raillery —a pox upon this Spain !—of passionate appeal that checked itself for lack of dignity and still broke out

[1] *Griphus* : "sed tu quoque hoc ipsum paulo hilarior et dilutior lege : namque iniurium est de poeta male sobrio lectorem abstemium iudicare."

[2] Vergilius Maro, *Epist. de Pron.* (Teubner), p. 123.

[3] *Epist.* 23. 24. 25. 26.

afresh, of bitter and wounding reproach.[1] Yet it seems not wholly to have been Paulinus' fault, unless that he had deliberately gone into retreat so strait that no rumour from his old world could reach him. At the end of the four years three letters came to him by a single messenger, and he hastens to make what amends he could.[2] At best, it is written from a great way off. Apollo, the Muses, the dusty laurels, what were these to the man

> " Whom Joy hath overtaken as a flood,"

whom " long eternity " has greeted with its " individual kiss " ? The small tuneful business of the old days is too clearly the dance of gnats above a stream in summer. Ausonius had not spared him ; there is a trace of Rutilius Namatianus' bitterness against this new Circe of a religion that made men's minds brutal, not their bodies ; but Paulinus has no resentment. He has chosen. Henceforth his mind is a torch, flaming through the secrets of eternity.[3] But his heart aches for his old master, and the gratitude, all but adoration, he lavishes upon him might have deceived most men. It did not deceive Ausonius. The letter in which he makes answer is poignant enough ; but the superscription is more poignant still—" To Paulinus, when he had answered other things, but had not said that he would come." [4] Eternity ? He words me, he words me. One thing was clear to Ausonius :

> " Nous n'irons plus au bois,
> Les lauriers sont coupés."

And this time he gives up argument, speaks no longer of a lost career, of great promise starved, but pleads for love's sake only.

> " And so, Paulinus, you cast off the yoke—"

[1] *Epist.* xxviii. xxix. " cum Pontius Paulinus iunior quartis iam litteris non respondisset, sic ad eum scriptum est."

[2] *Epist.* xxxi. [3] *Epist.* xxxi. 173.

[4] *Epist.* xxv. " Ad eundem cum ille ad alia magis responderet neque se venturum polliceretur."

There follow pages that have only one parallel, the cry from Po Chu-i in exile, four centuries later—" O Wei-chih, Wei-chih! This night, this heart. Do you know them or not? Lo Tien bows his head." Then Ausonius falls to dreaming; he hears the grating of the boat on the beach, the shouting of the people in the street, the footsteps, the familiar knock on the door.

> " Is't true? or only true that those who love
> Make for themselves their dreams?"[1]

That wounding spearhead of Virgil reached its mark. Paulinus answered in something like an agony of love and compassion. Once again he pleaded the mystery that no man sees from without: then the crying of his own heart silenced the sober elegiacs, and he breaks into one of the loveliest lyric measures of the ancient world.

> " I, through all chances that are given to mortals
> And through all fates that be,
> So long as this close prison shall contain me,
> Yea, though a world shall sunder me and thee,
>
> " Thee shall I hold, in every fibre woven,
> Not with dumb lips nor with averted face
> Shall I behold thee, in my mind embrace thee,
> Instant and present, thou, in every place.
>
> " Yea, when the prison of this flesh is broken,
> And from the earth I shall have gone my way,
> Wheresoe'er in the wide universe I stay me,
> There shall I bear thee, as I do to-day.
>
> " Think not the end, that from my body frees me,
> Breaks and unshackles from my love to thee.
> Triumphs the soul above its house in ruin,
> Deathless, begot of immortality.

[1] *Epist.* xxv. lines 131-2:

> " et sua praeteriens iam iam tua limina pulsat.
> credimus? an qui amant ipsi sibi somnia fingunt?"

> "Still must she keep her senses and affections,
> Hold them as dear as life itself to be,
> Could she choose death, then might she choose for-
> getting.
> Living, remembering, to eternity." [1]

After this there is silence. Whether Ausonius laid it to his heart, or wrote again above it, "But did not say that he would come," there is no showing. A few years saw him go down to his grave, a shock of corn fully ripe, full of years and honour, his children and grandchildren to mourn him: the same years saw Paulinus parish priest of the shrine of St. Felix at Nola.

> "To guard thy altar through the silent night,
> And sweep thy floor and keep thy door by day,
> And watch thy candles burn—"

"*voilà le rêve de ce sénateur et de ce consulaire.*" [2] Year after year his devotion to his saint brings an ode for his feast, the 14th of January, cheerful and sweet, like a robin singing in the snows: the loveliest written for that eternal April of the heart which was to flower in the twelfth century, the faint clear colouring of the first spring flowers, crocus and almond blossom. But never again is he the lark singing at heaven's gate: never again so stung by the *lacrimae rerum*, the blindness and the pain of solitary hearts, the suffering divinity of human passion, as to transmute its anguish into ecstasy.

There follow the idyllic years of a pastoral; scholarly letters, poems passionate only in brooding on the Cross; the story of how St. Felix brought back two pigs; visits of great ones, bishops and scholars; his own episcopate.

[1] *Epist.* xxx. For Latin text see Appendix A.

[2] Boissier, *La Fin du Paganisme*, ii. p. 107:

> "Et foribus servire tuis, tua limina mane
> Munditiis curare sines; et nocte vicissim
> Excubiis servare piis: et munere in isto
> Claudere promeritam defesso corpore vitam."

Carm. xii. Migne, *P.L.* 61, c. 463.

Sulpicius Severus recommends a cook; he hears that all Paulinus' cooks have left him in disgust at his scanty fare: wherefore he sends a slave, "innocent of pepper, but maker of a good vegetable soup, a hard man on a garden, and reckless in foraging for firewood. Take him as a son."[1] The last legend of his life has him still in a garden. In 410 when Rome had fallen and the broken rout of the fugitives came streaming down past Nola, Paulinus spent the last of that royal fortune in ransoming such as he could of the prisoners, made bare even St. Felix's shrine to buy back St. Felix's sons. At the last moment came a poor widow, pleading for her only son: Paulinus' hands were empty, but he sold himself, bought back the boy, and was shipped with the rest of the slaves to Africa. He was a good man in a garden and lived happily with the son-in-law of Genseric, no one knowing the rank of the old man who brought fresh fruit and salad every day to the table. Then the Vandal King came to dine, and recognised trembling the face that he had seen in a dream, the vision of his own judgment by such another: the gardener was questioned, confessed his old dignity and was sent back to Italy, and a ship-load of his fellow-captives for indemnity. Gregory the Great tells it, not vouching for the truth of it:[2] but it is a gracious soil from which such legends spring. The last act of his life blossoms in the dust; for on his deathbed this great lover of Christ and His Church restored to communion all those whom for grievous error he had barred from the Sacraments. Jews and infidels, says his biographer and disciple, followed him to his grave, weeping as for their father.[3] It is the most fragrant chapter in the history of the saints.

[1] Paul. *Epist.* xxii. Migne, *P.L.* 61, c. 255.

[2] Greg. *Dial.* iii. 1. Migne, *P.L.* 77, c. 216.

[3] Uranius Presbyter, *De ob. S. Paul.* Migne, 53, c. 860, 863.

II

The sharp severance in the life of Paulinus is the history in little of the literature that came after: of Sedulius of the *Carmen Paschale*, who had once been like to devote all the force of his mind to vanity and secular studies, but the mist cleared; his feet wandering in the deep thickets came out at last on the flowering sward of God:[1] of Sidonius Apollinaris, patrician turned churchman a little, like John Donne, against his will, and, again like Donne, misliking the poetry of his youth, shepherding his people against the shock of the Burgundian invasion, prisoner among the barbarians for two years and thereafter adored by them, a little to his own embarrassment—

> "They do not come to you at dawn,
> Breathing out leeks and ardour,
> Great friendly souls, with appetites
> Much bigger than your larder—"[2]

holding at Clermont the last stronghold of Roman culture in Auvergne, and dying at last in his cathedral, with the wailing of his people in his ears. Ennodius, born at Arles, brought up by Deuterius the grammarian whose reverend bald head was as the moon in its fulness,[3] whose boyish dream it was to be numbered with the goodly company of poets—"a poem swept me among the angelic host"—and if he might attain thereto the world was under his feet,[4] came at the last to "hate the very name of liberal studies."[5] "Those who seek Him from secular studies

[1] Migne, *P.L.* 19, c. 535.

[2] Sid. Apol. *Carm.* xii. *Ad Catullinum.*

[3] Ennod. *Carm.* ii. 104. Migne, *P.L.* 63, c. 354.

[4] Ennod. *Eucharist. Ib.* c. 245. Nam elevatus insanis successibus poetarum me gregi . . . indideram. . . . Angelorum choris me fluxum et tenerum poema miscebat, et si evenisset ut essem clarorum versuum servata lege formator, sub pedibus meis subjectum quidquid coeli tegitur axe, cernebam."

[5] *Ib. Epist.* ix. 1.

He refuses not: but that we should go to them from His brightness He will not suffer: one is the way and hard that leads to Christ."[1] The scholar's education as one sees it in Ennodius' college exercises[2] was still purely pagan, and the battle between the Muses and Christ, even as it was for Anselm of Bisate long after, "either company so sweet, so fair, my heart cried out for both." In its sharpness the gods who to the untroubled pagan, to Claudian for instance, are little but machines, recover something of their "faded splendour wan." Sidonius Apollinaris saw Venus asleep with her cheek pillowed on her rounded arm, and violets withering in her hair.[3] This is not the dignified figure of the Aeneid, "vera incessu patuit dea," but Botticelli's Venus, with "the roses browned a little at the stalk," the tender dangerous goddess of the mediaeval legends. Ennodius, who "hates the very name of liberal studies," saw her asleep by the sea, and Cupid coming to waken her, bitterly complaining,

> "Rare in the vast fields of the centuries,
> Rare is love's harvest:"

the grey cult of virginity has taken the colour from the world. "Fear not," says his mother, "the gods are never so dangerous as when they awake from sleep."[4] And, indeed, Venus is never so lovely as in the last centuries of her defeat, when her last poets even as her first

> "Fashioned the wave-born Dione from wedding of shower
> and spray."[5]

[1] Ennod. *Eucharist.* *Epist.* ix. 9.

[2] *Ib. Dictiones,* 25. 20. 16. 26. 28.

[3] Sid. Apol. *Carm.* x. lines 47-9:

> "Illa recurvato demiserat ora lacerto
> Mollia: marcebant violae graviorque sopore
> Coeperat attritu florum descendere cervix."

[4] Ennod. *Carm.* i. iv.

[5] *Pervigilium Veneris,* line 11. "Fecit undantem Dionen de maritis imbribus."

The old worn-out jest of the taking of Mars and Venus in the net is fresh again. They gather roses for her, solicitous that the thorns will not prick those tender breasts, spread her couch again, not with gold and purple, but with hyacinths and violets: Cupid does sentry-go, marvelling at the weight of Mars' spear. And when the old fraud is played again, and Vulcan's chain-net falls about the lovers, Mars will not try to break free, lest the chains should hurt her wrists.[1]

For though the cypress is withering at the top, the Latin genius is not yet sterile, and a new and lovely rhythm comes to supplant the old, the trochaic tetrameter of the *Pervigilium Veneris*, of "Amnis ibat inter arva valle fusus frigida." It belongs to the African school of the fourth century, but only as to its godfathers, its literary sponsoring, for it is a far older thing than that. It was the marching song of Caesar's legions,[2] as old as the tramp of marching men: and it was to have a long history. Hilarius took it for the Church Militant: it reached Ireland, where the legions themselves had never been, and became the basis of most Irish metres: [3] in the ninth century it is a wild lament for the slaughter at Fontenay: [4] at the end of the tenth century a wandering scholar sang it in the Rhine valley.[5] It sets itself again to trampling horses' feet, when Guillaume IX, Duke of Aquitaine, sang to it "Qu'una donna s'es clamada de sos gardadors a mei,"[6] and then in Venice to a chamber melody,

"A Toccata of Galuppi,"

[1] De concubitu Martis et Veneris. *Anthologia Latina*, 253. *Poet. Lat. Min.* i. 72.

[2] Suet. *Div. Jul.* c. 49. "Milites eius inter cetera carmina qualia currum prosequentes iocülariter canunt, etiam illud vulgatissimum pronuntiaverunt, 'Ecce Caesar nunc triumphat qui subegit Gallias.'"

[3] Kuno Meyer, *Primer of Irish Metrics*, p. xiii.

[4] Coussemaker, *Hist. de l'Harmonie au moyen âge*, p. 86.

[5] *Cambridge Songs* (ed. Breul), p. 54.

[6] *Chansons de Guillaume IX* (ed. Jeanroy), iii.

and so back to the soldiers again,

> "Where the dawn comes up like thunder outer China
> 'crost the bay."

But for the most part the old worn-out themes are set to the old tunes: Dracontius in Africa, with his *Medea, Orestes,* the obscure single-speech poets of the *Poetae Latini Minores.* But the flame leaps highest before its final sinking: it was left for an Etruscan, the subtle and luxurious race that was before Rome, to write the dirge of Roman youth.

The Elegies of Maximian were a mediaeval school text; so we gather from the indignant snorts of Alexandre de Ville-Dieu, who earnestly strove to supplant it with less inflammable matter.[1] It was an odd choice for schoolboys, for Maximian has the erotic psychology of Maupassant: yet it is a stout heart that could warm itself at that fire. It is one of the strangest documents of the human mind: Ecclesiastes without its austere reconciliation: the "*ossa arida* of the Valley of Dead Pleasures," but no breath from the four winds will blow upon these slain. One does not read Maximian without a strange catharsis, a purging by pity and—if not terror—fear: the legend of so many mediaeval gravestones cries out from it: "As I am now, so shalt thou some day be." It is an autobiography, written with a terrible sincerity, redeemed from over-intimacy by the inhumanity of the art: a consummate egotism, aware of every failing of its power, every circumstance and squalor of its decline, mocking even the impulse that drugs the present with its garrulous resurrection of the past.

The stories are as short as Maupassant's, and told with his irony: the innocent half-idyll of his schoolboy passion at sixteen, crumpling up under the older man's shout of

[1] Alexandre de Ville-Dieu, *Doctrinale,* ll. 3-4:

> "Iamque legent pueri pro nugis Maximiani
> quae veteres sociis nolebant pandere caris."

laughter " In love, and chaste ! " with yet one more twist of mockery at the close ;[1] his early manhood, fastidious and arrogant, bareheaded in wind and rain, swimming the Tiber in winter, but able to drink Father Bacchus under the table, swinging unmoved through the laughter and hurried flights of the soft Roman dusk : his dream-love of Candida, the dancer, seen for one night and dreamed of for many, and every song she sang running in his head —it might be Pendennis and the Fotheringay : the lament for Lycoris, the love of his life, who left him, and here the mood is for once not Gallic irony, but a heavy oppression of the senses shot through with the lightnings of the spirit that is nearer Donne than anything in Latin literature : the brief St. Martin's Summer of his Embassy at Constantinople, and the Greek who once again beguiled the Etruscan, and kindled the white ash to a momentary fire. It sank again : the girl falls to sobbing on the floor, and he to watching, grimly assuring her of a more adequate lover. She rounded on him, " It is not that ! It is the general chaos of the world," youth for the first time face to face with the knowledge that " this also will pass," the blankness of annihilation. Then comes the last elegy, the waking from the drug of memory, his cry on sluggish Death—

" I rise, a corpse already wept, and live,"

Rome's ghost since her decease.

III

If the " *crépuscule des dieux* " still lingers in the sixth century in Rome, the " rear of darkness thin " had long been scattered in Spain. It is characteristic that Prudentius should begin his Book of Hours with a song for cockcrow, for the simplicity, the clarity of his verse has something of that knife-edge cleaving of the darkness. He came to poetry late, after a lifetime of law and of high

[1] Oddly enough, it is Boethius who figures here as Lord Chesterfield.

office under Theodosius, the great Spanish gentleman whose life " lies like a ruined sea-wall amidst the fierce barbarian tide." [1] At fifty-seven, Prudentius renounced the world : entered the cloister, and with it the kingdom of heaven. He has the directness, the closeness to the object that is part of the physical necessity of childhood, and the experienced wisdom of old age. Blake has it, in whom the child and the Ancient of Days have equal parts : there are traces of it in the later work of Thomas Hardy. Compare with " The Oxen,"

" yet I feel
If some one said on Christmas Eve
Come, let us see the oxen kneel
. . . I should go with him in the gloom
Hoping it might be so."

the first verse of *Ad Gallicinium*,

" Thence is it, as we all believe,
At this same hour of quiet,
The jocund crowing of the cock,
Christ came back from the lower world." [2]

The verse is so simple that there is no translating it. Paulinus of Nola has a slow sweetness that gives a more cumbered language time to overtake him ; but here, to add a word for the sake of accent or rhyme is to smudge the outline. Again, in the *Hymn for Matins*—

" O Night and Dark,
O huddled sullen clouds,
Light enters in : the sky
Whitens.
Christ comes ! Depart ! Depart !

" The mist sheers apart
Cleft by the sun's spear.
Colour comes back to things
From his bright face." [3]

[1] Hodgkin, *Italy and her Invaders*, i. 197.

[2] Prudentius, *Cathemerinon*, i. lines 65-69. Migne, *P.L.* 59, c. 781. See Appendix A.

[3] *Cath.* ii. *Ib.* c. 785. See Appendix A.

One is a long way from rosy-fingered Aurora and the *quadriga* of Apollo ; but not so far from dawn. *Easter Eve* has the clear shining of the sixth century mosaics in San Apollinare Nuovo at Ravenna, where virgin after white virgin stands with scarlet anemones and lilies at her feet, in a field of living green.

" The earth is sweet with roses,
And rich with marigold,
And violets and crocus
Are wet with running streams.

" And through the grassy meadows,
The blessed spirits go,
Their white feet shod with lilies,
And as they go they sing." [1]

Loveliest of all, the *Burial of the Dead*.

" Take him, earth, for cherishing,
To thy tender breast receive him.
Body of a man I give thee,
Noble even in its ruin. . . . .

" Once again the shining way
Leads to ample Paradise,
Leading to the woods again
That the Snake once lost for men.

" Take, O take him, mighty Leader,
Bring again thy servant's soul
To that house from which he wandered,
Exiled, erring, long ago.

" But for us, the earth's above him.
Scatter violets and leaves.
Grave his name and pour the fragrant
Balm upon the icy stone." [2]

Prudentius is not an innovator ; Ambrose was before him in rhythm, Hilary in rhyme. But his verse has more of the swiftness of the lyric, less the tread of the processional chant. His hymn for Matins is even the first

[1] Migne, 59, c. 826. *Cath.* v. ll. 113-117. 121-125. See Appendix A.

[2] *Ib.* 884-8. *Cath.* x. ll. 125 et seq. See Appendix A.

aubade, though its cry is to the faithful heart, rather than to the sleeping lover. And in his Book of Martyrs he unlocks the treasure of the Golden Legend, the Lives of the Saints that Anatole France knew for the last and secret hiding place of romance. It was a long time before love captured the *chansons de geste*, of which the lives of the strong saints, the "Athletes of God,"[1] are the forerunners: but here it waits on the very threshold, the basket of red roses which the virgins trample under foot. The Church might decry bodily beauty, but not in the persons of its saints, and the first love scenes are the pleading of kings' sons and emperors with these fair women, vowed to the Eternal Lover. With what passion the scene of the renunciation could be handled is realised in the thirteenth century *St. Alexis*, when the young man, vowed to chastity, comes on his wedding night to the room where his bride is laid. He stands there, looking down at her—

"Asses y ardent candoiles et lanternes."[2]

The line is worth a page of passionate soliloquy: the intensity of the silence in which one is conscious of the quiet candle flame. That is eight centuries away: but Prudentius has the promise of it.

So, in his most famous and most considerable work, the *Psychomachia*, the Battle of the Soul, he has done more than set the stage for the struggle between the spirit and the flesh. The battle between the Virtues and the Vices, suitably habited, is everywhere, after him, in mediaeval literature. Herrad von Landsberg drew a picture of the rout of Luxuria for her nuns, the upset chariot, the roses and the trampled violets.[3] Faust sent

[1] Bangor Antiphonary. Muratori, *Anecdot.* ix. 139.

[2] *Li Roumans de Saint Alessin*, l. 125 (G. Paris, *La Vie de St. Alexis*, *Bibl. de l'École des Hautes Études*, vii. p. 225).

[3] *Hortus Deliciarum*, Herrad von Landsberg (Soc. pour la Conservation des Monuments Historiques d'Alsace, 1901).

her, called Lechery by that time, packing from the stage, to give place for the star-dawn of Helen, and in turn became an allegory for the Renaissance. But they have fallen from their first grace on the Elizabethan stage. This is Marlowe's "hot whore" as Prudentius saw her.

> "Come from the confines of the sunset world,
> Luxury, lavish of her ruined fame,
> Loose-haired, wild-eyed, her voice a dying fall,
> Lost in delight . . .
> Flowershod and swaying from the wine cup,
> Each step a fragrance." [1]

It is the first promise of *La Belle Dame sans Merci.*

> "I met a Lady in the meads
> Full beautiful, a faery's child.
> Her hair was long, her foot was light,
> And her eyes were wild . . . .
>
> "I made a garland for her head,
> And bracelets too, and fragrant zone,
> She looked at me as she did love
> And made sweet moan."

"O strange new war!" cries Prudentius; for Love and Pleasure and Beauty fought beside her, and their weapons were violets and the petals of a rose. The day is all but lost, when Temperance holds up the Holy Rood—

> "Dat tergum fugitivus Amor—"

he was to run the Middle Ages, with a price upon his head; Pleasure flies, heedless of the sharp stones under her tender naked feet; Luxuria dies choking at the feet of Faith, and the story ends in a triumph through the shouting streets.

The value of it is deeper than the provision of new and decorative machinery for poets; deeper than its lesson for faith and morals. It is the first artistic expression of the eternal problem, of Spenser's *Faerie Queen,* of Keats's *Hyperion.* This is no fight with dragons, of ugly lusts

[1] Migne, *P.L.* lx. c. 46. See Appendix A. *Psychomachia,* ll. 310-320.

conquered by ugly things, but the harder problem for the artist, the strife between Beauty and Beauty, the one destructive of the other. And the solution, for Prudentius, as for Spenser, as for Keats, is not the hideous mortifications of St. Simeon Stylites, but the vision that Marlowe caught at in a half-realized symbol—

> " Women and unwedded maids
> Shadowing more beauty in their airy brows
> Than have the white breasts of the Queen of Love "

—the vision of " Beauty not as luxury but as power." Once again for this austere and gracious allegory, as for so much of its mysticism and its chivalry, its ardours and endurances, the world is in debt to Spain.

CHAPTER II

FORTUNATUS TO SEDULIUS OF LIEGE

I

FORTUNATUS had his name out of a fairy tale: a good name for a man who was to be a sort of Mercury between two worlds. He had his youth and his learning in Ravenna: when he left it, it was to step into a world where the barbarians were masters, except where Gregory in Rome was building, without sound of axe or hammer, a stronger house than Caesar's: in North Italy the Lombards: the Goths in Spain: the Burgundians in Auvergne: the Franks in France and the Low Countries: and on every frontier the menace of the Huns. Yet the barbarians are no longer officially barbarians. Cassiodorus did a symbolic act when he sent a lute player to Chlovis in France, with the pious hope, aside to Boethius, that he might have the efficacy of Orpheus on the brutes.[1] The Church taught the good monsters language, and their profit on't was they knew how to swear and also to write verses. By the end of the sixth century Chlovis' grandson Chilperic is figuring on the portal of Notre Dame as Apollo, lyre and all,[2] and adding four new letters to the alphabet, demanding even that the old manuscripts be pumiced over, and rewritten with the improved spelling. He even wrote verses, about which Fortunatus was polite in other verses, though

[1] Cassiodorus, *Variae* ii. 40.

[2] Ozanam, *La Civilisation Chrétienne chez les Francs*, p. 417.

Gregory of Tours said they went on lame feet.[1] His father, Clothar I, captured a child princess in a raid on Thuringia, killed her kinsmen and brother, and had her formed in Latin letters, to make her the finer for his palate, to find in the end that he had fashioned the exquisite St. Radegunde of Poitiers. His brother Sigebert married Brunhild of Spain, and to the wedding of names straight out of a saga came Venus and Cupid, doves and wings and zone and all. They were part of the baggage that the last of the Italian poets brought with him to the North.

No one knows what errand brought him out of Italy. Born near Trevisa, he licked up, as he says himself, a few drops of grammar and rhetoric at Ravenna, and lost a little of his rust on the grindstone of the law.[2] There, too, he came near losing his eyesight. But a drop of oil from the lamp burning before the shrine of St. Martin in the church of St. Paul and St. John restored it ; [3] and possibly a visit to the sovereign shrine of the saint at Tours was the original motive of a sentimental journey a little like Sterne's. At any rate, the wedding of Sigebert and Brunhild found him at the Frankish Court in time to write them an Epithalamion : [4] the "seven feet of patron" does not scare him, as it scared the Muse of Sidonius Apollinaris.[5] His does not cough even at the name of Gogo, *primicier* of one of the barbarians, and by way of being a poet himself.[6] Fortunatus wanders through the terrifying courts of the giants, a little like Gulliver, timid, gay, and ready to admire, and his experiences, for the most part happy, gave him material for eleven books of collected verse. His wanderings brought him to Poitiers where Radegunde lived in the abbey she had founded,

[1] Gregory of Tours, *Hist. Franc.* vi. 46.

[2] *Vita S. Mart.* i. 25-35.

[3] *Ib.* iv. 687-701.

[4] *Carm.* x. 16 ; vi. 1.

[5] Sid. Apol. *Carmina,* xii. *Ad Catullinum* :

"How can I write a six-foot line
With seven feet of patron ?"

[6] *Carm.* vii. 1-4.

"an angel-watered lily." It was an apple-orchard in blossom to his luxury-loving, exquisite and peaceful soul: he settled down beside her, was ordained priest, and ended his days as bishop, a life so gentle and blameless that they made him a saint. He loved Radegunde and Agnes, the "daughter of her spirit," as Cowper loved Mrs. Unwin and Lady Hesketh, and when ill tongues said ill things about their intimacy, he cleared himself to her in a poem that is not yet cracked in the ring.[1]

His admirations are without number: and if he did not include his own verses among them, he enjoyed himself in writing them as few poets do. His life of St. Martin is the pipe of the least of his sparrows, he says: but it has immense zest. If St. Martin is going to cure a leper, never a leper so foul: the kiss that heals him has the waters of Jordan in it. The scene at the Emperor's Banquet spurs him to terrific efforts of upholstering; but at the vision of the Bridegroom the verse marches in a kind of carapace of precious stones. The doors of Zion set him off again: no renaissance tyrant, no Jew of Malta, gloried in jewels, their colour and sound, as Fortunatus did. In the fields, his thumb breaks off lilies and his nail snaps off roses, and he walks on violets and finally goes to sleep amid all odours at once.[2] At the last, the coat he has made for Martin is poor rough stuff, camelskin: it ought to be silk and gold thread, amethyst and white, with a crown of roses and lilies and precious stones.[3] But anyhow, go, little book, and ask your pardon at Tours, and thence to Paris, and trot through Italy, with greetings from Fortunatus to his friends and genuflexions at the tombs of the saints, till you come to Ravenna, to the church of St. Paul and St. John and the shrine of the Blessed Martin: and there abide.[4]

"Go, little book," said Sidonius, a century earlier, "but take not the great roads whose arches are marked with

[1] *Carm.* xi. 6.
[2] *Vita S. Mart.* iv. 1-6.
[3] *Ib.* iv. 621-30.
[4] *Ib.* iv. 630-712.

Caesar's eternal name: take you the little familiar ways."[1] It is the little byways that Fortunatus made accessible to men for whom the Roman road of the epic was too stately. He left the fashion for those little letters in verse that are so great a part of monastic literature, and that once or twice, in Notker, in Walafrid Strabo, in Hrabanus Maurus, even in Alcuin, come very near great lyric. His influence is everywhere in the earlier Middle Age: and when Angilbert attempts his shadowy forecasting of the Chanson de Roland, the hunt and the vision of the Holy War, he is thinking of Fortunatus, rather than of Virgil.[2] Sensitive and swift, a great occasion moved him to greatness: the coming of the relics to the church at Poictiers (always a moment of high and terrible emotion), gave him the inspiration of the greatest Processional of the Middle Ages, the "Vexilla Regis prodeunt" that became the chosen hymn of the Crusaders.[3] Both this and the other "Pange lingua gloriosi" are a mystic's Dream of the Rood. It is not as the Latins took it, the symbol and the sign: to Fortunatus, it is still the tree as it grew in the forest, foredoomed to its great and terrible destiny. In Northumberland again comes the Dream of the Rood, again in Cornwall. It is the dream of men who later made their cathedral aisles in the pattern of forest rides, in whose mythology, the mind of the race, not of the individual, was the other sacred Tree, Ig-Drasil, where Woden hung for nine days and nine nights that he might solve the riddle of the world. Radegunde came of that stock: and she was his finest inspiration.

He wrote for her, kindled by her passion of pity, the story of the little Spanish princess, brought north to marry Chilperic, and in a year so foully murdered by

[1] Sid. Apol. *Carm.* xxiv. *Ad Libellum*, ll. 1-10.

[2] Tardi, "Fortunatus et Angilbert." *Archiv. Lat. Med. Aev.* 1925, p. 30.

[3] Dante took it for the opening line of the last canto of the *Inferno*, "*Vexilla regis prodeunt Inferni.*" I am indebted for the reminder to Professor Saintsbury.

his mistress.[1] Her mother comes with her as far as Toledo, and there must turn. And the parting, haunted as it is, is agonising.

> " Who will come running now, arms held out, for my kisses ?
> . . . Big as you were, I carried you, so dear, so light.
> So many times I kissed you, in your sleep . . .
> You gone, it is from other children's faces
> That I must kiss the tears."

She was too innocent to hold a man who had known Fredegunde's satisfactions : in a few years her small tragedy was forgotten, and Fredegunde side by side with Chilperic at the Synod at Berny Rivière. One could have spared the felicitations of Fortunatus on that occasion,[2] but he was a courtier poet. He writes an epitaph, gravely and greatly, and his

> " Where are now the arms of Hector," [3]

is not unworthy of its great descendant. But he is happiest in the art that carves on a cherry stone, that fastens a lyric on the handle of a basket of chestnuts to send to his lady and abbess : [4] he ransacks the garden for roses, but can find only violets : may his love transmute them.[5] He loves good cheer and country things as Herrick did : an indifferent poet, but an artist, and aware of every fault he has. And in the grim if humorous world of Gregory of Tours, brutal and debauched, his *aperçus* of lovely things, a green parrot on a tapestry, violets and primroses on the altar at Easter, moonlight on a church floor,[6] are proof that the sense of beauty lingered, even in an age where Chilperic figured as Apollo.

II

Fortunatus died at Poictiers in 609 : Gregory the Great in 604 : Isidore of Seville, leaving the Encyclopedia Britannica of the Middle Ages behind him as his monument,

[1] *Carm.* vi. 5. [2] *Carm.* ix. 1. [3] *Ib.* vii. 12.
[4] *Ib.* xi. 13. [5] *Ib.* viii. 6. [6] *Ib.* iii. 13 ; viii. 7 ; iii. 7.

in 636: and for a while it seemed that they had taken Latin letters to their graves with them. It was low tide on the Continent of Europe,[1] except for one deep pool at Toulouse where the grammarian Virgilius Maro agitated strangely on the secret tongues of Latin, and told his story of the two scholars who argued for fifteen days and nights without sleeping or eating on the frequentative of the verb *to be*, till it almost came to knives,[2] rather like the monsters one expects to find stranded in an ebb. It is impossible that the tradition of Latin letters should be forgotten wholly in Provence and Aquitaine. Yet the Mediterranean is a tideless sea: and when the old learning comes again, it is with the urge of the Atlantic behind it.

Many extravagant things have been written about the Irish Golden Age: but in the sober scholar's prose of Bede, the story is miraculous enough. That fierce and restless quality which had made the pagan Irish the terror of Western Europe, seems to have emptied itself into the love of learning and the love of God: and it is the peculiar distinction of Irish mediaeval scholarship and the salvation of literature in Europe that the one in no way conflicted with the other.[3] Sedulius of Liège saw Christ a more gracious Apollo.[4] Zimmer has a theory that Ireland, secure from invasion in the shelter of the Four Seas, had long been the refuge of the timid scholars of Gaul, driven like thistledown before the barbarian blast, and that even in the fifth century the Irish schools were notable. There is support for it in a casual reference by Columbanus to the judgment of Irish scholars in the fifth century on Victorinus of Aquitaine, the philosopher.[5] Also, still earlier, one remembers Jerome

[1] Gregory of Tours, *Hist. Franc. Praef.*

[2] Virgilius Maro Grammaticus, *Epist. de Verbo* (Teubner, p. 138). *De Catalogo Grammaticorum*, pp. 88-90.

[3] Poole, *Illustrations of Mediaeval Thought*, p. 10 *et seq.*

[4] *Poet. Lat. Car.* iii. Sed. Scot. *Carm.* ii. 80.

[5] Epist i. Migne, lxxx, c. 261.

behaving very like Dr. Johnson to Pelagius, "sodden with porridge" as with heresy.[1] At any rate, by the sixth century the Irish schools were the most famous in Europe. The scholars came by the old trade routes, the three days' journey from the Loire to Cork—in 550 a shipload of fifty landed there—or up the Irish Sea to Bangor. That such a one "forsaking his own country sojourned in Ireland for the love of God and of learning" becomes a commonplace of biography. Bede, writing of the great plague of 664, speaks of its ravages among the scholars: "many of the nobles of the English nation and lesser men also had set out thither, forsaking their native island either for the grace of sacred learning or a more austere life. And some of them indeed soon dedicated themselves faithfully to the monastic life, others rejoiced rather to give themselves to learning, going about from one master's cell to another. All these the Irish willingly received, and saw to it to supply them with food day by day without cost, and books for their studies, and teaching, free of charge."[2]

They were not all of them saintly. St. Comgall had a master whose way of life perplexed his ardent disciple and grieved him: for he was a fine scholar "though of a nature frail in pleasure."[3] Side by side with the innocent story of the three clerks who went on pilgrimage to sea without provision, that being God's business, only that the youngest said, "I think I will take the little cat": how they came to an island and halted there to recite the Psalms for the day and the little cat went down and fished for them a great salmon: how they doubted, not seeing the hand of the Lord in the paw of the little cat, until they roused again from their devotions to see the salmon brandering on a fire of coals, which brought them too near the shore of Lake Tiberias to doubt:[4] and side by side with the story of St. Brendan who would listen to no

[1] "*Praegravatus Scotorum pultibus.*" Migne, xxiv. c. 682.

[2] Bede, *Hist. Eccles.* iii. 27.

[3] *Acta SS.* xv. 581.

[4] Whitley Stokes, *Lives of Saints from the Book of Lismore*, viii.

harping since the day that the Archangel Gabriel in the form of a white bird sat on the altar and sang to him, leaving him deaf to all earthlier music,[1] is another story, the far-off anticipation of Héloïse and Abelard: of the clerk who loved a nun, the handmaid of St. Molaisse: and when her time came she sent him away, fearing his curse upon her lover—"It is enough," said she, "that *I* should be ruined"—and herself faced the wrath of the Saint. So it was she who was cursed, and she died in childbed and was buried, not in consecrated ground, but in the middle of the Bog of Leighlin: and her lover came again to find her dead, and built himself a hut of wattles beside the grave, and prayed day and night for her soul. When more than a year had passed, St. Fursa came to see his brother saint, and as they sat he asked him what great saint was buried in the bog. "No saint," said the outraged holy man, "but an idol, a devil of a nun." "Nay then, a saint," said Fursa, "for I see a service of angels between heaven and her grave." So the dead nun was lifted from her grave in the peat, and buried in holy ground, and as for the clerk, St. Fursa took him with him, and he became a holy man.[2] The same St. Fursa crossed the sea to England where he founded a monastery in East Anglia, and thence to France, to die the patron saint of Peronne.[3] Cathaldus, patron saint of Tarentum, was once schoolmaster in the monastery of Lismore, and his office still recites the scholars of many nations who came to hear him.[4] Virgilius, Bishop of Salzburg and a thing of dread to Boniface, because he lectured on the antipodes which is to deny Christ and His Church, was once Abbot of Aghaboe.[5] They have an odd grace, the names of wild earth side by side with the sophistication of the older world, something of the strangeness of the

[1] Whitley Stokes, *Lives of Saints from the Book of Lismore*, xiii.

[2] *Ib.* x. [3] Bede, *Hist. Eccles.* iii. 19. [4] Ussher, *Brit. Ecc. Ant.* c. 16.

[5] Todd, *St. Patrick*, p. 64. Gougaud, *Les Chrétientés celtiques*, p. 243. *Annals of the Four Masters* (O'Donovan), i. 391.

Irish glosses in the ninth century manuscripts of Berne and Leyden and St. Gall :[1] "We are from Inch-madoc, Coirbre and I," and most moving of all to one who remembers the low grey ruins on the island in Strangford Lough, "Mahee of Nendrum."[2] It is a long way from the grey peace of Strangford Lough to the eagle's perch of St. Gall, but one manuscript went farther yet, to the monastery of St. Paul in Carinthia. It is the commonplace book of a scholar at Reichenau, but the compiler of it had known one of those moments of detached and humorous vision that are the salt of scholarship.

"I and Pangur Bán my cat,
'Tis a like task we are at:
Hunting mice is his delight,
Hunting words I sit all night.

. . . .

"'Tis a merry thing to see
At our tasks how glad are we,
When at home we sit and find
Entertainment to our mind.

. . . .

"'Gainst the wall he sets his eye,
Full and fierce and sharp and sly;
'Gainst the wall of knowledge I
All my little wisdom try.

. . . .

"So in peace our task we ply,
Pangur Bán, my cat and I;
In our arts we find our bliss,
I have mine and he has his."[3]

The other half-obliterated fragment is less the scholar than the exile dreaming at the fire.

[1] *Vide* Whitley Stokes, *Thesaurus Paleohibernicus,* ii. pp. xx; xxxii-iv; 290-96. Lindsay, "Early Irish Minuscule Script," *St. Andrews Univ. Publ.* vi. 1910. The Leyden Priscian was written by Dubthach and finished at three o'clock, 11th April, 838. Is this the same Dubthach who invented the Cryptogram of Bamberg for the confusion of all scholars at the Breton Court? (Gougaud, p. 244).

[2] These are in the margin of the Priscian MS. at St. Gall, Codex 904.

[3] Translated by Robin Flower.

"I wish the wood of Allabair and Argatbran between fire and wall. If this . . . may it be corn and milk that I see. If it be not . . . may it be wolves and deer and wandering on the mountains and warriors of the Feni that I see." And this:

"My heartlet: God from Heaven, He is the thatcher who
hath thatched it.
A house wherein wet rain pours not, a place wherein thou
fearest not spear points,
Bright as though in a garden, and it without a fence
round it."[1]

Another Irishman came to Carinthia, and found small hospitality there,[2] but an equal sickness for home.

"In all my wanderings round this world of care,
In all my griefs—and God has given my share—
I still had hopes my latest hours to crown,
Amidst these humble bowers to lay me down. . . .
Around my fire an evening group to draw,
And tell of all I felt and all I saw. . . .
And as a hare whom hounds and horns pursue,
Pants to that place from whence at first she flew,
I still had hopes, my long vexations past,
Here to return, and die at home at last."

There are nine hundred years between: but "wandering," as Walafrid Strabo, secure in his garden at Reichenau, wonderingly noted, was still "a second nature to the Irish race."[3]

Reichenau itself, where Walafrid weeded his garden, if not actually an Irish foundation, at any rate owed its fame to its Irish scholars. For when St. Columba turned his back on Derry with the lament that is the loveliest of the older Irish poems, and founded his monastery at Iona, it was the beginning of the other movement, the centri-

[1] Translations in *Thesaur. Palaeohib.* ii. 293-4.

[2] "Onward, where the rude Carinthian boor,
Against the houseless stranger shuts the door."

[3] Walafrid Strabo, *De Mirac. S. Galli*, c. 47. In *Carm.* 45 he teases his friend Probus for his "Irish fashion" of going away.

fugal, and this is more important even than the first, the centripetal, which had brought so many scholars to the Irish schools. Their fame persisted :[1] even in the twelfth century St. Bernard of Clairvaux speaks with honour of Bangor.[2] Clonmacnoise at the end of the eighth century had Coelchu, whom Alcuin himself called *Noster Magister*, and writes him from Charlemagne's court all the gossip of the journey and of recent politics, "for I know you curious of such things. . . . I know not wherein I have sinned, that for so long I have not deserved to see the sweetness of your letters." Charlemagne sends 50 siclos, Alcuin 50, and a phial of oil for consecration, "for I know it is hard to get it in Britain."[3] Clonfert on the Shannon, six times burnt, four times plundered by the Danes, survived till the Norman invasion in 1172. In the tenth century Maelbrighde, Abbot of Armagh, died, "head of the piety of Ireland and of the greater part of Europe," said the Four Masters, which may well have been, for the tenth century saw little piety anywhere else : he had presented King Athelstan with a marvellously illuminated gospel.[4] But the claim of the Irish schools is not so much in the intricate treasure of their manuscript, as in the other pattern which they wove into the history of Europe. Bangor, where Columbanus learnt the lighter Greek metres and the secret of his exquisite and melancholy prose, has now Marine Gardens and a promenade : Clonmacnoise, "St. Ciaran's plain of crosses," survives in a few ruined arches, and the echoing beauty of its name. But St. Gall is still a stronghold : and Bobbio, though fallen on degenerate

[1] Higden has a story (*c.* 1050) of a famous scholar in Ireland, Barbaras, a man of wonderful religion, who had a great school of clerks "and lewd men and maydens," but "for he schare the maydens in manere of his scolers, he was put out of Ireland." Trevisa's *Higden*, vii. p. 183.

[2] *Vita S. Malachiae*, vi. Migne, clxxxii. c. 1082.

[3] *M. G. H. Epist. Car.* ii. ep. 7. The intimacy of the letter suggests a strong personal affection, as though Alcuin himself had been a student at Clonmacnoise. Ducange rates the *siclus* at two silver denarii.

[4] Armitage Robinson, *The Times of St. Dunstan*, pp. 55-59.

and illiterate days, yielded at the end of the fifteenth century the remnants of a great classical library.[1] St. Martin's of Cologne, where the Archpoet saw his vision of the *terra ridentium,* the country of the laughing, and praised the Abbot for his free hand in wine,[2] was an Irish foundation, restored to them in 974, and only finally taken over by the other " Scots " in the fourteenth century.[3] St. Peter's of Ratisbon was founded in 1076 by Marianus Scotus. St. James, built by the aid of Conor O'Brian, King of Munster, in 1119, became the mother house of a dozen Irish monasteries, in Würzburg, Nuremberg, Eichstadt, Vienna, Prague.[4] But the great age is the century of Columba and Columbanus. Iona did for England what the Roman Augustine failed to do. On the Continent, Columbanus and his disciples founded over a hundred monasteries, some of them the greatest strongholds of learning in the Middle Ages: Luxeuil, Bobbio, St. Gall, St. Bertin, Jumièges, St. Riquier, Remiremont. In fifty years they had accepted the kindlier rule of St. Benedict, for the Rule of Columbanus was merciless to human weakness—" Let a man go to bed when he sleeps on his feet before he reaches it " [5]—but it had the positive austerity that is the driving force of the great apostolates. Columbanus himself was an austere man, for all his personal beauty: [6] " prince of Druids," John of

[1] There is a tenth century catalogue of the library at Bobbio: an astonishing number of grammarians and real intelligence in the method of entry. Muratori, *Ant.* iii. 43.

[2] Manitius, *Die Gedichte des Archipoeta,* ix. p. 54.

[3] Haddan, *Scots on the Continent* (*Remains of W. Haddan,* pp. 286-8). Wattenbach, *Irish Monasteries in Germany,* trans. by Reeves, *Ulster Journal of Archaeology,* 1859, pp. 227-246, 295-313.

[4] *Nuovi Studi Medievali,* i. 228.

[5] *S. Columban. Regula Cœnobialis,* cap. ix. (Migne, 80, 216). "Lassus ad stratum veniat: ambulansque dormiat, necdum expleto somno exsurgere compellatur."

[6] The Church has been an unconscious Platonist in insisting on the beauty of her saints.

Tritheim calls him:[1] he confronted Brunhild, Fortunatus' Brunhild, now wicked and old, like a second John the Baptist, and was driven from France for it. But squirrels came and sat on his shoulder and ran in and out of his cowl: he was a lover of Ovid and beguiled his wistful old age with experiments in Greek metres: and when Valery the gardener at Luxeuil came into his classroom and brought the smell of roses with him, Columbanus would stop in his lecture to cry, "Nay then, it is thou, beloved, who art lord and abbot of this monastery."[2]

It is to be observed of the Irish foundations that they were built in solitary places and then made of them a garden: the first reclaiming of the Vosges is the work of the monks of Luxeuil. It would have been better for literature if this craving for the soil which is the root and ground of Irish poetry had taken seisin of their Latin verse. It is too academic, for all its occasional loveliness: poetry that is to be read "by strong men and thieves and deacons" needs to touch the earth once in every generation. There is now and then a greenness in the dry tree, a single verse in a tenth century love song, a whole lyric early in the eleventh: but it is not till the twelfth that it finds where its great strength lies. There is nothing in the earlier Latin verse to equal the Exile Song by Columba, the meeting of King Guaire and the hermit (tenth century) or the fragment, once again a gloss from the Priscian MS. of St. Gall.

"A hedge of trees surrounds me: a blackbird's lay sings to me, praise which I will not hide,
Above my booklet the lined one, the trilling of the bird sings to me.
In a grey mantle the cuckoo chants to me from the tops of the bushes.
May the Lord protect me from doom! I write well under the greenwood."[3]

[1] "velut olim Druidum princeps." *De Script. Eccl.* (*Opera Historica*, 1601, p. 244).

[2] Vita St. Walerici. *Acta SS.* 1st April, p. 18.

[3] Translation in *Thesaur. Palaeohib.* ii. 290.

The wisdom of Irish verse is the vision of Finn after he had eaten the Salmon of Knowledge, not

> " The triple temporality
> Under the countenance of eternity,"

or Art on her knees to Nature craving the gift of life, or any of the complicated visions of the great clerk Jean de Meung at the end of the thirteenth century. " Finn, what do you see ? " And he said that he saw May Day, and swallows skimming and haze on the lake and the rushes talking, heather and black peat, and the sea asleep.[1] " What are the three lasting things ? " they asked Cormac, and the answer came, " Grass and copper and yew." [2] Their Latin verse is beaten copper : the Irish has the grass and the yew. It is the incommunicable gift, incommunicable in mere scholarship. But what the Irish scholars did give, was their feeling for classical literature : their handling, sensitive and fearless, of paganism. One sees it in Columbanus, whose verse is a mosaic of the old mythology, still more in Sedulius of Liège, two centuries later. He is writing a song for the Nativity : the choir is to sing it on Christmas morning.

> " It is the time of snow, sparkling with sincere light :
> The day that Christ was born : it is the time of snow."

He tells the story : the kindly oxen, the patient Joseph, the coming of the wise men from the East, with their gifts of royalty and death. From the West now they come, with no gift but their learning only. And Mary, says Sedulius, does not say them nay.[3]

[1] *Mac gnimartha Finn*, edited in the *Revue Celtique*, v. 195 *et seq.*

[2] Kuno Meyer, *Instructions of King Cormac*, p. 39.

[3] *P.L.C.* iii. Sedulius Scottus, *Carm.* ii. xi. p. 179.

III

At first derivative, never wholly unaffected by the Irish tradition,[1] is the English tradition of scholarship. Bede takes pains to show how much Northumberland and Mercia owed to the Irish scholars, but with the coming of St. Paul's fellow-townsman, Theodore of Tarsus, to the see of Canterbury with Hadrian the African as his *scholasticus*, the schools of Canterbury begin to rival those across the Channel. So at least thought Aldhelm, Bishop of Sherborne and pupil of Hadrian, and yearned for some occasion when the mighty boar, Theodore, might try his tusks on these yapping Irish hounds, with their sharp filed teeth of grammar. Aldhelm's friend, Eahfrid, had gone across the water, and Aldhelm, who doth something affect the letter, reproaches him for it in a really terrifying document, evidently intended to demonstrate that learning and elegance abode at home.[2] Aldhelm in this mood betrays something of the grandiloquent barbarian :[3] even his ordinary prose is full of surprises for the reader of Cicero, and something of a hurdle race. Nevertheless he was mightily learned for his age, and could drop the bishop's and the scholar's weeds and stand like a gleeman

[1] *Vide* William of Malmesbury on the restoration of Glastonbury by Irish scholars, and his critical appreciation of twelfth century Irish scholarship. (Stubbs, *Memorials of St. Dunstan*, pp. 256-7.)

[2] *M. G. H.*, *Aldhelmi Opera*, ed. Ehwald, Epist. v. p. 488.

[3] It has been suggested that Aldhelm is doing it for fun, and that this kind of language was highly esteemed on the other side of the "enormes dodrantium glareas." Yet all the prose documents, the letters of Columbanus, of Cummian, of the anonymous Irish scholar to Aldhelm himself (Ussher, *Epist. Hib.* 35) are as free from it as Bede, and there is not a trace of it in John Scotus Erigena. *Hisperica Famina* is a bantling no nation is anxious to claim. But the sources of the astonishing jargon would be an amusing if unprofitable quest. The style of Martianus Capella is thoroughly vicious, and Virgilius Maro of Toulouse with his secret Latin known only to the initiate sets just the kind of riddle to intrigue the barbarian mind. But perhaps it is better to read again "*Comment Pantagruel rencontra un Limousin*," and leave it at that.

on the bridge at Sherborne, singing fragments of the Gospels and scraps of clowning, that the Devil might not have all the good tunes. Of the experiments in Latin verse once ascribed to him (though Henry Bradley *bonae memoriae* was inclined to give them to his contemporary Ethelwald),[1] one is a description of a storm on the Cornish coast which the Northumbrian Swinburne would be hard put to it to beat.

> " Storm and destruction shattering,
>   Strike fear upon the world.
> The winds are out, and through high heaven
>   Their Bacchanals are hurled."

But the last line is a poor substitute for the very rip of thunder in the

> " Baccharentur in æthere,"

of the original.

> " Along the pathway of the sea
> The salt waves rise in foam." [2]

—for the first time, unless indeed the *Seafarer* be older, an English poet has entered on his kingdom of the sea.

Of Bede, of the next generation and of all time, there is no need to speak. He is the *massif* of English scholarship. His cell at Jarrow, and the books that Benedict Biscop brought in so many journeys from Rome, bounded him in a nutshell and made him king of infinite space. The historians claim him as the first modern historian: the critics as the first modern prosodist. He had a delicate ear: wrote an admirable book on metre with an appreciation of the new system of accent rather than quantity very rare in a classical scholar, even in the sixteenth century.[3] He is a greater critic than craftsman: there

[1] *English Hist. Review*, xv. 291.

[2]
> " Per pelagi itinera
> Salsa spumabant aequora."
>
> Aldhelm, *Carm. Rhythm* i. *Op. cit.* p. 524.

For text and discussion of authorship see Ehwald, *op. cit.* 519 ff.

[3] Bede, *De Arte Metrica*, c. xxiv. *De rhythmo.* Migne, xc. c. 173. See Ker, *The Dark Ages*, pp. 144, 200.

are cadences in his prose lovelier than anything in his poetry—"Burn now your candle as long as ye will: it has naught to do with me, for my light cometh when the day breaketh."[1] But the poet is in the strange burst of weeping that took him under a tree in the open, in a line or two of his vision of hell—

> "Where is no voice unless of bitter weeping,
> No face, unless the face of the tormentors."

and the wistful beauty of his heaven—

> "Nor any night
> To snatch the splendour of the gracious light:
> Nor sorrow comes, nor tears, nor tired old age."[2]

IV

It was at the Court of Charlemagne that three traditions met: the old rhetorical school of Italy in Peter of Pisa and Paul the Deacon, the old scholar and the young that Charlemagne brought back with him as booty from his Italian wars; the Irish, under Clement and Dungal; the English under Alcuin, Bede's grandson after the spirit; and, perhaps, a fourth in Theodulfus, the great Spaniard from the Narbonese. Peter of Pisa taught grammar, says Eginhard, noting that to grammar above all the arts the Italians cleave;[3] Paul writes court poetry, one exquisite line on the dead baby Hildegard,

> "So small a maid to leave so great a sorrow,"[4]

[1] Bede, *Eccles. Hist.* iv. 8.

[2] Migne, *P.L.* 94, c. 634, 636.

> "Dum sedi, subito planctu turbatus amaro.

> "Vox ubi nulla sonat, durus nisi fletus ubique,
> Non nisi tortorum facies ubi cernitur ulla. . . .
> Nox ubi nulla rapit splendorem lucis amoenae
> Non dolor aut gemitus veniet nec fessa senectus."

[3] Eginhard, *Vita Car. Mag.* c. 25. Cf. Rodulfus Glaber (*Hist.* II. xii.) on the heresy of Vilgardus. "studio artis grammaticae magis assiduus quam frequens, sicut Italiae mos semper fuit artes negligere ceteras, illam sectari."

[4] *Poet. Lat. Car.* i. Paulus Diac. *Carm.* xxiv.

but his heart is in Italy, and his loveliest sonnet is for Lake Como, with its scent of myrtles and its everlasting spring ; [1] his fame is less for his verse than for his History of the Lombards, written in the monastery of Monte Cassino, to which he wins his long desired return. For the Irishmen, there is the Monk of St. Gall's story of the two who came in a trading ship to France, and stood with the rest of the merchants crying in the fair that they had wisdom to sell ; for they knew that if men get anything for nothing they think little of it. It came to the ears of Charlemagne, that Athenian lover of strange things, and he sent for them and asked the price. " Proper places and noble souls," said they, " and such things as we cannot travel without, food and wherewith to be clothed." And Charlemagne received them joyously, and kept them in his own house ; but having to go on a campaign, he set one of them, Clement, over a school in which rich and poor sat together, and the other he sent into Italy, to the monastery of St. Augustine of Pavia.[2] In May, 1925, the University of Pavia celebrated its eleven hundredth anniversary, its foundation by decree of Lothair under Dungal the Irishman, as the centre of liberal studies for the minor schools of Lombardy.

But it is Alcuin who is the doyen of the Caroline renaissance ; the old piping shepherd of his own eclogues,[3] and much nearer that than the " Horace " of his own choosing. He came from the school of York because Charlemagne desired that his empire with himself should go to school ; and the picture of Charlemagne with his slate under his pillow so that he could sit up and make his letters in the middle of the night is very engaging.[4] He never learnt to write with ease, but he read with passion, and was a still more passionate musician. There

[1] *Poet. Lat. Car.* i. Paulus Diac. *Carm.* iv.

[2] Monachus S. Galli, *Gesta Car. Mag.* i. 1 (*M. G. H. Script.* ii. p. 731).

[3] *Conflictio Veris et Hiemis.* Alcuin, *Carm.* 58 (*Poet. Lat. Car.* i. p. 270).

[4] Eginhard, *Vit. Car. Mag.* c. 25. *M. G. H. Script.* ii. p. 457.

was nothing that Charlemagne did not wish to learn; and his scholarship is primary in the best sense. He is not content with Donatus and Virgil: he demanded a Frankish grammar and a collection of Frankish ballads.[1] "Why cannot I have twelve such ministers?" he cried, when they read him of Augustine and Jerome; to which Alcuin controlling himself with some difficulty replied: "The Most High had but these two: and wilt thou have twelve?"[2] With what mixture of poetry, pedantry and steady common-sense Alcuin managed his strange menagerie is evident in the text books that he wrote for it; he had ten years of it; and earned his retreat in the most gracious of all the French provinces, the aquatint landscapes of Touraine.

But he enjoyed himself; the evidence of it is a letter written during his two years absence in England to his friend, Joseph the Irishman, still at Court. He begins with news of their common friend and "master," of Clonmacnoise; encloses five pounds silver, with commissions for goatskins and paints, a really good sulphur and other colours for illumination. Then follows a *cri de cœur* that might be from Dr. Middleton. "But woe is me! There is death in the pot, O man of God! The wine is gone from our wineskins, and bitter beer rageth in our bellies. And because we have it not, do thou drink in our name and lead a joyful day; sad to us, for we have not wherewith to gladden us, and barely wherewith to strengthen. . . . Uinter the physician promised me two crates of wine, excellent and clear:" he proceeds to arrangements for its transport. "Alas! that you are so far away. I see you, a young goat among the vineyards. Farewell."[3]

[1] *Ib.* c. 29. "Inchoavit et grammaticam patrii sermonis." See Hauréau, *Charlemagne et sa cour*. Hauréau notes that the *Frankish Grammar* had to wait for the sixteenth century.

[2] Monachus St. Galli, i. c. 9 (*M. G. H. Scrip.* ii. p. 734).

[3] *M. G. H. Epist. Car.* ii. ep. 8.

This is hardly the heavy pedant of the text books; and though he himself initiated the "Charles—Father" type of school book, his own are written by a poet as well as a scholar. "What is speech?" says Pepin, Charlemagne's unfortunate eldest son. "The betrayer of the soul." "What is a man?" "The slave of death, the guest of an inn, a wayfarer passing." "What is sleep?" "The image of death."[1] There spoke Cynewulf's contemporary. The story of his enmity to Virgil in his old age may be true;[2] it hardly tallies with the evidence of his own verse, or with his trick of fastening the names of pagan poets to his friends and scholars. But the sensitiveness that had made him cry for Dido when he was a schoolboy never hardens: the transience of lovely things, the pitiful slow descent of strong men to tired old age, the cruelty of life that will not stay, is always with him,[3] and all heaven's height for him is only this:

> "The happy house where friend from friend divides not,
> And what he loves, he hath for evermore."[4]

Amor is friendship to Alcuin, as to all the earlier Middle Age,[5] and again to the sixteenth century Renaissance; and his loveliest lyric is his song to the cuckoo, the lament for his vanished scholar.[6] There is an equal gulf of years and imagination between it and "Too quick despairer, wherefore wilt thou go?" but Alcuin and Matthew Arnold

[1] *Disputatio Pippini* (Migne, 101, c. 975).

[2] *Vita Alcuini*, cap. x. *Mon. Alcuini*, p. 24.

[3] *Poet. Lat. Car.* i. Alcuin, *Carm.* ix.

[4] *Ib. Carm.* xi.

[5] *Ib. Carm.* 55:

> "Tu requies mentis, tu mihi dulcis amor.
> . . . O quando optandi veniet mihi tempus amoris,
> Quando erit illa dies qua . . . te cernere possim?"

[6] *Ib. Carm.* 57. *Cf. Epist.* 286:

> "Heu, cuculus nobis fuerat cantare suetus
> Quae te nunc rapuit hora nefanda tuis?
> . . . Non pereat cuculus, veniet sub tempore veris
> Et nobis veniens carmine laeta ciet.
> Quis scit, si veniat? . . ."

had heard the cuckoo's parting cry above the shining water meadows alike of Oxford and Touraine, and each had known it for the dirge of the unreturning springtime of the heart, the sorrow of Persephone's garden. It was in Touraine, in the abbey that he had made the most famous school of manuscript, out of Ireland, in Europe,[1] Touraine that was to be the cradle of many poets from the twelfth century to the sixteenth, that Alcuin died. The lament that his scholar Fredegis wrote for him and his cell left empty is the loveliest in the Middle Age :

> " O little house, O dear and sweet my dwelling,
> O little house, for ever fare thee well.
> The trees stand round thee with their sighing branches,
> A little flowering wood for ever fair.
> Small streams about thee, . . ." [2]

It has the silvered light of the Loire, the faint and exquisite landscapes of Ronsard and Du Bellay.

There was a good deal of verse about the court ; even if that famous clerk who surpassed them all for singing vanished suddenly from the Emperor's presence and left behind him only a little foully burning coal, evidence of the Satanic origin of his great gifts.[3] None of the verse that has come down to us is incendiary enough to justify that ; not even Angilbert's, the worldliest, courtier and counsellor, passionate, ardent and beauty-loving, successful lover of one of Charlemagne's jealously guarded daughters, abbot of St. Riquier in a mood of penitence, but still magnificent in his wearing, the first of the great princes of the Church. He loved a song with a refrain ; loved jongleurs and gauds (" thy care," said Alcuin sadly, who loved him, called him Homer, and shook his head over him, " should be for singing clerks rather than for dancing bears ").[4] It was a rich life, broken by penitence

[1] See Delisle, *L'École Calligraphique de Tours au IXe siècle.*
[2] *P.L.C.* i. p. 243. Alcuin, *Carm.* 23.
[3] Monachus S. Galli, *Vit. Car.* 1, 33 (*M. G. H. Script.* ii. p. 746).
[4] " nec tibi sit ursorum saltantium cura sed clericorum psallentium " (Ep. 244). The pun was made to Fredegis, but see Ep. 175, 237.

and passion ; he died in St. Riquier, even as his master lay dying in Aix la Chapelle ; left his magnificent library of 200 manuscripts to his monastery, and a memory so ardent that his very epitaph suggests something of the strong lover of life that lay beneath it :

> " O King, give Angilbert thy rest,
> Father and King.
>
> O Law, give him the eternal life of law,
> For thou art Law.
>
> O Light, give ever unto him thy light,
> For thou art Light.
>
> O Peace, give unto him eternal peace,
> For thou art Peace." [1]

Theodulfus in Charles' court has a little the countenance of Malvolio. For it was a lively court ; there are echoes of it in Alcuin's warning against the " crowned doves," the naughty princesses ; [2] even by contrast with the snowy days when Charlemagne moped like an owl, and even Delia would not sing, and the poet slinks away with an empty belly, and the boys sulk, till the sun comes out and David reaches for his harp, and all good things come again.[3] Theodulfus was a judge and wrote admirable verse, with judicial solemnity ; a man of taste, for they brought him vases to tempt him in the Southern circuit,[4] and he himself designed other vases, a fair woman suckling a child, for an image of the kind earth ; [5] a sound scholar, founder of the schools of Orleans beside which the University of Paris is a mushroom ; the first to antagonise Love, the winged wanton, the *sceleratus*, in his own name.[6] One other thing he antagonised, the Irish scholars at the

[1] *Poet. Lat. Car.* i. p. 356.

[2] " coronatae columbae," *Epist.* 244.

[3] *Poet. Lat. Car.* i. Alcuin, *Carm.* 40.

[4] *P.L.C.* i. Theod. *Carm.* Contra Iudices, line 79. See Delisle, *Les Bibles de Théodulfe.*

[5] *Ib. Carm.* 47.

[6] *Ib. Carm.* 45.

court, whom he describes in language which has since become almost traditional. Shall the Spaniard (Goth) make league with the Scot? as well with the south wind; could it be other than itself, it would be Irish. It is his levity he cannot abide—in eye, in hand, in mind and foot.

"And flashing now he pounces here, now there."

He has learnt all things, but to him nothing is fixed, nothing secure; swift to argument, "striking the living dead with a naughty gibe." [1] There, for Spanish gravity, was the rub. But the jest has evaporated, and the laughter; the spleen abides. Theodulfus was to suffer worse disaster; in prison, suspect of treason, he wrote the hymn that is still sung on Palm Sunday,

"Gloria, laus et honor tibi."

His is the first great name in the schools of Orleans that were to father many scholars and many poets.

Of the identity of the Irishman who provoked him, one knows nothing; Clement, Dungal,[2] Dicuil the geographer,[3] to whom certainly "nothing was fixed or secure." "This saith Solinus," writes Dicuil, "but I believe it not for——" and he goes on to tell what he heard from Brother Fidelis, talking to his master Suibhne when he himself was a boy.[4] Brother Fidelis had himself an inquiring mind; he measured one of the pyramids, which he took to be Joseph's granaries, and the measurements are still found exact; sailed from the Nile to the Red Sea by a canal, inspected the place where Moses crossed it, and wished to stop the boat so as to look for the wheel

[1] *Poet. Lat. Car.* i. Theodulf., *Carm.* xxv. lines 159 *et seq.*, xxvii. line 65.

[2] See Traube, *O Roma Nobilis*, pp. 332-357.

[3] See Dümmler, *Neues Archiv der Gesellsch. f. ält. deutsche. Geschichte.* 1879, Bd. iv. Mario Esposito, "An Unpublished Astronomical Treatise by Dicuil." *Proceedings of the Irish Academy*, vol. xxvi. pp. 378-446 (1907).

[4] Dicuil, *Liber De Mensura Orbis Terrae* (edited Parthey, 1870), p. 25.

tracks of Pharaoh's chariots in the sand, but the boatmen refused, which must have been a grief of mind to him.[1] Dicuil ranges from the marvel of the midnight sun to the habits of the "corcodrillus," and has an enchanting passage on the sea birds in the Faröes; he is a thorough scientist, for in his work on the changes of the moon he refuses to discuss the question of the tides, being now far inland, and leaves it to ingenious persons in the sea's neighbourhood.[2] It is John Scotus' contempt for authority, stripped of its veil of Platonism. Even "Hibernicus Exul," who sang his way into the Emperor's good graces, has left an epic that is an exaltation not so much of the Imperial greatness as of the dignity of poetry. "So long as the mighty axis of the starry sphere revolves, and dark night is driven off by the shining stars, so long as Phosphor rises splendid from towering waves, and the swift wind lashes the deep, so long as the rivers foam down to the sea, and the clouds touch the threatening peaks and the valleys lie low with their bogs, and the high hills rear their jagged crests, so long as the splendour of kings blazes with ruddy gold——" one expects the familiar climax of Latin compliment, the eternity of Caesar, but instead:

"Age after age the Muses' gifts abide." [3]

So that it is Charles, and not his harper, who is likely to be in debt. It is the eternal arrogance of letters, Hibernicus Exul at the court of Charlemagne: Jonathan Swift at the court of St. James.

[1] Dicuil, *Liber De Mensura Orbis Terrae* (edited Parthey, 1870), pp. 26-27.

[2] *Liber de Astronomia*, iv. 5. "Quamvis de concordia immutabiliter stabili maris et lunae convenienter in hoc loco narrari debuit, tamen quoniam sum procul separatus a mare, ingeniosis habitantibus iuxta mare eam nuntiare relinquo."

[3] *P.L.C.* i. Hibernicus Exul, *Carm.* ii. lines 24-33.

V

With the death of Charlemagne, "King David" to Alcuin and Angilbert, the genial tradition breaks. Louis the Pious succeeded him who "never showed his white teeth in a smile," said the Puritan chroniclers approvingly;[1] and the music makers and the jongleurs vanish from the presence like flies in winter. He had little of Charlemagne's immense curiosity, though his marriage with the beautiful Judith of Aquitaine brought him a late flowering; and in his reign the Church begins to bear hard on the wandering Irishmen. For the charmed circle that had so long saved Ireland from invasion is broken: in 795 the Northmen landed in Rechra and sacked the monastery, in 822, Bangor, "and the relics of Comgall were shaken from the shrine."[2] For the next hundred years the monasteries stand like battered rocks, washed over at every high tide, and in town after town of Europe one begins to find fugitive scholars. The St. Gall Priscian,[3] itself an exile, tells its own story: the lazy peace of the scriptorium is in the delicate leisurely script of the text, the little spurts of conversation, mostly from Cairbre, in the margin, after the fashion known to all who have sat side by side in "prep."; grumbles at new parchment and a bad pen: "I will go then, if you would rather." "It is dark to me." But Priscian has of course only one half of the conversation; some other manuscript once knew what Maellecan had said to provoke the heavy cynicism of "Love will last as long as property lasts, O Maellecan," and the romantic Maellecan's rejoinder. "O my hand!"

[1] Theganus, *De Gestis Ludov. Pii* (*M. G. H. Script.* ii. 594).

[2] *Annals of the Four Masters* (O'Donovan), i. 435.

[3] St. Gall. MS. 904. Traube (*Sedulius Scottus*, pp. 347-8) thinks it written by Sedulius' circle, and brought with them to the Continent. See Nigra, *Reliquie Celtiche*, i. 1-15. Mario Esposito, *Hiberno-Latin MSS. in the Libraries of Switzerland*, i. 78-9.

says Cairbre, and invokes the good offices of Patrick and Bridget on Maelbrigte, "that he may not be angry with me for the writing that is written this day." "A blessing on the soul of Fergus! I am very cold." One says Amen to that prayer; for Fergus' hands have been a great while cold. "Sunday of a warm Easter:" what magic is in two Irish words to bring again the April sunlight on the page, and the buzzing of the bees in the hives at the head of the cloister garden, bees that died of cold eleven hundred years ago.

"Bitter is the wind to-night; it tosses the ocean's white hair.
I fear not the coursing of the clear sea by the fierce heroes from Lochlann."[1]

Cairbre and Dungas and Maelpatric had found that there were worse things than writer's cramp or the wrath of Maelbrigte for a slovenly page; that terror brooded behind the stillness of quiet moonlight nights. And then the clear night came and the pirates with it; and Priscian, hurriedly snatched up and safe in the darkness of his scholar's wallet, did not see Clonfert or Clonmacnoise roaring red to heaven; or else, warned in time, the two had determined to "walk the world," which is the apostolic phrase of the Irish romances for all of Europe beyond the Four Seas, and had gone while the going was good. At any rate, some time in the middle of the century, Priscian was in Cologne, and lent a blank page for the rough draft of a Latin poem to Gunther, a bishop notoriously generous to wandering scholars; and a fellow-scholar and better Latinist corrects it here and there.[2] But whether or not Gunther came up to expectation does not appear; and it was not before the tenth century that

[1] Whitley Stokes, *Thes. Palaeohib.* ii. pp. xx-xxii, 290.

[2] Lindsay, *Early Irish Minuscule Script*, p. 43. Text in Nigra, *Reliquie Celtiche*, pp. 6-7, "Umbrifera quadam nocte." Also in *Poet. Lat. Car.* iii. 238.

Priscian found refuge in St. Gall. About 850 two famous Irishmen had halted there "to salute their compatriot," Ekkehard says, on their way back from Rome, the good bishop Marcus and his nephew Marcellus. Marcellus was not hard to persuade to go no further.[1] He was a mighty scholar, both in classics and divinity, and an exquisite musician:[2] the Abbot entreated him to take over the charge of the school, and let him and his uncle abide with them, and their countrymen go their way home. The bishop was persuaded, but the pilgrims knowing who had lost them their master so raged against the young man that he gave them their money through a window, fearing they would do him a mischief. Old Marcus came down to the courtyard, wearing his stole, to bless them, and watch them make their slow way down the pass and follow them with the eyes of the mind across France to the valley of the Loire and so to Nantes, or through Germany and the Low Countries, there to take ship for home. Marcellus was happy; he had three scholars, Notker, Tutilo, Ratpert, would have rejoiced any master. But the bishop was an old man; the Alps are not so friendly as the blue Wicklow hills, and though he never reached Ireland again he seems to have left "the nest that the Irishmen built" to live in quiet "a holy old man," says Heric of Auxerre, at St. Medard.[3]

St. Gall has his name in the Book of the Dead: the pallium and the gold were offered to the shrine; the manuscripts to the library. Priscian was not, it seems, among them, for the catalogue of the library made towards the end of the century does not mention him among the books "scottice scripti." He may have come to it when Notker, Marcellus' pupil, was librarian, when many works were added to the library, and if so, he lived through yet

[1] Ekkehard, *Casus S. Galli* (*M. G. H. Script.* ii. 78-9).

[2] *Ib.* p. 94. "In divinis eque potens et humanis: septem liberales eos duxit ad artes; maxime autem ad musicam."

[3] *Acta SS. July*, vii. 283.

another raid. In 925 the Huns swept up the pass, found the monastery deserted except for Heribald who was a little weak in the head, and had refused to leave because the chamberlain had not given him his shoe leather for the year. The Huns were uglier than the Danes, but better natured. When Heribald cried at them to stop when they were breaking in the wine casks, *for what are we to drink when you are gone away* ? they shouted with laughter and left them. And when he told them they ought not to talk in church and they beat him, they were sorry and gave him wine to make up for it ; " which is more than any of you would have done," said Heribald.[1] For the Huns rode away, and the monks came back again, and the books are carried back from Reichenau, and Priscian is back on his shelf, a new shelf, for they had set fire to the library.[2] That is the last alarm ;[3] he has lain there, mellowing his parchments, through the leisure of nine hundred years.

Not all Irish bishops were welcomed so heartily as Marcus, who after all had his *pallium* from Rome. Even in the eighth century the continental councils look a little crookedly at these odd phenomena, bishops without a diocese, like snails without a shell. It was the peculiarity of the Irish church that " bishop " denotes only spiritual rank, and involved no charge.

[1] Ekkehard, *Casus S. Galli*, iii. *M.G.H. Script.* ii. pp. 105, 106, 109. " When they [the monks on their return] asked Heribald how he himself had liked ' the so numerous guests of St. Gall,' he said, ' The very best ; take my word for it, I never remember seeing cheerier souls in our cloister, or better givers of meat and drink. . . . I don't deny there was one thing I did not like, that they had so little behaviour. I tell you the truth, I never saw such behaviour in the cloister of St. Gall, they were as wild in the cloister and the church as if they were in the fields."

[2] There is a chance that he may have been until now at Reichenau, where the books were sent for safety, and whence they returned, the same in number, but " not their very selves," says Ekkehard, so that the Reichenau Priscian may have supplanted St. Gall's. St. Gall had two Priscians before the raid, but neither of them in the Irish script.

[3] Not quite the last : there was the threat of the French Revolutionary Army in 1798. See Clark, *The Abbey of St. Gall*, 273-4.

"Not poor was the family of Mochta [abbot of Louth].
Three hundred priests and one hundred bishops,
Sixty singing men. . . .
They ploughed not, they reaped not, they dried not corn;
They laboured not, save at learning only." [1]

"Those who say they are bishops and are not" are to find closed doors, and no clerk is to accept ordination from them; nor are they to presume to take the cure of souls, or assist in Mass, unless the bishop of the diocese is satisfied of their genuineness.[2] It was doubtless necessary. A good many of the exiles had more scholarship than sanctity, and some little of either, with Bacchus nearer their elbow than Apollo. Most of the drinking songs of the ninth century come from the Irish[3] and the biographer of the blessed Rodbert[4] says harshly *de Scotis* that they are deceivers, wanderers, stragglers. The old guest-houses on the pilgrim roads, founded by pious Irish kings and nobles, fall into decay, and can give hospitality no longer; even the brethren who have served God all their lives, says one council kindly, are forced to beg their bread.[5] That Council was held under Charles the Bald, Louis' youngest and best loved son. For Charles had a good deal of his mother's intellectual ardour, and his grandfather's enormous zest. He loved foreigners, even as Charlemagne did; Greece, says Heric of Auxerre, wailed to see her best scholars go to France; and almost all Hibernia arrived, "a herd of philosophers,"

[1] Todd, *Life of St. Patrick*, p. 30.

[2] Council at Verneuil, xi. *De episcopis vagantibus.* Council at Chalons, 813, xliii. (See Appendix E).

[3] *Poet. Lat. Car.* iii. 198, 215, 690. See Zimmer, *Irish Element in Mediaeval Culture*, pp. 106-7, on the decay of the Irish monasteries in the thirteenth century. See also Nicolaus de Bibera, *Carmen Satiricum*, on the "Scoti qui cum fuerint bene poti," thirteenth century, at Erfurt (*Geschichts-quellen des Provinz Sachsen*, 1870).

[4] *Deceptores, gyrovagi, cursores.*" Baluze, *Capit. Reg. Franc*, ii. 743.

[5] *M. G. H. Capit. Franc. Reg.* ii. c. 34. Council held at Rheims, 846.

on our shore.[1] Heric did not intend to be funny; and the Irish scholar Martin lecturing on Greek at Laon is sober enough. His lectures had a success; even in the tenth century they are being copied, one manuscript crossing the frontier into Spain, to Ripoll.[2] But one man stands head and shoulders above his contemporary scholars: head and shoulders, some hold, above the Middle Ages: John Scotus Erigena, "the belated disciple of Plato, the last representative of the Greek spirit in the West."[3] Erigena belongs to the history of philosophy, not of literature, except that every Platonist is at heart a poet. A jester, too; he broke even on his patron the wit that had upset Theodulfus. "What is there between *sottum* et *Scottum*?" said Charles one night when the wine was in them both. "The breadth of the table, Sire," said John. His translation of the Greek pseudo-Dionysius is still scholarly;[4] his original work, *De Naturae Divisione*, is in a still greater tradition. The New Aristotle was condemned by the University of Paris in 1215, Erigena in 1225; it had taken the theologians three centuries to recognise, and then unwittingly, the order to which he belongs. John himself seems to have left France after his patron's death. Legend says that he was killed in an access of fury by his students at Malmesbury, and Dostoevsky, who knew the torture which the average mind endures in being forced to think, would have understood the murder, or the martyrdom.

[1] *Acta SS.* July 7th.

[2] Martin was a pupil of John Scotus: died 875. See M. L. Laistner, "Notes on Greek from Lectures of Martin of Laon." *Bulletin of John Rylands Library*, 1923, pp. 421 *et seq.* Greek verse in *Poet. Lat. Car.* iii. 696-7.

[3] R. L. Poole, *Illustrations of Mediaeval Thought*, p. 45. See also Hauréau, *Les Écoles d'Irlande* (*Singularités historiques et littéraires*): Bett, *Johannes Scotus Erigena*.

[4] "Jean Scot sait le grec . . . autant qu'un érudit du XVI siècle, et sa traduction du faux Denys est encore aujourd'hui dans toutes les mains." (Hauréau, *op. cit.* p. 31.)

It is to be observed that the centre of gravity of literature and learning is moving eastward ; has left the valley of the Loire for the Meuse and the Rhine. Liege in the ninth century inaugurates the tradition of scholarship in the Low Countries that reaches its height in Erasmus. John Scotus lectured in Rheims ; Hincmar, the archbishop, is the greatest power in France. For a century or two one will hear more of Fulda and Reichenau and Tegernsee than of Orleans or Tours. Alcuin lives again in his best scholar, Hrabanus Maurus, who came from Fulda to study poetry under him at Tours,[1] but went back to his own monastery to be *scholasticus*, served it as abbot for twenty years, and died archbishop of Mainz. He has left an unbridled metrical correspondence with bishops and archbishops, but one or two have other claims to poetry than their form.

> " Then live, my strength, anchor of weary ships,
> Safe shore and land at last, thou, for my wreck,
> My honour, my strong city, my sure peace." [2]

It is greatly said ; but he should not have said it twice, once to Bishop Samuel, and once to Grimoald, abbot of St. Gall. There is a descant on the old theme " Beauty vanishes, beauty passes," but with a rare freshness of direct observation :

> " Violets whiten, lilies darken ;
> Even while we speak, the grass
> Springs up, ripens, withereth." [3]

Finer still, " To Eigilus, on the Book that he Wrote "—

> " No work of men's hands, but the weary years
> Besiege and take it ; comes its evil day.

[1] *Poet. Lat. Car.* ii. Hraban. Maur. *Carm.* i.

[2] *Ib. Carm.* xxv. p. 188.

[3] *Ib. Carm.* xxxvii. p. 193.

> The written word alone flouts destiny,
> Revives the past, and gives the lie to Death." [1]

It is the first articulate *Credo* of the scholar's religion.

His pupil, Walafrid Strabo, came to him from Reichenau and was bitterly cold, and woefully homesick.[2] He wrote in sapphics; three centuries later another scholar will be hankering after his happy valley, this time in rhyme, but the heartache is the same, and the doubt if scholarship is worth the exile. It was, to Walafrid; his Gloss on Holy Writ, a kind of biblical encyclopedia, was one of the few mediaeval books which the Renaissance thought it worth while to print; it went into fresh editions, even in the seventeenth century. But the work that keeps his memory green is not the *Glossa Ordinaria*, but the garden that he made in the wilderness of academic verse, his plot of ground at Reichenau, of sage and rue and southernwood, poppy and penny-royal, mint and parsley and radishes, and, for love's sake only, gladioli and lilies and roses, even though only plain German roses, no Tyrian purple nor the scarlet splendour of France.[3] Like Johnny Crow, the abbot of Reichenau did dig and sow till he made a little garden; he tells us all about it, from the very beginning; how the nettles were everywhere, and how weeds link up underground; how his seeds, a tiny crop, sprang up, and how he watered them very carefully,

[1] *Poet. Lat. Carm.* xxi. p. 186. Hrabanus hands on the marvellous anticipation of the *Dies Irae* in St. Columba's *Altus Prosator*, in his *De Fide Catholica Rhythmus. Carm.* 39, 78; p. 202:

> " In quo cessit mulierum
> Amor et desiderium
> hominumque contentio
> mundi huius et cupido
> cum caelo, terra, ardore
> conflagrant atque lumine.
> *Tuba primi archangeli*
> *Strepente admirabili.*"

Admirable indeed, but not yet " Tuba mirum spargens sonum."

[2] *Poet. Lat. Car.* ii. p. 412. Walafrid Strabo, *Carm.* 75.

[3] *Poet. Lat. Car.* ii. p. 348. Walafrid Strabo, *De Cultura Hortorum*, 26.

sprinkling with his hands, it being dangerous to water from a bucket, by reason of its fierce impetus.[1] The spring showers were gracious, and the moon was tender to it; but bright Phoebus in his strength was too much for some of the weaklings, and they died. He grew ambrosia, but whether this was the ambrosia of the old gods he knows not,[2] and even though it is a vanity it pleases him to look upon his poppies and remember that when Ceres sought Persephone and found her not, they had given her a brief oblivion of her pain.[3] History has been very tender to the stooping figure with the watering pot, and in one poem that figure straightens itself with an undreamt-of dignity.

> "When the moon's splendour shines in naked heaven,
> Stand thou and gaze beneath the open sky.
> See how that radiance from her lamp is riven,
> And in one splendour foldeth gloriously
> Two that have loved, and now divided far,
> Bound by love's bond, in heart together are.
>
> "What though thy lover's eyes in vain desire thee,
> Seek for love's face, and find that face denied?
> Let that light be between us for a token;
> Take this poor verse that love and faith inscribe.
> Love, art thou true? and fast love's chain about thee?
> Then for all time, O love, God give thee joy!"[4]

He was a friend of the doomed Gottschalk, and if his name is hidden in the ascription "Ad Amicum"—Walafrid does not often leave his poems anonymous—one would gladly believe the imprisonment lighted by some such tenderness, for of tenderness Gottschalk had little and needed much. There is no halo about that scarred and tormented figure, unless the dark flame of his black and passionate sincerity. He was brought an oblate, like the child Samuel, to the monastery at Fulda, a knight's son with restless blood in him, and growing up

[1] *Poet. Lat. Car.* ii. p. 336. *II. Difficultas Assumpti Laboris. III. Instantia Cultoris.*

[2] *Ib.* xxiii. p. 348.

[3] *Ib.* xvi. p. 344.

[4] *Ib.* lix. p. 403.

fought for liberty like a caged panther. At sixteen a council of bishops granted his appeal, but his abbot, Hrabanus Maurus, strong on prerogative, carried the case to the Emperor, and Gottschalk was doomed, " condemned for life to the order of St. Benedict." But there are other ways of escape; at eighteen Gottschalk discovered St. Augustine, and wrung from him the secret of his passionate peace; in 835 he was ordained priest. There are natures doomed to be unfortunate, to find the bitter in the sweet; the doctrine which he wrested from Augustine and thereafter preached through France and Italy to the terror of many was predestination not only to grace, but to damnation. The Church in consternation brought in John Scotus to refute him, and though, " before the Irish philosopher could be checked, he had refuted Sin and Hell," [1] it took them three centuries to find it out. Gottschalk's book went to the flames first; he burnt it himself after torture, like one dead. They condemned him to solitary confinement; but somehow this indomitable malignant [2] secured ink and parchment and the book appears again. There followed further accusations, further vengeance on this man found *hereticus et incorrigibilis*. Twenty years later, in 870, the long misery ended. Gottschalk, dying, begged for the sacrament from which he had so long been barred. It was promised him, and Christian burial, after he should sign a recantation drawn up for him by Hincmar. He refused, and died without the sacraments. " A worthy end to such a life," says Hincmar, speaking more wisely than he knew.[3] There is no grace about Gottschalk; he had seen truth and it blinded him.

With that doomed history, there is a shadow on his

[1] Ker, *The Dark Ages*, p. 162.

[2] Hincmar, *De Una et non Trina Deitate* (Migne 125 c. 506):
" Gothescalcus pertinacissimus damnatus est."

[3] *Ib.* c. 613. " Sicque indignam vitam digna morte finivit, et abiit in locum suum." For the whole story with documents see Traube's Preface to Gottschalk's Poems, *Poet. Lat. Car.* iii. pp. 707-20.

verse, the most musical that was written in Europe for centuries. One with the refrain,

"O God, and what shall be the end of me?"

is cruel reading, in the light of what that end was indeed to be. Another, written in the Marches of Friuli,

"O quid iubes, pusiole,"[1]

has the aching sweetness of the flute, a melody of interwoven rhyme and echo that is heard nowhere else, unless in the Irish metres of the *debide*.[2] That same intricate rhyming has led Traube to insist on the influence of the Irish Dunchat, who was teaching in St. Remy at Rheims while Gottschalk was discovering Augustine at Orbaix.[3] It is not to say that rhyme had its origin in Ireland. Ennius was rhyming in the Republic; it may be that rhyme belongs to the original genius of the Latin tongue, the lyric Ariel imprisoned in the cleft oak of the Greek metres. Moreover, there is no rhyme in such primitive Irish verse as remains. But once crossed with the Latin genius, Irish rhyme becomes as intricate and subtle as the designs of the *Book of Kells*, and Thurneysen has counted two hundred and eighty measures, founded for the most part on the lovely rhythm of the *Pervigilium Veneris*.[4]

"O quid iubes, pusiole,
Quare mandas, filiole,
Carmen dulce me cantare
Cum sim longe exul valde
Intra mare.
O cur iubes canere?"[5]

[1] "O quid iubes, pusiole" is set to music in a ninth century MS., formerly of St. Martial of Limoges. Facsimile and musical score in Coussemaker, *Hist. de l'Harmonie au moyen âge*, pl. ii. p. v.

[2] See *Irische Texte*, iii. pp. 147-151.

[3] See Traube, *Poet. Lat. Car.* iii. 710-11, note.

[4] *Mittelirische Verslehren*: Thurneysen, *Irische Texte*, iii. 1-182.

[5] *Poet. Lat. Car.* iii. p. 731.

is the despair of translators, just as the loveliest of the Irish metres baffles the ear. Professor Raleigh caught the ghost of " Truagan Truag " in

" Though our songs
Cannot banish ancient wrongs,
Though they follow where the rose
Goes ; "[1]

and Browning's " Love among the Ruins,"

" Where the quiet coloured end of evening smiles,
Miles and miles "

is the echo of another, though deaf to its hidden recurring melodies.[2] Gottschalk says himself that he spent but one year in the study of verse ;[3] and if that were at Orbaix, where he read Augustine and wrote his first three *Carmina*, he had his revelation of poetry there, as well as of religion. His name is in the glosses of the Berne manuscript of Horace and Augustine,[4] and again in the Berne Epistles of St. Paul, the Greek text believed to be written by Sedulius ;[5] and applicable enough are the lines written in the Priscian manuscript :

" Take thy couch in the prison : thou shalt need neither down nor pallet.
Sad is it, thou servant of the rod, that the pack-saddle of ill luck hath stuck to thee."[6]

There seems to have been a colony of Irish scholars in the district round Liege and Cologne. Both Cologne and

[1] Quoted by Ker, *The Dark Ages*, p. 330.

[2] *Irische Texte*, iii. p. 150 :
" Aicnead in miled rodmarb isagarb.
etir domuintir dolam dolessad."

[3] Traube, *P.L.C.* iii. p. 710. Gottschalk to Ratramnus : " metri quoque iure solutus, quamlibet hoc modico usus sim sub tempore pauco, namque magisterio vix uno subditus anno."

[4] See Traube, *O Roma Nobilis*, pp. 348-52. The MS. (Berne, 363) contains Horace, Augustine, a fragment of Ovid, Bede, and the names in the margin are Fergus, Gottschalk, Sedulius, Dubthach, Comgan, Dungal, Conmac, Colgu, Ratramnus, Hincmar.

[5] See Traube, *op. cit.*

[6] *Thesaur. Pal.* ii. 290.

Liege in the middle of the ninth century had hospitable and scholarly bishops; one Irish scholar begging for the loan of a book, and offering Boethius, *De Musica*, as a hostage, calls his lordship "flower and paradox of the holy church of God."[1] Liege was on one route to Rome; and the Leyden manuscript edited by Dümmler is rather like an episcopal post bag.[2] There is the Scottish *peregrinus* returned from Rome, asking for a benefice—"I am not a *grammaticus*, nor am I skilled in the Latin tongue . . . yet is Christ hidden in the hearts of his poor." An Irish priest, old and ill, is hindered from Rome by the infirmity of the feet. He will say daily Masses for the bishop's soul, and writes him six devout verses. Another, a simple soul, entreats from Franco his stolen goods, a little in the manner of the Obscure Men. Because of his nation, he came back from Rome by way of this monastery (evidently an Irish foundation, like St. Martin's at Cologne); and certain men who were in the same ship (probably coming up the Meuse) stole an alb and a stole and two corporals and a good black cloak (*unam bonam nigram capam iij uncias valentem*) and a leather coat with *fasciolis* (puttees) worth ij sol. and a shirt worth ij sol., and four worn Irish garments and a skin-coat and other matters, "small things but necessary to me" (*reliquas minutas causas sed mihi necessarias*). Another writes with the indignant accent of the poor scholar that is to become so familiar in the twelfth century, the half-resentful astonishment that one cannot live by scholarship, and must yoke oneself to a benefice. "I cannot live in such poverty, having naught to eat or drink save exceeding bad bread and the least particle of abominable beer." The Irishmen liked beer as little as Alcuin did;[3] another Irishman from Soissons, a fellow scholar with the unhappy Carloman,

[1] *M. G. H. Epist. Karol.* iv. p. 197. [2] *Ib.* pp. 195-7.

[3] "I myself am a drinker of both," said John of Salisbury with his accustomed moderation, "nor do I abhor anything that can make me drunk." Epist. 85 (Migne, 199, c. 72).

writes of it as one who throws boots at it, and is on his knees to Bacchus, "invoked by thine ancient name."[1] But its great antagonist in the ninth century is the Irishman, Sedulius of Liege.[2]

It was some time after the year 840 that Sedulius came to the *évêché* at Liege, with two other scholars in as bad case as himself, tempest-tossed and sodden in a scurry of sleet, and crossed the threshold into warmth and light, where flowers fairer than in the gardens of the Hesperides bloomed on the tapestries, and shivered in no wind.[3] Hartgar had as good a taste in scholarship as in embroideries and recognised a fine Greek scholar in his salvage. Sedulius became his *scholasticus*, and slept sound of nights, even when the wind was quiet; Liege was far inland, and the Normans still happily employed in the Seine and the Loire, and the monasteries of Northern France. He met kings and emperors; wrote verses for the Empress to embroider, and a book of conduct for Christian princes, in no way resembling Machiavelli's, for the young sons of Lothair I. His grievances are the grievances of all scholars; a house that is dark, fitter for the habitation of moles than of philosophers, as he gravely points out to Hartgar; no key; abominable draughts, the east wind as much at home inside as out;[4] worse than all, a really horrible beer. No child of Ceres this, though it has the yellow of her hair; neither Jordan nor Moselle begat it, but the Brook Kedron; a beast of prey in a man's inwards. O gods, remove the creature to the Styx; and as you love me, Bishop, a poultice, a poultice! And the bishop chuckled, says Sedulius, and granted his request.[5] The

[1] *Poet. Lat. Car.* iii. p. 690.

[2] *Vide* Pirenne, "*Sedulius de Liège*" (*Mémoires couronnés de l'Académie Royale de Belgique*, xxxiii).

[3] *Poet. Lat. Car.* iii.; Sedulius Scottus, *Carm.* ii. 3-4, p. 168.
The Irishman Cruindmelus in his *Ars Metrica* claims Sedulius as his collaborator, *P.L.C.* ii. p. 681.

[4] *Carm.* ii. 4, p. 169.

[5] *Carm.* ii. ix. p. 177.

Arch Poet, three hundred years later, and he are at one on the superiority of verse well-soaked, "*carmina saturata*": one of them, sent to Count Robert, produced no less than a hundred flagons of the " dewy gifts of Bacchus,"[1] and he thumps out

" What a good man Robert is,
Robert's phrases flow "

on a barrel of the good Rhine wine.[2] Liege seems to have been a genial house. There is a song written for the brethren on the feast of St. Vedast, six brethren to a measure and six to a six-foot iambic, singing with one voice, so that the whole world hears it.[3] Then there is a lament in Goldsmith's mock-heroics for a sheep, a prelatic sheep that the bishop had promised him, and that the dogs worried, a good sheep that said no idle words, but mystically uttered BAA and BEE, that drank nor beer nor Bacchus, and walked upon its own feet in the way.

" Alas ! that thou wert never in my field !
I do confess I did desire thee ; now,
Desire wakes for thy widow and thy mother ;
Yea, and thy brethren shall I ever love. Farewell." [4]

One hopes that the bishop took the hint. His muse is Egla, fairest of the Naiads ; in praise of Hartgar he calls her to kiss him with her red lips.[5] Hartgar goes to Rome, and the wood nymphs wail for him, him whose learning shines in the Church,

" Even as Apollo wandering on shining Olympus
Lightens the whole earth with his magic lamp." [6]

He writes of his Irish friends, and the Celt comes out in his metaphors. Christ defend Dermot with thy shield ! [7]

[1] *Carm.* ii. 36, p. 201. [2] *Carm.* ii. 58, p. 215.
[3] *Carm,* ii. 32. *Verba Comediae,* p. 198.
[4] *Carm.* ii. 41, p. 204.
[5] *Carm.* ii. 1, p. 166. [6] *Carm.* ii. 3, p. 167.
[7] *Carm.* ii. 27.

Fergus is his arrow, Blandus the dove of God, Beuchele a flower among warriors ; these three with Marcus (is it the Marcus who came to St. Gall ?) are the four-horse chariot of God.[1] It was a peaceful life for long enough, interrupted only by visits of great ones, and the necessary odes.

" A writer am I, I confess it, Musicus, Orpheus the second,
And the ox that treads out the corn—" [2]

The serious business of scholarship goes on ; the Greek text of St. Paul's Epistles with an interlinear Latin translation,[3] a commentary on the Psalms, a commentary on St. Jerome ; *De Rectoribus Christianis,* written in a very pure Latin, the prose alternating with verse that goes lightly from strophe to varying strophe. Christmas brings snow and feasting ; Easter the sound of wandering bees busy in the flowers.[4]

" I read and teach and say my prayers,
And snoring sleep." [5]

Then Hartgar dies, and Franco, his successor, is oftener in the saddle than the pulpit, for the Normans have come a little nearer. But whether or not the enemy he had come so far to escape found Sedulius at the last, there is no telling. The last date that can be fixed is 874, the poem to celebrate the meeting of Charles and Louis. Seven years after, the

[1] *Carm.* ii. 33. *Ad suos,* p. 199.

[2] *Carm.* ii. 49, p. 211. His implication is that the ox is thirsty.

[3] MS. at Berne. See *Thesaur. Palaeohib.* ii. 34. Traube thinks that it is actually in Sedulius' script : the marginalia have the names of his circle : Dongus, Dubthach, Fergus, Comgan, Gottschalk, Gunther (Bp. of Cologne), Marcus.

[4] iii. 2. " Surrexit Christus sol verus vespere noctis,
Surgit et hinc domini mystica messis agri.
Nunc vaga puniceis apium plebs laeta labore
Floribus instrepitans pollite melle legit.

[5] ii. 74. " Aut lego vel scribo, doceo scrutorve sophiam,
Obsecro celsithronum nocte dieque meum,
Vescor, poto libens, rithmizans invoco Musas,
Dormisco stertens ; oro deum vigilans."

terrible beaked prows appear in the Meuse. At Stavelot, an escaped fugitive coming at sunset warns the monks of the attack planned at moonrise, and they fly with the precious relics to the woods.[1] It is the same at Liege, at Maestricht, Tongres, St. Trond, Malmédy. Anselm reproached the faint-heartedness of the flight in his history of the bishops of Liege, but it is easy to be brave a hundred years after.[2] Manuscripts perished everywhere ; Hucbald of St. Amand, sitting down to write his history, laments the loss of all his materials,[3] just as historians lament the blowing up of the Four Courts in Dublin. Some at least of Sedulius' manuscripts must have survived, for the verse was copied in the twelfth century, in the manuscript now in Brussels ;[4] the Greek St. Paul of the ninth century, probably in his own hand, is in Berne.[5] But whether Sedulius himself survived there is no record. One victory of Franco over the Normans roused him to a set of swinging Sapphics, but they were still a great way off.[6] Then came the plague, and moved him to a cry of intercession :

> "Saint of all saints, and King of all kingships."[7]

as straight from the heart as Herrick's *Litany*. There is no need to question his devotion ; the Bacchanalian verse is only the blown spray of a profound and serious scholarship ; and if the fragment of Irish verse in the *St. Paul* is his, "To go to Rome, much labour, little profit. The King whom thou desirest, if thou bringest Him not with thee, thou wilt find Him not "[8]—he had come at a truth that prophets and kings had desired in vain.

[1] *Vita St. Remacli, Acta SS. Sept.* 1, 705.

[2] *Gest. Pont. Leod. M. G. H. Script.* vii. 199.

[3] Migne, *P.L.* 132, c. 829.

[4] Discovered by Pertz, 1839. See Pirenne, *op. cit.*

[5] *Thesaur. Palaeohib.* ii. xx. 290-6.

[6] *Carm.* ii. 45.

[7] ii. 46, p. 209.

[8] *Thesaur. Palaeohib.* ii. 296.

CHAPTER III

THE TENTH CENTURY

THE tenth century has a bad name ; but good things came out of it. In the text-books it disputes with the seventh the bad eminence, the nadir of the human intellect. Archbishop Trench, a kind man, calls it the wastest place of European literature and of the human mind.[1] Radulphus Glaber, an ill-conditioned dog on his own showing, but a lively historian, declares that by the end of it, the year 1000, there was hardly a personage, religious or secular, in Europe.[2] He was unlucky in his choice of a date : the year 1000 saw the inscrutable master of all sciences, Gerbert, in St. Peter's chair ; his gallant and ill-fated scholar, Otto III, Emperor ; Fulbert, "*Socrates noster*" to the admiring younger generation, teaching music and the humanities in the school of Chartres ; and Robert, henpecked saint, poet and humourist, on the throne of France. The truth is that the tenth century does the old things, and does them not so well ; but it also does new things, and does them not so very ill. It saw the passing of Charlemagne's house in France in impotence and squalor, but in Germany the reigns of three great Emperors. It saw Clonfert and Clonmacnoise, St. Martin of Tours and St. Denis sacked by the Northmen and held to ransom, and wolves hunting in Auvergne ; but before the century was out the same Northmen were peaceful citizens among

[1] Trench, *Sacred Latin Poetry*, p. 47.

[2] Migne, *P.L.* cxlii. c. 644.

the apple-orchards of Normandy. The Huns burnt the library of St. Gall and spared the cellar; yet enough of both vintages was left to make the tenth century the Golden Age of the monastery. It saw a succession of Popes as short-lived and wanton as May-flies, but in England the reform of Dunstan, in France the founding of Cluny, the monastery that produced the great reforming Popes of the next century. "L'âme de Cluny, ce fut la prière liturgique": the office, the *opus Dei*, is restored to its place as the central task of the Benedictine order, to the incalculable enriching of the aesthetic and musical sense. The Office of the Sepulchre and the Office of the Star, the amazing moment when for the first time the three white-clad figures came slowly up the cathedral aisle, *pedetemptim*, as those who seek something, and the challenge,

> "Quem queritis in sepulchro, O Christicolae?"

first rang from the very tomb itself, belongs to the middle of the century:[1] the plastic, dramatic imagination is set free. From it, too, dates the beginning of modern music, ultra-modern even, for Hucbald of St. Amand[2] began that quest for the "perfect fourth" which Holst, unmoved by discord, still continues. The scholars of the century can almost be counted on the fingers of one hand; so can the lyrics. But they include the first *aubade* and the first love song; and in the manuscripts that contain them the lost tunes of the Middle Ages are for the first time caught and held.[3]

It is true that thanks to the dangers and squalors of

[1] *Regularis Concordia* of St. Ethelwold. Text in Chambers, *Mediaeval Stage*, ii. 309.

[2] Or rather, the unknown author of the *Musica Enchiriadis* which goes by his name.

[3] A tenth century MS. of St. Martial of Limoges (B. N. *MS. Lat.* 1118) contains "Iam dulcis amica": Vatican MS. *Reginensis* 1462, tenth century, formerly of Fleury, the aubade. For the facsimile and musical score of "Iam dulcis amica" see Coussemaker, *Hist. de l'Harmonie au moyen âge*, Pl. viii. p. x, xi.

the century, invasion, rebellion and faction, there is no longer, at any rate in France and England, an educated society. One misses the voluminous correspondence of the ninth century, of Alcuin and his Venerable Fowl, of Hrabanus Maurus, of Servatus Lupus, hoarding manuscripts like a magpie and clamouring like Petrarch for more. There is scholarship, but it is not present diffusedly. Bruno, young brother of Otto the Great and Archbishop of Cologne, does his best to maintain a school of the humanities there, and summoned to it an Irish bishop from Trier to teach Greek; there are colonies of Greek and Irish monks at Toul and at Verdun.[1] From Toul, indeed, or rather from a monastery prison in Toul, comes the odd little tale of the calf that ran away, and his adventures with the wolf and the hedgehog and the lion and the otter—the first rough draft of the *Roman de Renard*. The writer of it says frankly that he himself had misspent his youth nor plied his book, and the calf is his vagrant self, and that is why the metre is so clumsy.[2] At Glastonbury, Dunstan was brought up by Irish scholars (William of Malmesbury pauses to reflect on their continuing reputation in music and geometry, though their Latinity —he writes in the twelfth century—is no longer so pure as it was).[3] Begging letters addressed to his successor from Liège prove that the fire still burns there. One clerk with humility and confusion of metaphor pleads that as an unworthy pup he has licked up sufficient crumbs from under the bishop's table (Notker of Liege was a sound scholar) to qualify him to enter the English apiary as an obedient bee;[4] and another, about a journey and a loan of money and a borrowed horse, bears out the Vicar of Wakefield's experience that the conjunction of a

[1] Sandys, *History of Classical Scholarship*, i. 503, 505.

[2] *Ecbasis Captivi* (Grimm and Schmeller, *Lateinische Gedichte des X und XI Jahrhunderts*).

[3] *Vita S. Dunstani*, i. 4 (Stubbs, *Memorials of St. Dunstan*, pp. 256-7).

[4] *Ib.* p. 387.

scholar and a horse is not always fortunate.[1] The light never quite goes out ; though Gerbert in quest of it flickers across Europe like a will-o'-the-wisp.

Gerbert is not the first wandering scholar, but he is the most famous ; far greater than Nicholas Breakspear whose wanderings also ended in St. Peter's chair. " Can any man," said Panurge, " be so wise as the devils are ? " " Nay," said Pantagruel, " save by God's especial grace." But this explanation of Gerbert's amazing knowledge did not occur to his contemporaries ; and by the time the legend reached William of Malmesbury the light of the everlasting bonfire played about his head. He was, to William, a fugitive monk of Fleury, by whom the ordinary arts, arithmetic, music, astronomy and geometry, were lapped up as inferior to his genius ; he fled to Spain, studied magic at Toledo, stole a codex " conscious of the whole art " from his master's pillow by the aid of that master's daughter, fled, was pursued, and the direction of his flight betrayed by the stars, hung under a bridge between air, earth and water, so as to put the stars out of their reckoning, invoked the devil, and was assisted by him across the Bay of Biscay ; returned to France, and became *scholasticus* at Rheims, had Otto, future Emperor of Germany, Robert Capet, soon to be King of France, and Fulbert, future Bishop of Chartres, among his pupils, and made a water organ and a clock, as well as a brazen head which solved for him his problems in mathematics. Otto, Emperor after his father, made him Archbishop of Ravenna, and afterwards Pope. " So did he urge his fortunes, the devil aiding him, that nothing which ever he planned was left imperfect," except perhaps that unfinished Mass in the Chapel of Jerusalem, when the pains of death took hold on him. His death, says William, was terrible.[2]

[1] *Ib.* p. 390.

[2] William of Malmesbury, *Gesta Reg. Ang.* ii. 167. Stubbs (*Rolls Series*), p. 193.

William of Malmesbury's Gerbert is a legend out of the Arabian Nights ; and his learning, even in the sober testimony of Richer,[1] who loved and admired him more than any man living, is almost fabulous. But for scholarship of the academic indisputable kind, exact, pedantic scholarship, there is the evidence of an incomparable letter that came about 965 to the monks at Reichenau from Gunzo of Novara, appointed by Otto II to inaugurate humane studies in Germany.[2] The Ottos were scholars without Melville's damaging rider, "passing well, for a Queen ;" the youngest of them teases Gerbert for lessons in Greek and arithmetic, and threatens to send him as many poems as there are men in Gaul.[3] His father, coming back from one of the Italian campaigns that were the curse of every German Imperial house, brought with him Gunzo of Novara, very much as Charlemagne did Peter of Pisa ; and the long journey was broken by a halt to enjoy the famous hospitality of St. Gall. It was bitterly cold ; Gunzo had almost to be lifted from his horse, he complains, the recollection of his martyrdom mounting his indignation, so powerless had his frozen limbs become ; but he thawed in warmth and conversation, and unfortunately, his wits perhaps still sluggish with cold, blundered into an accusative instead of an ablative. And Ekkehard, the *scholasticus*, heard. One may imagine that Ekkehard was listening critically to the Inaugurator of Humane Studies ; conscious, as he well might be, that Otto could have found elegant scholarship a little nearer home. At any rate, the accusative registered upon his retentive mind, and in due course upon the common room. St. Gall rang with it, and with Ekkehard's unfeeling jest. Gunzo made no reply that he speaks of ; the mole subsides underground, though one suspects a frenzied activity. After a considerable interval he emerges, in a letter of

[1] Richer, *Hist.* iii. 45-65. Migne, *P.L.* cxxxviii. c. 101-109.

[2] Migne, *P.L.* cxxxvi. c. 1283 *et seq.*

[3] Gerbert, *Epist.* 153. Migne, *P.L.* cxxxix.

enormous length to the monks of Reichenau—Cambridge to the St. Gall Oxford—detailing the whole outrage, admitting his error, but adducing twenty-eight examples from approved and standard authors of equal eccentricity. It is academic comedy ; but the *milieu* which provides such situations is not illiterate.

"And indeed," Gunzo proceeds, "who knows not the verses of that wanton monk ? He openeth his mouth and emitteth a poem, ignorant of the economy of poetry, the interweaving of the purple patch [*purpureum pannum*] resplendent here and there, the personating of the manners of the time, the observation of the decorum of poetry. . . . I do confess that my own youth was touched with this vice. . . . Think not that I hold the art of poetry in contempt. I find verily that ecclesiastic persons make use of the form ; but I question if in our time a writer of the true poem could be found." *Scriptor veri poematis* —it is the contempt of the old classical scholar, the Gabriel Harveys, for the new-fangled rhyming. More than a century before, Paulus Albarus, the Jew of Cordova, had complained of it. Himself, he says, had written much rhyme in his youth, but purged his work of it later ; complains that few churchmen know their own tongue well enough to write so much as a letter of greeting to a brother, but that herds of them can learnedly expound the Arabic pomps of language, and adorn the end of their lines with the "co-artation" of a single letter.[1] The influence of Arabic poetry on the Sicilian school of Frederick II and Piero de la Vigne is an accepted enchantment. It is curious to find it anticipated by four hundred years.

It is likely enough that the rhyming of St. Gall was encouraged by the Irish humanist Marcellus, an even keener musician than scholar, says Ekkehard.[2] He had

[1] Traube, *Poet. Lat. Car.* iii. p. 123.

[2] "Maxime ad musicam." *Casus . . . Sancti Galli*, Ekkehard, c. iii. *M. G. H. Scriptores*, ii. p. 94.

charge of the monastic school; Iso of the "canonical," the oblates, "and joyous it is to recall how the house of St. Gall under these two began to increase, and how it flowered."[1] Iso was responsible for Salomon, future Bishop of Constance and Abbot of St. Gall; Marcellus for the great Three, Notker, Tutilo, Ratpert, "the Senators of our Republic," and famous for the oddest, most charming friendship of the Middle Age.

By the time Ekkehard's Chronicle has finished with them, one knows Notker, Tutilo, and Ratpert as intimately as Athos, Porthos, and Aramis. The Three-in-One, Ekkehard calls them, but he does not confound their substance.[2] Notker, the best beloved of the three, with his little stammer, a shy man yet "in divinis erectus," was gentle in all things: writing a book of instruction for young Salomon, the future Abbot, he dissuades him from the reading of the pagans (whom however he himself knew, and exercised some critical faculty upon): rather read Prosper on the active and contemplative life, and apply it, and you will indeed be worthy of the episcopate. *Eheu, sed mihi tum quam molliter ossa quiescent.* "Alas! but by that time how quietly my bones will rest!"[3] Tutilo, the artist of the three, was much in request for his skill in sculpture and design: *festivus*, says Ekkehard, of so ready a wit that Charles put his curse on whoever made such a man a monk; "chaste, as a true disciple of Marcellus, who closed his eyes to women; none seeing him could doubt him a monk of St. Gall."[4] He played exquisitely upon the flute, and his occasions took him much from the cloister, a little to Ratpert's uneasiness. For Ratpert, the scholar, historian of the monastery, rarely put his foot beyond the cloister, and hardly wore

[1] *M. G. H. Scriptores*, ii. p. 79.

[2] *Ib.* c. 3, pp. 94-101.

[3] Notker, *De Interpret. Div. Script.* vii.

[4] Ekkehard, *Casus S. Galli.* 3, pp. 94, 97.

out two pairs of shoes in the year.[1] Then there is the enemy, Sindolf, the server of tables, who rose to high place in the monastery, and worse than all caught the ear of the Abbot : a toad of a man, who found a manuscript delicately written, and cut four pages out of it with a cook's knife (" as indeed is so seen to this day "), and dirtied them, and put them back in the place whence they were stolen.[2] But the story of how they caught him spying through the window and took the vengeance of the Lord upon him is straight out of *Stalky and Co.* In its accomplishment, and the manner of its telling, it is a sufficient answer to those who accuse the Middle Ages of only rudimentary humour.[3]

The Bishop, though a little tarnished by his choice of an " auricular friend," was a great personage : and very nearly worthy, even in his wayward youth, of the affection that Notker lavished on him. There are three poems, all of them curious anticipations of the sixteenth century sonnet.[4] Salomon himself composed in both languages ; but whatever lovesongs he may have written to the frail beauty whom Notker dreaded, none have survived : the verse that remains is worthy, unless in its very human grieving, of a great ecclesiastic. But a charming story of the second decade of the tenth century proves his surviving charm, as well as the popularity of rhyming in St. Gall.[5] It was the Feast of the Innocents, afterwards the Saturnalia of the Church ; by old-established custom the boys had a holiday, and as their manner was they lay

[1] *Ib.* p. 95. " Scolarum ab adolescentia magister, doctor planus et benevolus, disciplinis asperior ; raro praeter fratres pedem claustro promovens, duos calceos annum habens, excursus mortem nominans ; saepe Tuotilonem itinerarium ut se caveret, amplexibus monens."

[2] *Ib.* p. 101. It happened to Notker, left solitary after the other two were dead ; and stabbed him to the heart, says Ekkehard. For it was a copy of a Greek text of the Epistles lent by the Bishop of Vercellæ and he had made the copy " *multis sudoribus.*"

[3] *Ib.* pp. 95-6.

[4] *Poet. Lat. Car.* IV. i. p. 335.

[5] Ekkehard, *Casus S. Galli*, p. 91.

in wait to capture a great one and hold him to ransom: as luck would have it, they found in their ambush the Lord Abbot himself. Gleefully they rush him to the *cathedra* of the Master, and there set him down; and the Lord Abbot regards them with his formidable smiling. "So you have made me *magister*: *eh bien!* the master's privilege. Strip!" There fell a gloom; but one gallant sparrow pipes up that on these painful occasions the victims may buy themselves off with a verse. Reprieve was granted; and two of them struck off rhyming couplets so adroitly *ad hoc* that the Lord Abbot set his arms about them, gave the whole school three days' holiday and feasting at the expense of the Abbey, and this moreover *in perpetuo*. Not often has a neck verse been so fortunate.

The couplets were in leonine hexameters: the most popular measure of the century. Notker occasionally used them, but his fame is in the Sequences, the *vers libre* of the Middle Ages, first composed to help the monks to carry in their minds the endless modulations of the Alleluia. The long vowels were intended, say the liturgists, to express that ineffable exultation when the heart is too full for speech;[1] but Notker confesses frankly that he could never remember them himself. Then one day, as he tells it, came a fugitive monk to St. Gall with his service book, a fragment of wreckage from the sack of his own monastery of Jumièges in Normandy.[2] He had words written under the notes; Notker was struck with the idea, found it excellent, but—like many artists—the execution paltry. So he wrote new words, and founded the most famous school of sequences, till Adam of St. Victor captures that supremacy for Northern France: the stateliest for the feast of St. Michael, with Urania restored again to verse.[3] It is emancipation, but dangerous.

[1] Paululus, *De Ecc. Off.* Migne, *P.L.* clxxvii. c. 381. See Frere, *The Winchester Troper.*

[2] Migne, *P.L.* cxxxi. c. 1003.

[3] *Anal. Hymn. Med. Aev.* 53, p. 307.

From this time on the complaints begin of clerks in the choir singing like *histriones*, even of introducing vain songs into the service; and by the twelfth century comes a descant for three voices, "*Et in fines*," accompanied by "*Dames sont en grant émoi.*" "*Vide et inclina aurem tuam*" interweaves and accompanies "*Dieus! je ne puis la nuit dormir*," but for other reason than the Psalmist's.[1]

There are other poets, of the historical kind; a lively epic written by the Ekkehard with whom Gunzo had words, the adventures of Waltharius and his gallant lady love escaping from the Hun to Burgundy again; sequences from no less a person than Robert of France, and the immortal story of how Constance of Aquitaine, who brought southern graces and southern morals in her flying squadron to the north, took it ill that her husband should write so many fine things, yet never one for her, whereupon Robert composed the

"O constantia martyrum,"

and solemnly presented it.[2] Flodoard of Rheims, in whom, says a French epitaph, "you will have all antiquity," wrote the Triumph of Christ and His Saints in Palestine, with a splendid invocation,

"Lux immensa Deus,"

and a life of Pelagia, the most neglected and perhaps the loveliest of the Magdalene saints.[3] Aymon, monk of Fleury, has pleasant poems on angels who showed St.

[1] Coussemaker, *Histoire de l'Harmonie au moyen âge*, facsimiles of B.N. MS. 813. Pl. 27. See Ælred of Rievaulx, *Speculum charitatis*, Migne, *P.L.* cxcv. 571: "God taught us through his organs, Augustine, Ambrose, Gregory, how to sing; and to it we prefer the idlest vanities of the scholars."

[2] *Chronicle of S. Bertin* (Bouquet, *Hist.* x. p. 299).

[3] Migne, cxxxv. c. 491. On the fragrance of Pelagia's passing:

"Quae quo migrabat, spargebat aromate ventos,
Sollicitis vacuum nidoribus aera replens."

Benedict the way, and about three crows who were his pensioners, and who followed him from Subiaco to Beneventum, almost fifty miles.[1] But the new things are the anonymous lyrics, the glorious rhythms of

> " O Roma nobilis, orbis et domina,"

and

> " O admirabile Veneris idolum,"

and still more significant in promise, the *alba* of the Vatican MS. formerly at Fleury, and the " Iam dulcis amica " of the MS. of St. Martial of Limoges. The *alba* is more precious for its Provençal burden than for other merit : it still holds to Prudentius, and the cry might be to waken faithful souls rather than sleeping lovers, the enemy in ambush the Enemy of souls rather than the jealous guardian. But in its own exquisite phrase,

> " Dawn is near : she leans across the dark sea." [2]

For *Iam, dulcis amica,* the quatrain halts a little, the rhythm wavers ; Ovid's upholstery is still in the background, a little the worse for wear. But its strength is in the sudden impatience with which the catalogue of attractions is thrust aside, the sudden liquid break like the first bird notes in the stuffy pedant-music of the Meistersingers :

> " Ego fui sola in sylva
> Et dilexi secreta loca—"

> " I have been in the woods alone,
> I have loved hidden places.
> Tumult of men I shun
> And the crowding faces.

[1] *Sermo de S. Benedicto,* ii., iii. Migne, cxxxix. c. 860.

[2] *Poet. Lat. Car.* iii. 703 *n.* :

> " *L'alba par umet mar atra sol,*
> *Poy pasa vigil miraclar tenebras.*"

Now the snow vanishes,
Out the leaves start,
The nightingale's singing :
Love's in the heart." [1]

It is the promise of the woods in *Tristan*, of a century of lyric. Not for another two hundred years will "Birds sing in every furrow," but the ploughing has begun.

Iam, dulcis amica was set to music ; so too Gottschalk's "O quid iubes, pusiole," and three of the lyrics of Boethius.[2] There is even a tenth century manuscript of Virgil in which some of the speeches of Æneas are noted to be sung.[3] Most astonishing of all, two odes of Horace, to Albius Tibullus, and to Phyllis : [3]

"A jar of the Albana, nine years old,
Still a full amphora, and in the garden
There's parsley, Phyllis, for twining coronals,
And trails of ivy
To bind your shining hair."

The rest of it is intricate with classical allusion, the other thornier still. To read them, and to reflect on the composer who chose them for setting, and the audience before which they were sung, is to revise our ideas of the tenth century.

It is easy to exaggerate the importance of the driftwood ; a broken twig does not mean a forest. But the rudeness

[1] "Ego fui sola in sylva,
Et dilexi loca secreta,
Frequenter effugi tumultum
Et vitavi populum multum.
Iam nix glaciesque liquescit,
Folium et herba virescit,
Philomena iam cantat in alto,
Ardet amor cordis in antro."

[2] B.N. MS. 1154. Coussemaker, *op. cit.* Pl. I. II. This is ninth century ; but there are two tenth century settings of "Iam dulcis amica," B.N. MS. 1118, formerly of Fleury, Pl. VIII, and a MS. of Vienna (Coussemaker, p. 108, Pl. IX).

[3] Coussemaker, p. 102. The *Ode to Phyllis*, Montpellier MS. 425, is given in facsimile, Pl. X.

of the century has been overstressed: there is courtliness in it, as well as savagery. The people fastened ill names on King Hugo's mistresses, but they were names of goddesses, Venus, Juno, and hapless Semele;[1] so Liutprand tells us in the liveliest history that has ever been written. Liutprand himself breaks out into all manner of verse, warning us beforehand with the phrase "Exclamation of the author upon him," which is as good a way as any of working off an historical prejudice. Lambert, monk of Ardres, writing a history of the Counts of Guines, works back through the marriage of Ralph with Rosella, some time in the eleventh century, "Rosella so called for her dewy fragrance and her colouring of a rose," to the tenth century tragedy of the loves of Sifrid the Dane and Elstrud (called after a daughter of Alfred the Great); he was an exile, and made welcome at the court of Arnold of Flanders, and remained after his death with Baldwin, the son; fell in love with Baldwin's sister, got her with child, fled to Guines and died there broken-hearted, because he was separated from his love, "suam amicam."[2] There is romantic passion there, as well as cowardice. Hroswitha came at twenty-three to the convent of Gandersheim, and learned Latin from the abbess Gerberga her contemporary, and a princess; Terence bewitched her, and, aware of his danger, she wrote herself six comedies as substitutes, "and if you do not much like them," says she to the learned bishops who are to judge them, "at least they have pleased myself." Hroswitha had learned something of the heart before she came to the convent, and phrases in her love scenes cry out from the printed page. The Roman general who has fought for Constantine, demanding his daughter's hand as the price of victory, comes back to claim it; the girl is bride to Christ (something very like it would have happened in the convent if Count Bernhard, Gerberga's

[1] *Antapod.* iv. 13.

[2] *Mon. Germ. Hist. Script.* xxvii. 568.

husband, had ever come back from his campaign), and waits in fear and dread. But the general has had his own vision on the battlefield ; when he comes, it is to renounce her, and vow himself Christ's bachelor. Constantine, immensely relieved, urges upon him the official rank of son-in-law, and residence in the palace : "—And risk the daily sight of her whom I love more than my friends, more than my life, more than my soul ? " It is not the speech of the plaster saint. So the two take leave of one another. " And may He grant," says the girl, " that for the severance of our bodies, it will be given to us to go together to the eternal joy." " Fiat, fiat ! " [1] A century later, and the old canon of Rouen who wrote the *St. Alexis* will finish not very differently :

> " Without doubt is Saint Alexis in heaven.
> He has God with him, and the angels for company.
> With him the maiden to whom he made himself strange ;
> Now he has her close to him—together are their souls.
> I know not how to tell you how great their joy is." [2]

Dulcitius, the governor who emerges complacent and smutty-faced from amorous encounter with saucepans and kettles which he has embraced in mistake for the virgins of the Lord, the said virgins meanwhile giggling through a peephole, is rattling farce.[3] The scene in the brothel in *Abraham*, where the desert saint goes to find and bring back his fallen niece, is Bellafront and her father over again. Some air of the desert is about the old saint in spite of the gallant hat which he has perched upon his head in his character of the elderly rip, and the girl, half conscious of it, begins to cry, is rebuked by the master of ceremonies, and by the saint himself, and tries as

[1] *Hroswithae Opera*, ed. Paul von Winterfeld. *Gallicanus*, p. 120.

[2] *La Vie St. Alexis* (*G. Paris. Bibl. de l'École des Hautes Études*, viii. p. 169. See Introduction, pp. 43-51). Translation by Professor Saintsbury.

[3] *Hroswithae Opera*, "Dulcitius," pp. 129-30.

best she can to play the wanton and be gay; left alone, he discovers himself, and his fashion of dealing with his penitent is the Age of Faith at its greatest.

"Manlike it is to sin, but devil-like to dwell in sin. Blame not him who falls, but him who fails to rise again . . ."

"The mercy of God is vaster than His creature."

"Who despairs of God sins mortally. Shall the spark struck from the flint set on fire the sea?"

"The day breaks: let us go."

He mounts her on his horse, lest the hardness of the roads should wound her tender feet, and goes walking beside her into the desert dawn.[1] The same compassion, the same understanding, is in the "*Callimachus and Drusiana*," the far-off promise of *Romeo and Juliet*. For Callimachus, desperately in love with Drusiana, a married woman, is challenged, not unlike Romeo, by his young friends: "I love."

"What?"

"A fairness; a loveliness."

"Meaning?"

"A woman."

"Having said that, you have said them all!"[2]

The love scene is of yesterday.

"What made you love me?"

"Your loveliness."

"My loveliness?"

"Assuredly."

"What has my loveliness to do with you?"

"Nothing, alas! as yet, but I hope otherwise."[3]

He swears by men and gods, and Drusiana, moved with terror, prays for death to save her honour. She dies, and is taken to the vaults. Callimachus bribes the ill-conditioned slave who watches them to let him enter; and finds her like Juliet as lovely fair as ever:

[1] *Hroswithae Opera*, "Abraham," pp. 154-9.

[2] *Hroswithae Opera*, "Callimachus," pp 135-6. [3] *Ib.* p. 137.

"O Drusiana, Drusiana, with what anguish of heart have I worshipped thee . . . and thou didst ever reject me. Now art thou in my power." Enter a serpent (if the play was ever acted in Gandersheim how fain would we have seen that serpent) and disposes of the slave, whereupon the lover dies for fear. Upon them, the corpse, and the serpent, enter St. John and the grieving husband. Christ appears, and restores the girl and Romeo, but not the slave. Why? asks the husband. "Because," says St. John with admirable subtlety, "through ignorance and deceived by carnal delight this one sinned, the other through malice only." The snake is dismissed, for it is felt that he might bite twice, and by the intercession of Drusiana the slave also revives, dislikes the new atmosphere, and prefers to go back to the place from which he came out.[1] It is preposterous; but it is very real "criticism of life." And it antedates by some centuries the discovery of romantic passion.

The "sweet south" is blowing in Germany, if anywhere. Ratherius of Liège, Bishop of Verona, has an ill word of the Italian bishops, and himself refused to ordain any man who had not served his apprenticeship to liberal studies in a monastic school, or under some learned scholar.[2] In France, except at Rheims, the humanities are little esteemed, and the reform of Cluny, though it meant a veritable renaissance in the plastic arts and in music, discountenanced classical scholarship. Yet its saintly abbot, Odo, had loved Virgil with passion, and even the dream which made him an anti-classicist for life—the exquisite vase with serpents twining out of it, and the voice telling him that this was the poetry of Virgil—shows him haunted by an amazing sensitiveness to beauty.[3]

[1] *Hroswithae Opera*, pp. 139-145.

[2] "They love Bacchanalians rather than philosophers, players than priests, minstrels than clerks." Migne, *P.L.* cxxxvi. 291. See Ozanam, *Documents Inédits*, p. 14.

[3] Migne, *P.L.* cxxxiii. *S. Odonis Vita*, c. 89.

It is laid down in the Customs of Cluny that in the hour of silence one asked for a book by the gesture of turning over pages with the hand; but if the work were by a profane author, one scratched like a dog behind one's ear, with implications that may be deduced, but are plainly stated in the text.[1] That rule has the impress of Maiolus, librarian of Cluny, and later abbot; to all who had to do with him "*exemplo fuit et terrori.*"[2] Maiolus himself had read the books of the ancient philosophers, and the lies of Virgil, with the result that he would henceforth neither hear them himself nor have others read. "Sufficient unto you," he would say, "are the divine poets; nor have you any need to pollute yourself with the luxurious eloquence of Virgil"; and some have it even that he mutilated the manuscripts, taking Jerome on the shaving of the captive maid in the letter as well as in the spirit. Yet something lingers. Rahingus, monk of Flavigny and charged with all its business affairs, felt his soul grow sterile in these things, and being bound to provide for so many bodily needs of the brethren set himself to do something for their souls' good also, and so fills his scanty leisure with collecting books. His Virgil is to be kept in the house for ever.[3] In the same century a monk gave Fleury a precious Horace, hoping for that good deed that his soul might be drawn from Hell.[4] But strangest of all is the anthology of Latin lyric that took shelter behind the vast respectable bulk of Isidore of Seville, in the lost manuscript of Beauvais, where the great Spanish doctor heaves himself like a breakwater for all the gay little craft in a perpetual Feast of Lanterns behind his back.[5] There is character in an anthology; and the unknown scholar masked by

[1] Martene, *De Antiq. Mon. Rit.* v. c. 18 (4).

[2] *Vita S. Maioli*, Migne, cxxxvii. 752.

[3] Delisle, *Un Virgile copié au Xe siècle* (1886). *Deux Mss. de l'Abbaye de Flavigny*, p. 5.

[4] Boutaric, *Vincent de Beauvais* (*Revue des Quest. Hist.* xvii. p. 16).

[5] *Anthologia Latina*, ii. pp. 153 *et seq.* Also *Praef.* iv.

the Codex Isidori Bellovacensis had burst the last grape of the pagan vintage against a palate sufficiently fine.

"Hither your goblets brimming deep with wine,
That Love aflame may his long vigil keep.
The fire of Love kindles from burning Bacchus,
For Love and Bacchus are like-minded gods." [1]

"O lovely restless eyes!
They need no tongue;
For there sits Venus, and the little Loves;
Between them sits Delight." [2]

"Julia but now let fly at me with a handful of snow.
I have said that snow was cold; now find I that snow is fire." [3]

"I was with thee, in falseness of a dream.
O far beyond all dreams, if thou wouldst come in truth." [4]

"But as for me, at least with maimed delight,
Still let me love, though I may not possess." [5]

Strangest of all, the wild fragment of a half-spent revel, the scattered oyster-shells, the ivy wreaths dishevelled, the eager dark:

"Nay, let the torches burn;
They watch to-night: to-morrow all's forgotten." [6]

They belong to the Renaissance in Italy, five centuries away, those torches. To find them burning in the tenth is to see strange shadows. Yet the gold lies there unminted; the wine undrunk. Catullus, the *Pervigilium Veneris*, the "Dancing girl": [7] they have them, and cannot use

[1] *Ib. Carm.* 710. [2] *Ib. Carm.* 714. [3] *Ib.* 706. [4] *Ib.* 702.
[5] *Ib.* 712. Professor Saintsbury's translation. [6] *Ib.* 711.

[7] Ratherius of Verona refers to Catullus (Migne, *P.L.* cxxxvi. c. 752) and also Walafrid Strabo. *Carm.* 62 is in Codex Thuanus B.N. 8071, a late ninth century MS., also the *Pervigilium Veneris*; *Copa Syrisca* in Vatican 3252, ninth century Lombard, and B.N. 7927, tenth century. The last lines of the *Copa* appear in the *Carmina Burana*, 178 *a*—

"Pone merum et talos, pereat qui crastina curet."

them: the creative impulse is not yet come. It is the legend of the treasure of the Caesars that lay buried in the Campus Martius, beneath the statue with the outstretched arm that said "*Percute hic*," and many men struck the arm and went away disbelieving. But Gerbert, by this time Pope Sylvester II, watched and saw where the shadow of the outstretched finger fell at noon, and marked the place, and came back at night alone with his chamberlain and a lantern and a pick. And where he struck, the earth opened, and they went down into a great hall, where a king and queen of gold sat feasting with servitors of gold, but all the light came from a great carbuncle in the ceiling, and in one corner stood a boy with a bow, and the arrow taut on the string. And Gerbert stooped to handle the marvels that lay about him and stayed his hand, for a shiver ran through the still figures about him, and he was afraid, and stood gazing only. But his chamberlain saw a knife with a handle curiously worked and coveted it and secretly picked it up. The bow twanged; with a crash the carbuncle splintered into darkness, and round them they felt the shadowy figures rising *cum fremitu*. Gerbert snatched the knife and flung it from him; blind and stumbling they rushed from the place, and so by lantern light back to the world they knew.[1] It is another of William of Malmesbury's legends: and a parable for other scholars than Sylvester II.

[1] William of Malmesbury, *Regum Gesta*, ii. 167. Rolls Series.

CHAPTER IV

THE REVIVAL OF LEARNING

"I," SAID Benedict of Clusa, disputing with the bishops of Aquitaine, "I am the nephew of the abbot of Clusa. He led me about through many places in Lombardy and France for the sake of grammar. My learning stood him at 2000 sol. which he paid to my masters. For nine years I stood at Grammar, and now am become a *scholasticus*. We were nine *scholastici* who learned grammar, and I indeed am thoroughly learned. I have two large houses filled with books, and at this moment I have not read them all, but I meditate upon them daily. There is not in the whole earth a book that I have not. After I have left the schools, there will be no one under heaven so learned as I. I shall be abbot of Clusa after the death of my uncle. I am already chosen by all and but for the malice of some evil monks who care for nothing but hypocrisy and rusticity, I should have been consecrated abbot long ago. I am the prior of Clusa, and I know well how to make discourse, and how to write. In Aquitaine there is no learning, they are rustics all: and if any one in Aquitaine has learnt any grammar, he straightway thinks himself Virgil. In France is learning, but not much. But in Lombardy, where I mostly studied, is the fountain of learning." [1]

[1] *Mon. Germ. Hist.*, *Script.* iv. 109. Migne, cxli. 107-8. It is no wonder that Adhémar was roused. "For forty days of August and September the young man alternately ate and drank, and blasphemed the Blessed Martial," at his own table.

That speech has made the unhappy Benedict immortal. For Adhémar, an elderly scholar, although of Aquitaine, has the reporter's flair. He was present at that council, and wrote an account of its controversy in admirable Latin; but when the nephew of the Abbot of Clusa rises to speak, Adhémar reports in full: it is *oratio recta*. With what yearning affection must his eyes have rested upon the young man, with what flattering eagerness the stylus must have rushed along the tablets. It is superb reporting; never a comment, never an aside. He would not spoil its bouquet for the world.

The council was held in 1028; and historically, the egregious Benedict was justified. In Lombardy, at any rate in Italy, was the fountain of learning. Himself was hardly more than damped by its spray, and the 2000 sol. of his uncle the abbot might have been better bestowed; but one unlucky scholar went deep enough to drown. He was the poor little grammarian, Vilgardus of Ravenna, who saw Virgil and Horace and Juvenal in a dream, like unto gods, and was thanked by them for his good offices to their memory and promised a share in their immortality. After that he taught openly that the words of the poets are in all things worthy of belief, even as Holy Writ, but expiated that heresy in the fire.[1] One remembers the other heretics, burned at Paris in the next century, of whom Caesarius von Heisterbach speaks with bated breath, "who say there is neither paradise nor hell, but he who hath the knowledge of God in himself, which they have, hath paradise in himself: and he who hath mortal sin hath hell in himself, as it were a rotten tooth in the mouth." Some of them were Doctors at the University of Paris, and one of them ten years in the Faculty of Theology, but they held that God hath spoken in Ovid, even as in Augustine.[2] The old quarrel which had lapsed in the harsher noises of the tenth century is roused again. St.

[1] Rodulfus Glaber, *Hist.* II. xii. (Migne, cxlii.).

[2] Caesarius von Heisterbach, *Dial. Mirac.* v. 22.

Peter Damian is hot against the monks who challenge the grammarians at their own idle game, and bandy vanities with the seculars as if it were the din of a fair,[1] but Damian himself was in his youth a passionate classicist. "Once was Cicero music in my ears, the songs of the poets beguiled me, the philosophers shone upon me with their golden phrases, the sirens enchanted my soul nigh unto death. The Law and the Prophets, Gospel and Epistle, the whole glorious speech of Christ and His servants, seemed to me a poor thing and empty. I know not what the son of Jesse whispered in my ear, so gracious in its consonance of speech and thought, that all these others whom I once had loved fell inarticulate and silent."[2] Not wholly inarticulate: the haunting rhythms of his own prose betray his debt. "*Caligaverunt in mortem oculi sui, et illa luminaria quae illuminant orbem ad horam extincta sunt.*"[3] "Darkened in death his eyes, and those lights which lighten the earth at that hour went out." The mysticism of the twelfth century is in his sermons—on the reticence of Holy Writ, wherein "silence itself cries out that some greatness is nigh"[4]—and he has what the twelfth century mystics had not, a style that has the plangent resonance of the violin. There are moments when the bow scrapes wildly across the strings, and when the terrific invective that descends like another fiery hail on the sin of the cities of the Plain falls equally upon his unlucky travelling companion, the poor bishop who sat up in the inn playing chess while Damian was at his prayers, the effect is purely comical.[5] But some divinity hedges him. They could nickname that other accuser of the brethren at Geneva "The Accusative Case," but for Damian there is his own lightning-flash on Hildebrand, "My holy Satan." The aura about him is of a man

[1] Damiani, *De Perfectione Monachorum*. Ozanam, *Documents Inédits*, p. 15.

[2] Migne, cxliv. 852. [3] *Ib.* 763. [4] Migne, cxliv. 754.

[5] Migne, cxlv. 454.

"surer of eternity than time;" with all his denunciation of man's flesh, he loses himself, unlike St. Bernard, in an *O altitudo*! before the high aspiring of his mind. "How strange a thing is man! But half a cubit of him, and a universe full of material things will not satisfy it." It is not the man whose senses are blunt who makes the sternest ascetic, and a great lover wrote the passionate strophes of his sequence on the Song of Songs—

> "Who is this that knocketh at my gate,
> Breaking the sleep of the night?"[1]

But it is in his most famous poem,

> "Ad perennis vitae fontem,"[2]

that the long struggle of his soul is laid bare. It is by its satisfactions that one judges a soul, and there are stanzas in the *Paradise* that have an echo in Walton's great sentence on Donne, "His mind was liberal and unwearied in the search of knowledge, with which his vigorous soul is now satisfied."

> "For the fount of life undying
> Once the parched mind did thirst,
> Cramped within its carnal prison,
> Sought the soul its bonds to burst.
> Struggling, gliding, soaring free,
> Comes back the exile to its onw country.
>
> . . . . .
>
> "Cleansed from all its dregs, the body
> With the spirit knows no war,
> For the mind and flesh made spirit
> One in thought and feeling are.
> Deep their peace and their enjoying,
> From all shame and scandal far."

All the contrary desires of the poets are here: Wyatt's

> "Nothing on earth more do I crave
> Save that I have, to have it still."

[1] Migne, cxlv. 939. *Carm.* lxii. [2] *Ib.* 980. *Carm.* 226.

Shelley's

> "Thou lovest—but ne'er knew love's sad satiety."

—— *Avidi et semper pleni quod habent desiderant.*

> "What they have they still desire,
> Eager, and yet satisfied:"

Shakespeare's

> "Wishing me like to one more rich in hope,
> Featured like him, like him with friends possessed,
> Desiring this man's art and that man's scope,"

——"*Licet cuiquam sit diversum pro labore meritum*
Caritas hoc facit suum, quod amat in altero.
Proprium sit singulorum fit commune omnium.

> "Let there be a different guerdon
> Unto each man for his pain,
> That which I loved in another
> Love hath brought to me again;
> Thine and mine in full possession,
> Yet 'tis common unto men:"

Milton's longing for something fixed where all is moving "in all the changes of that which is called fortune from without, or the wily subtleties and refluxes of man's thought from within"—

—— "*Hinc perenne tenent esse, nam transire transiit.*"

Damian is the greatest name in the century: the next greatest are, like him, Italian, though they made their name in France, Lanfranc, who came from the law school of Pavia to Bec in Normandy, and thence with the Conqueror to Canterbury: Fulbert, Chancellor and Bishop of Chartres.[1] He was born in Rome, about 960; for apologising to Einhard for not sending on a manuscript he explains that he himself had borrowed it from a library in Rome "*ex natali patria.*" He was Gerbert's pupil at Rheims, while that admirable scholar was simple *scholas-*

[1] *Vide* Clerval, *Les Écoles de Chartres au Moyen Âge*, pp. 58-107. Manitius, however, gives Fulbert to Aquitaine.

ticus and not yet archbishop of that see: and about twenty-seven came as master and chancellor to the episcopal school at Chartres, the first of the almost unbroken succession of humanists and Platonists whose memory still makes Chartres a holy place. "The streets are full of the genius of Fulbert," said an English monk, a hundred years after his death:[1] they are so still. "Almost every man of letters in that age in France had him as master," said Orderic Vitalis. "At his death," says the author of the Life of St. Odilo, "the study of philosophy in France perished, and the glory of the priesthood wellnigh went out." They likened him to a spring, from which rivers went over all France, and history confirms them.[2] Rainaldus restored the schools of Angers, so famous in the last half of the century that many English scholars came to study there: Berengarius the heretic, yet so gracious that the Council had hardly the heart to damn him, revived the glories of Tours, and was himself the adoration of the still finer scholar Hildebert. "Do you remember," writes Adelmann to Berengar, "the evening talks he used to have with us, our venerable Socrates, in the garden beside the chapel . . . entreating us with tears that now and then would break out in the midst of his talk not to be turned aside, not to slip into a new and deceptive way."[3] "Our venerable Socrates" knew the dangerous crossroads: but, strong lover of Plato that he was, he counted beauty no enemy to holiness. St. Augustine's dread of music is far from him: his pupil, Franco of Cologne, is the author of the first treatise on counterpoint, and his own song to the Nightingale, in the famous trochaic "fifteener" is for accompaniment by the lyre, the monochord, and the organ. It has the first spring ecstasy in it, for the poets before him have been

[1] See Clerval, *Les Écoles de Chartres au Moyen Âge*, p. 96.

[2] Migne, cxliii. c. 1295. Adelmann, *De Viris Illustribus*.

[3] *Ib.* c. 1289. *Epist. ad Berengar*, "sub nostro illo venerabili Socrate."

greatest when their theme was autumn and the falling of the leaf

"When the earth with spring returning buds again,
And the branches in the woods again are green,
And the sweetness of all flowers is in the grass,
Lilts the nightingale all passionate with song,
With the thrilling of her tiny swelling throat,
Flings the prophecy of spring and summer tides.
Beyond all birds that sing, clearer than flutes....
Filling the woods and every little copse,
Most glorious with the rapture of the Spring....
The snarer in the green wood holds his peace,
The swan falls silent, and the shrilling flute.
So small art thou, to take us all with singing,
None gave that voice, unless the King of Heaven."[1]

The verses go heavily: there is monotony in the single final assonance on the vowel ā: but it is a prophecy to unawakened earth.

The humorous breadth of the man, as well as some very adroit rhyming, is in the skit that he wrote upon the Abbot John. It is worth quoting in full, for it is the reverse of the shield, of Damian's strained and tortured ardours: humanism is at the gate.

"The Abbot John, in stature small,
  But not in godly graces,
Spake thus unto his elder friend
  —Both lived in desert places—

"'I wish,' said he, 'to live secure
  As angels do in heaven:
No food to eat, no garment wear
  Whereon men's hands have striven.'

"His senior said 'Be not too rash,
  Brother, I counsel you,
For you may find you've bitten off
  More than your teeth can chew.'

[1] *De Philomela.* Migne, cxli. c. 348.

" But he—' Who goes not to the war
Nor falls, nor wins the fight,'
He spake, and to remoter wilds
Naked, went out of sight.

" For seven days he painfully
Endured a grassy diet,
The eighth, his famine drove him home,
He can no more abye it.

" Night, and the door fast shut, all snug
Sat in his cell the other,
When a faint voice without the door
Cried ' Open to me, brother.

" ' John, poor and needy, is without
The old familiar gate,
Let not your kindness scorn the man
Whom want did overtake.'

" Then answered he, safe shut within :
' John to an angel turned him,
He contemplates the doors of heaven,
And men no more concern him.'

" John had his bed without, and bore
The chills of night contrary,
And thus did penance rather more
Than was quite voluntary.

" Now with the dawn, he's safe within,
And scorched with caustic sayings,
But he, intent upon his crust,
Endures it all with patience.

" All warm again, he thanks returns
God and his friend unto,
And even tries, with feeble arm,
To wield the garden hoe.

" Cured of his folly, he'll let him
An angel be who can,
Himself he finds it hard enough
To be a decent man." [1]

[1] Latin text in *Cambridge Songs*, ed. Breul, p. 60 : Du Méril, *Poésies Populaires Latines Antérieures au XIIe siècle*, p. 189.

THE REVIVAL OF LEARNING

The Gulf Stream, diverted for almost a century from France, is flowing again: the rawness gone from the air. Radulfus Glaber is genial with it: his odd prose goes with a sudden lightness when the earlier decades of the century are past, and climbs to an exaltation at his story of the council where the people made their truce with God. And though it was transient, though the horror of the great famine of 1033 made the earth brutal, the exaltation comes again in his speech of the first pilgrimage to the Holy Sepulchre.[1] By the time Guibert de Nogent is writing his autobiography—Guibert was born in 1053—he can almost fix the date of the change, the breaking of the frost. "Shortly before that time and indeed partly in my own time was so great a dearth of grammarians that almost none could be found in the towns and scarce any in the cities, and if it befell that any were found, their learning was so slender that it could hardly equal that of a wandering clerk in modern times."[2] The old man who was his own tutor had been caught up late into the new currents, and the poor small scholar suffered many things for not understanding an explanation which the master could not understand himself. But there was an immense affection between them: and when Guibert's mother suspected the gallant lying and stripped the shirt from the small scarred shoulders and cried over them, declaring that he must give up going to school, the youngster burst out "If I die for it, I shan't stop till I have got my learning and am a clerk."[3] That same mother's great beauty is one of the things Guibert thanks God for—another proof that the rigour is passing. "Assuredly," he says in his own defence, lest some think he has spoken profanely and idly in calling her fair, "assuredly, although beauty is momentary and fickle with the restlessness of the blood, as is the way of imaginary good, nevertheless it cannot

[1] Radulfus Glaber, *Hist.* iv. 5. Migne, cxlii. 678-80.

[2] Guibert de Nogent, *De vita sua.* Migne, clvi. 844.

[3] *Ib.* clvi. 847.

be denied that it is good. For if whatever God hath willed from all eternity is fair, then all that which hath a temporal fairness is as it were a mirror of the eternal beauty."[1] So good a Platonist was bound to be a poet, but Guibert thinks with less complacence of the next stage of his studies. He was now professed at Fly, and "immersed" in poetry. Holy Writ was contemptible to him: Ovid and the Bucolics were his pattern, the suavity of the amorous poets bewitched him, and nothing will do him but he must play the sedulous ape, "fashing myself for this only, if I might but once get even with some poet in a courtly phrase." But from suavity he fell to wantonness, from wantonness to sheer obscenity, and chewed the cud of many a song so outrageous that he could not for shame's sake confess he was the writer of it, so fathered it on some other poet, and then basked in his friend's praises. It passed: the Blessed Gregory gave him something to break his mind upon,[2] and the Abbot of Nogent is remembered for his prose, his Chronicles of the Crusade, and an autobiography in the manner of Augustine. But the story is interesting, for it suggests the new passion for verse in the schools.

Latin verse composition had always, of course, been taught. Charlemagne bent his great brows on the young dandies of the palace school who failed to produce tolerable verse,[3] and Hrabanus Maurus came to Alcuin at Tours to study metres.[4] But it is towards the end of the eleventh century that one recognises the beginning of the craze for verse, which is almost universal in the twelfth,[5] just as in Elizabethan England any man of breeding was expected to know what to

[1] Guibert de Nogent, *De vita sua* Migne, clvi. 839.

[2] *Ib.* 872. [3] *Gesta Carol. Mag.* (Monk of St. Gall), i. 3.

[4] Hrab. Maur. *Carm.* i.

[5] See William Fitzstephen on the verse-combats of the London scholars, *Descriptio Nobilissimae Civitatis Londoniae*: Stow, *Survey of London*, p. 476.

do with the music sheet set down before him after dinner. The verse was of two sorts, the scholar's verse in the classical metres of Hildebert and Alphanus of Salerno and the school of Liège, and the *cantilena*, the *rhythmus*, which the young men sang at the corners, "pleasant," says dear old Tetbald de Vernon who wrote the *St. Alexis*, "because of its sound like a bell." They all wrote it, *en pantoufles*: even the great Bernard himself in his youth at Citeaux. He was guilty of great ease and proficiency in it, as Abelard's indiscreet terrier, Berengarius, reminds him:[1] and by the end of the twelfth century, the writing of rhyming verse was absolutely forbidden to the members of the Cistercian order:[2] its associations were too dangerous. Not much of it from the eleventh century survives: perhaps small loss, judging by the specimen Ivo of Chartres refers to, as one who holds it in the tongs. The story is one of the liveliest of the minor dramas hidden in that great bishop's correspondence. What became of her, the girl of servile birth who had married a man of rank, when he found out, and appealed to the bishop for annulment of the marriage? "Both canon and secular law permit," says Ivo magnificently, "but the law of Nature says Nay: before her there is neither bond nor free."[3] Did they force the marriage on their unwilling girl, the parents who appeal to Ivo to join with them in coercing her, and he refuses—"That is not marriage which is the coition of two bodies: but the union of two minds."[4] Ivo had the granite virtues: and when his hoe lights upon the more pestilential type of weedy manhood, there is little left for the bonfire. Now John, Archdeacon of Orleans, was a peculiarly pernicious weed: and to Ivo's immense disgust, had just been elected Bishop of that see. Ivo, writing

[1] Migne, *P.L.* clxxviii. c. 1857: *cantiunculas mimicas et urbanos modulos.*

[2] Hauréau, *Poèmes Latins attribués à St. Bernard*, p. 2.

[3] Ivo, *Epist.* 221 (Migne, clxii.). [4] *Ib. Epist.* 134.

to the Pope, does not mince matters: he does not spare the Bishop of Orleans lately dead, who had made John Archdeacon, nor the present Archbishop of Tours, who had secured this final preferment, nor John himself, who has been nick-named Flora by his fellow-canons in Orleans (Flora being the name of a famous courtesan), and under that name is the heroine of innumerable songs sung at the corners by idle young men throughout all France; "and as you well know," says Ivo, "there are too many of the sort. For proof of it, here's a specimen that I caught a young man singing and took from him with some violence." One sees it, the graceless pup bawling it cheerfully on his way to the *Maîtrise,* and the whirlwind of the mighty Bishop round the corner, and the full buffet. Yet apparently the election was confirmed. "Flora" had the ear of the queen, and his moneybags were heavier than his rival's, the Abbot of Bourgeuil. A year or two, and Ivo is writing, not cordially, but with full consideration, to John, Bishop of Orleans, to advise him on a point of canon law.[1]

The disappointed abbot of Bourgeuil was a poet, of that valley of the Loire that is so rich in poets.[2] Baudri first learnt his grammar in the school of Meung that Theodolfus founded, and which was afterwards to produce a more famous poet, the Jean de Meung who wrote the sequel to the *Roman de la Rose*: from Meung he went to Angers, to study under Rainaldus, once pupil to Fulbert at

[1] Ivo, *Epist.* 66, 67, 162. Migne, clxii. 83, 86, 163.

[2] Much of Baudri's poetry is still in manuscript. The original—MS. of Queen Christine, Vatican, 1351—was copied by the Abbé Salmon, and the copy bequeathed by him to Tours. Delisle in *Romania,* Jan., 1872, and H. Pasquier—*Un Poète Latin de l'XIme siècle*—have printed a good deal of it from the Tours MS.; the more serious verse is in Migne, clxvi. The famous poem to Adela, Countess of Blois, describing the Bayeux tapestry, has been edited separately by Delisle, and much commented. But a complete edition of Baudri, as well as Marbod and Hildebert, would be worth doing. A grudging account of him is given in the *Histoire Littéraire,* xi. 96-113.

[Since going to press, this note has been happily nullified by Miss Abrahams' *Baudri de Bourgeuil,* a critical edition of the Vatican MS.]

Chartres. His poems are no great matter, but they suggest the ampler ether in which poetry is possible. He has nothing of Hildebert's stark grandeur of phrase, the iron structure of thought that lies behind the conceits, nothing of Marbod's rich and vivid temper. He trims his verses to fit the exquisite tablets that his friend the Abbot of Séez gave him (he died Archbishop of Canterbury in 1122), broad enough to hold an hexameter, long enough to take eight lines, and coated with green wax, not black, because green is more pleasing to the eye.[1] He has a little of Petrarch's childlike vanity, and, like Petrarch, rejoices in having found a new scribe, a *vagus*, young and malleable :[2] the other, Hugh, though admirable, was too slow, in spite of being promised immortality in the future, and his expenses to Rome on account.[3] The green tablets filled faster than they were emptied : Baudri chafes and frets, because the inspiration is upon him, and there is no room to write.[4] Baudri was very particular about the colouring of his capitals—Gerard, who had the Arabic art, did the illumination—because since the verses are very indifferent, he would like to make sure of readers by the beauty of the MS. Mabillon declares that the Abbey of Bourgeuil was more famous for its verses than its discipline, but it was a pleasant place, of running streams and arbours, and in its Abbot's verses a little vanity and an over-sensitiveness to the luxury of things are the gravest faults. His gift is in that sensitiveness to beauty, his love of nature, not yet wild, perhaps, but bird-haunted : a garden with the sound of running water, not too loud, but a just accompaniment to the reading of verse. It is to be sure a place remote from Cicero, says Baudri, Cicero who had more pleasure in the stylus and the tablets than in cabbages : yet it might be apt enough for poets.[5] His

[1] *Carm.* xlvii. *Romania,* 1872, pp. 29-30.

[2] *Carm.* xxxvi. *Romania,* 27.

[3] *Carm.* cxlvi. *Romania,* 34. Pasquier, 71.

[4] xliv. *Romania,* 29.

[5] ccxv. *Romania,* p. 45.

friends are scholars: to Godfrey of Rheims who reads the masters, Virgil and Ovid, he writes pleading that if he gives the great ones a year, give me, for friendship's sake, a day.[1] His hospitality is encompassing, he is for ever inviting, for ever wailing a departure: "The Muses look askance at me when you're away."[2] He is the perfect host, and although his friends might learn to dread the production of the little green tablets, many of them were poets too, and he lures them by the promise of the garden, cherry trees and pear trees, olive and pine, narcissus and daphne and thyme, and you will read me your verses, and I will read you mine, for I have been writing a lot too.[3] He has one poem "On the Day on which I was Happy": he was up early, and there were the tablets ready, and the Muses.[4] He likes to have poetry read to him before he himself begins to compose: and a nightingale singing in the copse.[5] He loves the Loire, the river in which the young girls bathing shine all the whiter in its silver water:[6] his worst grief is that some one has extorted his Ovid from him—he thinks he must have put magic on him to make him lend it[7]—and that a friend has made a poem on a mole. *Vae mihi!* If only he had thought of it himself![8] Charming *religieuses* are among his correspondents, Muriel and Emma and perverse Beatrice who will not write,[9] and Constance who thinks him worth many Aristotles.[10] Once only is there a spark

[1] clxi. Pasquier, p. 140.

[2] clxxi. Amicis qui ab se recesserant. Pasquier, p. 143.

[3] cxci. Ad Avitum ut ad eum veniat. Pasquier, 141.

[4] clxiii. Ad diem in qua laetatus est. Pasquier, 65.

[5] ccxxxv. Pasquier, 68. clxxviii. De sufficientia votorum suorum.

[6] Delisle, *Poème à Adèle*, 891-2:

> "Unda quidem Ligeris teneris infusa puellis
> corpora lotarum candidiora facit."

[7] clxxiii. Ad eum qui Ovidium ab eo extorsit. Pasquier, p. 134.

[8] cxciii. De talpo se reprehendo. Pasquier, p. 69.

[9] cii. Beatricem reprehendit. Pasquier, 169.

[10] ccxxxix. "Multos Aristoteles, alter Homerus."

of passion, when Constance writes to thank him for his poems—" And I have touched your songs with my bare hand." [1] He does not mind confessing to Constance that the commentary on Genesis is not getting on very fast,[2] but he defends himself against masculine critics, righteously hurt. He does make sermons : if he reads it is while other people are snoozing in the siesta, and his poems he writes at night, or when he is on horseback.[3] Some think his disappointment about Orleans turned his thoughts to gravity : in a few years he becomes Archbishop of Dol in Brittany, and his garden knows him no more. The prose works, the History of Jerusalem, On the Sword and Shield of Michael, on the Visitation of the Sick, date from the episcopate. " But roses like the roses of Bourgeuil, I have not found them here . . . and I begin to sigh. . . . Not that I would go back, but I would fain see flowers fairer than are here." [4]

Marbod, *scholasticus* of Angers and Bishop of Rennes, is a more robust type. His love is there, frankly and heartily, for all the world to read, the type that the twelfth and thirteenth century lovers sang of more lightly and more tunefully, but with no more sincerity: snow white and rose red, star-eyed, soft laughter, and the scarlet flame of tenderly swelling lips, all these had the maid who sought to give herself to me. And a handsome young man desired her, but her eyes were on the *scholasticus* of Angers. He is very stern : he reminds himself that kisses are to be scorned. The worst of it, as he ruefully discovers, is that to scorn kisses is to fasten them still more securely in one's thoughts.[5] Malachy, the old Irish bishop who died thirty years later at Clairvaux,

[1] ccxxxix.

[2] ccxxxviii. Ad dominam Constantiam.

[3] clxi. . . . xxxvi.

[4] *Epist. ad Fisc.* Migne, clxxi. c. 1173.

[5] Migne, *P.L.* clxxi. c. 1635. *Carm.* 16:

" Oscula dum sperno, spernens tamen oscula cerno."

was wiser in his sequence of the wisdom of the spirit—

> "To scorn the world, to scorn one's self, to scorn no man at all." [1]

And so he begged his kisses, and thought them a kingdom, kisses that seemed to mingle the strength and sweetness of the rose. A rose the face seemed then, that's white and buried now.

> "Out of my door, O boy with wings, thou the love-bringer,
> And in my house no place for thee, O Cytherea!" [2]

Marbod regretted the light-winged verse of his youth, but spoke of it bravely. Once the word is spoken, there is no recalling it: better look to the future than regret the past.[3] But he is no Puritan. Death is a harsh word, and life a lovable.[4] If a man can look out on a spring day, the nests with the unfeathered birds, and not be touched by it, and go unsmiling, he is intractable, and there is strife in his heart.[5] His reproof written to a censorious monk is annihilating: "I greet you not, nor do I wish you well.

> "Nam cum sis purus, et forsitan abbas futurus."

all the rest of us are *extorres*, outcasts from the kingdom of heaven. Know that God's mercy knows not how to measure. *Te non consulto,* He pities, and He hardens; nor does any man know, till he is out of the body, on which hand of the Most High he will find himself: the thief on the cross: the hermit who fell at the last. So spare, I pray, while you yourself are still at sea, to vex with words

[1] "Spernere mundum, spernere sese, spernere nullum." See Hauréau, *Mélanges Poétiques d'Hildebert de Lavardin,* p. 123.

[2] Marbod, *Carmina,* xvii. Migne, clxxi. c. 1655.

[3] *Decem Capitulorum Liber. Ib.* c. 1693.

[4] *Carm.* xxxvii. c. 1671:

> "Asper quippe sonus, incultaque syllaba mors est;
> At affabilis est, jucundaque dictio, vita."

[5] *Carm.* iv. c. 1717.

a bark so tempest-tossed.[1] Marbod's wisdom is the wisdom of open country: when the town wearied him, he took refuge on his uncle's farm. Green grass and quiet trees, a soft little wind and gay, a spring well in the grass, these things give me back to myself, they make me abide in myself. Town takes a man out of the truth of himself, says Marbod, with a wisdom beyond Juvenal, and dreaming under the trees, he watches the eager present slip back into the still grave of the past.[2]

Marbod was a famous master: but less famous than Hildebert of Le Mans, whose stormy life of conflicting loyalties and ardent scholarship brought him in the end to the archbishopric of Tours.[3] He is the only modern author whom John of Salisbury with his unerring judgment included among the classics. His contemporaries get the richness, the ornament; Hildebert, not always but unmistakably, their austere economy. The lines on the bar of a man's own conscience,

> "Myself accuser, and myself accused,"[4]

the bitter but experiencing satire on Love and Fortune:[5] the appeal to the girl of his discriminating worship to write to him in his exile:[6] on the fading rose of the world, the eternal Rose of God:[7] they have a new accent. And that accent is clearest in the two lines that are the herald's

[1] Marbod, *Carmina*, xxxv. Migne, clxxi., c. 1679.

[2] *Carmina*, xxvii.:

> "Herba virens et silva silens et spiritus aurae
> Lenis et festivus, et fons in gramine vivus
> Defessam mentem recreant et me mihi reddunt
> Et faciunt in me consistere: nam quis in urbe
> Qui non extra se rapitur. . . .
>
> "Tempora praeterita mortis consumpsit imago
> Illud tantillum spatii brevis atque pusillum
> Quod vivens praesens iam praeteritum fit et absens.
> Haec et plura mihi licet atque libet meditare,
> Fronde sub agresti dum rure moror patrueli."

[3] See Hauréau, *Mélanges Poétiques d'Hildebert de Lavardin*.

[4] Migne, clxxi. c. 1280.

[5] *Ib*. c. 1423.

[6] *Ib*. c. 1445.

[7] *Ib*. c. 1238.

blazon of a new order of thought, the lines that came to the mind of Magister Gregorius when for the first time he saw Rome lie below him with its towers :

> " What wert thou, Rome, unbroken, when thy ruin
> Is greater than the whole world else beside ? " [1]

For the first time since the passing of the Empire a man's eyes turn to Rome, not as the inheritance of Peter, but the grave of a buried beauty.[2]

With every rediscovery of antiquity comes the discovery of the goodness of the earth. It is so seen in the scholars of the Loire valley, still more in Sigebert of Liège.[3] It is the freshest verse in all the century, as fresh as the names of his virgins in the fields of the Blessed.

> " Gertrude, Agnes, Prisca, Cecily,
> Lucia, Thekla, Petronel,
> Agatha, Barbara, Juliana,
> Wandering there in the fresh spring meadows,
> Looking for flowers to make them a garland,
> Roses red of the Passion,
> Lilies and violets for love." [4]

On early morning : he has been lying listening to the crowing of the cock : hourly at first, now every minute : let him take the road. It is a lyric on walking, rather than

1 " Quam cum primo a latere montis a longe vidissem, stupefactam mentem meam . . . cum incomprehensibilem decorem diu admirans deo apud me gratias egi, qui magnus in universa terra in opera hominum inestimabili decore mirificavit. Nam licet tota Roma ruat, nil tamen integrum sibi potest equiparari. Unde quidam sic ait,

> ' Par tibi, Roma, nihil, cum sis prope tota ruina :
> Fracta docere potes integra quanta fores.' "

Magister Gregorius, *De Mirabilibus Urbis Romae*, Rushforth (*Journal of Roman Studies*, ix. p. 45).

2
> " Non tamen annorum series, non flamma nec ensis
> Ad plenum potuit hoc abolere decus.
> Non potuit natura deos hoc ore creare
> Quo miranda deum signa creavit homo."

Hauréau, *Mélanges Poétiques d'Hildebert de Lavardin*, p. 60. Migne, clxxi. c. 1409.

3 Sigebert of Liège (1030-1112). See Dümmler, *Abhandlungen der Kgl. Akad. der Wissenschaft. zu Berlin*, 1893.

4 *Ib.* p. 24. *Passio S. Luciae.* See Appendix A.

on dawn: all things are happy in the morning, and it's good to cover the ground swinging, when the body's rested and the mind vivid, and the birds singing, so that even a tired man would forget his weariness.[1] The glorious entry of the Theban Legion is a riot of jewels and sound, but loveliest at its close—

> "No lily for me, violet or rose,
> Lilies for purity, roses for passion denied,
> Nor violets wan, to show with what pure fire
> The bride for the bridegroom burns.
> I know not how to gild my marigolds,
> Proud poppies and narcissus not for me,
> Nor flowers written with the names of kings.
> All that this blockhead zeal of mine could find
> Was privet blossom, falling as I touched it,
> That never boy or girl would stoop to gather,
> And of it, badly woven, ill contrived,
> I twisted these poor crowns.
> Will you but deign to wear them,
> Hide neath the victor's laurel this poor wreath—
> Clumsy the work, a silly weight to carry,
> And yet revile it not, for it is love." [2]

Sigebert rejects the old fountains:

> "I never drank of Aganippe's well," [3]

yet Liege at the end of the century held one poet who recaptured the older lyric measures fallen so long into rust. It is an allegory, a complaint of the Bride against the Bridegroom, and the historical basis of it is the struggle between Pope and Anti-Pope, Urban II and Clement III, but there are good moments in it. The Church is sometimes "Any wife to any husband"; and the metres are astonishingly varied, glyconics, asclepiads, adonics, iambic dimeter. The whole is a credit to the school of classics at Liege,[4] but it looks back. The promise of the future is

[1] *Ib.* p. 69. [2] *Ib.* p. 124. [3] *Ib.* p. 67.

[4] *Notices et Extraits,* xxxi. pp. 165 *et seq.* Seifrid, Abbot of Tegernsee, excusing his own illiteracy by his frequent infirmity, professes that he once drank "quidquid . . . fluentis Leodiscensibus discendi aestibus flagrans" (c. 1048). Migne, cxlii. 723.

in a less learned manuscript, that some traveller in the Rhine valley brought back with him to the monastery of St. Augustine in Canterbury, or that the Augustine monks themselves copied from the songbook of a wandering clerk.[1] It is an odd mixture, fragments from Statius and Virgil, laments for dead emperors, sequences for Easter, for the feast of St. Katherine, the patron lady of all scholars, Fulbert's song to the nightingale, the sad story of the Abbess' donkey, reminding one of the cow belonging to Miss Betsy Barker in *Cranford*, who went meekly forth to pasture clad in grey flannel, the really Chaucerian malice of *The Snowchild*, and one or two scraps of good fooling.[1] But the new things are the spring songs, one in clumsy sapphics, only here and there the authentic note, and still impersonal.[2] But in the other the marvellous close of the *Pervigilium Veneris* wakens the first echo,

> " With the strange cry of swans the pools are shrill :
> The nightingale beneath the poplar shade
> Singeth, as though remembering the passion,
> Forgetful of the pain.
> She sings, I hold my peace :
> For when will come my spring ? "

It came, in literature, sometime in the first half of the eleventh century.

> " Softly the west wind blows,
> Gaily the warm sun goes.
> The earth her bosom showeth,
> And with all sweetness floweth,
>
> " Goes forth the scarlet spring,
> Clad with all blossoming,
> Sprinkles the fields with flowers,
> Leaves on the forest.
>
> " Dens for four-footed things,
> Sweet nests for all with wings,

[1] *The Cambridge Songs : A Goliard's Song Book af the XIth Century* : ed. K. Breul (Cambridge, 1915).

[2] *Cambridge Songs*, p 63, " *Vestiunt silve tenera merorem.*"

On every blossomed bough,
Joy ringeth now.

"I see it with my eyes,
I hear it with my ears,
But in my heart are sighs,
And I am full of tears.

"Alone with thought I sit,
And blench, remembering it.
Sometimes I lift my head,
I neither hear nor see.

"Do thou, O Spring most fair,
Squander thy care
On flower and leaf and grain,
—Leave me alone with pain." [1]

By some miracle, that song has escaped destruction. For some austere brother of St. Augustine has used his best gall on half a dozen others, sometimes even the knife. But there are obstinate palimpsests, and the scarred folios have an odd enchantment. Letters stand out here and there, V, that may be *ver*, for spring, or *veni*, come ; single words, *pulchra*, *nidis*, *flores*, *studium*, enough for any scholar's love song : a single phrase, "In *languore pereo*."[2] Still the soft pipes play on,

"Pipe to the spirit ditties of no tone."

The nest has been torn to pieces : but enough remains to show it was a singing-bird's.

[1] Latin text in *The Cambridge Songs*, p. 64, *Levis exsurget Zephirus*. See Appendix A.

[2] *Ib.* facsimiles 440 *v*, 441 *v*.

CHAPTER V

HUMANISM IN THE FIRST HALF OF THE TWELFTH CENTURY

" CAR en enfer vont li beau clerc," says Aucassin, affirming his own willingness to go there. It is the jongleur's recognition of the new temper of scholarship. So far, humanism had really been, in Jerome's metaphor, the captive maid of the theologians. The great scholars, from Alcuin to Hildebert, had been men of approved sanctity, some of them titular saints: Gerbert, in this as in all things the exception, was at least a great and austere ecclesiastic. Theoretically, the tradition holds that literature and logic are the gymnasium of a good wit, which will in time apply itself to divinity, but in practice men come to the schools from benefices and parishes and canonries, and there abide. " One must come to the schools to be a good theologian," says a parish priest, bitten with these strange new ardours. " Not a bit of it," says Robert de Sorbon, " the great doctors save not one soul in the year." [1] " Grammar forges the Sword of the Word," says another sermon, " dialectic sharpens it: theology uses it," but too many busy themselves with the forging and the tempering only: " they do spend their

[1] Hauréau, *Les Propos de Maître Robert de Sorbon* (*Mémoires de l'Académie des Inscriptions*, xxxi. 2e partie, p. 147). See the rebukes in the sermons quoted by Hauréau, *Notices et Extraits*, vi. 209, 210, 213, 214, 230, 233, 237. Also the complaint of Urban III in 1187 to the provost of the chapter at Maguelone: " Your canons go without leave to study civil law and profane letters " (Luchaire, *La Société française sous Philippe Auguste*, p. 116).

best years in fine speaking, and come in their old age to theology, which should be the wife of their youth.[1] "Think shame to yourself," cries Peter of Blois to one obstinate humanist. "Think shame to yourself, O schoolboy centenarian, O antiquity still at the elements! Your contemporaries have passed on to a higher knowledge: you still dispute of nouns and syllables. Lucan and Priscian, these be thy gods! See to it, for Death is on the threshold."[2] Peter spoke consciously virtuous: he had denied himself with frequent and vehement sighs a distinguished career in Bologna, the stronghold of civil law.[3] Bologna was the "nursery of young archdeacons"; Gilbert Foliot, when he was Bishop of London, had sometimes two archdeacons studying there. The statutes of St. Paul's allowed non-residence for student canons; such must go for not less than one year, and leave might be given for two or three.[4] But the difficulty was rather to get them home. "If I had had five or six marks a year to keep me in the schools," said the masterful Abbot of Bury St. Edmunds, "I should never have been monk or abbot."[5] An anonymous sermon from Tours tells the story of a scholar of Paris who shared a room with a

[1] Robert of Sorbon. Quoted by Haskins, *Paris University in XIIIth Cent. Sermons*, p. 9.

[2] Peter of Blois, Ep. vi. (to Radulfus of Beauvais), Migne, 207. See also *Epist.* 76 to his namesake, another Peter of Blois, who spent his days in civil law, worse still in vain and amatorious poems. Peter in his own youth had given some talent to these amorous toys, but the dragon of Moses devoured the dragons of Pharaoh, and he left these behind him on the very threshold of youth.

[3] *Chart. Univ. Paris*, p. 32 (c. 1160), "Bononensis castra milicie crebro suspiransque vehementer citius et premature deserui."

[4] Stubbs, *Learning and Literature under Henry II.* (Seventeen Lectures, p. 160).

[5] *Jocelini de Brakelonde Cronica*, Camden Society, p. 27. *Vide* Jean de St. Gilles, preaching to the University: "It is to be observed that the Mother of the Lord suffered him not to be in the schools, save three days only, nor was he Magister save for three years and a half; and in this are those rebuked who dally forever in the schools." (Hauréau, *Not. et Ext.*, vi. 234).

friend, and how, moved by divine prompting, he determined to enter the cloister, and tried to persuade his room-mate to do likewise. But the young man shaking his head replied that he meant to stay the three years' course—the *triennium*—at Paris, and take his master's degree, and then to Montpellier to take his degree in medicine, and thence to Bologna, the seven years' course, and proceed Doctor of Law. And in the morning the other rising early came to the bedside of his friend and found him stark: struck by sudden death, "he who had planned to live so fully."[1] A good man asked the masters of Paris if it were better to learn what one did not know or to apply what one knew, and when they approved the second, concluded upon them that they were fools and astray in the wits, since they came to Paris from divers places, abandoning parishes and prebends, and studied a reading which they knew not, and the next day yet another and so perpetually.[2] It is the stumbling paraphrase of Marlowe's

> "Still climbing after knowledge infinite,
> And ever moving as the restless spheres."

Abelard is the first of the new order: the scholar for scholarship's sake. Patrimony and knighthood he left to a younger brother, recognising in himself a vocation for letters as some men might for religion:[3] and though he died in such a fashion that Peter the Venerable writes of it with a sort of heartbroken passion of reverence, he knew it for the breaking of the proudest scholar in Europe. It is easy to belittle Abelard's achievement, the depth and originality of his thinking, the harmony of his poetry, the quality of his prose. It remains that he is one of the makers of life, and perhaps the most powerful, in twelfth century Europe. Paris would have had its university

[1] Tours MS. 468, quoted by Haskins, *The University of Paris in the Sermons of the Thirteenth Century*, p. 12 n. (*American Hist. Review*, x.).

[2] Hauréau, *Notices et Extraits*, iii. p. 243 (Sermon by Robert of Sorbon).

[3] *Hist. Cal.* Migne, *P.L.* clxxviii. c. 114-5.

without the magnet that drew all men thither in the great years when "Rhinoceros indomitus"[1] lifted up his horn on Mont St. Genevieve and the schools became a bull-ring, where opponent after opponent tosses on the horns of his deadly logic. His tremendous weight flung into dialectic and philosophy did but incline a balance already swaying, for north of the Alps, in this as in the other Renaissance, the current always flows from pure humanism to speculative theology.

> "O nightingale, give over
> For an hour,
> Till the heart sings,"[2]

would have been written, even if Abelard had not come to neglect the schools for a windflower of seventeen growing in the shadow of Notre Dame, and set her lovely name to melodies lovelier still. But he stamped himself on the imagination of the century in a fashion beside which Petrarch's influence on the sixteenth becomes the nice conduct of a clouded cane. "Lucifer hath set," said Philippe of Harvengt when he died.[3] "Was there a town or village," cried Héloïse, "but seethed at the word of your coming? What eye but followed you as you went by?"[4] "Sublime in eloquence," wrote a man who hated him.[5] Even Guillaume of Saint Thierry who loosed the storm upon him, said "And yet I loved him."[6] In the schools he kept his sword like a dancer: Goliath they called him with the

[1] *Vita B. Gosvini*, i. 18, p. 79.

[2] *Carmina Burana*, cxl. 6:

> "Sile, philomena,
> pro tempore,
> surge cantilena,
> de pectore."

[3] *Epitaphia Abelardi*, v. Migne, clxxviii. c. 103. Mediaeval epitaphs are notoriously extravagant; yet these men have seen some majesty:

> "Nec mors cujusquam fit tanta ruina Latinis."

[4] *Epist. Hel.* ii. Migne, clxxviii. c. 185.

[5] *Vita B. Gosvini*, cap. iv. p. 12.

[6] Rémusat, *Abelard*, i. p. 185. "Dilexi et ego eum." S. Bernard, *Epist.* 326.

club of Hercules, another Proteus, flashing from philosophy to poetry, from poetry to wild jesting:[1] a scholar with the wit of a jongleur, and the graces of a *grand seigneur*.[2] His personality, no less than his claim for reason against authority, was an enfranchisement of the human mind. Two things show the efficacy of that dynamic, almost daemonic force, the vibrating fear in the letter of St. Bernard of Clairvaux, *vehementissimus Christi amator*,[3] but a good hater of the brethren—"He hath ascended into heaven: he hath descended into hell:"[4] and the last paragraph of the letter in which Peter the Venerable, Abbot of Cluny, broke to Héloïse, now Abbess of the Paraclete, that he who had been hers, *tuo illo*, Master Peter Abelard, was dead. Their love had been a street-song in Paris: the outrageous vengeance of the girl's uncle on her lover and tardily made husband had been a blazoned scandal; Abelard himself had come to write of it as a surgeon cauterises a wound. Peter the Venerable was an austere man, a stern disciplinarian of his order: but the tragic splendour of it, the marred beauty of these star-crossed lovers whose violent delight had had so violent an end, triumphs over the ecclesiastic's prejudice, and at the last the gracious compassionate prose quickens into a strange, almost lyrical exaltation. He has written of the last days in the great monastery where Abelard, the heretic hounded by two councils, had come to die, "and by so coming enriched us," says its Abbot, with almost a shout of defiance at St. Bernard and his eager pack, "with a wealth beyond all gold." Peter had done what he could, had forced him to take senior rank; and

[1] *Vita B Gosvini*, iv. p. 12. "Sublimis eloquentiae sed inauditarum erat et assertor novitatum. . . . Dicebat quod nullus autea praesumpserat . . . plus vices agere joculatoris quam doctoris." See Otto von Freisingen on Abelard, *Gesta Fred. I.* c. 47 (*M. G. H. Script.* xx. 376).

[2] "Elegantia morum tanta tua," Hugues Metel, quoted by Rémusat, i. 181.

[3] *Hist. Pontifical. M. G. H. Script.* xx. 521.

[4] Quoted by Otto von Freisingen, op. cit. p. 377.

now stands abashed before the mystery of this man's life whom the love of God and the hate of men had broken, yet left greater in his ruin. Content with the barest, he asked for nothing; Peter, walking behind him in the procession of the relics, *pene stupebam,* all but halted amazed at the bearing of this man who had had the proudest name in France, "humbler than St. Martin, lowlier than St. Germain." Constant at the sacraments, often in prayer: for ever silent, speaking only familiarly with the brethren at meals, or when urged sometimes to speak of divine things in assembly: even to the last, for ever bowed over his books (*semper incumbebat libris*). "Thus Master Peter brought his days to their end: and he who for his supreme mastery of learning was known well-nigh over the whole world and in all places famous, continuing in the discipleship of Him Who said 'Learn of me, for I am meek and lowly in heart,' so to Him passed over, as I must believe. Him therefore, O sister most dear, him to whom once you clung in the union of the flesh and now in that stronger finer bond of the divine affection, with whom and under whom you have long served the Lord, him, I say, in your place or as another you, hath Christ taken to His breast to comfort him, and there shall keep him, till at the coming of the Lord, the voice of the archangel and the trump of God descending, He shall restore him to your heart again." [1]

Abelard died in 1142: his stormy life is bounded by what is perhaps the greatest half-century of the Middle Ages. The thirteenth century is the full harvesting, the richer in accomplishment, yet the Paris of St. Thomas Aquinas and Saint Bonaventura has lost something of the first madness,

> "The divine intoxication
> Of the first league out from land."

[1] *Pet. Ven. Epist.* Migne, clxxxix. 347 *et seq.*

That first league, that first half of the twelfth century: Abelard lecturing in Paris; Peter the Venerable travelling in Spain and commissioning a translation of the Koran: Adelard of Bath in Syria and Cilicia, writing his book on natural philosophy and dedicating it to the Bishop of Syracuse; Hermann of Dalmatia translating the *Planisphere* of Ptolemy and dedicating it to Thierry of Chartres, "the soul of Plato reincarnate, firm anchor in the tempest-tossed flux of our studies": Thierry lecturing on the new Aristotle, just restored to scholarship: Paris for the first time become the *patria* of the mind, the rival in men's hearts of Rome.[1] By the thirteenth century she has a University with statutes and privileges and set books and courses that prescribe Priscian *magnum et minorem*, and then alas! omit the classics altogether.[2] But in the glorious liberty of the children of Paris of the twelfth, the scholars come up, young and old, and demand the point and the line, the nature of universals, of Fate and Free Will, the sources of the Nile,[3] dividing in the taverns the undivided Trinity,[4] and one calls to the other to abandon this for that. Literature was to make a man's fortune. Had not Maurice de Sully come to Paris begging his bread, and now behold him its Bishop? And Nicholas Breakspear, the shabby Englishman, the "spoiled monk" of St. Albans, sheltering under St. Denys, picking up what crumbs of learning he could; behold him Bishop of Albano, Cardinal Legate, Lord Pope himself. Petrus Pictor had in vain prophesied

> "How to be a beggar and a fool? Would you know it?
> Let you read books and learn to be a poet."

had in vain seen Ignorance go by in full pontificals, on a

[1] See Clerval, *L'Enseignement des Arts Libéraux à Chartres et à Paris.* John of Salisbury speaks of it as "roused from the dead or from sleep by the knocking at the gate of an ardent talent."

[2] *Chart.* i. 228, 278; ii. 678; iii. 145.

[3] *Chart. Univ. Paris,* i 27, Peter of Blois.

[4] *Ib.* 48, Stephen of Tournay.

good horse, clean and splendid and well washed in warm water, and Aristotle barefoot on the road, the dust on his feet and his stick, a few books of grammar in his knapsack.[1] Their disillusionment was to fill Europe with disgruntled scholars who could not dig, but to beg were not ashamed,[2] who died under the ban of the Church, and made great verse and grievous scandal. But that is still to come. Men do not yet know which is *utile* among the arts, but write hopefully home that "as Cato saith, to know anything is praiseworthy," [3] and they live in a garret, with one gown for lectures among them,[4] and play at dice with the neighbour's cat for a fourth.[5] The whole brief sweetness of it in the opening sentence of a story told by an unknown Irish scholar: "In those first days when youth in me was happy and life was swift in doing, and I wandering in the divers cities of sweet France, for the desire that I had of learning, gave all my might to letters." [6] John of

[1] *B.N. Fonds Lat. MS.* 14193, f. 1, 7*v*.

[2] Wright, *Latin Poems . . . Walter Mapes*, 41:

"Postquam sentit pontifex nihil posse dari:
Non est qui pro paupere spondeat scolari.
Iam mendicat misere chorus poetarum,
Nulli prodest imbui fonte literarum."

Hauréau, *Notices et Extraits*, i. p. 367:

"Nihil prodest mathesis,
Nil logos, nil poesis,
Aurum plus quam phonesis
Ponderat."

[3] *B.N. MS.* 1093, f. 82.

[4] Rashdall, *Mediaeval Universities*, ii. 659. Told of St. Richard of Chichester (1253), *Acta SS.* 3rd April, i. 278.

[5] Haskins, *Univ. of Paris in Thirteenth Century Sermons*, p. 25, n. MS. Tours, 468. "Certain clerks of Paris were playing dice, and one who lost took a neighbour's cat that frequented the house, and said, 'Let this fellow play with you, who is for ever eating and never pays a penny,' and setting the dice in the four paws of the cat he made him throw, and he lost. And they wrote about the cat's neck that he had lost at play a quart of wine, and must lose his pelt unless he paid, which his master perceiving bound the money about his neck, asking that he be not again compelled to play, as he could not count his throw."

[6] *Mon. Germ. Hist. Script.* xx. 512.

Salisbury writes of Paris with the subdued warmth, the steady heat of his affection transfiguring his sober prose.[1] Guido de Bazoches becomes sheerly lyrical: "Paris, queen among cities, moon among stars, so gracious a valley [as it is to this day from the terraces of St. Germain], an island of royal palaces. . . . And on that island hath Philosophy her royal and ancient seat: who alone, with Study her sole comrade, holding the eternal citadel of light and immortality, hath set her victorious foot on the withering flower of the fast ageing world." [2]

Philosophy, which is dialectic, was already the queen science of Paris, as it was in the degenerate days when Panurge disputed with the Englishman Thaumaste by signs only: inevitably so, considering Abelard's great fame, the discovery of fresh matter of controversy in the New Aristotle, and the mediaeval passion for debate. John of Salisbury, who held the *religio grammatici*, feared it, very much as Milton did—"a sterile science, except it conceive from without." [3] "An infamous tract of rocks," said Milton, ". . . not here the sounding of Apollo's lyre: not here the dance of goddesses." [4] Giraldus Cambrensis, a much smaller man than either, but a shrewd observer, saw it for a facile and superficial triumph, and already with the strangle-hold on literature. John is never weary of poking fun at the new breed of the Cornificians who come up to the schools and emerge fully qualified Masters of Arts in so much time as a chicken shall be feathering; [5] the same jest that was in Samuel Butler's mind when he marvelled that a chicken should be ready for all the uses of life in three weeks, whereas it takes three and twenty years to make a curate. It was a

[1] *Epist.* 134. Migne, 199, c. 113. [2] *Chart. Univ. Paris*, i. 55.

[3] *Metalogicus*, ii. 10. Migne, *P.L.* 199, c. 869.

[4] *Prolusions.*

[5] *Metal.* ii. 3. Migne, cxcix. c. 829. "Fiebant ergo summi repente philosophi: nam qui illiteratus accesserat, fere non morabatur in scholis ulterius quam eo curriculo temporis quo avium pulli plumescunt."

showy trick, and impressed the neighbours: consider your man and your pig going to market: doth the man or the rope lead the pig? [1] "Mouse is a syllable," mocks Giraldus Cambrensis; "A mouse eats cheese: *ergo*, a syllable eats cheese." And he tells a long tale of a young man who spent five years at great expense in Paris, and came home able to prove to his father that the six eggs on the table were twelve: whereupon the father ate the six eggs apparent, and left the young man those which the hen of his logic had laid. He was sent back to Paris with a caution.[2] In Giraldus' own youth, he says, he was at the University and mad for logic: but an old priest of his acquaintance took him aside, and bade him think of the future. This logic, what avails it without an opponent to dispute, and, even given the opponent, without a crowd to applaud? But the man of letters sits in his chimney corner with a book, and is his own best company.[3] John of Salisbury, fifty years before, had written on the same theme, with that meditative gravity that brings him so near the *Religio Medici*.[4]

The Battle of the Seven Arts, that Henri d'Andely described in the middle of the thirteenth century, was by that time a Hundred Years War. John of Salisbury, writing in 1159, has seen the first campaign. In Henry's time Orleans was the stronghold of humanism, of the poets, already a little discredited, as they are in Elizabethan England, for their legendary licence of lying. But in the great age, the first half of the twelfth, it is Chartres, Chartres where Donatus and Cicero and Aristotle still sit meditating on the west front of the Cathedral.[5] Of the teaching of Bernard of Chartres Dr. Poole has given

[1] *Metal.* i. 3. Migne, *P.L.* cxcix. c. 829.

[2] *Gir. Camb. Gem. Eccl.* ii. 37 (Rolls Series, ii. 349).

[3] *Ib.* p. 350.

[4] *Polycrat. Prologus.* Migne, cxcix. c. 385 *et seq.*

[5] The west front was in building while the brothers Thierry and Bernard were Chancellors.

a summary in pages that have John of Salisbury's own grave charm.[1] Nothing of his work survives, except a fragment of verse[2] on the Scholar's Regimen, and the great saying that the moderns are but dwarfs on the shoulders of giants,[3] which has the feeling for the past, the sense of power in other things, that is one secret of the efficacy of Chartres. John himself seems not to have been taught by him, but by men whom he had taught: but scholarship of that quality survives to the second and third generation. The experience of literature, the critical appreciation of it, is evident in every page. No man of his age has the same grace of quotation, the same clean structure of thought, the sense of the perfect period: and when an inquiry into the Greek root of the heroic merges into a delicate meditation on the truth of things as the only constancy, and thence, because his imagination is haunted by its loveliness, through the paradox that that which is may be the symbol of that which is not yet, to the line from the Georgics,

> "A crimson sky at dawn, and rain: at evening, light,"[4]

one knows oneself in the power of a great master of prose. The submerged city of the poets is always in John's consciousness: and in the strongest tides of controversy he hears the sound of its bells.

Of the other Bernard, Bernard Sylvestris of Tours, also it would seem a Breton, one knows less, and criticism

[1] R. L. Poole, *Illustrations of Mediaeval Thought*, pp. 99-106.

[2] "Mens humilis, studium querendi, vita quieta,
Scrutinium tacitum, paupertas, terra aliena,
Haec reserare solent multis obscura legendo."

Quoted by John of Salisbury, *Polycrat.* vii. 13. "Humility of mind, a questioning desire, a quiet life, silent scrutiny, poverty, a strange land, these will resolve their problems for many."

[3] "We are as dwarfs mounted on the shoulders of giants, so that we can see more and further than they: yet not by virtue of the keenness of our eyesight, nor through the tallness of our stature, but because we are raised and borne aloft upon that giant mass," *Metal.* iii. 4, translated by Dr. Poole, *op. cit.* p. 102.

[4] *Metal.* iv. 34. Migne, cxcix. c. 937.

has reluctantly given up the endeavour to identify the two, arguing that Bernard of Chartres might have lectured also at Tours, even as his still more famous brother Thierry,

"The Chartrian doctor with tongue like a sword,"

lectured in Paris.[1] If Bernard Sylvestris is not Bernard of Chartres, then twelfth century scholarship was the richer for it, in that two great Platonists were lecturing, one in Chartres, the other in Touraine. It matters very little, except that one covets so great a piece of imaginative prose as the "*De Mundi Universitate*"[2] for the town which of all towns in France has kept the secret of the Middle Ages, yet brought them into the current of ageless and hereditary beauty. For the rediscovery of the dignity of the human body which is in every sculpture of Chartres, of the beauty and the abiding value of "the whole sensible appearance of things" is brought to the twelfth century as to the sixteenth, by the Platonists. Bernard Sylvestris in his *De Universitate* did for the poets and sculptors of the twelfth and thirteenth centuries what Giordano Bruno in *Gli Heroici Furori* did for Sidney and Spenser in Elizabethan England. "God creating the Sun and Moon" on The North Portal of Chartres is the mediaeval and Puritan godhead, powerful and serene: but "God creating the Day and the Night," that face of meditation and of dream, is the artist and the philosopher, as well as the moralist: the Logos in stone.

It is not to say that every thirteenth century sculptor every down at heel goliard poet, had read the *De Univer-*

[1] See Clerval, *L'Enseignement des Arts Libéraux à Chartres et à Paris dans la première moitié du XIIe siècle; Les Écoles de Chartres au moyen âge*, p. 160; R. L. Poole, *Illustrations of Mediaeval Thought*, iv. *The Masters of the Schools at Paris and Chartres* (*Eng. Hist. Rev.* xxxv. 326-331, 1920); Hauréau, contradicting his first conviction of identity, *Mémoires de l'Académie des Inscriptions*, xxxi. (2), p. 99 *et seq.*

[2] Bernard Sylvestris, *De Mundi Universitate*, edited Barach, *Bibliotheca Philosophorum Medii Aevi*, i.

sitate any more than the "rakehelly rout of ragged rhymers" in Elizabethan England had read Giordano Bruno. But these things are in the air. Provençal poetry demands no other intellectual background than that of its century, a May morning, the far-off singing of birds, a hawthorn tree in blossom, a Crusade for the Holy Sepulchre. It is the Middle Ages in the medium of a dream. William IX of Aquitaine, the first and the earthiest of them, has no conception of life other than the Church would have recognised.

> "Since now I have a mind to sing,
> I'll make a song of that which saddens me,
> That no more in Poitou or Limousin
> Shall I love's servant be.
>
> . . . . . .
>
> "Of prowess and of joy I had my part,
> But now of them my heart hath ta'en surcease.
> And now I go away to find that One
> Beside whom every sinner findeth peace.
>
> . . . . . .
>
> "All that which I have loved I leave behind,
> The pride and all the pomp of chivalry.
> Since it so pleases God I am resigned,
> I pray Him have me of His company.
>
> "And all my friends I pray when I am dead
> They'll come in honour of my burying.
> For I have known delight and dalliance
> Both far and near, yea and in my own dwelling.
>
> "But this day, joy and dalliance, farewell.
> Farewell to vair and gris and sembeli."[1]

That is a scheme of life which the Church has regretted, but admitted. But the Latin poetry of the twelfth and thirteenth century scholars is pagan, as Keats is pagan.

[1] Jeanroy, *Chansons de Guillaume IX*, xi. "Pos de chantar m'es pres talenz."

"O tender laughter of those wanton lips
That draw all eyes upon them,
Love's own lips,
Soft-swelling,
And instilling
Sweets of honey in their kissing,
Till I deny that ever I was mortal." [1]

Something has unshackled it from gauging the whole of life by measuring right and wrong. It does not defy heaven and hell: it is unaware of them.

"When I think upon her eyes
Like twin stars,
And the mouth that were a god's
Bliss to kiss,
I've transcended far, it seems,
Treasuries of ancient kings." [2]

And though pagan, it is not corrupt; its altars are to Cupid and his mother: not Priapus. The cry of Urania to Nature "I, Natura, sequar"—

"Go thou, I follow
For no man goes astray in following thee," [3]

is the bedrock of their philosophy, as it is of Bernard's. It is a philosophy a good deal more dangerous than that

[1] *Carmina Burana*, 42:
"Lasciva blanda risus
Omnes in se trahit visus,
labea venerea
tumentia
sed castigant errorem
leniorem
dum dulcorem
instillant, favum mellis, osculando,
ut me mortalem negem aliquando."

[2] *Die Gedichte Walters von Chatillon* (Strecker), xxiii. p. 39:
"Dum contemplor oculos
instar duum syderum,
et labelli flosculos
dignos ore superum
transcendisse videor
gazas regum veterum."

[3] Bernard Sylvestris, *De Universitate Mundi*, lib. ii. c. 4, lines 53-55.

which the University of Paris burned in 1225, yet the Church seems to have ignored it, disarmed perhaps by the utter guilelessness of the philosopher. The treatise was immensely popular; by the middle of the thirteenth century it was a school book,[1] and the scholars were fortunate. For Bernard handles antiquity as Milton did, in whose Paradise

> "Pan
> Knit with the Graces and the Hours in dance
> Led on the eternal spring."

"Pan, and the Fauns and Nereids, a harmless company," says Bernard, describing his world;[2] and they are harmless, in the presence of this dreamer. "Nature made the world brazen," said Sir Philip Sidney, "the poets only deliver a golden," and Bernard is of that company. It is a mind like Shelley's.

His book has two sources, the *Timaeus* of Plato and the comment of Chalcidius; but the driest of the Platonic dialogues is only the fuel for his fire. The poet in him never sleeps; the sheer mechanism, the skeleton of philosophy, stuff like the theory of the four elements, becomes a succession of visions. "From the confused, from the turgid, came forth the power of Fire, and *broke up its native darkness with sudden quivering flame*. . . . water, whose plain and smooth surface gave back a rival image, *assailed by flying shadows*."[3] The very baldness of his argument—"Nature brings to *Nous*, that is, the Providence of God, a complaint of the confusion of the primal matter, that is, *Hyle*, and demands a fairer world"[4]—is the dream of the *Faerie Queene*, of *The Tempest*, of *Hyperion*. And of that Providence, his prose is the prose of Shelley's Defence of Poetry.

[1] *Laborinthus*, lines 683-4 (Faal, *Les Arts Poëtiques* . . . p. 361).

[2] "Illic Silvani, Panes et Nerei innocui conversatione aetatis evolvunt tempora longioris." *Ib.* ii. 7, lines 111-115.

[3] *Ib.* i. 2, lines 100-107.

[4] *Ib. Breviarium*, p. 5.

"This Nous, then, is the intellect of God, God the supreme, powerful beyond all power: its nature born of his Divinity. There are the types of all things living: the eternal ideas, the intelligible world, the knowledge of the things that are to be. There as in a clear mirror may one see the generations, the mysterious destiny of the creation of God. There, in kind, in species, in very idiosyncrasy, are written those things which the first chaos, which the world, which the elements themselves shall bring to birth. There, graven by the finger of the Supreme Accountant, the texture of time, the foredoomed consequence, the disposition of the centuries. There are the tears of the poor and the fortunes of kings; there the soldier's pomp, and the happier discipline of the philosophers: there, whatever the reason of angels or men may comprehend: there, whatever heaven holds in its wide arches. And since these th ngs are so, not disparate is it from eternity, nor separate from the nature and substance of God."[1]

There are prosaic reasons for its immense success: the first book, on the making of the world, gave opportunity for a good deal of geography, much astronomy, a little *materia medica*, and a lively zoo of animals, more recognisable than Milton's. But the power of transfiguration that illumines a trade route in

"As when far off at sea a fleet descried
Hangs in the clouds, by equinoctial winds
Close sailing from Bengala, or the isles
Of Ternate and Tidore, whence merchants bring
Their spicy drugs."

is here: the forests of Broceliande and the Celtic woods and the Ardennes, the waters of Shiloh that go softly, and Simois so happy if Paris had loved not or loved wisely, the Tiber that bears Rome upon its shoulders, the Po, that rolls towards Venice its imperious way, Silo that sees from its pine-clad crest the white sails of twin

[1] *De Mundi Universitate*, lib. i. 2, 152-167, p. 13.

seas.[1] But the stars are his passion—another manuscript of his on astronomy once belonged to Pepys [2]—and the firmament for him is not a blue and shining arch, but a depth where the starry Argo is nightly launched upon a vaster sea, where Ariadne's crown blazes behind the shoulders of Hercules, and Helen shines between the Great Twin Brethren.[3] The good Benedictines of the *Histoire Littéraire* hold up their hands at his clashing tale of stars: the fate of Hippolytus, the fall of Hector, the beauty of Helen are written there, and with them the mystery of the Incarnation.[4] Bernard saw no incongruity; his is the supreme beatitude of the scholar watching the divine travail of the centuries to that diviner birth, and of the poet, besieged by memories of the beauty that had made beautiful old rhyme. He does not trespass on holy places: he has seen the Light that makes about itself a darkness. It is the theologians and not the poets who divide the undivided Trinity in the pot-houses of Paris: Urania and Nature cover their faces and worship before the mystery of the triple-shafted fire.[5] But there is no incongruity in their slow descent, though Urania loses something of her radiance, to the house of Jupiter, at whose doorposts the twin figures stand bearing cups of absinthe and honey, which every soul must taste: past the evil house of Saturn where no flowers grow, to the radiant house of the Sun, one zone green as Egypt with flowers of the spring, another dry and hot, a third splendid in crimson and saffron for the light of Autumn, a fourth of ice and snow. There they find the god of the bow and

[1] *De Mundi Universitate*, i. 3, lines 233 *et seq.* 347-352.

[2] Bernardus Sylvestris, *De Virtute et Efficacia Constellationum.* See *Histoire Littéraire*, xii. p. 273.

[3] *De Mundi Universitate*, i. 3, lines 105-124:

> "... Temptarit aquas famosior Argos
> Aethecum nullo Tiphyde temptat iter."
>
> "... In Geminos Helenae lucentia sidera fratres."

[4] *Ib.* i. 3, lines 31-54.

[5] *Ib.* ii. 5, lines 23-35.

the lyre, and with him his two daughters, Psyche and Swiftness. The rising of Lucifer sends them on their way; they all but lose it in the intricate confusion of the ways of Mercury and Venus, note her fairness, with Cupid at her left breast (even Venus, to Bernard, is something of the Madonna): and so to the Kingdom of the Moon, above it the Elysian fields, below a confused and passionate world. They find Physis, in a place of woods and streams, a river plunging by into the plain yet not with tumult, but rather with a friendly murmuring; and there the three goddesses devise the creation of man.

The poet in Bernard, as in Shakespeare himself, has his moments of rebellion against the muddy vesture of decay, of lament for the "poor soul, the centre of my sinful earth," for "the gross body's treason." One of his most splendid *tirades* is the vision of the spirits wailing at the house of Cancer the Crab: "From splendour to darkness, from Heaven to the Kingdom of Dis, from eternity to the bodies by the House of the Crab are these spirits doomed to descend, and pure in their simple essence, they shudder at the dull and blind habitations which they see prepared."[1] But when he comes to the making of man in that place of green woods and falling streams, he holds, plainly and determinedly, the dignity of his creation. He has his discrimination among the senses: in his glory of sight he is in the tradition that begins with Augustine's "O queen light, sovereign of the senses," and ends with Milton's invocation.[2] Of the others, he speaks generously, yet without that transport. Of generation itself, plainly and fearlessly, the Greek ideal of moderation, of discretion: and then the poet sees in the very physical act the eternal war between life and death, the reweaving of the thread that has been snapped by Atropos' shears.[3] Only, he would have a man fix his

[1] *De Mundi Universitate*, ii. 3, lines 64-69. [2] *Ib.* ii. 14, lines 15-48.

[3] *Ib.* ii. 14, lines 153-182.

eye upon the stars, and his term ended, thither let him go: "*hospes haud incognita*," a guest not unknown.[1] Someone, remembering it, made it the last line of Bernard's epitaph.

"Integrescit ex integro, pulchrescit ex pulchro, sic exemplari suo aeternatur aeterno." "Perfect from the perfect, beautiful from the beautiful, eternal from the eternal: from the intellectual world the sensible world was born: full was that which bore it, and its plenitude fashioned it full."[2] The war between the spirit and the flesh has ended in a Truce of God, even as the Last Judgment of the Western rose-window in Chartres melts into "heaven's own colour, blue." St. Bernard of Clairvaux spoke of the dungheap of the flesh: Bernard Sylvestris saw in their strange union a discipline that made for greatness, and the body itself a not ignoble hospice for the pilgrim soul.[3] The spirit is richer for its limitations; this is the prison that makes men free. His Adam is the Summer of Chartres Cathedral, naked, fearless, and unbowed. He saw him as Michael Angelo did, wistful, beautiful, potent for evil or for good, already prescient of the travail that God hath given to the sons of men that they may be exercised in it. "He hath made everything beautiful in his time," continues the voice of Ecclesiastes which John of Salisbury found so strangely poignant,[4] "Also He hath set the world in their heart, so that no man can find out the work that God maketh from the beginning to the end." And if the world of Bernard Sylvestris is a dewdrop too crystalline for philosophy or experience, it is for that moment of vision that poets are born.

[1] *De Mund. Univ.* ii. 14, lines 53-4.

[2] *Ib.* i. 4, lines 93-97.

[3] *Ib.* ii. 10; ii. 12, lines 10-60:

"Humanumque genus quamvis mortale trahatur
Conditione sua,
Tale reformandum, quod demigrare superbos
Possit ad usque Deos."

[4] *Metal.* iv. 35.

CHAPTER VI

PARIS AND ORLEANS

"I BELIEVE," said Master Konrad Unckebunck, "that the devil is in these poets. They destroy all universities. And I heard from an old master of Leipsic who had been Magister for xxxvi years, and he said to me that when he was a young man then did the University stand firm, for there was not a poet within xx miles."[1] It is the last round of the fight between the humanists and the schoolmen: the first was fought in the twelfth and thirteenth centuries, between Paris and Orleans: and it was not the humanists who won. Henri d'Andeli made a mock epic of it: he was for the poets, as how should he not, being so great a lover of the wine of St. Jean d'Angely, and so good a hater of doctors and Lombards and lawyers.[2] "Paris et Orliens, ce sont ij," says Henri, and describes the parties in each others' language, every clerk of Orleans worth four Homers, when it came to drinking, anyhow, and can make you fifty verses about a figleaf: to which the poets reply by calling Dialectic cockadoodledoo.[3] It

[1] *Epistolae Obscurorum Virorum*, ii. 46.

[2] Héron, *Œuvres d'Henri d'Andeli*, p. xxiii.

[3] Paetow, *Bataille des Sept Arts*, ll. 6-16:

"Car Logique, qui toz jors tence,
Claime les autors autoriaus,
Et les clers d'Orliens glomeriaus,
Si vaut bien chascuns iiij Omers.
Quar il boivent a grans gomers,
Et sevent bien versifier
Que d'une feuille d'un figuier
Vous feront il l. vers.
Mais il redient que por vers
Qu'il claiment la Dyaletique
Par mal despit quique le quique."

comes to blows. Grammar sets up her *barrière* among the cornfields outside Orleans : Homer and Claudian in the van, Perseus and Donatus and Priscian, Dan Juvenal and Dan Horace, Virgil, Lucan, Statius, Terence, Sedulius, Prudentius, with a rearguard commanded by Ovid and Primas of Orleans, Martial and Bernard Sylvestris. Paris, on the other hand, has *le clerc Platon* and Aristotle, Law richly mounted and Decretals riding orgulously. Theology, *Madame la haut science,* withdraws to Paris, by the advice of the Chancellor, to drink the wine in her good cellar and leave the secular studies to fight it out. Donatus hit Plato such a blow on the chin with a verse that he made him stagger, but Plato hit back with a sophism so hard that Donatus fell in the mud. Aristotle unhorsed Priscian and would have trampled him, but for his two fine nephews the *Graecism* and the *Doctrinale,* who made for Aristotle's horse and left him three-legged. Grammar is winning, but up come reinforcements for Logic, the *Categories* and the *Six Principles,* "two good buyers of tripe," said Henri rudely, for he referred to the esteemed Chancellor of Chartres, Guibert de la Porrée. There is charge and countercharge, but Logic wins the day. Grammar fled to Egypt, whence she came : Sir Versifier the courteous lies in hiding somewhere in the country round Blois : "It will be thirty years," says Henri, "before he dares to show his face again." When he does, in the person of Jean de Meung, he is no longer noble, and no longer courteous : but Henri did not live to read the sequel of the *Roman de la Rose.*

It is regretfully that one finds a Chancellor of Chartres in the camp of the enemy : but by the middle of the twelfth century the supremacy is gone from her to Orleans. Guibert de la Porrée was a profound scholar, but his interests were theological rather than humanist. Nevertheless one holds him dear if only for his reply to the great Bernard, who had broken Abelard. Guibert was the next to engage the Saint's attention, and Guibert "is the one man whom Saint Bernard of Clairvaux unsuccessfully charged with heresy."[1] He stood at bay, a solid phalanx of the Fathers in folio literally behind him, for his clerks followed him thus armed into the council. Some time after the trial, comes a friendly overture from the Saint, suggesting a little informal conference on some points in the writings of St. Hilary, to which the Chancellor replies that if the Abbot wishes to come to a full understanding of the subject, it would be well for him to submit for a year or two to the ordinary processes of a liberal education. John of Salisbury savoured that story ; and yet, he adds, with characteristic fairness, though Bernard made small account of secular studies, I have known no man pursue the art of poetry with so much grace.[2]

The truth seems to be that the late twelfth century saw the beginning of the reaction, partly utilitarian, partly Puritan, against the purely humanistic studies of the earlier years. "Alas," says Helinand in a university sermon preached in Toulouse in 1229, "how seldom in these days do virtue and learning come together. By some—I know not what—factious bond, lust and literature cling together, a union no less prodigious than pernicious."[3] Herrad von Landsberg, the very able abbess of Hohenberg, made an ingenious sketch for her nuns, a rose window design of Philosophy with Plato and Socrates at her feet, the seven liberal arts in a circle, but in the corners of the page are four figures inscribing naughtiness, the poets, the magicians, the idle story-tellers, each inspired by a lean black fowl of portentous neck who sits on his shoulder and whispers in his ear.[4] Alexandre de Ville Dieu worked himself into an ecstasy of denunciation about the schools of

[1] R. L. Poole, *Mediaeval Thought*, p. 113.

[2] *Hist. Pont. M. G. H. Script.* xx. 526.

[3] Quoted by Wulff and Walberg, *Vers de la Mort*, Anc. Textes franç. p. xxv.

[4] *Hortus Deliciarum*, Herrad von Landsberg (Facsimiles published by the Société pour la Préservation des Mon. Hist. d'Alsace).

Orleans, where the scholars are busy trying to set Dagon on his seat again. The fathers have eaten sour grapes—the sour grape, says Alexandre, is the cult of the pagans—and now the next generation worship Apollo and Venus, Jupiter and Bacchus. There is a regular sect of such scholars, and the masters are as bad, above all at Orleans where is the scorner's chair in which the righteous does not sit. Peter Riga, now, in the versified Bible, has watered the clergy with vivifying dew, and invites us to the river that flows from Paradise. But at the moment the road to Paradise does not pass through Orleans.[1] Arnulfus the Red-headed (the off-scouring of the human race, says Matthew kindly)[2] was lecturing on the *Fasti* with a wealth of antiquarian detail that kindles modern critics to enthusiasm,[3] but awakened in the breast of his contemporaries such hate as only scholars know. Matthew of Vendôme is responsible for perhaps the dullest Art of Poetry that has ever been written, but the preface is lively with squibs about Arnulf, and his hair, and his wench, also it would seem red-headed; and red being the colour of infidelity, that circumstance is full of matter. And now, says Matthew, wiping his pen, he will be more sparing of his barking. The sacrificing to Bacchus was hardly more than the invocation which is in the drinking songs from the ninth century to the round danced on Pompey's galley,

> "Come thou monarch of the Vine,
> Plumpy Bacchus with pink eyne."

and Pope John XII was deposed for similar practices.[4]

[1] See Thurot, *Notices et Extraits*, xxii. 2, 114-116:

> "Aurelianiste via non patet ad Paradisum,
> Non prius os mutet."

[2] "Obprobrium hominum et abjectio plebis," Matthew of Vendôme, *Ars Versificatoria. Prologus* (Faral, *Les Arts Poëtiques du XIIe siècle*, p. 109).

[3] *Hist. Litt.* xxix. pp. 375-7. Arnulfus commented the *Fasti*, *De Remedio Amoris*, and Lucan's *Pharsalia*.

[4] *Mansi*, xviii. c. 466: "Diaboli in amorem vinum bibisse. . . . In ludo aleae Jovis, Veneris ceterorumque daemonum auxilium poposcisse."

But a scrap of delicate irony in a letter of John of Salisbury suggests the respectful, half antiquarian attitude to paganism. The Bishop of London, it seems, had declared that he owned no obedience to Canterbury, and avowed that the arch-episcopal see should be in London, where the Archflamen of Jupiter had his seat in the days of the *religio Jovialis*. "And perchance that prudent and religious gentleman intends to restore that cult, so that if he can in no way set up for an archbishop, he may at least adorn himself with the title of the Archflamen."[1] There are odd traces of almost pagan luxury.[2] Gilles de Corbeil was no Puritan; held in fact that a love affair was the best cure he knew for excessive megalomania, nothing better than a love *blandus, lascivus,* to prick the balloon of a dangerously swelled head; but he denounces the wanton extravagance of the wealthier prelates as hotly as any vagabond scholar. The episcopal visitation that he describes suggests rather a prelate of the Italian Renaissance than of twelfth century France, above all the last exaction wrung from the unhappy priest—half a mark to buy roses for the garlands of the handsome young men who wait upon the bishop at table.[3] Gilles of Orval has an odd story of the excesses of the clerks at Liege, under the easy discipline of Albero the Bishop, how on holy days such as Easter and Pentecost when they should frequent the church even more devoutly than on other days, they choose instead one of their mistresses, deck her in purple and crown her and set her queen on a throne veiled behind curtains, and sing and dance all day long

[1] John of Salisbury, *Epist.* 289. Migne, *P.L.* cxcix.

[2] See Ozanam, *Documents Inédits*, p. 19. Hauréau, *Un MS. de la Reine Christine*, xvi., *Altercatio Ganymedi et Helenae*.

[3] Veillard, *Gilles de Corbeil*, 396. On the luxury of the Italian bishops, see S. Peter Damian (Muratori, *Ant.* ii. 310): "in chrystallinis vasculis adulterata mille vina flavescunt." And in a later century, John of Salisbury, *Polycrat.* viii. cap. 7, on the banquet in Apulia, "Memini me ipsum . . . interfuisse," with delicacies from Constantinople, Alexandria, Tripoli, and Tyre.

before her, the goddess of their idolatry.[1] Henry, Bishop of Winchester, albeit heavily bearded and of a philosophic gravity, bought statues in Rome, to the astonishment and jesting of the light-minded, with whom Rome is always full,[2] and the regret of Magister Gregorius for the havoc wrought among the Roman marbles by the Blessed Gregory is very evident.[3] Jacques de Lausanne has a story that is the rude anticipation of Gautier's *La Morte Amoureuse* ; a young regent-master whose dead love haunted him, sleeping and waking, till he opened her grave, and scarred his imagination with that horror : [4] and Caesarius von Heisterbach tells the livelier tale of John, *scholasticus* of Prüm, whom the devil beguiled in the guise of a fair woman, so that he lay with her, and in the morning when the fiend with *empressement* declared himself, John replied with a word " so marvellous that I blush to say it," says Caesarius, and went his way, mocking the devil and in no way concerned for the affair.[5] Caesarius, who is as good as the Duchess at finding what the moral of that is, is baffled for once. Not so with the tale of the scholar of Paris " at the time our Abbot was a student there," who emitted contumelious words about the holy Abraham, and died on the third day, so that all knew that God had avenged his saint.[6] The typical scholar of mid-century Paris is not John of Salisbury, grave, sardonic, remote, nor yet young Peter from Denmark, studying theology in

[1] Aegidius Aureavallis, *Gesta Pont. Leod.* (Bouquet, *Hist.* 13, p. 616.) See also Abelard, *Theologia Christiana,* ii. (Migne, clxxviii. 1211), " Ante ipsi Christi altaria . . . Veneris celebrantur vigiliae."

[2] *M. G. H.* xx. 542, *Hist. Pontificalis.* " . . . barba prolixa et philosophi gravitate . . . spectabiliorem idola coemere, subtili et laborioso magis quam studioso errore gentilium fabrefacta."

[3] On the destruction of the Temple of Pallas, see Magister Gregorius. *J.R.S.* ix. 1, 52.

[4] Hauréau, *Not. et Extr.* iii. p. 129.

[5] Caesarius von Heisterbach, *Dialogus Mirac.* iii. 10.

[6] *Ib.* iv. 20.

St. Geneviève, who falls ill of a quartan ague, and is sent home in the hope that his native air may restore him—"a willing spirit in a fragile body"[1]—but the Englishman,[2] Serlon of Wilton, whose brilliant and dissolute figure was as famous in his own generation as his spectacular conversion in the University sermons of the next.[3] A collection of Serlon's verse, for the most part still in manuscript, would be an addition, not wholly edifying, to the records of English literature in the twelfth century: he has the morals of Captain Macheath, the manners of Restoration Comedy, with a suggestion of Walter Pater's preciousness at the last that goes not ill with the white robes of the Cistercian Abbot. One of his least graceless performances is a variant of

"How happy could I be with either;"[4]

there is a lyric of seduction with the full mannerism of Renaissance subtlety—wherefore beauty, if not for use?

"And who knows honey sweet, who tastes it not?"
"Nature demands; Deny? It is a crime."[5]

—Bernard Sylvestris' "I, Natura, sequar," in its inevitable consequence: a salute to the memory of the

[1] Stephen of Tournai to Absolon of Laon, *Chart. Univ. Paris*, i. p. 43.

[2] The English disliked foreigners in high places at home; but they themselves are everywhere in the twelfth century. See Stubbs, *Learning under Henry II* (*Seventeen Lectures*). Robert of Melun was English, Adam du Petit Pont, and Alexander Neckam, all famous scholars in Paris. Nicholas Breakspear became Pope, Robert Pulleyn, Papal Chancellor, Thomas Brown, advisor to the King of Sicily, Herbert, Archbishop of Compsa, Richard, Bishop of Syracuse, Walter, Archbishop of Palermo, John of Salisbury, Bishop of Chartres. See Hauréau, *Not. et Extr.* xxxii. p. 297, on the debt of the University pulpit to English preachers, Alexander of Hales, Grossetête, Bacon, Duns Scotus, Richard Middleton, William of Ockam.

[3] See Walter Mapes, *De Nugis Curialium* (Wright), p. 70. Hauréau, *Not. et Extr.* i. p. 303 *et seq.* Jacques de Vitry, xxxi. 3 (Crane). The MS. containing most of his poems is B.N. MS. Lat. 6765, transcribed in part by Hauréau. I was unable to use it, as it was on loan.

[4] Hauréau, *op. cit.* p. 305.

[5] *Ib.* 323.

dead poet and mighty drinker, Primas of Orleans:[1] praise of a small town in the Maritime Alps, where a man might almost forget England:[2] and a sudden eagle soar in

> "Yea, the gods fear thee, O Cyprian,
> Stronger art thou than Jove."[3]

He was a master much sought after, a bold and daring logician, very much *le Byron de nos jours*; till one day the University rang with the tale of his sudden conversion. His favourite scholar had died: that night his master saw him in the Pré aux Clercs weighted down with a cope of parchment inscribed with the pagan learning that had been his damnation, that crushed him even as if the tower of St. Germain had hung about his neck. The sweat of his agony stood on him in beads; a drop fell on Serlon's hand, and burnt it to the bone. Serlon vanished from the University, never to appear again, unless as "a certain master of Paris" in thirteenth century sermons.[4] He had entered religion, in the monastery of La Charité-sur-Loire, found the Cluniac rule too slack for his new-found austerity, which gave his poetic vein fresh argument of bitterness, and abandoned it for the stern discipline of the Cistercians at L'Aumône, of which he became Abbot in 1171. There is one last glimpse of him, still characteristic, in the charming gossip of Giraldus Cambrensis: how Giraldus in his youth paid a visit to Archbishop Baldwin, then bishop, and found him sitting with a gaunt old man in the white robes of an Abbot of the Cistercians, who looked intently upon the young man as he came forward, murmuring, "And can such beauty die?"—"a brief discourse," says Giraldus, "but not without efficacy in touching my heart. And indeed," he continues, with his wonted modesty, "I was a young man of extraordinary charm."[5] That story is the perfect colophon.

[1] *Not. et Extr.* xxix. 2. p. 261. [2] *Not. et Extr.* i. 321. [3] *Ib.* p. 313.

[4] Jacques de Vitry, *Exempla* (T. E. Crane), xxxi.

[5] Gir. Camb. *Speculum Ecclesiae,* ii. cap. 33 (Brewer, iv. 105).

It is significant that the Dominicans, in the first austere years of the order, forbade the brethren to read the classics, though they might look upon them, say, for an hour :[1] and in the *Metamorphosis Goliae*, the great debate between Pallas and Aphrodite, it is the "cowled folk," *populus cucullatus*, who rush in and force silence on the poets.[2] But the reaction is due to other enthusiasms than the religious. Absalon of St. Victor complains that the students wish to study the conformation of the globe, the nature of the elements, the place of the stars, the nature of animals, the violence of the wind, the life of the herbs and roots.[3] Peter of Blois makes the same complaint : he himself was brought up on the classics, and he naturally concludes that no other foundation can safely be laid.[4] For a time the classics even in Paris had been fashionable and poets on every bush. Philippe of Harvengt complains that too many blossom suddenly into verse, who have scarcely been damped by the spray from the Caballine fountain : that it is not enough to have caught a glimpse of the Muses and of Helicon.[5] But their day, brief anywhere, was briefest of all in Paris. Magister Mainerius, who had been one of Abelard's favourite pupils, cried one day with the voice of prophecy in the schools, "Woe to the day when law shall kill the study of letters," and Giraldus Cambrensis, who heard him, saw it fulfilled.[6] Law, either civil or canon, had become the "scientia

[1] "In libris gentilium et philosophorum non studeant, etsi ad horam inspiciant. Seculares scientias non addiscant, nec etiam artes quae liberales vocant . . . sed tantum libros theologicos tam juvenes quam alii legant." Denifle, *Archiv für Lit. und Kirch.* ii. 222, quoted by Mandonnet, *Siger de Brabant*, p. 31.

[2] Wright, *Latin Poems . . . Walter Mapes*, p. 30.

[3] Luchaire, *La Société française sous Philippe-Auguste*, p. 82. See *La Bataille des Sept Arts*, l. 91 :

"Et li arcien [the arts students] n'ont mès cure
Lire fors livres de la nature [*libri Aristotles de naturale philosophia*]."

[4] *Chart. Univ. Paris*, i. 27.

[5] *Chart. Univ. Paris*, i. 53.

[6] *Gem. Eccl.* ii. 37 (ed. Brewer, ii. p. 349).

lucrativa."[1] It is the lawyers to whom the key of the well is given, says Guiard, Chancellor of the University in 1238; a young man goes to theology for two years and gives it up for law, and is made an archdeacon,[2] and though the more devout questioned as to whether an archdeacon could be saved, a good many were prepared to risk it. Decretists, says Gautier de Chateau-Thierry, are more honoured and preferred to abbacies and bishoprics than theologians and good confessors, for they love dung more than souls.[2] By Roger Bacon's time civil law had become more important than canon for an ecclesiastical dignitary.[3] Again and again in the collections of student letters comes the request that his father will allow him to read law, an expensive course, but of great future profit and honour. "He who maketh his son a lawyer," says Ponce de Provence, "hath fashioned an engine against his enemies, a machine for his friends."[4]

Literature suffered from the new rival even more than theology. "Here be these superficial, surface-sown gentlemen," says Ralph of Beauvais, "who have the impudence to go straight from Donatus and Cato to law, both human and divine, leaving out literature, the foundation of the poets of love, the philosophers and the arts."[5] Giraldus Cambrensis quotes him with approval. With what colours of rhetoric and grace of quotation he himself lectured, he has himself assured us: and one course of lectures given in Oxford during which he entertained most of the University to dinner in his lodging, was crowded out. Giraldus is undisturbed by memories of Lucian's advice to authors, "First dine them well, and the feet of your friends will be loud upon the floor." It was a noble and costly act, he says simply, and brought back the authentic days of the old poets.[6] And indeed

[1] Sermon by Guiard, Hauréau, *Not. et Extr.* vi. p. 226. [2] *Ib.*

[3] Roger Bacon, *Opus tertium*, p. 84 (ed. Brewer, *Opera Inedita*).

[4] B.N. MS. Lat. 8653, f. 3, 50 *v*. [5] *Gem. Eccles.* ii. 37.

[6] Gir. Camb. *De Rebus a se Gestis*, ii. 16 (Brewer, i. 72-3).

Giraldus' conception of himself as the last of the humanists is very nearly justified. Vincent of Beauvais was strong on the necessity of grammar as a foundation, but divorced it from any serious study of the texts: the authors and the poets are a kind of added grace, "an appendix to the arts," and very pleasant if one has time for it. Vincent is a monument of patience and erudition, but there was one author whom he conspicuously had not had time for, or he would not have said that Petronius Arbiter was a good bishop of Bologna, who lived under Theodosius, and wrote the lives of the Desert Fathers.[1] The imps who wait on mediaeval scholarship were busy that day. Grammar's foes were of her own household. "*La perverse gent grammaire*," says Henri d'Andeli crossly, "such of them as are left in Paris, have given up Claudian and Persius, the best books they had: it is the collapse of all good antiquity."[2] *La bone ancientez* was further clouded: by the middle of the thirteenth century the *Doctrinale* by Alexandre de Ville-Dieu had supplanted Priscian, to the utter degradation of the poetic standard.[3] For Priscian's closely-reasoned paragraphs were interrupted by strange lightnings, just as some of us who would be hard put to it to define metaphor and simile with the old glibness can still remember the unearthly glory of the "example,"

"and with the setting sun
Dropt from the zenith like a falling star
On Lemnos the Aegean isle."

In place of the pagan memories of Horace, of Tibullus,

"the brand that set on fire
Strong Ilion and all the Phrygës' land"

[1] Boutaric, *Vincent de Beauvais* (*Revue des questions historiques*, xvii. p. 50). Vincent died c. 1264.

[2] *La Bataille des Sept Arts*, ll. 93-98.

[3] He was detested by Roger Bacon: "nunquam fuit dignus auctoritate." Brewer, *Opera Inedita* i. 477.

Alexander produces

> Est coluber factus vel facta mistica virga.
> The Serpent's made, or made the mystic wand.

and illustrates the gerund by

> Presbyter essendi causa vis, clerice, radi. [1]
> For sake of being a priest, O clerk, you fain would shaven be.

Eberhard's *Graecismus* has more tincture of the classics, less leonine rhyming, and one chapter on "the Names of the Muses and the Pagans" rather like an abridged classical Dictionary.[2] But on the whole, John of Garland was right when he branded them both as "the monkey twins."

> "Nec sunt scripta bona quae diminuunt Helicona,"

he pleads, with almost pathetic earnestness, "They are not good books that diminish Helicon," and he invokes Orleans as the last stronghold of the art of eloquence, whose foundations are everywhere crumbling.[3] Helinand, the scholar-trouvère turned monk, gives her the same distinction in his whirlwind summary of the Universities of mediaeval Europe. "In Paris the scholars seek the arts, in Orleans the authors, in Bologna codices, in Salerno gallipots, in Toledo demons—and nowhere good manners."[4]

[1] *Doctrinale*, 1447; 1513 (Text in Kehrbach, *Monumenta Germaniae Pedigogica*, xii, 1886).

[2] *Eberhardi Bethuniensis Graecismus*, ed. J. Wrobel, 1887.

[3]
> "Vos vates magni . . .
> . . . quos Aurelianis ab urbe
> Orbe trahit toto, Pegasei gloria fontis,
> Vos deus elegit per quos fundamina firma
> Astent eloquii studio succurrere, cuius
> Fundamenta labant,"

Quoted by Delisle, *Les Écoles d'Orléans*, p. 8.

[4] Migne, *P.L.* 212, c. 603. Helinand had studied at Beauvais under Radulfus the grammarian, a former pupil of Abelard. He was before his conversion a famous trouvère, "as unfit for serious labour as the bird that can only fly," *De. Repar. Relapsi*). See G. Paris, *Bibliothèque de l'École des Chartes*, 1889.

That broadside was delivered in a sermon to the students of Toulouse in 1229, but already the old supremacy was being undermined. In 1219 civil law was driven by papal decree from Paris, where it was strangling theology: it bore down on Orleans where it strangled literature.[1] When in 1235 Gregory IX gave permission for civil law to be read in Orleans, he had pronounced sentence of banishment on many a "fallen old divinity," sunning himself for one brief century in the pale sunlight of the Loire.

> "From haunted spring and dale
> Edg'd with poplar pale,
> The parting Genius is with sighing sent,"

but not before he had left the springs for ever haunted: the Latin lyrics of that brief century are still fragrant with the flowering limetrees of Touraine. "Sir," said Dr. Johnson sportively, "we are a nest of singing birds." Whether or not it were true of eighteenth century Pembroke, it was certainly true of twelfth and thirteenth century Touraine.

Yet Orleans, the stronghold of humanism, was herself responsible for the tarnishing of her greatest glory:[2] above all towns in France she fostered the *Ars Dictaminis*, that bastard of literature and law, the art that undermined the serious study of antiquity.[3] Its professors gave a thorough secretarial training in official and literary cor-

[1] See Prévostin, Chancellor of Paris, Hauréau, *Not. et Extr.* iii. 166. Fournier, *Hist. de la Science de Droit*, iii. 5: *Statuts des Univ. françaises*, i. 2. Early in the fourteenth century a master wishes to come to Orleans to teach rhetoric and logic, but is dissuaded; the scholars in arts are few, poor, and superficial; he will have no audience worthy of him (Haskins, "Life of Mediaeval Students in their Letters," *Amer. Hist. Rev.* iii. p. 222).

[2] "Parnassus vertex cedet uterque tibi." Alexander Neckam, quoted by Delisle, *Les Écoles d'Orléans*, p. 146.

[3] See Stephen of Tournai, complaining of the collapse of learning in Paris (1192-1203) on the beardless boys, who sit in the seats of the Masters. "Conscribunt et ipsi summulas suas . . . omissis regulis artium abiectisque libris autenticis . . ." *Chart. Univ. Paris*, i. 48.

respondence: Latin for working days; a prose style without Cicero. The *Summa Dictaminis* is a cross between a Polite Letter-writer and "Every Man his own Lawyer": guaranteed, without the fatigues of classical scholarship and the long discipline of the law, to make a young man an admirable secretary. The scholar in Orleans crying to his friend to abandon the stagey and meretricious art of verse for this solid employment was justified: it did, as he said, bring a man into kings' palaces: and kings recommended him to great prelates for preferment.[1] A secretaryship was a sure road to honour. Alberic de Montcassino, who compiled the first *Ars Dictaminis*, had taught John de Gaeta, who in turn became Chancellor to Urban II, and himself Pope. Albert of Morra, Chancellor to three Popes, becomes Pope Gregory VIII.[2] Three papal secretaries came from Orleans to Pope Alexander II and Lucius III. Stephen of Tournai, writing to John of Orleans, "domini papae scriptori," warns him against the Roman climate in summer, and urges him to return to golden poverty and good health in Orleans; but meantime he might put through the little business of the excommunication of Meaux. And again, a little unkindly, to William and Robert, secretaries to Lucius III, that some people are gold abroad who were hardly even silver when they were at home.[3] Again and again in the letters which the students painstakingly copied comes the request, to set the mouth watering, of king to bishop, to give my faithful clerk N. the next canonry, and when the bishop dallies, he is sharply reminded that opportunity hath a baldness behind.[4] It was the easiest and most economical reward in a king's power, nor was it confined to the thirteenth century. What else was the Deanery of St. Patrick's but the shabby payment of the Tory debt to

[1] B.N. MS. Lat. 1093, f. 61; 18595, f. 17 *v*.

[2] R. L. Poole, *The Papal Chancery*, p. 78.

[3] Stephen of Tournai, *Epist.* 65, 85. (Migne, ccxi. 356, 381.)

[4] B.N. Lat. MS. 1093, f. 59; 8653, f. 34 *v*.

Swift? And if Queen Anne's feelings towards Swift were such as he believed, there is a parallel in the delightful story of a King Henry (surely the English Henry II) and a certain clerk, who had long besieged him for a bishopric. A see fell vacant; the chapter met, and elected another. The clerk in some fury taxed Henry with perfidy, in that he had not lifted a finger to secure his election, to which the king replied that it was so: he had not judged it necessary, having observed that a chapter, left to itself, invariably chose the worst. But lo! they have found a worse than thee. Have courage, brother, it cannot always be thus![1] These were the golden prizes held out to tempt wavering students. Some were fortunate: some like the Arch-poet, displaying their shabby wares for a great man's patronage, declare that they have learned to *dictare*.[2] Reginald von Dassel was a patron of letters, and there exists a copy of the great *Summa* of Bernard Sylvestris written at his court. In the same MS. are poems by the disreputable genius who was his laureate: and it is a pleasant speculation if the whole is the work of the most enigmatic figure of the Middle Ages: if the *Summa* is a memory of lecture notes from Orleans, or from the classrooms of the great Bernard himself.[3]

The Art came quickly to terms with its subject. The letter is divided into five parts, salutation, exordium, narration, petition, conclusion. Salutations vary. Any

[1] Sermon by Jacques de Lausanne. Hauréau, *Not. et Extr.* ii. 153.

[2] "Vide, si complaceat
tibi me tenere
in scribendis litteris
certus sum valere . . .
vices in dictamine
potero supplere." *Carm. Bur.* 162.

[3] Pertz, *Archiv*, 1839, vii. p. 1008. "Twelfth century MS. formerly at Stavelot; contains a book *De Arte Dictandi*, written under the Archbishop Reginald of Cologne, and a poem to the Emperor Frederick I, '*Salve mundi dominus.*' Then *Aestuans intrinsicus* to the Archbishop Rainaldus, *Archicancellarie* to the same, are added, in different ink, but the same handwriting. The poems are transcribed (*Diese Gedichte sind abgeschrieben*)."

ecclesiastical personage, whether clerk, or priest, or bishop, or abbot, is John the unworthy, or the undeserving, or the sinful, but this qualification is unnecessary for the laity.[1] The scale in love-letters is nicely graded from "To the noble and discreet lady P., adorned with every elegance, greeting and whatever happiness and service can perform," to the lyrical fervours of "Half of my soul and light of mine eyes . . . greeting, and that delight which is beyond all word and deed to express."[2] But the love-letters are at best an attractive side line: the sterner theme prevails. "Sit thema," that a student is in Paris, and hard up for funds[3]: how shall he best approach the fountain, whether father, or uncle, or archdeacon? This is the exordium: and on the exordium Ponce de Provence is most helpful. There is nothing so necessary, says Ponce, as to induce a suitable frame of mind in the reader of the petition: and in no way is this so well accomplished as by a proverb. Ponce has the happy thought of providing emollient proverbs for every situation: and for the better convenience of his students these are classified and graded: rubrics in red.

"Proverbs for sons to fathers.
Proverbs for fathers to sons.
Proverbs for nephews to uncles.
Proverbs for uncles to nephews.
Proverbs for relations to relations.
Proverbs for enemies to enemies
Proverbs for friends to friends.
Proverbs for debtors to creditors.
Proverbs for creditors to debtors.[3]
Proverbs for laymen to prelates.

[1] Alberic of Monte Cassino; Rockinger, *Briefstellen und Formelbücher*, p. 1; *Quellen zur Bayerischen und deutschen Geschichte*. Munich, 1863.

[2] B.N. MS. Lat. 8653, f. 51 (Guido Faba).

[3] Giraldus Cambrensis before he left Paris, was sorely harassed by importunate creditors. See also the fatherly kindness of the authorities in Bologna, Guido Faba, *op. cit.* f. 52.

Proverbs for prelates to laymen.
Proverbs for minor clergy to prelates.
Proverbs for prelates to minor clergy.
Proverbs for prelates to prelates." [1]

That is the climax : the speech of the great whales.

Bernard's *Summa*, a really massive treatise on prose composition, was abridged by the smaller Bernard of Meung : it had an immense success ; there are manuscripts everywhere. He was a mighty scholar : not so his successors and rivals, Ponce de Provence and Buoncompagno. Ponce was a braggart, and worthy of his name : he is rather like Ancient Pistol, and his comedy is purely accidental. But Buoncompagno is the *dictator* par excellence, the prince of letter-writers, the new untravailed scholarship at its transient and epigrammatic best. He never read a page of Cicero, but his prose marches with incredible vivacity, and his running fire of satire against his reader never flags. If Mercutio and Touchstone had come together to compile an *Art of Writing*, it would have been very like Buoncompagno's. "Magnus trutannus et magnus trufator," says Salimbene, and shakes his head over him.[2] He was a professor at Bologna, and his quarrels with the University and the tricks he played upon it had the malice of a jackdaw. But he became puffed up and judged his talents too great for the provinces : came to the Roman Curia, and found, as so many better men had done before him, that the Dative Case was the only one to which the Curia responded. He hung about for a while, drifted north to Florence, perhaps ashamed to come back to the town he had left with kettledrums, and died in great want, in hospital. One of his own best model letters is an appeal from a dying scholar in hospital in Paris.[3] It is not easy reading.

Buoncompagno had the dramatic sense. His letters

[1] B.N. MS. Lat. 8653, f. 3, 4.

[2] Salimbene, *Cronica, an.* 1233 (*M. G. H. Script.* 32, pp. 77-78).

[3] B.N. MS. Lat. 8654, f. 16.

are little novels of Italy, but he is most radiantly himself when he describes his wrestling with his jealous colleagues in the University. For two years "perfect love and perfect hate"[1]— the phrase is his—came to their ripening. then upon his secure hour the envious stole, and carried off a series of lectures on "salutations" on which Buoncompagno prided himself not a little: damped it: stained it: smoked it like a haddock, and produced it triumphantly as a century-old manuscript from which Buoncompagno had been "cribbing" without acknowledgment: "Depositis alienis plumis, remanetis ut cornicula denudatus"—precisely Robert Greene's language about the upstart crow. For once the crow lost its self-possession: it retired confused and shamefaced, dismissed its auditors, and lay close for nine days, in which it composed the book called *Palma*, emerging with a nine times repeated "I pretended that I had gone away," to recite an entire fresh MS. in the presence of his stricken foes, and his ineffably exultant friends. On the crest of that wave he left Bologna. Common report had it that he was gone a great way off: but he was plotting a more exquisite vengeance. In July "when it was hot," he came secretly back to town, and in a day or two the University received a letter from a distinguished scholar, just returned from abstruse researches in astronomy and magic in Toledo and Arabia. For ten years he had conversed with Arabs and Satraps: had journeyed beyond the Sarmatians where he heard Uranath who maketh even the deaf asp to hear by his enchantments, and Catarath who distinguishes upon the Astrolabe of Solomon, had glanced through most of the works on the faculty of magic, and learned from Zinziniath the comprehension of the barking of dogs and the language of birds, even to the sparrow and the wren. There are secrets not for the vulgar; but for the love that he bears to the University he is prepared to reveal to it something of the majesty of his art. "Wherefore I intimate to you

[1] B.N. MS. Lat. 8654, f. 12.

that on this day about or shortly before the hour of noon, at which time the sun shall be in its strength, let you come to the Piazza of St. Ambrose and there shall I transform an ass into a lion, and thence into a winged fowl, which shall fly before you through the air. . . . And yet in the end the ass shall remain." All Bologna rang with it. Long before the hour the entire University, masters and scholars, crowded the piazza and the roof tops, gazing intently, while the sun grew hotter and hotter. Hours passed: and slowly it dawned upon the University that the ass indeed remained.[1]

It is a wickedness that never sleeps: in a note on "What is irony?"[2] a congratulation to those scholars who are the "nephews" of bishops and other distinguished ecclesiastics:[3] the lady who suspects her husband of reading in another codex and proposes to read a little in the Digest herself:[4] the bland and exquisite satire of the sentimental newly elected bishop, looking back to the happy days in the University when the Castalian fountain sprinkled him with its dews. "From the harbour of quiet, from the paradise of scholastic discipline hath the prelatic function dragged me. Weak are these shoulders for that load. . . . I see you pacing at your pleasure about the ancient wells. . . . I smell the nard. Think not I envy you your happiness: I do but grieve that I myself am no longer a sharer of your joy. Pray you, write to me: tell me how it goes with you: I pray in all things well."[5] Follows the reply from paradise, a suave impudence it would be hard to rival, even in the eighteenth century. Even before his promotion to the episcopal dignity they were his, voluntarily and freely: but their devotion has grown with his growth. "We well believe that your little ship is as you say so tossed in the sea of secular affairs that you can no longer savour your accustomed joys. Yet we who remain in the paradise of scholastic

[1] B.N. MS. Lat. 8654, f. 13*v*. [2] *Ib.* f. 6.
[3] *Ib.* f. 15. [4] *Ib.* f. 22. [5] *Ib.* f. 19.

discipline would fain be in your hell, perceiving that all who are called to that pain abide therein with constancy nor tremble at its torments, they being such as the victim may at any moment decline. Sweet and suave is that pain which all men desire and none refuse. Nevertheless it seems strange to us that you commend yourself to our insignificance: for the less are commended to the greater; yet humility was in that voice that once rang out so brazen. Know that our state is joyous by God's grace; and by yours in your exalted station, might yet blossom as the rose. For we desire a bishopric, and he who desireth a bishopric, saith the Apostle, desireth a good thing: and still more earnestly do we desire to exercise that function, because we would emulate you in that divine emulation with which you emulated the prelatic honour." [1]

The *Ars dictaminis* has never yet had the study it deserves. The various *Summae,* still in manuscript in every great European library, are a quarry not only for legal formulae, but for life. Side by side with the formal business of a royal chancery, letters of commendation from a bishop for his clerk, requests for knighthood, forms of bequest, are love-letters ranging from doubtful equivoque to exquisite and fantastic dreaming: [2] strange *aperçus* into tragedy, a husband pleading with his wife to forgive him and come back, "for day and night my conscience scourges me more inwardly and tears me more cruelly than ever I struck you, innocent, with my guilty hand. Come back, and comfort him with thy so longed-for presence, whom now thy absence hath made desolate": the wife's low-toned desperate reply, "I had thought that you would be a husband to me, not a torturer, but my hope was cheated. . . . I cannot bear so hard a man, and now you continually entreat and pray me to come back. I shudder, and I fear, for to my present ills my mind conjures up the past. If some man of great name will put his hand to it that you will not be cruel to me, I shall

[1] B.N. MS. Lat. 8654, f. 19 *v.* [2] *Ib.* f. 22.

come back to your bed. But I dread and fear."[1] A father writes to a bishop to use his influence with his son-in-law to come back to his wife; he has left her on her father's hands, and doubtless wastes his substance on some harlot: follows the bishop's grave expostulation: the young husband's passionate reply that it is easier for one to bear poverty than two; he left her where at least she might not be in actual want; for himself his hands are daily turned to an unaccustomed toil, that some day kindlier fate may smile on him and he may claim her as his wife again. "God who knows all things, knows that I have gone to no woman's breast but hers."[2] But the *Summa* is above all the Book of Youth. The scholars have it. *Sit thema*[3] is eternal. There is the shabby scholar, nobly born—"would to God I had been born a peasant, that I might not be a laughing stock. They call me noble, point me out as I go by, and I go with my head down and my eyes on the ground, for my beggary devours me. And to help things I am side by side with *parvenus*, sons of nobodies, who go everywhere, entertain everybody, live in the best digs., and I sit up in my garret, or come out in my coat with the fur worn bare, and so gloriously poor that I can't even buy bread to fill myself. I can't write home to my people for more, for there's my brother to be knighted, and sisters to be married, and no end of daily expenses that they can't avoid. And so I come to you as to my other God, to dip your little finger in the fountain of your liberality, and touch your wretched nephew's tongue."[4] Another, sick for home and ill; will his sister come to see him—"I think the sight of your face would make me well again":[5] another, mournful in gaol—"Dearest father, when I was lately in Orleans, I had a row with a young man and the devil ministering unto me,

[1] B.N. MS. Lat. 1093, f. 66 *v*. [2] *Ib*. 1093, f. 59.

[3] I am in want. I have no books and no clothes. Paris drinks money. What tiger would refuse its kitten? (Matthieu de Vendôme, *Sitzungsberichte*, Munich, 1872. p. 612.)

[4] B.N. MS. Lat. 8654, f. 15 *r*. [5] *Ib*. 8653, f. 13.

I hit him on the head with a stick, and now am shut up in Orleans gaol. But the young man is free, and better of his wound, and demanding his expenses off me, £10 Tours, and I can't get out until it's paid." There are alternative replies to this, one kindly and without reproach, wishing his son "health and joy," the other "health and full repentance of your folly. People who get into prison are as well to stay there till they realise their folly, and I am not going to impoverish and destroy my house for the likes of you."[1] To his lady, that it has come to the ears of her goddess-ship that he boasts of her favours—far be it from him.[2] To his love, that she will take no other into her kindness, for though his body is far from her, his mind is not, and when the two years' course is ended, please God he will come back to her.[3] To his father, from hospital: he has many times told him of his poverty, but could never yet find his way to his compassion; "and now, brought as I am to the last extremity of shame and wretchedness, I ask your help no more." Starvation brought on a fever that ended in consumption, *lacerationem pulmonis*: he had himself brought to hospital, for there was no one to reach him a cup of water. But it is squalid: he has lost all appetite: his lungs are gone. Will his father please come before he dies, "for I would have you give the son of your loins the gift of a grave."[4] Less tragic, the poor scholar begging about the doors, lost in a humorous contemplation of all the varieties of staleness that can still be bread, and coming home with his stomach barking:[5] the outrageous jester watching the marching and counter-marching of certain insects upon his tattered quilt like a procession of ecclesiastics[6]—it is

> "the image of the emptiness of youth
> Filled with the sound of footsteps, and that voice
> Of discontent and rapture and despair."

[1] B.N. MS. Lat. 1093, f. 12. [2] *Ib.* 8654, f. 10. [3] *Ib.* 1093, f. 68.
[4] *Ib.* 8654, f. 16 *v.* [5] *Ib.* f. 16. [6] *Ib.* f. 16.

There are other sources for his life and manners, vivid enough: the University sermons, with their *exempla*, of Guéric d'Auxerre sitting at his window and hearing a song sung in the street,

> "Temps s'en va
> Et rien n'ai fait,
> Temps s'en vient
> Et ne fais rien."

which so moved his heart that he entered religion, to become first prior of the Dominicans at Metz:[1] of the poor clerk who was promised a benefice and danced all day, and perhaps, poor soul, may never see it:[2] of the naughty scholars more often in the *pâtisseries* than in the classroom, singing,

> "Bad people, good town
> Where a ha'penny buys a bun."[3]

There are the records of the Nations, where after the election of Magister John of Stralen as procurator, the first act of his tenure was to move the adjourning of the English nation without dissentient voice to the tavern of the Two Swords in the Rue St. Jacques, where the elect should be drunk in: this being done to the pleasure of the masters then present to the amount of xxis. and ijd., of which xvis. were due from the elect, it being his first procuratorship, and the remaining 5s. ijd., the same did pay and expend, explaining that he was in no way called upon to do so, but willing so to do, to the well pleasing of the masters:[4] or where in congregation of the English nation on the 2nd of October the procurator of the Norman nation complained that a college scout of that nation had been enormously beaten without cause by a certain person named (here there is a blank, as the accused was a friend

[1] Hauréau, *Notices et Extraits*, iii. 341.

[2] *Ib.* p. 288.

[3] *Notices et Extraits*, xxxii. p. 290.

[4] *Auctuarium Univ. Paris*, i. 441. *The Book of Procurators of the English Nation*, Feb. 10, 1374.

of the Bishop of Lisieux). On Tuesday, 26th October, he who struck the Norman was summoned and did confess that he had indeed beaten the aforesaid, but subjoined that he had not done it in despite of the University. The witnesses agreed that a certain one wearing a white cloak had struck the aforesaid scout, giving him one or two buffets, and when he cried out that he was in the safeguard of the king and his lords, the other did but beat him the more.[1] There are the Law Reports, where the University holds itself aggrieved in the person of its scholar, in that the Provost had taken a cask of wine from his lodging and emptied it into the gutter, to the great grief, damage and prejudice of the said University, its Rector, doctors, bachelors and scholars.[2] But it is *oratio obliqua* at best: in the actual manuscripts, the earnest appeals for love, for money, for an assignation, for lecture notes, for—the eternal impossibility of human relations—the assurance "that you care for me even as I do for you," for a moment time stands still; the wall of glass, impalpable and deadening, is broken; and one hears the very voices of the Paris streets.

> "And did you once see Shelley plain?"

Shelley? This man may have spoken to Peter Abelard.

[1] *Auct. Univ. Paris,* i. 318, 2nd Oct. 1368.

[2] Fournier, *Statuts,* i. p. 79.

CHAPTER VII

THE ARCH POET[1]

Out of the bruyant, turbulent confusion of peoples and languages, Breton and Limousin, English and German—for the clangour of the German tongue once so rang in the streets of Orleans that one would have thought oneself in the Fatherland, says a German lament for the decay of the University in the fourteenth century[2]—came forth singing, in the ageless and marmoreal tongue. For Latin is the language of the mediaeval commonwealth, in Paris, in Bologna, in Orleans, in Oxford: the scholar's "realm of Flora and old Pan." With all other lyric, provenance is easy.

"Quan li jor sont lonc en mai,"

—twelfth century Provencal, softer than sleep:

"Unter den Linden,"

Walther von der Vogelweide, and no blackbird in that meadow more liquid than he:

"Main se leva Bele Alys,"

street song in Paris, clean cut and clear:

"Bytwene Mershe and Averil
When spray biginneth to springe,"

[1] For text and comment on the whole subject see Manitius, *Die Gedichte des Archipoeta*, 1913; Schmeidler, *Die Gedichte des Archipoeta*, 1911: Grimm, *Gedichte des Mittelalters auf König Friedrich den Staufer* (Kleinere Schriften, iii. 1844).

[2] Fournier, *Statuts des Univ. franç.*, i. 145.

English, early fourteenth century, sweet and uncertain as the first thrush:

> " Lassa! la vita m'è noia,
> Dolze la morte a vedere,"

thirteenth century Italian, the Sicilian school:

> " Dum Dianae vitrea
> Sero lampas oritur,"

—as well find the provenance of that moon rise; over a valley in the Hartz, or the linden trees of Orleans, or the quick flowing of the Seine, or the vast gentle Lombardy plain. "There is no speech or language where that voice is not heard."

> " When Diana lighteth
> Late her crystal lamp,
> Her pale glory kindleth
> At her brother's fire:
> Little straying west winds
> Wander over heaven,
> Moonlight falleth,
> And recalleth
> With a sound of lute strings shaken,
> Hearts that have denied his reign
> To Love again.
> Hesperus, the evening star,
> To all things that mortal are,
> Grants the dew of sleep.
>
> " Thrice happy sleep!
> The antidote to care,
> Thou dost allay the storm
> Of grief and sore despair;
> Through the fast-closèd gates
> Thou stealest light;
> Thy coming gracious is
> As Love's delight.
>
> " Sleep through the wearied brain
> Breathes a soft wind
> From fields of ripening grain;

The sound
Of running water over clearest sand,
A mill wheel turning, turning slowly round,
These steal the light
From eyes weary of sight.

" Love's sweet exchange and barter, then the brain
Sinks to repose;
Swimming in strangeness of a new delight,
The eyelids close.
Oh sweet the passing o'er from love to sleep,
But sweeter the awakening to love!

" Under the kind branching trees
Where Philomel complains and sings,
Most sweet to lie at ease.
Sweeter to take delight
Of beauty and the night
On the fresh springing grass,
With smell of mint and thyme,
And for Love's bed, the rose.
Sleep's dew doth ever bless,
But most, distilled on lovers' weariness." [1]

It is one of the timeless things: it has the memory of two antiquities: it dreams on things to come.

Dum Dianae vitrea is the height of secular Latin poetry, even as the *Dies irae* of sacred: the twin peaks of the mediaeval Parnassus. But in this same scholar's commonwealth, comedy never sleeps, and the parody provided a few pages later in the same MS. brings the scholar, the *vagus*, from bas-relief into the round, a globe of sinful continents.

" When the pub is sighted
In the market square
Every face is lighted
With its rosy flare,
Then says every cheery soul,
'Could you find a better hole?'

[1] *Carm. Bur.* 37. For the Latin text see Appendix A, p. 229.

"Bacchus wrangleth,
Venus wangleth
Purses that have stood long strain
To vent again,
And suborneth
And transformeth
Clothes the wearers still have on
To pledge in pawn.

"Food's rich consumption, and the bacon fat——"[1]

These are the happy spirits who went to mass at St. Rémy on Maundy Thursday in procession, each clerk leading a herring on a string, the object being to step on the herring of the man in front, while guarding your own herring from the assault of the man behind. Mediaeval parody[2] is graceless, even blasphemous, delighting even more than the scorpion to sting the faces of men, and the *Beginning of the Gospel according to the silver Mark* has blasted the entire Roman Curia with one triumphant breath.

"In those days the Pope spake unto the Romans, 'When the son of man cometh to the seat of our majesty, first say unto him, "Friend, wherefore art thou come?" But if he shall continue knocking and giving nothing unto you, cast him forth into the outer darkness.' And it came to pass that a certain poor clerk came to the *curia* of the Lord Pope and cried, saying, 'Have mercy on me, ye doorkeepers of the Pope, for the hand of poverty hath touched me. For I am poor and needy, and I pray you that ye should have compassion upon my calamity and my affliction.' But they hearing it had indignation among themselves and said, 'Friend, thy poverty go with thee to perdition: get thee behind me, Satan, for thou savourest not the things that be of pelf. Verily, verily, I say unto thee, thou shalt not enter into the joy of thy lord, until thou hast given thy uttermost farthing.'

"And the poor man went away and sold his cloak and

[1] *Carm. Bur.* 176. See Appendix A, p. 231.

[2] See Novati, *Carm. Med. Aev.* p. 66: Lehmann, *Die Parodie im Mittelalters* (1922).

his tunic and all that he had, and gave to the cardinals and the doorkeepers and the chamberlains. But they said, 'And what is this among so many?' And they cast him out, and he going out wept bitterly and could not be comforted. And thereafter came to the *curia* a certain rich clerk, fat and well-fed and puffed up, who for sedition had committed murder. He first gave to the doorkeeper, and then to the chamberlain, and then to the cardinals. And they took counsel among themselves, which of them should have received most. But the Lord Pope hearing that his cardinals and his servants had received many gifts from the clerk fell sick nigh unto death. Then sent unto him the rich clerk an electuary of gold and silver, and straightway he was recovered. Then the Lord Pope called unto him his cardinals and his servants and said unto them, 'Brethren, see to it that no man seduce you with vain words. For I have given you an example, that even as much as I take, ye should take also.'"[1]

As for authorship, it is the paradox of letters that the lyric, the most personal, most individual of the literary kinds, is often likely to go fatherless, the love-child of the Muses. We know the great preachers of the Paris pulpit, Jacques de Vitry, Robert de Sorbon, Grossetête of Lincoln: we know that Matthieu de Vendôme wrote the tale of Pyramus and Thisbe, of Tobias and the fish: that Walter of Châtillon composed an Alexandreid which embarrassed both Homer and Virgil, and Alain de Lille a Complaint of Nature, full of elaborate female figures, and Nigellus Wireker, precentor of Canterbury, the really excellent story of how Burnellus (Burnellus being the concrete, as opposed to the abstract, idea of the Ass) went to Paris to become a scholar and perhaps even a bishop, but lost his tail and gained very little else.[2] All these

[1] *Carm. Bur.* xxi.

[2] Wright, *Satirical Poets of the Twelfth Century*, i. 11-145. See also Sandys, "English Scholars of Paris" (*Camb. Hist.* i 192). Dan Russel quoted him to Chaunticlere (*The Nonnes Preestes Tale*).

works, *de longue haleine,* yet leave the author breath enough to recite his authorship. But the lyrics, like their masters, went like leaves before the wind. They light on this man's heap or on that, Walter Map, Gautier de Châtillon, Primas of Orleans, Primas of Cologne: are shuffled here and there in the caprice of scholarship. The greatest of them all, a craftsman so individual that one can say *Aut Archipoeta aut Diabolus* is nameless: Punchinello, with a mask half comic, half tragic: a ghost, but a ghost with a cough.

He is coughing in the first lyric we have from him, dated from internal evidence and much patient research about 1161, a dramatic cough, that suggests the gift of a cloak: and he is coughing in the last, safe housed in St. Martin's cloister at Cologne.[1] At the date of the first lyric, Barbarossa's great Chancellor, Reginald von Dassel, Archbishop elect of Cologne, had been for three years ambassador, with Otto, the Count Palatine, to the Pope. The Archpoet addresses him as a *transmontanus* and cries his mercy for one, like himself, a man from beyond the mountains: they are both exiles in Italy. The Archpoet had a fine taste in patrons: Ragewin of Freising, writing of Reginald von Dassel, is kindled to a paragraph of splendid prose. He is describing both the Chancellor and the Palatine: "in these were innate grace of presence, nobility of race, a wise and powerful brain, a soul undismayed: to them no labour come amiss, no situation harsh, no enemy seemed to them formidable. They showed no mercy to themselves for lust, or for default. Eager for fame, lavish of largesse, they sought a mighty glory, their riches in their honour. Young in years, marvellous in oratory, in character wellnigh balanced, except that in the one, by reason of his office and his order there was a certain gentleness and compassion,

[1] Continuam tussim patior tanquam tisicus sim,
Sentio per pulsum quod (non) a morte procul sum.
Manitius, ix. p. 14. Grimm, p. 60.

to the other, the severity of the sword which for good cause he bore, did add a certain majesty. . . . From this time forward nothing was done greatly, nothing was done exquisitely, but these two were at the doing of it." [1]

"Lavish of largesse, they sought a mighty glory":

but when the Chancellor demands an epic on Barbarossa's Italian campaign in one week, the Archpoet has reason for an indignant howl.[2] It is not only that the spirit of poetry comes and goes in a whirlwind—do we not know that the spirit of prophecy fled from Elias ?—but consider the subject. Would you have me do in a week what would take Virgil or Homer seven years, or Lucan a quinquennium ? Moreover, is it for a beggar to write the conquests of an Emperor ? A poet—and poorer than all poets : nothing have I, I tell you, beyond what you see. Tears for me, but a jest for you—it is the far-off anticipation of the amazing prologue to *I Pagliacci*—and think not I am vicious, and so I'm poor Can I dig, I that am a scholar, and of knightly blood ? but—the clown's mask is on again—the fighting scares me : rather would I follow Virgil than thee, Paris ! To beg I am ashamed "—if that were so, the Archpoet wore his shame like a garland. He has the diabolic rhyming of *Don Juan*, the Ariel lightness of *Iolanthe*, and he made his own tunes : Gilbert and Sullivan in one. In June or July, Reginald held a mighty hosting in Vienne.[3] The whole herd of the jongleurs and the jugglers and the clowns came jigging into town, breathless, to be there before the ninth day : but a greater poet in hiding watched them with despairing eyes. Only yesterday, the Chancellor's favourite, a horse to ride, and money to spend, and Life going by like a festival : hot blood, and a scandal about a wench—

[1] Pertz, *Script. Rer. Germ.* *Ottonis Frisingenis opera*, ii. 188.

[2] Manitius, p. 32, "Archicancellarie, vir discrete mentis." Grimm, p. 57.

[3] Manitius, viii. p. 49, *n.* Grimm, p. 54.

"they showed no mercy to themselves, for lust or for default"—and the Archpoet is fleeing on the roads,

> "Nunc vesanus plus Oreste,
> Male vivens et moleste,
> Trutannizans inhoneste."

He fled, like Jonah: and like Jonah, the whale, poverty, swallowed him.

> "But, if prayer can avail,
> Speak thy word unto thy whale.
> And the whale, whose mouth's enormous,
> Vomiting thy poet foremost,
> Bidden, in thy great compassion,
> Yawning widely in his fashion,
> To eject him, now a bald head,
> Thin and lean and famine-scalded,
> But once more thy poets' poet,
> Writing that all men may know it."

The translation is a travesty of the original, the breathless impudent rhyming on one word only, and yet never a rhyme that is not inevitable through all the ten lines of it. Truly, his successor after two centuries was justified in saying that the Archpoet maketh verses for a thousand poets: "Yea," replied the Pope, his patron, "and he drinks for them too." [1] Droll, shameless, spendthrift and importunate, he is inscrutable still. Now and then comes a gleam of the dangerous agate knife-edge of genius, a gesture of the singing robes about him, and for a moment he stands head and shoulders above the great Chancellor. He never sustains it: a verse or two of haughty defiant sincerity, and the comic mask is on again, the hand outstretched palm upwards, the impudent grin. But something remains—"a moulted feather, an eagle's feather." *Confessio Goliæ* is something more than the arch-type of a generation of vagabond scholars, or the greatest drinking song in the world: it is the first defiance by the artist of that society which it is his thankless business to amuse:

[1] Grimm, p. 15.

the first cry from the House of the Potter, "Why hast thou made me thus?"

Reginald von Dassel was much at Pavia in the years of the breaking of Milan, and Pavia, already old in scholarship, had altars to Aphrodite as well as to Athene and her owl.

> "Let you bring Hippolytus
> In Pavia dine him,
> Never more Hippolytus
> Will the morning find him."

The Archpoet was no Hippolytus, on any day of the week, and Reginald seems to have checked him for it sharply. But this time the poet turns at bay,

> "Seething over inwardly
> With fierce indignation,
> In my bitterness of soul,
> Hear my declaration.
> I am of one element,
> Levity my matter,
> Like enough a withered leaf
> For the winds to scatter.
>
> "Since it is the property
> Of the sapient
> To sit firm upon a rock,
> It is evident
> That I am a fool, since I
> Am a flowing river,
> Never under the same sky,
> Transient for ever.
>
> "Hither, thither, masterless
> Ship upon the sea,
> Wandering through the ways of air,
> Go the birds like me.
> Bound am I by ne'er a bond,
> Prisoner to no key,
> Questing go I for my kind,
> Find depravity.

"Never yet could I endure
  Soberness and sadness,
Jests I love and sweeter than
  Honey find I gladness.
Whatsoever Venus bids
  Is a joy excelling,
Never in an evil heart
  Did she make her dwelling.

"Down the broad way do I go,
  Young and unregretting,
Wrap me in my vices up,
  Virtue all forgetting,
Greedier for all delight
  Than heaven to enter in:
Since the soul in me is dead,
  Better save the skin.

"Pardon, pray you, good my lord,
  Master of discretion,
But this death I die is sweet,
  Most delicious poison.
Wounded to the quick am I
  By a young girl's beauty:
She's beyond my touching? Well,
  Can't the mind do duty?

"Hard beyond all hardness, this
  Mastering of Nature:
Who shall say his heart is clean,
  Near so fair a creature?
Young are we, so hard a law,
  How should we obey it?
And our bodies, they are young,
  Shall they have no say in't?

"Sit you down amid the fire,
  Will the fire not burn you?
Come to Pavia, will you
  Just as chaste return you?
Pavia, where Beauty draws
  Youth with finger-tips,
Youth entangled in her eyes,
  Ravished with her lips." [1]

[1] Manitius, *op. cit.* p. 24.

Young, consumptive, in love, the Archpoet had a short life of it. He is sent down to Salerno to study medicine and become a useful member of society—" It is a better and a wiser thing to be a starved apothecary than a starved poet, so back to the shop, Mr. John, back to plasters, pills and ointment boxes." The Archpoet, more submissive than Keats, trundles obediently down south, falls ill of a fever, is given up, but slowly mends again and comes home, the pallor still upon him, selling every rag he can spare to buy bread, and begging for the rest.[1] 1165 finds him in the cloister of St. Martin, the cough still " undefeated " and his voice gone, but still impudent and still gay. He had a vision of heaven last night, he tells his patron, saw neither Homer nor Aristotle, but had a long talk with Augustine and got the whole truth of it at last, of the Nominalists and the Realists, of kinds and species, of names and things. Unluckily, later on in a little chat with Michael the Archangel, he was warned to keep his knowledge to himself. Had the Archpoet even then an impish vision of the busy spiders of the next three hundred years? One thing he may tell his Chancellor: he has a guardian angel of great ability, and the Sicilian campaign will be an immense success. But no man is perfect, and I warn you that the Blessed Martin has a crow to pluck with you. Certain evil-disposed persons have defrauded his cloister here in Cologne, and you suffer it. I met the Blessed Martin going hot foot to tell on you, and I had to weep myself almost dead to beg you off. So see to it. Myself, I weeping left the country of the laughing. *Terra ridentium*—he has the gift, peculiar rather to his age than to himself, of a sudden nobility of phrase, an echo of the

" Tuba mirum spargens sonum,"

even while the thorns crackle most briskly under the pot. Here it is the " drenched with sudden light " of the first

[1] Manitius, x. p. 61. Grimm, p. 64.

moment of vision, " the holy people, the immortal folk," and the aching sweetness of

> " The final peace, the quiet of the heart."

The end is very near now, he says complacently : a good deal of pain, so that it's hard to enjoy the old jokes. But even in this state of grace

> " I cannot love the name of Palatine,
> For thanks to him the price is up for every cask of wine."

If it's true, says the Archpoet firmly,

> " I shall make such verses as I never made before,
> All the woes that may be read in the Apocalypse
> Shall fall on him, unless he frees the vine from its eclipse."

But for himself, the Abbot is his good shepherd : however it goes with the rest of the Abbey, for him there's no stint in the wine, and with that the curtain drops on the twisted grin.[1] Whether or not he recovered to follow the Chancellor in his last fatal campaign, when the plague, rather than the Papal armies, defended Rome, there is no evidence. Reginald von Dassel died on that plague-stricken plain, and the news cast its shadow even in Paris : Maecenas was dead.[2] So too, Eberhard, Bishop of Spires : there is no room for a vagabond poet among such great ones. Better to go from St. Martin's cloister, St. Martin who was notoriously kind to vagabonds, to find again the country of the laughing, and this time to come no more out.

Three generations later, Salimbene told the tale of Philip, Archbishop of Ravenna and papal legate, who was wont to pace through his palace chanting a responsory or an antiphon to the praise of the Glorious Virgin, from one corner of the palace to the other : and in every corner in the summer time, stood a flagon of a truly remarkable

[1] Manitius, ix. p. 54. Grimm, p. 60.

[2] John of Salisbury, *Chart. Univ. Paris*, i. 21.

wine, cooling in ice-cold water.[1] For he was a mighty drinker, and liked not water in his wine, for which reason he greatly delighted in a tractate that Primas made against the mixing of the same. And this Primas, says Salimbene, was a canon of Cologne, *magnus trutannus et magnus trufator*, an astonishing versifier and a swift, who, if he had given his heart to the love of God, would have been mighty in divine letters, and mightily availed the Church of God. His *Apocalypse* which he made I have seen, and many other writings also. . . . and when his archbishop checked him for his incontinence, he defended himself in those verses which are called his *Confessio*.[2] The business of false ascription has already begun. The *Confessio* will turn up in an English manuscript with a dedication to the Bishop of Coventry (notoriously generous to lively wits) instead of the Archbishop of Cologne: [3] its author will be credited with the thirteenth century *Apocalypse*, a rattling broadside against the higher clergy, with Ezekiel's vision of the four living creatures moving on wheels, the pope as lion, and the archdeacon as the eagle, for he seeth his prey afar off. And Primas, the thirteenth century canon of Cologne, will not only be identified with the Archpoet half a century earlier, but with another Primas of Orleans, contemporary of Abelard, an unmitigated scoundrel, but of amazing verve, who begged and lectured and vilified and versed from Sens to Beauvais, from Beauvais to Amiens, from Amiens to Orleans, from Orleans to Paris, and very subject to being kicked downstairs by enraged ecclesiastics.[4] And finally one and all are comprehended in the great name of Golias,

[1] *M. G. H. Script.* xxxii. p. 430. "Did Addison know of the Archbishop of Ravenna when he had the bottles put at *both* ends of the Holland House library?" (G. S.)

[2] *Mon. Germ. Hist. Script.* xxxii. p. 83.

[3] Wright, *Walter Mapes*, p. 75; perhaps Hugh of Nunant, who expelled monks from Coventry in favour of seculars.

[4] See Wilhelm Meyer, *Die Oxforder Gedichte des Primas, Magister Hugo von Orleans*, 1907, edited from MS. Rawlinson, G. 109. Note especially Nos. xv. p. 152; xxiii. p. 158.

the Philistine turned Bishop, father of many sons, a humour compact of many simples, hearty as Friar John, malicious as Panurge, yet touched by the bouquet of white roses that Quintessence Queen of Entelechy carries in her exquisite hand. Primas, Archpoet, Golias, the name is given indifferently, the same mask, and the eyes looking out from it, alike at least in mockery and hope. Rebels against authority, greedy of experience, haunted by beauty, spendthrift and generous, fastidious and gross, the temperament abides. "There was in our own time a certain parasite, Golias by name, notorious alike for his intemperance and his wantonness . . . a tolerable scholar, but without morals or discipline . . . who did vomit forth against the Pope and the Roman curia a succession of famous pieces, as adroit as they were preposterous, as imprudent as they were impudent . . . and of his own life and morals also, even writing his own epitaph at the last. . . . What punishment might have been his, if the Curia did exact corporal penalty? Yet although he may escape the vengeance of men, hardly might he shirk the divine fury, which suffers not that sin shall go unpunished, unless it be redeemed by penitence."[1] "Not inferior to any of the former in Atheism and impietie and equall to all in manner of punishment was one of our own nation of fresh and late memorie . . . by profession a schollar, but by practice a Play-maker and poet of scurrilitie who by giving too large a swinge to his own wit and suffering his lust to have the full reines, fell (not without just desert) to that outrage and extremitie that he denied God . . . affirming . . . all religion but a device of policie . . . the manner of his death being so terrible . . . not only a manifest figure of God's judgment but also a horrible and fearfull lesson to all that beheld him."[2] The mask of Golias: the death-mask of Christopher Marlowe.

[1] Giraldus Cambrensis, *Speculum Ecclesiae*, ed. Brewer, iv. 15.

[2] Thomas Beard, *The Theatre of God's Judgements* (second edition 1612), p. 149.

CHAPTER VIII

THE ORDO VAGORUM

"It is a strange madness," said Petrarch to his out-at-elbows secretary, "this desire to be for ever sleeping in a strange bed." He had been a good secretary; had endeared himself to his master by learning eleven canzone in nine days; had copied his patron's verses in a fine and clear script. But the task given him of transcribing Pilato's translation of Homer was more than he could bear; he spoke wildly of going to Constantinople to learn Greek himself, and disappeared: was next heard of in Pisa, penniless and starving; came back to Petrarch a reformed prodigal, and again vanished. Ten years later Petrarch writes to him in Rome, in friendly admonition, the sentence of perplexity already quoted: the touchstone of two temperaments. Selden would have agreed with Petrarch, and his dislike of sleeping out of his own bed may account for his taking no part in the Civil Wars. Selden would have made a good mediaeval churchman; and Petrarch, though indifferent even for an archdeacon,[1] was in this point sound.

For the mediaeval church had never much approved of wandering. "Sit in thy cell," said the Blessed Antony, "and thy cell shall teach thee all things. The monk out of his cell is a fish out of water."[2] "Dig and sow," said the old Abbot Luan, founder of Clonfert, little thinking

[1] See the provision in Petrarch's will, if he should die in Parma, "Et si Parmae, in ecclesia majori, ubi per multos annos archidiaconus fui inutilis et semper fere absens." *Epist.* (edited Fracasetti), iii. 539.

[2] Verba Seniorum, ii. Migne, 73, c. 858.

that he spoke to the men who were to be the scholar-gipsies of Europe, "that you may have wherewith to eat and drink and be clothed, for where sufficiency is, there is stability, and where stability is, there is religion (*ubi stabilitas, ibi religio*)."[1] *Stabilitas,* perseverance in that place where a brother had made his profession, was one of the three obligations of the Benedictine vow. And the rule which was absolute for the monk, the *clericus religiosus,* holds, though with more elasticity, for the clerk, the *clericus saecularis.* No clerk may leave the diocese without permission and letter of license from the bishop; no bishop may receive him without such letter. Movement by order of one's superiors is a different matter; the strategy of the church sends a man here and there, and so Theodore of Tarsus founds a school of Greek studies in England, and a Greek monk plants vines at Malmesbury, and John of Salisbury dies bishop of Chartres. But the natural state of the clerical soul is static. Brother Ratpert went about but little and hardly wore out two pairs of shoes in the year; Tutilo the artist had commissions here and there, and Ratpert peers anxiously over the top of his great folios after him, for the devil walks even more briskly without than on the pavement of the cloister. The stability of the Church goes far to stabilise Europe; it is seen in so concrete an instance as the growing of the towns round the episcopal palaces.[2] King and Count live in and by perpetual progresses, so much of their revenues being in kind, and of the sort best consumed on the premises. But the bishop is bound by canon law to abide in his diocese,[3] and industry first begins under the walls of the *évêché* or the great abbey.

If one wished to abuse an antagonist, one called him

[1] *Acta SS.*, August 4th, p. 353, note.

[2] See A. Pirenne, *Mediaeval Cities,* pp. 63-4. "Civitas becomes synonymous in the ninth century with the bishopric and the episcopal city."

[3] See the *Conc. Chalcedon.* v. "De episcopis vel clericis qui a civitate in civitatem transeunt" (Mansi, *Concilia*, vii. 362. See Appendix E.)

a *gyrovagus*. Abelard, who left St. Denys for the wattled hut and oratory of the Paraclete, was a *gyrovagus*; Arnold of Brescia, that firebrand tied to a fox's tail, comes off still worse; Gottschalk, three centuries earlier, was a *gyrovagus*; so was the recreant who betrayed the Christian pilgrims to the Saracens. The word was consecrated. St. Benedict had used it in a stern chapter of his rule, of those monks whose whole life is spent, three days here, four days there, in the hospitality of different monasteries, ever wandering and never in one stay, and minding only their own pleasures and their wretched gullets: "of whose unhappy conversation it is better to be silent than to speak."[1] His anonymous commentator in the eighth century was not so reticent; and his sketch of their habits is one of the liveliest things in mediaeval prose. These vagabonds count, he says, on the hospitality which the Apostle enjoined, and the pleasure of unexpected arrival, so that all kinds of exquisite relishes will be brought out, and many chickens give up the ghost under the knife. Their feet are weary with the hardness of the way, and they would like them bathed; but they would rather have their inwards drenched with infinite refilling of the cup than the fomentation of the feet, and when the table has been cleared by their starving host, and the crumbs swept up, they shamelessly insist on their mighty thirst, and if by any chance there is no goblet handy, they'll mix it up in the same plate, and when they are stuffed and sodden to the pitch of vomiting, they say it is all their hard life. And before they go to bed, more exhausted after their labours at table than by their journey, they tell all the toils of the way, and beguile still more relishes and still more cups from their host; as for the reason of their wandering, a pilgrimage, we'll say? or perhaps captivity. Soon they enquire as to the whereabouts of any neighbouring monk or monastery. And there they'll go, as men wearied, men to whom the whole

[1] S. Benedict, *Regula*. Migne, *P.L.* lxvi. 246. See Appendix E.

world is closed, who can find nowhere a place of rest and refreshing for the soul, nowhere a complete observance of discipline: do they not well to wander? Wherever they go the traveller's thirst demands goblet hurried on goblet; pilgrims for their bellies' sake rather than their souls'. Two days pass: the supply of relishes diminishes: on the morning of the third day the host betakes himself, not to the kitchen, but to the ordinary toil of the day: our friend begins to meditate another visit. Suddenly he starts up as though impelled from behind: already he sees a fresh dinner on the horizon: not far off from that same monastery he finds another; he halts for a little rest. Behold him now come from the Italian frontier, and a good fresh tale all about pilgrimage or captivity, entering the house with humbly bowed head, and lying hard till all the poor host's poverty goes into the pot and on to the table: that host will be a well-picked bone in a day or two. Three days, and himself and his monastery and his habits and his discipline will be found displeasing: the knapsacks full of dry bread are strapped up again: the unhappy donkey recalled from his lean pasture, which would have pleased him well enough if two days' hospitality had not displeased his master. Once again he is loaded up with tunics and cowls, for you can always strip your host by declaring you've only rags to cover you. Farewell, say you to your host, and away, where other feasts already beckon. Beaten, thumped, poked, the poor donkey humps along, and then stands stock still, and its ears are beaten, efforts on its rear being in vain. Pushed and pulled, it gets along somehow: one must be in time for dinner. Once arrived, hear the hearty voice crying: "Benedicite!" and hardly inside the monastery, what a thirst! . . . They go to bed, always for these a strange bed: in the morning, their bones tired with the fatigues of the road, they cannot rise, even though strong and hearty at table the night before. But matins once safe over, they get up, groaning and exhausted. A little wine warms them, and just a morsel of bread: they creep about the monastery, bowed with their infirmity, though their step livens wonderfully out of sight. . . . Day after day, walking, begging, sweating, whining, on they go, rather than stay in one place, there to toil, and there abide: humble at their incoming, arrogant and graceless at their outgoing, as if no monastery had morals or discipline holy enough for them. For ever wandering, they know not when the last weariness will come upon them: nor do they know what place will give them burial.[1] The type is eternal: Jacques de Vitry, six centuries later, tells his tale of the dormouse that went from monastery to monastery, till finding one where the rats scampered on the larder floor said: "Here is my place: here will I stay."[2]

Isidore of Seville with his monumental common sense goes to the root of the matter. The *clericus* is like the Levite, who had no allotment of land: his portion was the Lord. But there are two kinds of clerks: those who live in obedience to their head, the bishop; those who owe no allegiance to any man, but follow their own will: they are a hybrid, like the hippocentaurs: they have neither religion to restrain them, nor the ordinary business of the world to occupy them; *solutos et errantes*, free-lances and vagabonds, they embrace a life of baseness and wandering.[3] The argument is that if they who serve the altar have a right to live by the altar, then those who live by the altar must at least serve it. The same argument is in the mind of Ivo of Chartres, when the Bishop of Paris writes to the great canonist for advice about a canon who has married. To Ivo, the clerk above the rank of subdeacon who marries does not indeed lose his clerical privilege, but must lose his benefice. His point is that the faithful layman does not pay the clerk to live precisely as he

[1] *Regula Magistri*, c. I. Migne, ciii. 736.

[2] Jacques de Vitry, *Exempla* (Crane, T. F.), p. 31, No. 71.

[3] Isidore, *De Ecc. Off.* ii. 5.

does.[1] He is to offer to the Lord an offering in righteousness. Exactly how far the Church supported its clerks is a question: and especially towards the twelfth and thirteenth centuries the indignation against the canon discountenancing a clerk who engages in secular business,[2] yet makes no provision for him, accounts for some of the fiercest and bitterest invective of the scholars.[3] Clerical privilege in itself was conferred by receiving tonsure at the hands of a bishop.[4] It secured relief from every tax

[1] Ivo, *Epist.* 218 (Migne, 162, c. 221). See the later decretals of Gregory IX. (*Decret. lib. III. Tit. III.* cap. 7, 8, 9) penalising marriage of clerks even below the rank of subdeacon. The whole question is one of the thorniest in canon law. For a full discussion, see Genestal, *Privilegium Fori en France.* Rockinger (*Briefsteller und Formelbücher*, p. 560) quotes a letter from a bishop excommunicating the *praetor et aluaciles* because they exacted taxes from and denied clerical privilege to a cleric in major orders who had married.

[2] Gratian, *Decret.* i. Dist. xxiii. c. 3. "Saecularia officia negotiaque abnuant." But in practice there was much elasticity; suggested even in the canon of the Lateran Council 1215, "maxime inhonesta." That a clerk should turn grocer was less intolerable than jongleur, an occupation disgusting even in a layman. See Innocent IV. *Appar. Decret.* iii. *Cf.* Canons at Mayence, 813; Tribur, 895; Trosley, c. 909; Lateran, 1215; Montpellier, 1258; Pont-Audemar, 1279; Liege, 1287; Rodez, 1289. (See Appendix E for texts.)

[3] *Vide* the terrible story in Caesarus von Heisterbach of the clerk who could get no benefice, committed murder to get money, and died at the stake (*Dial. Mirac.* iii. 15). Cf. Richard de Bury, *Philobiblon*, Prol. 7, and Wright, *Latin Poems attributed to Walter Mapes*, p. 63, *Goliae Querela ad Papam.*

"Turpe tibi, pastor bone,
Si divina lectione
Spreta, fiam laicus.
Vel absolve clericatu
Vel fac ut in cleri statu
perseveram clericus.
Dulcis erit mihi status
Si prebenda muneratus
redditu vel alio
vivam, licet non habunde,
saltem mihi detur unde
studeam de proprio."

[4] Genestal, *Privilegium Fori*, p. 3, *et seq.*: "On ne comptait point seulement dans le clergé ceux qui par une ordination avaient reçu quelque part de pouvoir d'ordre, c'est a dire ceux qui avaient au moins l'un des ordres mineurs. Les simples tonsurés, n'ayant reçu aucun

and imposition of the secular power: from military service (Louis XI demanded recruits for his army from the University of Paris, was told that the Church had no weapon but prayers, and offered a weekly mass instead: on the other hand, it is pleasant to remember that after the victory of Bouvines the University danced for seven days and nights without stopping),[1] above all, it meant freedom from trial in a secular court of law.[2] The neck verse that could save a man from hanging is a survival of

ordre, faisaient cependant partie de l'*ordo clericalis*. . . . La tonsure . . . put de bonne heure être donnée avant les ordres. . . . Les canonistes sont unanimes à affirmer sans justification speciale que les tonsurés sont des clercs et jouissent des privilèges de ceux-ci. *Per primam tonsuram clericalis ordo confertur*, dit Innocent IV., sur le c. 11. x. *de aetate et qualitate praeficiendorum*, I. 14. Cette règle étendait dans d'enormes proportions le privilège clérical. Nombreux étaient ceux qui avaient reçu regulièrement la tonsure, et qui cependant ne remplissaient aucune fonction ecclésiastique. L'exagération était telle que l'Eglise finira par la reconnaître elle même, et que le concile de Trente exclura des privilèges les clercs mineurs qui ne sont pas attachés au service de l'Eglise" *Trid. Sess.* xxiii. De reform. c. 6. "Nullus prima tonsura initiatus, aut etiam in minoribus ordinibus constitutus ante dec. quat. ann. beneficium possit obtinere. Is etiam fori privilegio non gaudeat, nisi beneficium habeat aut clericalem habitum et tonsuram deferens, alicuius ecclesiae ex mandato episcopi inserviat vel in seminario clericali aut in aliqua schola vel universitate de licentia episcopi quasi in via ad ordines suscipiendos versetur."

[1] Luchaire, *La Société française sous Philippe Auguste*, p. 79.

[2] A good many points have practical illustration in the struggle between the "consuls" of Toulouse and the Bishop, Hugues Mascaron. In the episcopal towns of Languedoc, clerical privilege had been made accessible all round; *i.e.* freedom from all but ecclesiastical dues, *et quasi impunité en matière de crimes*. Butchers, innkeepers, grocers, bakers, were clerks, and flouted the secular authorities. In 1295 married clerks or those who exercised mechanical arts are ordered by the Seneschal to choose between the tonsure and the trade. The bishop appeals to the King, Philippe le Bel, who rebukes the consuls, but asks the bishop to remind his clerks of the canon against secular business. In 1292, Philip had instructed the consuls not to torture the bishop's delinquents, nor drown them by night in the Garonne (which had evidently been a rough and ready way of securing justice). In 1295 it is ruled that clerks who abandon tonsure and habit in order to escape the Bishop's justice "quod frequenter contingit" are still in his jurisdiction. See Baudouin, *Lettres inédites de Philippe le Bel*, pp. 11-27; *Histoire de Languedoc*, ix. pp. 174-175.

See also the complaint of the Chancellor Philippe le Grève against persons who assume the student's garb in order to commit a crime with it :[1] for the Church never inflicted the death penalty. The Inquisition itself handed its condemned to the secular power, with a recommendation to mercy. This practical immunity in the gravest offences[2] was one of the causes of quarrel between Henry II and Thomas à Becket : and again between King John and the Papal legate, where the story goes that the king threatened to hang a clerk in prison for forgery, Pandulfus threatened excommunication on the spot, went to look for a candle, and returning with it and bell and book found the king shaking in his shoes. In February, 1323, there is a long and amusing suit brought by the University against Nicholas Brouillart, provost of Orleans and certain sergeants for offences against certain scholars, Guillaume Jean, canon of Angers, Bernard Evrard, canon of Orleans, Guillaume Bertrand and Hugues his brother, clerks studying at the aforesaid *studium* : these coming *de spatiando in campis*, from a country excursion, late one Sunday evening, and passing through the Rue de la Brettonerie to their lodging, peacefully and without weapons, were set upon by the provost and his sergeants, with drawn swords, dragged along by their garments and beaten, and shut up in the prison of the *Castellum*, a dungeon vile and unclean. When it was night, Jean Angelart, clerk to the provost, came to ask

safety, " because the provost dare not lay hands upon them " (Haskins, " Paris University in Thirteenth Century Sermons," *Amer. Hist. Review*, x. p. 20).

[1] See Richard De Bury, *Philobiblon*. iv. 54. Firth, " Benefit of Clergy in the Time of Edward IV.," *E.H.R.* 1917, p. 175.

[2] See Beugnot, *Les Olim. Registre des Arrêts par la Cour du Roi*, vol. ii. p. 275. A clerk had committed murder at Mont Désir, and was taken by the mayor and the jurats : the Bishop of Amiens demands the clerk and his property from the mayor, who is willing to give up the prisoner, but not to bring him to Amiens, whereupon the Bishop puts the town under interdict (1287). In 1311, the Bishop of Morin complains that his clerk, Gerard de Wiserne, was taken from his prison by the Bailie of Amiens, the prison broken, and the prisoner done to death " de nocte, viliter, inhumando " (Beugnot, ii. 542). In 1208 two prisoners in the *Castellum* are claimed by the official of Paris as clerks, because they are tonsured ; but it was proved that they had managed to tonsure themselves in prison (Beugnot, ii. 501).

them what they would pay to be set free: they offered 30 sols. Paris: he comes swiftly back, saying he could do nothing with his lord, and that indeed he had been hit for naming such a sum. Moreover it being observed that one of the prisoners was looking out through a window to get some fresh air, they were taken to another vile prison, and the window then shut with an iron bar.

Representations were made to the provost that the imprisoned scholars were noble and wealthy men, of good report and conversation and of great status: to which the provost replied that £12 would set them free, and if they were indeed of such wealth and worth, they should not haggle over so small a sum, and that he had had £40 from other students for less. Agreed finally on £6 Paris.

Further charge against the sergeants: that they took Nicholas du Chef de Bois by his body and his garments, he at the ninth hour wearing clerical habit and tonsure and entering the schools to hear Nones, took him to the *Castellum*, and shut him up in a wooden ark, so short and low and narrow that a man could not abide therein *nisi in quodam globo*, unless in globular form so that his mouth kissed his knees, and moreover offered to the said Nicholas insults numerous and atrocious.

Also, they set on Guillaume de Paris, canon of St. Aniane, scholar of Orleans, coming on his horse from the outskirts of the town, and threatened to take him to prison, putting upon him that he was a monk but rode in secular garb. Up came Jean le Chrétien, known to the said scholar, and bargained with them for £12. He paid them 50s. down, and they held him up till his servant brought from home his *Infortiatum*, which was worth £40. The remaining £10 was finally borrowed from Jean de Belvoir: final result that the scholar was damnified to the sum of £20 Tours.

The provost's case is: first, that the scholars were

carrying weapons, and thereby lost clerical status: that on the Sabbath day between Christmas and Candlemas he had learned that malefactors were abroad, and was *ad guietum* with certain persons, to the number of 20: that between midnight and matins he found in the Bretonnerie in a certain brothel the before-named clerks; the said brothel they had forced to be opened to them, using violence, as the women therein said, and made complaint to the provost. Moreover they were carrying weapons, sticks and knives, and *in vestibus garcionum*, meanly habited, so as not to be recognised: and since they had entered the brothel by force, the provost took them in charge.

The finding of the Court was that the provost be deprived of all royal office for ever, return the £6 Paris, and pay to the court a fine of £500.[1]

This, however, like immunity from Income Tax, is a negative privilege at best: how was a clerk to live? Every clerk actually employed about a church in any capacity got something,[2] although the authorities had a nasty habit of making distribution at unpopular services, such as matins. A certain anthem, *lucrative et nourrissante*, sung before Christmas entailed at Notre Dame de Paris a distribution of 70 rolls and 70 quarts of wine to the cathedral clerks,[3] and when John, Duke of Bedford, was made Canon of Notre Dame at Rouen he received his *possessio*

[1] Fournier, *Statuts*, i, 69 *et seq.*

[2] See the Capitulary of Louis the Pious, A.D. 827, vi. 127, enjoining that a bishop shall not ordain a multitude of clerks, but regulate the number "*secundum meritum vel reditum ecclesiarum.*" In 1294, Narbonne, called on to count its *foyers* for the tax of 6 sols tournois *par feu*, makes return that there are 2016 hearths, not counting the poor (those whose goods were under 50 sols. tournois) nor the married clerks, 26 fires; the clerks who had benefices, 54; the unmarried clerks, without benefices, 21. All these clerks were "pas de la communauté." *Hist. de Languedoc*, ix. p. 174. Langlois quotes a good story about Primas, the preposterous cleric of Orleans, who would only sing with half of his mouth in church, and when taxed, explained that he had only a half-prebend; why therefore work full time? *La Littérature Goliardique: Revue Bleue.* 1892, p. 810.

[3] Luchaire, *op. cit.* p. 116.

panis et vini as part of the ceremony.[1] The person in charge of these financial arrangements was the archdeacon; hence the popularity of the *summa* "which contained two-and-twenty different ways of approaching an archdeacon on this ever delicate subject."[2] A good many of the clerks at the Universities had benefices;[3] Odo, Bishop of Paris, complains that the church of St. Marcel has been deserted by its canons; henceforth a canon must spend eight months in residence. If he fails to do so he is not to receive from his prebend more than xx sol. beyond the daily distribution. After he has completed his residence, if he wishes to go on pilgrimage or to study, the canons resident must not prevent him: but even a bona fide scholar may be recalled. The absent canon must find a suitable vicar, to whom he must give at least xx sol. per annum, besides the distribution which is made to vicars.[4] Some benefices were given in extreme youth, just as commissions were in the early nineteenth century, and the story of the flustered nursery-maid: "Please ma'am, I can't get the Colonel to take his porridge" is capped by Gilles de Corbeil's canon whose roving eye espied an apple which a wicked bystander had rolled, and who dropped the book on which his uncle the bishop was receiving his vows to crawl after it under the feet of the crowd.[5] The Abbot Samson of Bury St. Edmund's

[1] Beaurepaire, *Fondations pieuses du duc de Bedford à Rouen* (*Bibl. de l'École des Chartes*, 34, p. 365).

[2] Haskins, "Student Letters," *American Hist. Review*, iii. See B.N. MS. 8653, f. 32, on the defrauding archdeacon.

[3] Henry II. in 1167 recalls clerks from France: "ut diligunt reditus suos," let them return within three months or they lose their income. Rashdall, *Mediaeval Universities*, ii. 330. In 1348, Clement VI. granted the scholars of Orleans privilege of enjoying their benefices for three years without residence; Fournier, *Statuts*, i. 115. See the complaints of Eudes de Châteauroux and Gautier de Château-Thierry; Hauréau, *Not. et Extr.* vi. 209, 210, 214. See the Council at Girone, 1274, canon 25 (Appendix E).

[4] *Chart. Univ. Paris*, i. 63.

[5] Veillard (C.), *Gilles de Corbeil*, p. 376. The youngster had been sought for everywhere, for investiture, and was found riding a stick.

was kept at college by a poor priest, out of the offerings he received for holy water.[1] John of Salisbury made his living for a while by teaching pupils, and found it a quickening of his own studies,[2] and Abelard, says Fulk, might have made a mighty fortune if it had not been for his reckless extravagance.[3] One finds the legitimate schoolmaster at St. Denis complaining of unofficial rivalry, a wandering scholar with a fiddle who has got round the parents with his flatteries, and emptied the regular school.[4] But again and again comes the almost indignant cry from a starving scholar, that he can bear it no longer : that hunger is too hard a step-mother to learning : once to a bishop, that a man who has come through hardship himself should have some sympathy.[5] The delusion died hard that to come to the University was in itself a meritorious act, deserving all the support of one's relatives or one's church.[6] And in one point the tonsure and the *soutane* had a positive value : it gave a poor clerk a claim on the charity of all good men : it was moreover a real security, for to strike a clerk meant excommunication, released only by a visit of penitence to the Pope himself.[7] For this reason, bishops are cautioned

[1] *Jocelini de Brakelonde Cronica* (Camden Society), p. 32. See Council at Exeter (Appendix E) on the " Beneficia aquae benedictae " as the perquisite of poor clerks in the schools, 1287.

[2] *Metalogicus*, ii. 10.

[3] Abelard, *Epist.* xvi. Migne, 178, c. 373.

[4] Hauréau, *Not. et Extr.* iv. p. 270.

[5] " Qui passus est scolarium egestatem et eorum debet libentius et maiore misericordia misereri . . . Mihi dedit hanc comitem et novercam acerrimam usus scolasticus qui submergit nobiles in profundo lacu miseriae et paupertatis, et compellit per ostia mendicare . . . precor . . . quoddam mihi bonum ecclesiasticum concedendum." B.N. MS. Lat. 1093, f. 57 *v*. 71 *v*°.

[6] " Ex denario parentum vel ex denario ecclesiarum." Gautier de Château-Thierry (Hauréau, *Not. et Extr.* vi. 210).

[7] See Fournier, *Statuts des Univ. franç.* i. 2.

Gregory IX. (Jan. 1235) writing to the Bishop of Orleans, regrets the interruption of studies caused by perpetual excommunications, seeing that in such a concourse of students *rixes* are bound to occur. Hence-

against giving the tonsure and habit unless to fit and proper persons, as it is so often a cloak for wandering.[1] For that matter the kindness for the poor scholar still lingers; Irish students in the eighteen thirties walking across Scotland to Edinburgh for medicine or divinity would find a bed in the barn and milk and oat cake left ready. One of the kindliest of the fabliaux turns on it: the poor scholar who had stayed at the University till he had nothing left to pawn, and reluctantly left it to make his way as best he could home. He came that night after a hungry day to a farmer's house, but was chased from the door like a dog by the angry mistress, not before he had seen a cake go into the oven, pork into the pot, a flagon of wine to the shelf, and the parish priest into the house, his cloak plucked about his ears. But there was no malice in the little clerk; he went his hungry way, met the husband returning and was heartily bustled back again with much loud talking. The priest vanishes into the manger, through which he anxiously regards the situation, the host and guest sit down at the fire, while the virtuous and aggrieved hostess protests that there is nothing in the house—of course he has forgotten to bring anything from town, *et patati et patata*. Meantime the host begs for a story: he knows it isn't a clerk's job, of course, but a great reader like him must know all kinds of fine things. So the little clerk begins; a dull story, a dream that he had, about walking in a wood, and meeting a swineherd, and how the swineherd had a drove of pigs, round pigs, fat pigs, just as round and just as fat as the little pig that's plumping in the pot there. " Mon Dieu ! "

forth let the Bishop absolve at discretion, unless the excess is " difficult and enormous." " They rush with their tonsured pates into frays armed knights would hesitate to enter." Hauréau, *Not. et Extr.* vi. 250. At a council at Rheims, 1148, the visit to Rome is deprecated; it affords too much opportunity to the curious and dissolute " sub pretextu adeundi dominum papam curiosis et dissolutis libertas evagandi." Pertz, *M. G. H. Script.* xx. 519.

[1] Council at Salzburg, 1274. (See Appendix E.)

from the rapturous host, the lid comes off—hasty explanations from Madame. The party subside to await the fruition of the little pig, and the story continues : how a wolf, a large wolf, a wicked wolf, came up and pounced on a little pig, and how the blood flowed, red, red blood, as red as—as the wine in yonder flagon. Fresh ebullition. Story continues : how the clerk, furious at the wolf, looked about and found a stone, a big stone, a round stone, as big and round as the cake in yonder basket. A cake! Again general post. Story continues : how the clerk took the stone, and lifted it and looked at the wolf, and the wolf looked at him, with great eyes, with wild eyes—just like the eyes of the priest, looking through the bars of the manger. There is a very fine scene, in the best fabliau manner : and in the end the clerk goes off with the priest's comfortable cloak hugged round him. But mark you, says the teller anxiously, he would never have said a word if the lady had only been kind.[1]

II

Given clerical privilege, the abuse of it existed at least from the fourth century. Augustine complains of the clerical vagabonds who sell sham relics and come inquiring for relations that they never had,[2] and a Greek father of the fifth century says that better scholarship is another excuse for the road : [3] Benedict, Isidore, *Regula Magistri* said their say, and the Church Councils follow monotonously, but with fiercer animosity in the thirteenth century where the *peuple grouillant*, reinforced by so many disappointed scholars, becomes more articulate, abler, more dangerous. Some are born wanderers; some have it thrust upon them ; but the word *vagus* denotes often a mental

[1] Montaiglon-Reynaud, v. p. 132, *et seq.*, *Le Pauvre Clerc.*

[2] Augustine, *De Op. Monach.* c. 28. Migne, 66, 257.

[3] St. Isidore of Pelusium. Migne, 66, 258.

quality, as well as the physical condition.[1] Ekkehard's use of it is interesting: he tells a story of a young monk of St. Gall, of a mind incorrigibly *vagus*, with whom discipline could do nothing, and how on a certain day being forbidden to go beyond the monastery, he climbed in his restlessness the campanile—"O that I were where I but see"—to look abroad, and missing his foot, crashed to the ground. They sent for Notker, and all his stammering tenderness comes out in his telling of how the boy caught at his hand and held it till he died, commending his soul to All Virgins (it was on the Common of All Virgins he died), for he said he was at least on that score innocent. And Notker saw to it that masses should be said yearly for his soul.[2] Some men no monastery could hold: like the two fugitives from St. Sebastian in Auvergne, who could bear its discipline no longer and fled to live tumultuously: poverty brought them like the prodigal to their senses: they begin to hanker after the old comfortable tranquillity, the ordered peace. But they had reason to dread their reception, and cast about them for an emollient of their Abbot's greeting. They were in Rome. Relics were as yet plentiful, and for sale: they found to their delight that a complete St. Sebastian was going at a moderate price, and made haste to secure so suitable a present. But the *custos* of the relics was a thorough scoundrel: his St. Sebastian was no other than a Roman Emperor of a peculiarly malignant kind, well drenched in perfumes, for as is well known, a fragrance as of violets is one of the

[1] Notker, speaking of Horace, quotes, evidently from memory:

> "Pallida mors aequo pulsans pede, sive tabernas
> Aut regum turres, Vivite ait, venio."

with approbation; for the rest he is to be avoided as "lubricus atque vagus": Hartmann, *Vita S. Galli*. Cf. the Glossary, c. 1325, in Muratori, *Ant.* ii. 33, when vagus = *cupido, amator, venustus*. Helinand, the trouvère who turned monk, describes his former temper, "Behold him closed in the cloister to whom the whole world seemed once to be not even a cloister, but a prison."

[2] Ekkehard, *Casus S. Galli*, iii.

criteria of sanctity defunct. The money is paid; back go the vagabonds to Auvergne with their precious burden. Their reception at the Abbey surpassed their dreams; Imperial Cæsar has an ovation equal to anything he can have known in the days of his divinity: he is safely lodged beneath the altar, during a most moving day of ceremonies and processions and chanting, and in the evening the exhausted brethren retire to the refectory to a feast worthy of the occasion. Emotion and exhilaration was at its height when a terrific crash and horrified shrieking from the chapel brought them running. Whether it was that his unaccustomed surroundings irked him past bearing, or whether, as the monks thought, the holy place itself could not endure him, the Emperor blew up, precisely like a bad egg, wrecking the altar in his explosion. The sequel is very painful.[1]

There is also the type that the monastery itself could not endure: men like Radulfus Glaber, who confesses himself as frankly intolerable to live with: impudent to his superiors, a nuisance to his equals, and a bully to the juniors: so insufferable "with the inflation of a truculent mind" that his first monastery drove him out, with the less compunction that they knew him to have some "notion of letters," and therefore sure to be received elsewhere. Four monasteries in turn endured him and in turn cast him out: in one of them, St. Germain at Auxerre, he was employed to restore the Latin inscriptions on the tombs in the chapel.[2] Cluny finally received him, but it was the wise old Abbot of St. Benigny who turned his intractable genius into its fitting channel: set him to write a history of his own times, to the enriching of the more comic kind of mediaeval scholarship. He had a gift for visions, especially of the devil. Once in the monastery of St. Benigny, he saw him at dawn, a little thin man, black eyed, retreating chin, and hair on end, humpbacked

[1] *Vita S. Odilonis.* Migne, cxxxii. c. 608 *et seq.*

[2] Rodulfus Glaber, *Hist.* v. i. Migne, cxlii. 686.

and dirty, who rushed out of the dormitory crying: "Where is my bachelor?" and next day a young brother, Theoderic, a light-minded youth, threw aside the habit, and fled to the world, but moved by compunction returned. Another brother, from St. Mary at Meaux, fled and remained six days "tumultuously with the seculars," but on the seventh day returned, and was received again after correction. Radulfus himself fled from St. Benigny to another monastery, fearing his abbot's displeasure about something, but saw another vision, his abbot entreating him to finish the work he had begun.[1] The monasteries took no small pride in their distinguished members and there is a good deal of jealousy among them. Even in the seventh century an abbot writes in very strong terms to a bishop who has given his countenance to a fugitive monk, also ordained,[2] and the Abbot of St. Denis writes a very nasty letter to the Abbot of Saint Ayoul, where Abelard had taken temporary refuge.[3] The Abbot of Bury St. Edmund's appointed a good but unlearned man a prior, and his brethren murmured saying that no distinguished clerk would now come to a monastery where scholarship was so little thought of and a log of wood set in office.[4] For ambition is a great while dying, even in the religious heart: Edward, archdeacon of London, moved by grace, entered the monastery of Canterbury, and became secretary, thanks to his knowledge of affairs. But the first ardour flagged: it irked him that he should receive public correction from men inferior to him both in rank and learning: the world, the embraces of women, gracious homes and easy society called him: he made all ready for flight, and went on the appointed night to the tomb of St. Dunstan to plead for his understanding and his grace. Leaving the church

[1] Rodulfus Glaber, *op. cit.* 718.

[2] Baluze, *Formulae.* Migne, *P.L.* lxxxvii. 867.

[3] *Hist. Calam.* x. Migne, 178, c. 156.

[4] *Jocelyn of Brakelond* (Camden Society), p. 93.

he found the door barred by a monk of terrible aspect, the Saint himself: tried in vain to pass him; the third time received the sentence: "Thou shalt not go: but thou shalt die, and here." For two months he languished, confessed himself, and died a penitent.[1]

One sees the making of a *vagus* in a good many stories; the clerk in the chapel of Queen Constance who stole a candlestick, being hard driven for money, and lived in terror of her wrath: and the kindly King, who had seen it from his stall, sent for him and bade him sell the candlestick and make his way home: for Robert was very like the Abbé in *Les Misérables*.[2] There is another story about a *vagus* and candlesticks told by Caesarius von Heisterbach: a disreputable clerk who came to the Cistercians at Clairvaux for what he could pick up, stayed a year, but found himself no nearer the altar, religiously guarded; took the vows, to secure his object, and then to his amazement found himself coveting the grace of God rather than His candlesticks, and so changed his heart that he died Prior, and would many a time tell the story to the edifying of his novices.[3] The twelfth century injunction that no monk or canon regular is to read either medicine or civil law ("though they make a pretence of doing it for the weal of the brethren's bodies, and the better guidance of their business")[4] is responsible for some defections: a monk so doing and failing to return in two months is excommunicated. There is a letter from a scholar-monk in one of the Italian *Summae*, entreating restoration: desire of learning had beguiled him to the

[1] Eadmer, *Vita S. Dunstani*, 19. (Stubbs, *Memorials of St. Dunstan*, pp. 241-5).

[2] Helgaldus, *Vita Roberti Regis Franc.* Migne, 141 c. 194.

[3] Caesarius von Heisterbach, *Dialogus Miraculorum* (Strange) i. 3. "Quemdam clericum actu trutanum, quales per diversas vagari solent provincias." Cf. "*Du clerc Golias qui volt rober s'Abaie.*" Méon, *Nouveau Recueil*, ii. 447.

[4] Alexander III., 1163. *Chart. Univ. Paris*, i. 3, repeated by Boniface VIII. "ut periculosa religiosis evagandi materia subtrahatur" (*Sexti Decret.* iii. *Tit.* 24. c. 2). See Appendix E.

University, but want and remorse have disciplined him: may he come back?[1] And there is the worst type, as in the inquest in Oxford, for instance, on the body of poor Margery of Hereford, stabbed under the left breast, who died on Sunday, 27th April, 1299; she had been brought by an unknown clerk to his lodging in Brasenose, and when she asked for the money he had promised her, he drew out his knife and stabbed her.[2] "Non inventus est" nor any goods either, not even the "weak coverlet" which one man left behind him in his haste. But these enforced recruits are not the true *vagus*, though the like of them made the order an abomination to all decent men. The *vagus* is born, not made: none shall be accounted fit, say the "new decretals" of the Ordo Vagorum who is not of an inconstant and jocund mind, a world's wanderer—

> "et recurrat
> et transcurrat
> et discurrat
> in orbe rotunda."[3]

There are minor conditions: that he shall never be up in time for matins, for there are *phantasmata* abroad in the early morning, which is the reason why early risers are never quite sane: that no man may have two coats: if he is given a tunic he must, to live honestly, immediately dice away his cloak, and he who enjoys the possession of a shirt shall in no case extend the privilege to breeches: two pairs of boots means excommunication. But first and last, it is the life of the road.

> "Let no one in his travelling
> Go against the wind
> Let him not, because he's poor,
> Look as though he whined.

[1] Guido Faba, B.N. MS. 8653, f. 52.

[2] Rogers, *Oxford City Documents*, p. 154.

[3] *Carm. Burana*, 177: "Nunquam erit habilis
Qui non est instabilis
Et corde iocundo
Non sit vagus mundo . . ."

Let him set before himself
Hope beguiling.
Ever after sorrow comes
Fate that's smiling." [1]

"They live by their vices," say the Church Councils: a hard saying, but not so damning as it sounds. From the mediaeval point of view it would have applied equally well to Goldsmith, who jigged his way through Europe with a flute and a trick of Latin disputation: the flute got him bite and sup from the country folk; his argumentative tongue and dog-Latin three days board and lodging in a monastery, for that was the prize of a victory in debate: and possibly it was in some of the older monastic libraries that he picked up his odd and unexpected knowledge of the Middle Ages, of Luitprand for instance, whom he thoroughly enjoyed. The twelfth and thirteenth century *vagus* was very like him: and the music-making that would have damned Goldsmith damned these also. From the fourth century the "*clericus inter epulas cantans*," singing at banquets, had been singled out for discipline: he was to lose his office, though not yet his privilege.[2] For the Puritan attack on the

[1] *Carm. Burana*, 193:

"Ordo noster prohibet
Matutinas plane
Sunt quedam phantasmata
que vagantur mane,
per que nobis veniunt
visiones vane;
sed qui tunc surrexerit
non est mentis sane . . .

Nemo in itinere
contrarius sit ventis,
nec a paupertate
ferat vultum dolentis,
sed spem sibi proponat
semper consulentis,
nam post grande malum
sors sequitur gaudentis."

[2] See Appendix E, p. 245.
The jongleur's profession was the most degrading a clerk could have; but it was also the most natural. It was a clerk's business to sing. A

stage in the seventeenth century is emasculate in comparison with the mediaeval onslaught on the jongleur and the mime : above all on the goliard, the clerk who had abandoned his business of edifying for this degrading business of the *amuseur.* A set of clerical reprobates keep company down the centuries : the *clericum inter epulas cantantem* ; *clericum scurrilibus joculatorem* ; *clericum qui tabernas intraret* ; *clericum vel monachum fugitivum vel vagum.*[1] Not many councils refrain from pillorying one at least : and sometimes all four appear in the dock together. There are interesting variations in the attack. Toledo in the seventh century uses Petrarch's own word "illa vesania," and empowers any ecclesiastical authority to lay the vagabond by the heels and do his best to reclaim him, though one feels that the severity tails off at the last : and canons less wordy come from Autun, Berghamstead, Ireland.[2] Boniface in the eighth century speaks his mind on pilgrimage, on which the gravest minds in the church had always some reserve : forbids the pilgrimage to Rome wholly to women and nuns : "there is not a town in France or Italy," he says, "where there is not an English harlot or adulteress."[3] In the ninth, Benedict of Aniane rehearses what everyone else has said : the ninth century councils are a small body of divinity, and explain the reason of things at length, how music, for instance, softens the virility of the mind, and is to be dreaded by ecclesias-

singing master, touting for custom, declares it is the foundation of all ecclesiastical functions (B.N. MS. 8654, f. 14), and the tragic emperor, Henry IV., the mediaeval Lear, came begging to his own church at Spires, to be taken in as a clerk, urging that he could read and sing in the choir. See the story in Caesarius von Heisterbach (iv. 9) of the clerks who sang loudly and proudly, and then were *gloriantibus* as those who *bene et fortiter* praised the Lord, but found that the Devil had put all the voices in a sack. And the clerks who sang so that they scared the crows from the steeple. Hauréau, *Robert de Sorbon*, p. 16.

[1] See Appendix E.

[2] Mansi, *Concilia*, x. 769 ; xi. 123 ; xii. 112, 121.

[3] Labbe et Cossart, *Concilia*, vi. 1565. *Ep. Bonifac. ad Cuthbert*, "De corrigendis vitiis Anglorum."

tics,[1] and even by laymen: while the Irish vagabonds come in for a full share of denunciation. The Emperor is implored not to encourage absentee clerics about the court, and to have a strict inquisition made in Italy to recall fugitives, for Italy seems to have become a kind of Paradise for free souls.[2] They were already at their trick of parody, for San Zeno's first communion addresses were made the basis of a wicked *Feast of St. Cyprian*, attended by most of the worthies of both Testaments, not at their best, but with just enough dreadful resemblance to make it a useful help to memory. So at least the great Hrabanus Maurus saw it; and actually commends it to Lothair II.[3] Also the good wine of Angers which the Three Musketeers so loved got its fame early, in

"Once there was an Abbot, Abbot of Angers,"

whose long saturation in it ended in making him incorruptible, at least as to the flesh.[4] It may have been one of the songs sung by the three young men of the *familia*, the household of the timid Abbot of Ferrières, who sat up late at night when all decent monks were in bed, roaring catches without mitigation or remorse of voice till they rolled in drunken slumber above the very pavement where the good St. Aldricus slept his last sleep. Yet God unwilling to have his saint's repose thus profaned, removed the three delinquents, and the faithful coming to mass next morning found them variously disposed in the street beyond the bridge.[5] Shortly after, the Abbot gave up his riotous charge, and died in peace, a simple monk of Fleury: the rule passed into the stronger hands of Servatus Lupus, whose scholarship did not interfere with

[1] Mansi, xiv. 813.

[2] *M. G. H. Concilia Car. Aev.* i. 635, 675. See Appendix E.

[3] *Poet. Lat. Car.* iv. 857 ff. *Epist. Car.* v. 506. See Novati, *Studi critici*, p. 178 ff.: Lapôtre, *Mélanges d'archéologie* . . . 1901.

[4] *Poet. Lat. Car.* iv. p. 591.

[5] Migne, *P.L.* cv. 807.

his sense of discipline.[1] In the first decades of the tenth century, under Walter of Sens, appears the council, the bone of controversy, against the ribald clerks "who are vulgarly called the family of Golias," the first apparition of the genial Pantagruelian prelate whose sons are as the sands of the sea, who ate and drank more at one sitting than the Blessed Martin did in his whole life,[2] and whose countenance appears so often in the thirteenth century councils,

"As though through dungeon grate he peered
With broad and burning face."

The authenticity of the council has been justly disputed: Golias makes that one meteoric appearance, and darkness swallows him until the first decade of the thirteenth century: his presence in the text is almost certainly a clerical error.[3] But the presence of his offspring, the ribalds, in the century is past controversy:[4] and the familiar quartet continues to appear in the dock. The sack of so many monasteries by the Northmen, the intrusion of lively secular clerks, and their final expulsion (leaving the monasteries like rotting timber, says an English charter indignantly)[5] added enormously to the

[1] Radulfus Tortaire, Migne, clx. 1200, on Gaubert, "vir timoratus qui etiam abbatis officio functus fuerat, sed sibi subjectorum mores nequaquam emendare valens." I am indebted for the reference to Mr. J. W. Thompson's extremely interesting article on the authenticity of the Council of Sens, in *Studies in Philology*, 1923, but the monastery is Ferrières, not St. Columba of Sens.

[2] Summa of Simon of Tournai, c. 1202, "praelatus ille Golias qui una nocte millia michas et venalia exhausit et fora, et in salsamentis plus illa nocte quam sanctus Martinus tota vita sua consumpsit." Hauréau, *Not. et Extr.* i. 169.

[3] See Genestal, *Priv. Fori*, p. 165. Quoted in Appendix E, p. 254.

[4] See Appendix E. The *Ecbasis Captivi* was written to beguile the tedium of a monastic prison, evidently by a *vagus* under discipline—*Me vero vacuo, claustrali carcere septo.* St. Goslin, Bishop of Toul, 922, took in hand a general reform. St. Aper especially had sunk very low. See Voigt, *Quellen und Forschungen zur Sprache . . . der germanischen Völker*, viii. pp. 4-8.

[5] Mansi, xix. 47. Edgar's Charter to Malmesbury, 974 A.D.

crowd on the roads:[1] and the glimpses that one gets of the clerks of St. Ghislain, who lost their saint by taking him about to fairs,[2] is worthy of the worst traditions. Eleventh century letters of licence for a clerk going on a journey describe the *vagus* as the fraud that he is, but hasten to add, "The present bearer is not such."[3] The twelfth century with its craze for scholarship and the utter disillusionment that followed it increased still further the wandering population.[4] There are the genuine scholars, like Nicholas Breakspear or John of Salisbury, or later, Reuchlin and Ulrich von Hutten, making their difficult way from one great school to another,[5] or the less ambitious, going home for the holidays.[6] There is the baser type, the unfrocked or runaway monk or clerk, and the

[1] William of Malmesbury complains that that monastery was become a *stabulum clericorum*; yet the body of the blessed Aldhelm was discovered by these *irregulares et vagos*. (*Gesta Reg. Ang.* ii. 147). The clerks at Winchester were offered their choice between regular profession or surrender of the monastery, and chose "mollem vitam, tunc tota insula incertis vagabantur sedibus."

[2] *Analecta Boll. Rainer. Miracula St. Ghislani*, ix.; Armitage Robinson, *Life and Times of St. Dunstan*, p. 137.

[3] From Alberic de Montecassino: Rockinger, *Briefsteller und Formelbucher*, p. 35.

[4] *Carm. Bur.* 89:

"O ars dialectica
Nunquam esses cognita,
Quae tot facis clericos
Exsules et miseros."

[5] Dr. Johnson himself would have been a *vagus*, if the mood had lasted that took him in his rooms above the gateway in Pembroke, when Dr. Panting, the Master, passing underneath, heard a burst of soliloquy, "Well, I have a mind to see what is done in other places of learning. I'll go and visit the Universities abroad. I'll go to France and Italy. I'll go to Padua—and I'll mind my business." Ulrich von Hutten ran away from Fulda to appear an undergraduate at Cologne, thence to Erfurt, Frankfort, Leipsic, read law at Bologna, and there discovered Aristophanes and Lucian, whence the *Epistolae Obscurorum Virorum*. Reuchlin studied at Freiburg, was singing-man to the Margrave of Baden, studied Greek at Paris and at Basle, jurisprudence at Orleans and Poictiers.

[6] "When I came home from the schools in the summer, my father hardly knew me, I was so blackened (*denigratus*) with tramping in the sun" (Robert of Sorbon, quoted by Haskins, "Paris University in Thirteenth Century Sermons," *Amer. Hist. Rev.* x. 24).

type, not so base but just as irreclaimable, "the drunken M.A.," the scholar without influence or money to get him a benefice, who has found that Homer himself, without money in his purse to get him an audience, may go and live as the flies do. For himself he has done with the scholar's vigils and the scholar's fasts: a roast is better than cheerless salads, and your warm bed, and a wench,[1] and his Litany runs "From scanty dinner and a bad cook: from a poor supper and a bad night: and from drinking wine that has turned, Good Lord deliver us."[2] By the beginning of the thirteenth century they have actually a burlesque order, with Golias for its legendary Grand-master. An English goliard, writing, like Mr. Verdant Green, to headquarters in France, propounds a series of points on which he would be resolved, such as whether it is better to make love to Rose or Agnes: to eat boiled beef or little fishes driven into the net: resolve him that no longer he may live without decorum.[3] The late twelfth and early thirteenth centuries saw religious orders springing up like mushrooms, and there is probably little more substance in the *ordo vagorum* than in the rest of their impish parodies. But something of the kind must have existed, for the Church councils speak of it as both an *ordo* and a *secta*.[4] And now at last the battle is joined.

[1] *Latin Poems . . . Walter Mapes*, 157:

"Adora pecuniam, qui deos adoras.
Cur struis armaria? cur libros honoras?
longas fac Parisiis vel Athenis moras?
Si nihil attuleris, ibis, Homere, foras! . . .
ipse licet venias musis comitatus, Homere. . . .
quis ferret vigilias frigidam-que cellam
tutius est iacuisse toro et tenuisse puellam. . . .
malo saginatas carnes quam triste legumen."

See Petrus Pictor, B.N. MS. Lat. 14191, f. 1:

"Poenitet esse probum, poenitet esse poetam,
Qui numquam duco noctemve diemve quietem."

[2] Montaiglon, *Recueil des poësies françaises*, vii. p. 67.

[3] *Latin Poems . . . Walter Mapes*, p. 69. See also *Carmina Burana*, 177, on the visit of Simon to the brethren in Alsace; 193, on the Constitution of the Order; 195, on its resemblance to the Apostles.

[4] Council of Salzburg, 1291. See Appendix E.

The long patience of the Church is exhausted; and in 1231 she launches, not indeed excommunication, but the second heaviest thunderbolt, degradation:[1] the *clericus* found *vagus* is henceforth *clericus* no longer: he is to be shaven, so that no trace may be left of that order to which he is a disgrace: henceforth he will go out from the bishop's or the monastery prison, an Ishmaelite indeed.[2] The *vagus* is stripped of his dearest possession, the one thing that set him apart from the "people without the law," the other gentlemen of the road, the clowns and the tumblers and the performing monkeys and the dancing bears, he who had held his head so high, because he knew his Lucan and his Ovid, and broke his wildest jests in the ancient tongue.[3] To lay him by the heels, the Church will even call in the secular arm: repudiation—in the Middle Ages—could no further go. Any ecclesiastic harbouring or countenancing such persons is himself liable to fine and suspension.[4] It has its effect: after this, degeneracy is swift.

[1] Council at Rouen, 1231; Château-Gonthier, 1231; Sens. 1239. See Appendix E. From one standpoint excommunication is the lighter, for a clerk, though excommunicate, has still the protection of the Church.

[2] Salzburg, 1291.

[3] Cf. the Arch-poet (Manitius, p. 37):

> " Presules Italici, presules avari,
> potius idolatrę debent nominari
> vix quadrantem tribuunt pauperi scolari,
> qui per dona talia poterit ditari ?
> Doleo, cum video leccatores multos
> penitus inutiles penitusque stultos,
> nulla prorsus animi ratione fultos,
> sericis et variis indumentis cultos."

[4] Council at S. Hippolyte (Passau), 1284. See Appendix E.

Cf. Salimbene's account of the Bishop of Parma (*op. cit.* p. 62), who was all things to all men, *cum clericis clericus . . . magnus dispensator; largus, liberalis, curialis,* but gave over much *trufatoribus,* for which he was accused before the Pope. A fine scholar, notably in canon law, and an expert at chess. He had for a long time indulged one Gherardino Segalelli, who had founded an Apostolic order; after a horrid scandal he dismissed them the diocese; and to so great madness did their leader come that he turned jongleur, "in habitu histrionum incedit et factus joculator per plateas et vicos salticando vadit" (pp. 256, 619.)

The word goliard soon becomes the vilest in the language. By the end of the fourteenth century the law courts use it as equivalent to the brothel-keeper.[1]

There is no denying that the Church had good reasons for its exasperation. If Homer knocked at the gates of the Curia in vain, and was driven off to live with the flies, he soon develops the wasp's, not to say the hornet's, sting. The Albigensian heresy had left the Church sensitive; a good deal of dirty linen had been washed in public, and the *vagi* undertake that task with a dreadful glee. They say no harder things than Innocent III said at the Lateran Council in 1215, but they say them in portable form: a folio of parchment is less dangerous than an indecent distich about the morals of the Papal legate sung all over Paris.[2] And the distichs are not all of them indecent. Golias, the jovial shepherd of so many black sheep, is the archtype of the loose-living prelate; but a good many of his satires against his fellow-churchmen have the weight of a real indignation behind them, and something of the coldness of Swift's steel. "Their God is their belly: and they obey that which is written, *Seek first the Kingdom of God.*"[3] And once or twice there is the apocalyptic power, the genius of Ezekiel or of Blake—

> "O truth of Christ,
> O most dear rarity,
> O most rare Charity,
> Where dwellst thou now?

[1] See Genestal, *Privilegium Fori*, p. 235.

[2] Matthew Paris, *Chron. Maj.* 1229. Cf. *Hilarii Versi et Ludi*, Champollion Figeac, xiv. *Papa Scholasticus*. Compare Hamlet on the ill word of the players with Salimbene's story of the wisdom of the Cardinal Octavian, Papal Legate in Lombardy, 1247, when during a procession a joculator cried, "Room for the man who betrayed the Roman curia, and many times tricked the Church." And the cardinal sent money, saying, "pecuniae obediunt omnia," so well judging that the joculator crossed over to another place on the route, and cried that there was no better cardinal, and worthy to be Pope on his return.

[3] Wright, T., *Latin Poems, attributed to Walter Mapes*, p. xl. "Magister Golias de quodam abbate."

In the Valley of Vision ?
On Pharaoh's throne ?
On high with Nero ?
With Timon alone ? "

Follows a vision of Truth bound and tortured at the judgment seat. . . . Then Love replied :

" Man, wherefore didst thou doubt ?
Not where thou wast wont to find
My dwelling, in the Southern wind.
Not Decretal and not Bull,
Not in casque nor yet in cowl.
But on the road from Jericho,
I come with a wounded man." [1]

Moral indignation is a heady wine on an empty stomach, and their stomachs were often empty. " The hunger of the order," " famine de povre clerc" passed into a proverb.[2] The *vagus* who wrote his animal story in the monastery prison at Toul says that if you speak it right through it may get you a piece of bread.[3] One of their songs ends suddenly and dramatically, with a clutch at a proffered shirt.[4] " They go about in public naked," says the Council at Salzburg, " lie in bake-ovens, frequent taverns, games, harlots, earn their bread by their vices and cling with inveterate obstinacy to their sect, so that no hope of their amendment remaineth." [5]

" *Et ne nos inducas* : desire
Must take you, God, such life to share.
Barefoot in your shirt you go
Through the heat and through the snow." [6]

[1] *Carm. Bur.* xciii. [2] Bedier, *Les Fabliaux*, p. 391.

[3] *Ecbasis Captivi*, l. 42. " Si recitas totam, panis mercabere tortam.'

[4] " Camisia
Detur ! Pia
Virgo solvat pretium ! "
Notices et Extraits, xxxii. p. 297.

[5] Mansi, xxiv. 1077. See Appendix E.

[6] Jubinal, *Jongleurs et Trouvères*, " Paternoster du Vin," p. 69 :
" *Et ne nos inducas* : envie
Vous doinst Diex de mener tel vie,
S'irez en langes et deschaus
Et par les froiz et par les chaus ! "

" Many a jest I've broken,
Many a penny spent,
In many a square and many an inn,
And whoe'er it displeases, I'll do it again;
For if they chase me, I shall fly,
And if they kill me, I shall die." [1]

" They cling with inveterate obstinacy to their sect," say the perplexed Bishops in council: for " the wind that lifts when the sails are loosed " did not stir in the chapter house of Salzburg. But it stirs in everything the goliards have written.

" a l'entree de mai
A Orliens, la bone cité
Ou j'ai par mainte fois esté,
L'aventure est et bone et bele,
Et le rime fraiche et nouvele." [2]

The goliard of the later days is Panurge at his ungentlemanly worst: but the original goliard, starved cat though he is, has more of Pantagruel than Panurge. His oracle is the oracle of the Holy Bottle, *Trinq*! Bacchus and Scacchus are his gods, but he can sing, and the songs that he jigged out in taverns and alehouses, in monastic refectories after supper, at the tables of easy-going prelates,[3] caught the ear of Europe. Whatever his life was, the songs that were his repertoire would challenge most Elizabethan or seventeenth century anthologies

[1] " J'ai mainte parole espandue,
Et mainte maille despendue,
Et dedans taverne et en place,
Encore ferai, cui qu'il displace,
Car s'on me chace, je fuirai
Et s'on me tue, je morrai."
" Le Dit des Boulangiers," *Jongleurs et Trouvères*, p. 138.

[2] Montaiglon-Raynaud, vi. 139.

[3] See the complaint of Absolon of St. Victor on the secular prelates, " in palatio ubique resonat cantus de gestibus Hectoris, mensa ferculis, thalamus iocis impudicis jocundus est " (Hauréau, *Not. et Ext.* iv. 30), and the continual complaint of Church councils. There were not many like Foulques, Bishop of Toulouse, who " when he heard any song sung which he had composed while yet he was *in saeculo* [Foulques, the scourge of the Provençal heretics, was once a famous trouvère], on that

either for melody or for romantic passion, and for comedy, go far beyond them. Even at his wickedest, he is never *louche*: he is only *magnus trutannus et magnus trufator*, like Salimbene's crow.[1] He was not really Salimbene's crow: he belonged to the papal legate, Gregory of Montelongo, but he was a *maximus truffator*, and when the house was full of pilgrims, for it was near the river, the crow would get up in the middle of the night when all were sound asleep and cry in a shipman's voice: "Who's for Bologna? Come! come! come! Quick! quick! quick! Up! up! Come! come! Bring your baggage! All aboard! All aboard! Port your helm!" and up would rise the stranger guests, who knew not the *truffas* and deceptions of that crow, and wait with all their goods all night on the river bank, marvelling greatly. That fowl was inspired by Golias, and came to a bad end: a blind beggar whose shins he used to nip threw his stick at him, and he trailed a broken wing.

The goliard, too, trails a broken wing. One hears of jongleurs who came to fortune. William the Conqueror gave his minstrel "three vills and five carucates of land" in Gloucestershire:[2] Walther von der Vogelweide, in a higher rank, got his little fief, tired at last of warming himself at another man's fire. But one seldom hears of a goliard coming to good. Nicholas, a *clericus vagus*, whom they called the arch-poet, fell

same day did eat naught but bread and water. And it befell that once when he was at the court of the King of France, at table a certain jongleur began to sing one of his songs and straightway the bishop demanded water to be brought to him, and did eat nothing save bread and water."—Sermon by Robert de Sorbon (Hauréau, *Mem. Acad. Inscr.* xxxi. 2). "You know Foulques' glorious speech to Dante in the IXth *Paradiso* on the way certain things are *not* repented of in heaven?" G.S.

"Non però qui si pente, ma si ride
non della colpa, ch' a mente non torna,
ma del valor ch' ordinò e provide."

[1] Salimbene, *M.G.H.* xxxii. p. 391. The phrase haunts Salimbene like a refrain: he never wearies of it.

[2] Chambers, *The Mediaeval Stage*, i. 43.

sick and thought he was going to die and came to the Cistercians at Heisterbach, and was received with some ado into the order. But when the devil was well, *cum quadam irrisione,* he cast aside the cowl and fled.[1] And Theobald, famous all over Cologne for his wild jesting, given wholly to wine and dice, came to the order and was received as a novice and edified them all for a while, washing clothes and drinking the water they were washed in, to the discomforting of his inwards and the casting out of the devil of pride. And then he took leave, to go to see his friends in France, he said, and indeed came back, but the old habit had gripped him. He disappeared, this time for good. Another *vagus,* drifting past the monastery, gave them news of him. He had gone back to his old life but in the end died in penitence, confessing himself to a secular priest.[2] They are clear-sighted enough. They know what ails them. Surian, parodist of Eberhard II, Archbishop of Salzburg, knew the brevity of that summer day, the swallow's restlessness, and with it, *inerti stultitia,* the inertia of folly. Driven out by the laymen, turned away at the door by the clerks, "bats are we," says the Archbishop of the Wanderers, "that find no place either with beast or bird." [3] They know the full rigour of their inordinate order, *rigorem inordinati nostri ordinis,* but they abide by it. They will write a Dicers' Mass with a

[1] Heisterbach was kinder than some monasteries. Philip of Ottisberg, canon of Cologne, studying under Rudolf in Paris, was touched by divine grace and left the school, giving all his fine clothes to the poor scholars, and came to the Cistercians at Bonnevaux, asking to be made a novice. But the brethren seeing him *cappa trita atque vetusta* judged him to be a *scholarem pauperem et vagum* and at first refused him admission. Caes. von Heisterbach, i. 38 : ii. 15.

[2] Caes. von Heist. iv. 6.

[3] Surian is writing a burlesque dispensation to free the church of which the good Sighard is archdeacon from any further extortion by the Wanderers. It is an astonishing document; the Arch-poet's *Confessio* in prose, with the bitterness distilled from half a century of vagabondage added. The full text is a complete commentary on the church councils denouncing the order. For text and translation see Appendix C.

"Fraud to thee, Decius," [1] but Decius is the third person of their Trinity, and they politely offer membership to the Almighty Himself if he will learn to throw a main.[2] One thing they share with Villon: they have no sentiment in them. The word is a naked sword. Ronsard wrote an epitaph for a dead actor,

> "Never while you lived, Mernable,
> Had you either house or table.
> Never, poor soul, did you see
> On your fire a pot to be.
> Death to you is profitable,
> Now you need not pot nor table,
> And what you never had before,
> You've a house, for evermore."

It is consummate, but no goliard would have written it; it is too tender. What they did write was the *Credo au Ribaut.*[3]

A goliard is dying: the priest sent for in haste speaks comfortable words: have comfort, good son: let him but recite his *Credo*.

> "That will I, Sir, and hear me now.
> *Credo*—in dice I well believe,
> That got me often bite and sup,
> And many a time hath had me drunk,
> And many a time delivered me
> From every stitch and every penny.
> *In Deum*—never with my will
> Gave Him a thought nor ever will.
> The other day I took a shirt
> From a ribald and I diced it,
> And lost, and never gave it back.

[1] *Carm. Bur.* 189, "Incipit Officium Lusorum." *Vide* Barbazon, *Fabliaux et Contes*, iv. 485:

[2]
> "Et je vous dis par fin convent
> que vous serez de nostre gent,
> S'aus trois dez vous poez amordre
> Par tens porrez entrer en l'ordre.
> *Et ne nos inducas*, envie
> Vous doinst Diex de mener tel vie."

"Paternoster du Vin" (*Jongleurs et Trouvères*, p. 70).

[3] *Barbazon-Meon.* iv. p. 445.

If I die, he can have mine.
Put it in writing, 'tis my will,
I would not like it were forgot.
Patrem—at St. Denis in France,
Good Sir, I had a father once,
Omnipotentem in his having,
Money and horses and fine wearing,
And by the dice that thieveth all things
I lost and gamed it all away. . . .
Creatorem who made all
I've denied—He has his will
Of me now. I know I'm dying,
Nothing here but bone and hide.
Coeli—of heaven ever think ?
Nay, but the wine that I could drink.
Et terrae—there was all my joy.
Do you think that I believe
More *in Jhesum* than the tavern
Better love I him who's host
There, than *Christum filium eius*.
Watch the roast turn on the spit,
And the wine that's clear and green,
Orleans, Rochelle, Auxerre,
That's the joy that's *unicum*

. . . . . .

To drink and wench and play at dice
Seem to me no such mighty sins. . . .
Never man I know *descendit*
Ad infernum for a game.
Ask thou something else of me. . . .
Ad caelos will no man go
Because he aped a holy show.
But he who *sedit* by a lass
And hath his three dice in his hand
Is in the tavern better set
Than *ad dexteram Dei patris*.
I'd like well to be come again
Venturus where I squandered most—
'Twould be in Paris, by my soul,
There was a girl there, she was fair. . . .
Credo in wine that's fair to see,
And in a barrel of my host

More than in *the Holy Ghost.*
The tavern is my sweetheart, yea,
And *Holy Church* is not for me.
Remissionem of the bill
You'll not get that, my dear, for nothing,
You'll give your hat, or cape, or coat. . . .
But when I've drunk a good strong wine
That leaves me well and warm within,
Little I care for *peccatorum.*
Et corporis—the body's lust
I do perform. Sir Priest, I chafe
At thinking of that other life.
I tell you, 'tis not worth a straw.
And I would pray to the Lord God
That He will in no kind of way
Resurrectionem make of me,
So long as I may drench the place
With good wine where I'll be laid,
And so pray I of all my friends
That if I can't, themselves will do't,
And leave me a full pot of wine
Which I may to the Judgment bring. . . .
Vitam aeternam wilt Thou give,
O Lord God ? wilt Thou forgive
All my evil, well I know it,
Amen. Priest, I now am through with't.
Through with life. Death hath its pain.
Too much. . . . Too much. . . . This agony—
I'm dying. I to God commend you.
I ask it of you—Pray for me."

CHAPTER IX

THE SCHOLARS' LYRIC

"AND thereafter," said Abelard, "I made no new songs of the mysteries of philosophy, but of Love's secrets only."[1] In this, as in so many things, Abelard is the protagonist of the new scholarship. He came to love late: fastidiousness and a white heat of the intellect had kept him chaste, and he had small interest in lay society.[2] The old canon had no scruple in bringing the mightiest scholar in Paris under the same roof with his niece;[3] was inordinately flattered that this man who had cardinals as scholars should think the girl, Hypatia though she was,[4] worth his pains. Abelard was to read with her in such leisure as his weightier studies left him. No opportunity was wanting: the same trance fell on the quiet house in the Rue des Chantres as on the ship becalmed off the Cornish coast: and the two drank together a cup as fatal as the

[1] *Hist. Cal.* cap. vi. *P.L.* clxxviii. c. 128.

[2] *Ib.* v. c. 126. "Quia igitur scortorum immunditiam semper abhorrebam, et ab excessu et frequentatione nobilium feminarum studii scholaris assiduitate revocabar, nec laicarum conversationem multum noveram, prava mihi . . . fortuna . . . nacta est occasionem qua me facilius de sublimitatis huius fastigio prosterneret."

[3] Cap. vi. "Quanta eius simplicitas esset vehementer admiratus." Abelard was at least moved by it. "Non facile de his quos plurimum diligimus, turpitudinem suspicamur," and bitterly accused himself "de summa proditione" (c. 128, 129).

[4] "Tu . . . et mulieres omnes evicisti, et pene viros universos superasti." Peter the Venerable, *Epist.* Migne, clxxxix. c. 347.

love draught of Tristan and Isolde. As famous too: the songs that he made for her went over all France. He had two gifts, to win any woman's heart, said Heloïse, gifts rare in a philosopher, of making and singing, making both in the classic metres and the new rhyming, and setting them to airs so lovely that even the unlettered knew his name.[1] Not one of them remains. All that is left of Abelard's verse are the Hours that he wrote for her when the sword lay between them and she was Abbess of the Paraclete, and half a dozen laments, of Dinah for her ruined lover, for the daughter of Jephthah dead in her virginity, of David over Jonathan.[2] The metres are exquisite: the matter like enough his own sorrowful fortunes and the treatment poignant enough to suggest what that gift might have been, with passion triumphant instead of crucified.

"Low in thy grave with thee
Happy to lie,
Since there's no greater thing left Love to do,
And to live after thee
Is but to die,
For with but half a soul what can Life do?

"So share thy victory
Or else thy grave,
Either to rescue thee, or with thee lie;
Ending that life for thee,
That thou didst save,
So Death, that sundereth, might bring more nigh.

[1] *Epist.* ii. Migne, *P.L.* clxxviii. c. 185. "Duo autem, fateor, tibi specialiter inerant, quibus feminarum quarumlibet animos statim allicere poteras, dictandi videlicet et cantandi gratia. Quae ceteros minime philosophos assecutos esse novimus . . . pleraque amatorio metro vel rhythmo composita reliquisti carmina, quae prae nimia suavitate tam dictaminis quam cantus saepius frequentata, tuum in ore omnium nomen incessanter tenebant, ut etiam illiteratos melodiae dulcedo tui non sineret immemores esse. . . . Et cum horum pars maxima carminum nostros decantaret amores, multis me regionibus brevi tempore nuntiavit."

[2] Migne, *P.L.* clxxviii. *Planctus Varii*, c. 1817 *et seq.*

"Peace, O my stricken Lute!
Thy strings are sleeping.
Would that my heart could still
Its bitter weeping!"[1]

Abelard himself was merciless to that memory, and one may be sure that no fragment of the love songs would be found among his own papers. But it is hardly possible that the songs of so famous a singer should perish wholly: and here and there in the anonymous songbooks of the century, a lyric may have caught something of the "shattering ecstasy of their fire."

"Take thou this rose, O rose,
Since love's own flower it is,
And by that rose
Thy lover captive is."[2]

"I suffer,
Yea, I die,
But this mine agony
I count all bliss,
Since death is life again
Upon thy lips."[3]

[1] "Vel confossus pariter
Morirer feliciter
Quum, quod amor faciat
Majus hoc non habeat.

"Et me post te vivere
Mori sit assidue,
Nec ad vitam anima
Satis est dimidia.

"Triumphi participem
Vel ruinae comitem.
Ut te vel eriperem,
Vel tecum occumberem.

"Vitam pro te finiens,
Quam salvasti totiens,
Ut et mors nos jungeret
Magis quam disjungeret.

"Do quietem fidibus.
Vellem ut et planctibus
Sic possem et fletibus!" Migne, clxxviii, c. 1822.

[2] *Carmina Burana*, 147:

"Suscipe Flos florem
quia flos designat amorem.
Illo de flore
nimio sum captus amore."

[3] *Ibid*, 42:

"Amare crucior, morior
vulnere, quo glorior.
Eia si me sanare
uno vellet osculo
que cor felici iaculo
gaudet vulnerare."

The influence of the actual lyric must have been potent enough : the power of the actual story on the imagination of his student generation incalculable. It is not that the undergraduate of any generation needs notable examples : but there was a difference between this over-mastering passion staged before their eyes, with its tragic end to give it consecration like that of Tristan or of Lancelot, and the casual encounters of the Rue St. Jacques, the amorous hesitations between Rose and Agnes. The proof of it is the fashion in which the story was remembered. In the *Metamorphosis*, the twelfth century Love's Assize, Heloïse comes solitary among the great lovers of the world, still seeking the "Palatine," now a stranger to the heart where once she held him.[1] Jean de Meung was the *vrai bourgeois*, the type of clerk whose conception of love was based chiefly on Juvenal and the Ars Amandi and his own apparently squalid experiences: but he translated the Letters, and in his speech of Heloïse comes as near reverence as his ill-conditioned and extremely able mind permits. That is at the end of the thirteenth century: by the fifteenth Villon has set Heloïse among the *Dames du temps jadis*,

> " Où est la tres sage Hellois,
> Pour qui fut chastré et puis moyne
> Pierre Esbaillart à Saint Denis ?
> Pour son amour ot cette essoyne . . .
> Mais où sont les neiges d'antan ? "

It was more than two hundred years since Peter the Venerable had brought Abelard's body to be buried in the Paraclete, and had been thanked in Heloïse' stark phrase, "You have given us the body of our master."[2] But for such as these the memory of youth is long.

Already, in the earlier decades of the twelfth century,

[1] *Metamorphosis Goliae*, 213-17. (Wright, *Latin Poems . . . Walter Mapes*, p. 29.)

[2] Petrus Ven. *Epist.* xxi. (Migne, *P.L.* clxxxix. c. 427).

the scholars were praising their ladies in rhymes and verses. The war between Athene and Aphrodite that is the conceit of so many of their songs, and that beguiled Shakespeare himself into writing the undergraduate comedy of Love's Labour Lost, had already begun. Sometime, probably towards the middle of the century, a lively clerk invented a burlesque church council, held at Remiremont in the ides of April, to decide whether it is better to be loved by a clerk than by a cavalier.[1] Remiremont had a gallant reputation: and its beautiful Abbess Judith II was the sovereign lady of the unknown Spanish poet-monk of Ripoll.[2] No layman was present at the council, only *honesti clerici* from Toul, true lovers: also were all veteran ladies excluded, to whom all joy and desire of youth is tedious. The *quasi evangelium* was from Ovid, *doctor egregius*, and thereafter love songs were sung by the two Elizabeths. The cardinal lady opened the session garlanded with a thousand flowers of May, herself flower of the world, Spring's own child.

"If you were April's lady,
And I were Lord of May—"

"Vos, quarum est gloria amor et lascivia
Atque delectatio Aprilis cum Maio—"

"You, whose glory is love and dalliance and the delight of April with May, to you hath Love, god of all lovers wheresoever they be, sent me to visit you and inquire into your manner of life: so hath May determined and April counselled it. Mine is it to correct, and mine to spare." The two Elizabeths, de Fauçon and de Granges, uphold

[1] *Concilium in Monte Romarici*, edited from MS. Trier, 1081 by Waitz (*Zeitschrift für deutsch. Alterth.* vii) and by W. Meyer, *Das Liebesconcil in Remiremont*, 1914. See Langlois (E.), *Origines et Sources du Roman de la Rose*, 1891, pp. 6 *et seq.*; P. Meyer, *Romania*, 1886, pp. 333 *et seq.* The nightingale is the champion of the clerks in *Florence et Blanchefleur*, and conquers the perroquet. But in the English version, *Melior et Ydoine*, the knights have it.

[2] *L'escole poetice di Ripoll*: *Archivum Latinitatis medii ævi* (1925), p. 196.

the courtly and honourable love of the clerks, their erudition in loving, and their "industry"; what they have loved with sweetness, they leave not lightly. A daring voice is raised on behalf of the knights, their courage, and their deeds to win their lady's grace, but borne down. The knight blazons his love everywhere: he cannot hold his tongue about it. But the clerks are discreet, as well as courtly. The whole country laughs with their joyousness: they praise us in all manner of rhymes and verses. Henceforth let there be no more knightly lovers: one lover shall suffice: and transgression be atoned by no light penitence. Follows excommunication of the rebels, and a universal Amen. The clerks prided themselves as much as the trouvères on their knowledge of the subtleties of love,[1] and one of the most ambitious poems in the *Carmina Burana* is a midnight vision of Love in anger at the spoiling of his temple and the profaning of his mysteries by the vulgar.[2] Chrétien de Troyes had translated the *Ars Amandi* about the middle of the century, and Ovid was a mystery no longer. But Love might have spared his wrath. The secret of the scholar's lyric is not in Ovid, but rather in the "wish" copied at the back of a vocabulary of Guillaume le Breton, "And I wish that all times were April and May, and every month renew all fruits again, and every day fleurs de lis and gillyflower and violets and roses wherever one goes,

[1] *Vide* Langlois, *op. cit.*; also *Pamphilus* (ed. Baudouin), twelfth century, and André le Chapelain, *De Amore*, who records the judgments of the Courts of Love. See also the romance of *Galeran*, on the chaplain of the Abbess of Beauséjour, good, debonair and compassionate, who knew

"biau deduitz
En francoys et en latin,"

and the *Roman de Guillaume de Dol*, on the preferences of the Bishop of Chartres (ll. 356-63),

"li vesque de Chartres
S'amast miex iloec qu'en .i. sane [synod], . . .
Tantes faces cleres, vermeilles.
Et ces douz viz lons et traitiz
Et ces biaus sorcils porvoutiz."

[2] *Carmina Burana*, 156.

and woods in leaf and meadows green, and every lover should have his lass, and they to love each other with a sure heart and true, and to everyone his pleasure and a gay heart."[1] If that world ever was, it is between the folios of the manuscript of Benedictbeuern: and if too many of the writers had forgotten Hildebert's warning, have

"Lost the eternal April for the sake of a passing spring,"[2]

they have left another April, eternal in another fashion, in its stained and wrinkled pages.

For this thirteenth century manuscript,[4] copied not always intelligently from various lost originals, one of them evidently a scholar's songbook, and found a hundred years ago among the debris of a secularised monastery, is the evidence of a lost world. One of its most sounding odes is a commination, as remorseless as Milton's, of the flocking shadows pale, and the yellow-skirted fays:

"By that unspoken name of dread,
The tetra-grammaton of God,
I exorcise you, Ghosts and Fauns,
Nymphs and Sirens, Hamadryads,
Satyrs and ye Household Gods,
Get ye gone and make your home
In Chaos: trouble us no more."[4]

[1] *Hist. Litt.* xxix. 597.

[2] Hildebert, *Carmina*. Migne, clxxi. c. 1285: "Ne pro vere brevi longo careamus Aprili."

[3] See the full description of the MS. in Meyer's *Fragmenta Burana*, pp. 5-17 (1901), and, with important modifications, in the preface to the critical text by Hilka and Schumann (1931). The MS. is an anthology copied by three hands, and has delightful illuminations, a kind of fantastic fairyland, two young lovers for *Suscipe Flos florem*, a drinking scene for *Potatores exquisiti*. Meyer judged it written in the Moselle valley *c.* 1225, Schumann in Bavaria *c.* 1300 (*vide* p. vii, *supra*.)

[4] *Carmina Burana*, xxx.

"Per nomen mirabile atque ineffabile
Dei tetragrammaton,
Ut expaveatis et exhorreatis:
Vos exorcizo, Larve, Fauni, Manes,
Nymphe, Sirene, Hamadriades,
Satyri, Incubi, Penates,
ut cito abeatis, chaos incolatis,
ne vas corrumpatis christianitatis."

But, again like Milton's folk, they escape from the mirk: and the scholars even in broad sunlight see the Dryads slip from the bark of a linden tree of Touraine—

> " Estivantur Dryades
> Colle sub umbroso." [1]

To the Augustans, as to Dr. Johnson, the gods were "images of which time has tarnished the splendour." But to the twelfth and thirteenth century, they have been dead and are alive again: they are part of the resurrection miracle of the Northern Spring.

For this is the amazing discovery of mediaeval lyric. Spring comes slowly up that way, but when it comes it is an ecstasy. In the North far more than in the South, Persephone comes actually from the dead. It is a new thing, and their own. With the exception of the *Pervigilium Veneris*, the spring song hardly exists in Latin literature. Here it wells up in the theological centuries very much as the lyric *Ab æstatis foribus* springs from the dry ground of the Benedictbeuern play of the Nativity. There has been a long and scholarly discussion between the Archisynagogus and St. Augustine on the possibility of the Virgin Birth: a Flight into Egypt, Joseph with a prolix beard,[2] say the stage directions, leading the Mother and Child. They are met by the King of Egypt and his *comitatus*, singing, and this is the song.

> " At the gates of summer,
> Love standeth us to greet.
> The earth, to do him honour,
> Burgeons beneath his feet.
>
> " The flowers that aye attend him
> Laugh at the golden prime;
> Should Venus not befriend them,
> They die before their time.

[1] *Carmina Burana*, 49.

[2] *Ib.* p. 85:
" Cui assedeat Joseph in habitu honesto et prolixa barba."

"Of all things the beginning
Was on an April morn;
In Spring the earth remembereth
The day that she was born.

"And so the feast of Venus,
Wherever Love holds sway,
By mortal and immortal
Is kept a holiday." [1]

The scholars were strong in faith when they challenged Mary Virgin with that enchantment.

Nor is it the full-blown spring, the May morning of Provence, of the *Roman de la Rose*, of English fifteenth century convention. These, like Meredith, are the poets of February, when this year's birds begin calling in the twilight trees, of January itself, those days of incredible sweetness, the first stirring of the blood, the first mounting of the sap, so much more poignant than the full burgeoning.

"New Year has brought renewing, winter's gone,
Short daylight lengthens and the winds are still.
The year's first month of January's here,
And in my mind the tides still ebb and flow
For a girl's sake." [2]

It is the background of wild earth, of rain-washed April, that gives their earthiest passion its amazing cleanness. The background of Ovid's love, of Tibullus, of Propertius, is urban Roman society; the barred door and the lamp, the wine-cup and the garlands, the bed where the exquisite body is laid: at its most rustic in Horace, a garden, and the figure of a garden god: or in the *Copa*, the arbour in

[1] *Carmina Burana*, p. 91 (from the *Ludus scenicus de nativitate Domini*). See Appendix A.

[2] *Ib.* 51:

"Anni novi rediit novitas,
hiemis cedit asperitas
breves dies prolongantur,
elementa temperantur.
Subintrante Januario
mens aestu languet vario
propter puellam quam diligo."

the inn garden outside the city wall. Tibullus only is haunted by visions of a wider sky, of the old druid stone with the garlands on it: of himself at the plough, his love's white feet in the wine press. But he rouses himself: dreams, dreams—

> "Dulcius urbe quid est? An villa sit apta puellae?"
>
> "Is there aught sweeter than town? And see you your love on a farm?"

That, he knows, belongs to the youth of the world, *le beau temps de jadis*, when Venus herself went straying to the fields. But for these, *le beau temps de jadis* is come again, with the memory of a thousand springs in the blood.

"O Spring the long-desired,
The lover's hour!
O flaming torch of joy,
Sap of each flower,
All hail!
O jocund company
Of many flowers,
O many-coloured light,
All hail,
And foster our delight!
The birds sing out in chorus.
O youth, joy is before us,
Cold winter has passed on,
And the Spring winds are come!

"The earth's aflame again
With flowers bright,
The fields are green again,
The shadows deep,
Woods are in leaf again,
There is no living thing
That is not gay again.
With face of light
Garbed with delight.
Love is reborn.
And Beauty wakes from sleep."[1]

[1] *Carm. Burana*, 118. See Appendix A.

For the love of these poems, it is not Dante's, nor Petrarch's, nor the dream love of Provence. Take Jaufré Rudel's "*l'amour de lonh*"—

"When the days lengthen in the month of May,
Well pleased am I to hear the birds
Sing far away.
And when from that place I am gone,
I hang my head and make dull moan,
Since she my heart is set upon
Is far away.

"So far, that song of birds, flower o' the thorn,
Please me no more than winter morn,
With ice and sleet.
Ah, would I were a pilgrim over sea,
With staff and scrip and cloak to cover me,
That some day I might kneel me on one knee
Before her feet.

"Most sad, most joyous shall I go away,
Let me have seen her for a single day,
My love afar.
I shall not see her, for her land and mine
Are sundered, and the ways are hard to find,
So many ways, and I shall lose my way,
So wills it God.

"Yet shall I know no other love but hers,
And if not hers, no other love at all.
She hath surpassed all.
So fair she is, so noble, I would be
A captive with the hosts of paynimrie
In a far land, if so be upon me
Her eyes might fall.

"God, who hath made all things in earth that are,
That made my love, and set her thus afar,
Grant me this grace,
That I may some day come within a room,
Or in some garden gloom
Look on her face.

"It will not be, for at my birth they said
That one had set this doom upon my head,
—God curse him among men !—
That I should love, and not till I be dead,
Be loved again." [1]

Set it beside this, the nearest approach in Latin lyric to the translunary passion of Provence.

"By the dread force of love am I thus worn,
On the wheel of desire am I thus torn,
I stifle in the fire.
O Merciful, bid thou my torment cease. . .

"Mourns now the heart for that which made it glad.
The day that first of thee it knowledge had,
It chose thee for its love,
Chose thee, unsullied, none beside thee, none.

"O virgin lily, come thou to mine aid,
Thine exile prays thee to be comforted,
He knows not what he does,
And if thou wilt not succour him, he dies.

"O thou on whom Desire hath no power,
Thou in whom Chastity's reborn in flower,
Sweet still regard,
Thou who hast Truth about thee for a cloak,

"I sing to thee, I sing to thee alone,
Despise him not who asks this only boon,
That he may worship thee,
Thou who dost shine above him like a star." [2]

This man has not "fallen in love with the Countess of Tripoli for the good that he heard tell of her from the pilgrims that came from Antioch." [3] The woman is flesh

[1] Jeanroy, A., *Les Chansons de Jaufré Rudel*, v :
"Lanquan li jorn son lonc en may
M'es belhs dous chans d'auzelhs de lonh."

[2] *Carm. Bur.* 158. See Appendix A.

[3] *Chansons de Jaufré Rudel*, p. 21. "Jaufres Rudels de Blaia si fo mout gentils om, princes de Blaia : et enamoret se de la comtessa de Tripol, ses vezer, per lo ben qu'el n'auzi dire als pelegrins que venguen d'Antiocha."

and blood. It is this directness, the *I* and *thou* of passion that is their strength. It is sensual enough : there is no disguising that its end is possession :

> " If she whom I desire would stoop to love me,
> I should look down on Jove,
> If for one night my lady would lie by me,
> And I kiss the mouth I love,
> Then come Death unrelenting,
> With quiet breath consenting,
> I go forth unrepenting,
> Content, content, content,
> That such delight were ever to me lent ! "[1]

Now and then, but very rarely, it is the speech of the libertine and the braggart ;[2] now and then the bluntness of the pastoral,[3] and the pastoral is better in old French than in the scholar's speech. Once there is the directness of a child's song, even of folk song—

> " She stood in her scarlet gown,
> If any one touched her,
> The gown rustled.
> Eia !
> She stood in her scarlet gown,
> Her face like a rose,
> And her mouth like a flower.
> Eia ! "[4]

But even this has an exquisite sophistication. At its most sensual, the woman confers. There is not a snigger nor a sneer from end to end of it : downright anger : once a wholly delightful defiance,

> " I would have a man live in manly fashion,
> Yea, I shall love, but with an equal passion."[5]

Yet even this ends, laughably, ruefully, with Benedict on his knees for mercy. And this from the clerks, who are credited with having brought the scorn of women into mediaeval literature, *cette haine des femmes, faite de mépris,*

[1] *Carm. Bur.* 167.
[2] *Ib.* 45, 57.
[3] *Ib.* 63.
[4] *Ib.* 138.
[5] *Ib.* 139.

de curiosité, de crainte, de désir.[1] There is not much scorn or hatred here, and if fear, it is in Milton's sense, of the terror that is in love and beauty—

"I trembled at the shining of thy star."[2]

The truth is that the *Carmina* are not only the last flowering of the Latin tongue: they are, like the Cavalier lyric, the poetry of an aristocracy of privilege. Diverse as the authors are, from the Chancellor of Paris to a nameless goliard, they belong alike to the *ordo clericalis*: and that goliard, as one thirteenth-century canonist grimly observed,[3] wore his tonsure *patentem et latam*, flaunted the evidence of the order he disgraced. Long before the century ended he was stripped of it:

"Vente, gresle, gelle, j'ay mon pain cuit.
Je suis paillart, la paillarde me suit . . .
Nous deffuyons onneur, il nous deffuit,
En ce bordeau où tenons nostre estat."

But the *Carmina*, many of them written in the twelfth, all of them before the last decades of the thirteenth, century, belong to the moment before the degradation, when scholarship was still of great price, and the clerks held by their order. Their contemporaries are *Tristan*,[4] the prose romances of the Vulgate Arthur (themselves attributed by the MSS. to clerical authorship), the *Roman de Guillaume de Dol*, with its snatches of lyric intolerably sweet: the good brief moment before the bourgeois shoulders himself into literature, before Jean de Meung laid his not overclean hands upon the rose. The middle class come late into literature, as into history. In the twelfth century the merchant has ceased to be the "piepoudrous," and is a recognised factor in the community.[5]

[1] Bedier, *Les Fabliaux*, p. 398. [2] *Carm. Bur.* 157.

[3] Hostiensis, quoted by Genestal, *Priv. For.* 165.

[4] "Béroul, à en juger par sa connaissance de l'antiquité, par certaines de ses prétentions, serait un clerc . . . Chrétien de Troyes, esprit tout muni de souvenirs érudits auxquels on reconnaît le clerc." Faral, *Les Jongleurs en France au moyen âge*, p. 199.

[5] Pirenne, *Mediæval Towns*, p. 127 ff.

In the thirteenth century literature, always sensitive to a new public, adapts itself to this new audience, lusty, humorous, and gross. It is true that there is no water-tight division, the romance and the epic to the château, the fabliau to the town. A knightly audience was not squeamish. William IX, Duke of Aquitaine, has a chanson of two ladies and a cat that need not blush to find itself beside any fabliau, and the *Jeu de la Reine* produced as scandalous equivoques in the hall as on the village green. But roughly, Shakespeare's finding on the taste of the groundling holds, "Give him a jig, or a tale of bawdry, or he sleeps," and Chaucer's fitting of the tale to the teller is equally significant. The Knight and the Squire and the Man of Law and the Clerk have it, over against the Shipman, and the Miller and the Reeve.

> "It is an impossible," said the Wyf of Bath,
> "That any clerke wol speken good of wyves
> But if it be of holy seintes lyves—"

but in practice it is the clerk of Oxenford who tells the tale of the patient Griselda, and it is the Marchant wedded but two months who lets his burden down. It is true that the Church denounces woman as incarnate temptation, denounces bodily beauty;[1] love itself, *gratissimus error*,[2] is too near the sweetest sin of the seven to be much countenanced,[3] and marriage is the last shift.[4] It is the inevit-

[1] Gregory the Great, *more suo*, sums the whole matter, "A certain nun, fair after the putridity of the flesh." *Dialog.* I. 4.

[2] John of Garland, quoted in *Romania*, 1875, p. 384.

[3] "The sirens have the faces of women, because nothing so estranges men from God as the love of women." Honorius d'Autun, *Speculum Ecclesiae* (Migne, clxxii. c. 855-7).

[4] Cf. *Gryll Grange*, ch. vii.

"*Dr. Opimian*: I never pretended to this sort of spiritualism. I followed the advice of St. Paul, who says it is better to marry . . .

Mrs. Opimian: You need not finish the quotation."

Yet there is good divinity in praise of marriage. Even in the late Middle Ages, Robert de Sorbon in a sermon on marriage is tolerant, even idealistic (Hauréau, *Notices et Extraits*, i. 188). Cf. *supra*, the judgment by Ivo of Chartres.

able result of its ascetic ideal, its absolute severance between the physical and spiritual nature of man. When asceticism is the positive good, love and licence are but degrees of negative comparison. But in practice, the situation is nearer the old story, surely the second oldest in the world, in the form Caesarius von Heisterbach tells it, of the Abbot and the monk riding out together and the young man seeing women for the first time. "They be demons," said the Abbot. "I thought," said the young man, "that they were the fairest things that ever I saw."[1] "There is no such solace under heaven," says Robert of Brunne,[2] "of all that a man may have, as the true love of a good woman." The whole story is in the statue above the South Portal of Chartres, the Devil carrying the Courtesan to hell, the Devil a gross fantastic humorous horror, but the woman slung across his shoulders has been modelled in a passion of pity, the tenderness of the breasts, the despair of the beautiful doomed head and the trailing hair. It is Blake's Triumph of Satan over Eve, the serpent about her coil upon coil, the terrible triumphant head at peace upon her breasts, and the look frozen upon the unconscious face, Heloïse' cry of despair upon herself as the ruin of her lover.

It is not to say that satire upon woman is not a distinct branch of mediaeval clerical literature. It is to this day the *fonds* of most music-hall jokes, thanks to that obscure instinct for which "woman, in herself and without any effort on her part, is always News." But the bourgeois is a far richer vein than the clerical. Bernard of Morlaix is rough tongued enough in the *De Contemptu Mundi*: and Golias in his *De Conjuge Non Ducenda* is profoundly grateful to

[1] Cf. Chaunteclere's free translation for Dame Pertelote of

"*In principio,*
Mulier est hominis confusio.
(Madame, the sentence of this Latine is,
Woman is mannes joye and mannes bliss)."

[2] Robert of Brunne, *Handlying Synne*, *E.E.T.S.* p. 69.

the three angels who come to dissuade him from matrimony. But there is nothing in Latin to touch the sheer brutality of the vernacular. "I always bless God," said William Morris, "for making anything so strong as an onion;" it is the ideal temper in which to approach the grosser half of mediaeval literature. It is true that Jean de Meung, the mediaeval Diogenes, is a clerk, but he is too often taken as the representative of his order, his *Roman* as the outrage of clerical prejudice on the chivalrous Dream of the Rose. But the author of the first *Roman* seems himself to have been a clerk: his successor wrote at the end of the thirteenth century, in the first blast of the east wind that blows for nearly two centuries. And still earlier than Guillaume de Lorris, another clerk dreamed of the garden and the lover and the Rose: the first rough draft of it is in the *Carmina*.[1] Henri d'Andely, himself a clerk, ended his *Lai d'Aristote* with a warning to those who think evil of love and lovers: just as Lyly, for all his aspic, laid down the rules of governance: "In those that are not in love, reverent thoughts of love: in those that be, faithful vows."[2] A good many of the fabliaux have been laid to the clerical charge, but it is to be observed that those most certainly of clerical authorship are the funniest, and the least indecent.[3] They are ribald enough, but not often obscene, and the *Lardier qui parle Latin* is glorious comedy. Such malevolence as they have is unleashed not against the woman, but the full fed porker, the priest. It is the eternal rancour of the Have-nots against the Haves. The situation as the clerk saw it was very simple, guilty Capital and innocent Labour, the clerk thin and scholarly, over against Dives, fat and sleek with good

[1] *Carmina Burana*, 50.

[2] *Love's Metamorphosis*, Act II., Sc. 1.

[3] *Le Pauvre Mercier, Les Trois Dames qui trovèrent l'anel, Le Pauvre Clerc, Le Credo au Ribaut, Le Lardier qui parle Latin, Le lai d'Aristote.*

living and incontinence.[1] There is nothing in Protestant literature fiercer, though a good deal that is grosser, than the invective of the *Carmina* when Rome and the great ones are in question.

"Wilt thou have a love song or a song of good life?" asks Feste, and Sir Andrew's hasty "A love song, a love song. I care not for good life" is representative enough of the goliard's audience. Yet the songs of good life (including too often the bad life of his ecclesiastical superiors) are almost a third of the *Carmina*: and carefully arranged by themselves. The Archpoet himself told the story of the Gospels with some tenderness to his monkish audience, though it winds up, adroitly enough, with the outstretched begging hand. Some clerks, like Garnier de Pont-Sainte-Maxence, who made a scoop in the martyrdom of St. Thomas à Becket, reciting it on the tomb of "le baron" himself, profited mightily by the gifts of the faithful.[2] Such as these, who kept their tongues off their superiors and told devout tales, are described even in a Penitentiary as rather more tolerable.[3] But the immortality of the *Carmina* is in the love songs and the drinking songs. *Mihi est propositum* is surely the greatest drinking song in the world;

"In taberna quando sumus
Non curamus quid sit humus,"

shares the second place with

"Back and sides go bare, go bare":

and whoever was the author of the first, vagabond or episcopal secretary, the other lies at the door of a learned

[1] *Notices et Extraits*, xxxii. p. 286:

"Est scolaris humilis, simplex, iustus, castus,
Pallidus et gracilis, labor premit vastus.
Dives est horribilis, plenus magni fastus,
Luxuriae facilis, plenus vini, bene pastus."

[2] *La Vie de S. Thomas le Martyr*, ed. Walberg, pp. 210-11.

[3] *Penitential of Thomas of Cabham, Bishop of Salisbury.* Text in Chambers, *The Mediaeval Stage*, ii. p. 262.

Prebendar of Durham. The writer of the *Paternoster aux Goliardois* rounds on his greedy tavern-keeper, but checks himself with one of those stabbing thrusts of recognition, so poignant because so unconscious, that are Villon's strength—

> " *Da nobis hodie* : domage
> Ne lui doit fere, ne anui,
> Quar tout le bien me vient de lui." [1]

These, too, found their warmest welcome in an inn. And if their women are its lights o' love, there is little trace of it in their verse : they have youth lambent about their heads. Primas himself, scurrilous dog that he is, broke his heart when Flora left him at the time of flowers, though she was all men's stale.[2] The grace is upon them that is on Greene and Marlowe and Peele,

> " Beauty, the silver dew that falls in May."

Of the prosody of the Latin lyric compared with the vernacular, a book may some day be written : would have been written, if Professor Ker had lived to finish his study of metre. But to handle it demands a knowledge of five vernaculars at their thorniest transition, Provençal, Middle German, Italian, Old French, Anglo-Norman, as well as Middle English : lacking that equipment the amateur is like to find himself launched in a cockleshell upon a very dangerous sea. And indeed upon the whole question of origins, ballad, lyric, dramatic, there is wisdom in the nursery story of the centipede, who

> " was happy quite
> Until the Toad, in fun,
> Said ' Pray which leg goes after which ? '
> Which worked his mind to such a pitch,
> He lay distracted in a ditch,
> Considering how to run."

[1] " Paternoster du Vin," Jubinal, *Jongleurs et Trouvères*, p. 70.

[2] " Tempus erat florum, cum flos meus, optimus horum,
Liquit Flora thorum, fons fletus, causa dolorum."
Meyer, *Die Oxforder Gedichte des Primas, Magister Hugo von Orleans*, vi. p. 127.

"Such affliction," says Daniel, "doth laboursome curiosity still lay upon our best delights." Which came first:

"Ich sih die liehte heide
in gruner varwe stan.
dar süln wir alle gehen,
die sumerzit enphahen,"

or this—

"Ut mei misereatur,
Ut me recipiat,
et declinetur ad me,
et ita desinat!"

or this—

"Quan la douss' aura venta
deves vostre pais
vejaire m'es qu'en senta
odor de paradis."

The resolving of precedence might be an agreeable exercise: but it is almost enough to know that each exists: that as early as the twelfth century the loveliest of all rhythms was shaping itself in three languages to its last and absolute perfection—

"By brooks too broad for leaping
The light-foot boys are laid,
The rose-lipt girls are sleeping
In fields where roses fade."

Of its combination, richer though not lovelier, with a second quatrain of triple rhyme, and final echo, the stanza of "In a drear-nighted December," and of

"There go the loves that wither,
The old loves with wearier wings,
And all dead years draw thither,
And all disastrous things.
Dead dreams of days forsaken,
Blind buds that snows have shaken,
Wild leaves that winds have taken,
Red strays of ruined springs."

there is no instance earlier than Dryden. Adam of St Victor is fumbling for it, the mesmeric beat of the triple rhyme, with the break in the fourth line for relief, but he uses a longer line, and trochees are brisker than iambics. His metre is too stately for most of the Vaganten. The Archpoet's *Confession*,

> " Down the broad way do I go
> Young and unregretting,"

gave the tempo to most of his brother-vagabonds : when they break from it, it is when some forgotten tune has caught their ear, sometimes as in

> " Vidi
> Viridi
> Phyllidem sub tilia," [1]

the whistle of a blackbird. One thing at least is beyond controversy, that Latin was the schoolmaster of both the Romance and the German tongues : and the scholar's practice in a language immutable yet all but infinitely adaptable is invaluable to hobble-de-hoy languages not quite sure what to do with their feet. The folk-song origin, at any rate, seems to have gone by the board. M. Bédier, once its apostle, joyously rends his own pamphlet of twenty years ago, and scoffs at the " mugissements vagues de la Muse populaire." Only Tibullus, that obstinate lover of country things, still insists that the first metres were beaten out to the rhythm of the flails : and perhaps Joachim du Bellay writing the *Vanneur* would have agreed with him. It is a piece of sentiment : a memory of the Before Time of which Sir Philip Sidney said rudely that " what that Before Time was, I think scarcely Sphinx can tell."

Provenance is another riddle, but here one is on surer ground. The Benedictbeuern Manuscript has fifty German lyrics scattered among the Latin, and is written by German scribes : Benedictbeuern itself was a Benedictine monastery in Upper Bavaria : the heaviest

[1] *Carmina Bur.* 57.

and most continuous broadside of Church Councils was directed from Würzburg, Salzburg, Cologne, St. Hippolyte in the diocese of Passau : the Eberhardini, an alternative name for the *goliardi*, are possibly nicknamed after Eberhard, Archbishop of Salzburg, once gloriously parodied by a wandering scholar.[1] But this proves nothing. The first threats of degradation come from Sens and Rouen, are echoed in Liege, Cahors, Toul. A Tarragon council complains of clerks turning jongleurs.[2] Bishop Wolfger gives half a talent in Rome to a French *vagus* with a guitar, and sets it among his travelling accounts.[3] The originals from which the *Carmina Burana* were copied may have been the property of a German scholar, and one is tempted to connect them with the days when the German tongue rang in the streets of Orleans as in the fatherland.[4] One of the most naive of the German lyrics,

> " Were the world all mine
> From the sea to the Rhine,
> I'd give it all
> If so be the Queen of England
> Lay in my arms." [5]

is surely the work of a German student, haunted by a passing glimpse of Eleanor of Aquitaine, and perhaps as surely her slave as Bertrand de Born. But the best things in the *Carmina* are in other manuscripts, in St. Omer, in the Vatican MS. of Queen Christine, in the Harleian and Arundel MSS. of the British Museum, and scattered singly

[1] See Frantzen, *Die Vagantendichtung*, *Neo-philologus*, v. 1920, pp. 62, 63. Mayer, *Archiv f. öst. Gesch.-Quellen.* vi. (See Appendices B and C). On the scribes, see Schumann, *Carm. Bur.* ii. p. 70.*

[2] *Vide* Appendix E.

[3] See Appendix B.

[4] Fournier, *Statuts*, i. p. 145.

[5] *Carm. Bur.* 108 *a* :

> " Were div werlt alle min
> Von deme mere unze an den Rin
> Des wolt ih mih darben
> Daz div Chünegin von Engellant
> Lege in minen armen."

through every great European library. The Germans claim the *tilia* for the Fatherland, but there are *tilleuls* in Touraine: the Italians will have *Phyllis and Flora* for Italy, because of the landscape and its pines. The macaronics are sometimes German, sometimes Italian, sometimes Provençal.[1] The truth is that the goliard, like the Latin tongue, knew no frontiers: "se nuls me dit, 'Guarniers, ou vas?' tuz li munz est miens envirun:"[2] and the nightingale needs no interpreter.

"Veni, veni, venias,
ne me mori facias.
hyrca, hyrca, nazaza,
Trillirivos!"[3]

But the good minute goes. By the end of the thirteenth century the vernaculars have come to their strength: Latin in creative literature is doomed, though so great an artist as Milton, four centuries later, had not yet realised it. The revival of learning brought only contempt for this bastard-rhyming, such contempt as a professional gardener might have for the small scarlet buds of a rose that has grown wild. Some of the gayer choruses are still shouted in German Universities: *Mihi est propositum* is in every anthology: *Phyllis and Flora* appears as "The sweete and civill contention of two amorous Ladyes Translated out of Latin by R. S. Esquire. Aut Marte vel

[1] *Carm. Burana,* 79, "Audi bela mia
mille modos Veneris
da hizevaleria."

81, "*a remender*
statim vivus fierem
per un baiser."

138, "Stetit puella, *bi einem boume,*
scripsit amorem *an eime loube.*"

141, "O mi dilectissima
vultu serenissima . . .
Manda liet, mande liet,
min geselle chumet niet."

[2] Garnier de Pont-Sainte-Maxence, *Vie de St. Thomas*, ed. Walberg, p. 211.

[3] *Carm. Bur.* 136.

Mercurio. Imprinted at London by W. W. for Richard Jones, 1598." But they are fragments of a sunk argosy.

Of the absolute value of the *Carmina* as literature, there can be two opinions. The verse is sometimes pedantic: it makes love a little like Gabriel Harvey at Cambridge who used "everie night after supper to walke on the market hill to show himselfe," and if "the wenches gave him never so little an amorous regard, he presently boords them with a set speech of the first gathering together of Societies and the distinction of *amor* and *amicitia* out of Tullie's offices."[1] The classical scholar airs his Chronos, the logician his distinctions: though for its lovers, even this has its own odd pleasure. Even at its most spontaneous, it has not the sudden miracle of the earliest vernacular lyric. It can hold its own against Provençal, but hardly against

> "Lenten ys come with love to toune."

or—

> "O man that diggest the tomb,
> And puttest my darling from me,
> Make not the grave too narrow."[2]

or—

> "Christ! that my love were in my arms,
> And I in my bed again!"

and the snatches of German verse in the *Carmina* are like dew on the grass of a heavy summer. Whatever one's prejudice in favour of the older, richer language, there are times when all the scholar's verse is no better than "Aristote," watching from his window the young girl barefoot in the dew, ungirdled in her smock, plucking flowers for her hair and singing "not too loud,"

> "Or la voi, la voi, la voi,
> La fontaine y sort serie,"

[1] "Have with you" (*Works of Thomas Nash*, McKerrow, iii. 79).

[2] *Irische Texte*, ii. 174.

and suddenly finding himself lean and dry and old.[1] It is the contrast between the thrushes in February and the violin. Even the rock-hewn crystal of *Dum Dianae vitrea* seems sophisticated beside the shaken dewdrop of the oldest French lyric. But to grant this is to give away nothing.

> " Whenas that Rubie which you weare,
> Sunk from the tip of your soft eare,
> Will last to be a precious stone,
> When all your world of Beautie's gone."

In the last resort, the mediaeval scholar's lyric has value only for those to whom the richest thing in life is the sense of the past: who believe as Milton did in his exultant scholar's youth that to read history so is " to be present as it were in every age, to extend and stretch life backward from the womb, and thus extort from unwilling Fate a certain foregone immortality "; who have little use for Keats in his first Spenserian mood, but recognise his godhead when contact with the older literatures has brought him austerity and power.

> " A pigeon tumbling in clear summer air,"
>
> " Sweet peas on tiptoe for a flight,"

are good, but

> " Far from the fiery noon and eve's one star
> Sat grey-haired Saturn, quiet as a stone . . .
> Forest on forest hung about his head
> Like cloud on cloud."
>
> " Mother of Hermes and still youthful Maia,"
>
> " O Hearkener to the loud clapping shears,"

this is the utterance of the early gods. Anatole France in this at least conservative, dedicated " *Le Génie Latin* " as " un acte de foi et d'amour pour cette tradition grecque et latine, toute de sagesse et de beauté, hors de laquelle il n'est qu'erreur et trouble ": an exaggeration, but a valiant exaggeration in an age when the classics have met

[1] Montaiglon-Reynaud, ii. 137, *Le Lai d'Aristote.*

a deadlier enemy than the Blessed Gregory. Some altars are safe: some debts will never be dishonoured.

> "O Proserpina,
> For the flowers now, that frighted thou let'st fall
> From Dis's wagon! daffodils
> That come before the swallow dares, and take
> The winds of March with beauty;"

—that is the English genius,

> "violets dim,
> But sweeter than the lids of Juno's eyes,
> Or Cytherea's breath;"

and this the Latin. Who shall choose between them?

> "That faire field
> Of Enna, where Proserpin gathering flours,
> Herself a fairer Floure, by gloomie Dis
> Was gatherd, which cost Ceres all that pain
> To seek her through the world."

> "to have quite set free
> His half regain'd Eurydice."

> "And the brown bright nightingale amorous
> Is half assuaged for Itylus,
> The Thracian ships and the foreign faces,
> The tongueless vigil and all the pain."

—these are the eternised sacrifices, on which generation after generation throws its incense. But these others, who served a ruinous altar and got a scanty living by it: the grammarians of Toulouse sitting up at nights to argue the frequentative of the verb to be: Rahingus of Flavigny filling his scanty leisure with copying Virgil: Froumund of Tegernsee collating manuscripts of Persius with chilblained hands: Primas shivering and mocking in his shabby cloak, writing a lament for Troy with Bacchanalian tears: the Arch-poet coughing his heart out on the Lombard roads; a century of nameless vagabonds: on these the iniquity of oblivion hath blindly scattered her poppy. They kept the imagination of Europe alive: held untouched by their rags and poverty and squalor the Beauty that had made beautiful old rhyme. And for those of us who are the conservatives of letters, for whom literature obeys the eternal movement of the tides, for whom the heavens themselves are old, there remains the stark simplicity of Terence—" In truth they have deserved to be remembered of us."

> " O no man knows
> Through what wild centuries
> Roves back the rose."

APPENDIX A

LATIN ORIGINALS OF LYRICS TRANSLATED IN THE TEXT

I

Paulinus of Nola to Ausonius

Ego te per omne quod datum mortalibus
  et distinatum saeculum est,
claudente donec continebor corpore,
  discernar orbe quolibet,

Nec ore longe, nec remotum lumine,
  tenebo fibris insitum,
videbo corde, mente complectar pia,
  ubique praesentem mihi.

Et cum solutus corporali carcere,
  terraque provolavero,
quo me locarit axe communis Pater
  illic quoque animo te geram.

Neque finis idem qui meo me corpore
  et amore laxabit tuo.
mens quippe, lapsis quae superstes artubus
  de stirpe durat coeliti.

Sensus necesse est simul et affectus suos
  teneat aeque ut vitam suam,
et ut mori sic oblivisci non capit,
  perenne vivax et memor.

Carmina, XI.

APPENDIX

II

Prudentius

Ad Gallicinium

Inde est, quod omnes credimus
  illo quietis tempore,
quo gallus exsultans canit,
  Christum redisse ex inferis.

Cathemerinon, I. ll. 65-69.

III

Hymnus Matutinus

Nox, et tenebrae, et nubila
  confusa mundi et turbida,
lux intrat, albescit polus,
  Christus venit, discedite!

Caligo terrae scinditur
  percussa solis spiculo,
rebusque iam color redit
  vultu nitentis sideris.

Cath. II. ll. 1-8.

IV

De Novo Lumine Paschalis Sabbati

Illic purpureis tecta rosariis
  omnis fragrat humus, calthaque pinguia,
et molles violas, et tenues crocos
  fundit fonticulis uda fugacibus.

Felices animae prata per herbida
  concentu parili suave sonantibus
hymnorum modulis dulce canunt melos,
  calcant et pedibus lilia candidis.

Cath. V. ll. 113-117, 121-125

V

Hymnus circa Exsequias Defuncti

Nunc suscipe, terra, fovendum
  gremioque hunc concipe molli,
hominis tibi membra sequestro,
  generosa et fragmina credo.

. . . Patet ecce fidelibus ampli
   via lucida iam paradisi,
licet et nemus illud adire
   homini quod ademerat anguis.

Illic, precor, optime ductor,
   famulam tibi praecipe mentem,
genitali in sede sacrari,
   quam liquerat exsul et errans.

Nos tecta fovebimus ossa,
   violis et fronde frequenti;
titulumque et frigida saxa
   liquido spargemus odore.

Cath. X. ll. 125 *et seq.*

VI

Venerat occiduis mundi de finibus hostis
Luxuria, extinctae iamdudum prodiga famae,
delibuta comas, oculis vaga, languida voce,
perdita deliciis . . .
      lapsanti per vina et balsama gressu,
ebria calcatis ad bellum floribus ibat.

Psychomachia, ll. 310-320.

VII

Hrabanus Maurus

Ad Eigilum de libro quem scripsit

Nullum opus exsurgit quod non annosa vetustas
   expugnet, quod non vertat iniqua dies.
Grammata sola carent fato, mortemque repellunt,
   praeterita renovant, grammata sola biblis.

Carm. XXI.

VIII

Dulcissimo Fratri . . . Grimaldo

Vive, meae vires, lassarumque anchora rerum,
   Naufragio et litus tutaque terra meo,
solus honor nobis, urbs tu fidissima semper,
   curisque afflicto tuta quies animo.

Carm. VI.

IX

Dum loquimur, seges alta viret, maturiet, aret,
  canescunt violae, lilia fusca cadunt.

Carm. XXXVII. ll. 9, 10.

X

WALAFRID STRABO

Ad Amicum

Cum splendor lunae fulgescat ab aethere purae,
Tu sta sub divo cernens speculamine miro,
Qualiter ex luna splendescat lampade pura
et splendore suo caros amplectitur uno
corpore divisos, sed mentis amore ligatos.
Si facies faciem spectare nequivit amantem,
hoc saltim nobis lumen sit pignus amoris.
hos tibi versiculos fidus transmisit amicus,
si de parte tua fidei stat fixa catena,
nunc precor, ut valeas felix per saecula cuncta.

Carm. LIX.

XI

ST. PETER DAMIAN

De Gloria Paradisi

Ad perennis vitae fontem mens sitivit arida
claustra carnis praesto frangi clausa querit anima,
gliscit, ambit, eluctatur, exsul frui patria.

. . . Omni labe defaecati carnis bella nesciunt
caro facta spiritalis et mens unum sentiunt,
pace multa perfruentes scandalum non perferunt.

Carm. CCVI.

XII

ST. FULBERT OF CHARTRES

De Luscinia

Cum telluris, vere novo, producuntur germina,
nemorosa circumcirca frondescunt et brachia ;
Fragrat odor cum suavis florida per gramina
hilarescit Philomela, dulcis sonus conscia,
et extendens modulando gutturis spiramina,
reddit veris et aestivi temporis praeconia.

. . . Vocis eius pulcritudo clarior quam cithera,
vincitur omnis cantando volucrum catervula,
implet sylvas atque cuncta modulis arbustula
gloriosa valde facta veris prae laetitia.
. . . Cedit auceps ad frondosa resonans umbracula.
Cedit cignus et suavis ipsius melodia ;
quamvis enim videaris corpore premodica,
tamen cuncti capiuntur hac tua melodia.
Nemo dedit voci tuae haec dulcia carmina,
nisi solus Rex caelestis qui gubernat omnia.

Carmina XVIII.

XIII

De Johanne Abbate

Johannes abba, parvulus
statura, non virtutibus,
ita maiori socio
quocum erat in heremo :

'Volo,' dicebat, 'vivere
sicut angelus secure,
nec veste nec cibo frui
qui laboretur manibus.'

Respondit frater, 'Moneo
ne sis incepti properus,
frater, quod tibi post modum
sit non cepisse satius.'

At ille, 'Qui non dimicat
non cadit, neque superat.'
Ait, et nudus heremum
inferiorem penetrat.

Septem dies gramineo
vix ibi durat pabulo,
octava fames imperat
ut ad sodalem redeat.

Qui sero, clausa ianua,
tutus sedet in cellula,
cum minor voce debili
appellat, 'Frater, aperi :

Johannes opis indigus
notis assistat foribus,
nec spernat tua pietas
quem redigit necessitas.'

Respondit ille deintus,
'Johannes, factus angelus,
miratur celi cardines
ultra non curat homines.'

Foris Johannes excubat
malamque noctem tolerat,
et prȩter voluntariam
hanc agit pȩnitentiam.

Facto mane recipitur
satisque verbis uritur,
sed intentus ad crustula
fert patienter omnia.

Refocillatus domino
gratias egit et socio,
Dehinc rastellum brachiis
temptat movere languidis.

Castigatur angustia
de levitate nimia,
cum angelus non potuit
vir bonus esse didicit.

Carmina XXV.

APPENDIX

XIV

Sigebert of Liege

[Dümmler, *Abhandlungen der Kgl. Akad. der Wissensch. zu Berlin,* 1893, p. 23 *et seq.*]

Hinc virginalis sancta frequentia
Gerdrudis, Agnes, Prisca, Cecilia,
  Lucia, Petronilla, Tecla,
  Agatha, Barbara, Juliana . . .

Hę pervagantes prata recentia,
pro velle querunt serta decentia,
  rosas legentes passionis,
  lilia vel violas amoris.

Passio Sanctae Luciae, 19.

XV

Conatus roseas Thebeis ferre coronas . . .
lilia nulla mihi, violę nullę, rosa nulla,
lilia munditię rosa carnis mortificandę,
nec per pallorem violę testantur amorem
quo pia sponsa calet, quo sponsus mutuo languet,
proximus atque deus, non bis tingunt mihi coccum.
Nescio luteola vaccinia pingere caltha,
non cum narcisso mihi summa papavera carpo,
hic flores desunt inscripti nomina regum.
Quod solum potui studio ludente socordi
alba ligustra mihi iam sponte cadentia legi,
pollice nec pueri dignata nec ungue puellę,
inde rudi textu, non coniuncto bene textu
conserui parvas has qualescunque coronas.
Vos, O Thebei, gratissima nomina regi,
votis posco piis, hęc serta locare velitis
inter victrices lauros ederasque virentes.
Si rude vilet opus, si rerum futile pondus,
at non vilescat, pia quod devotio praestat.

Passio Sanctorum Thebeorum, Epilogue, ll. 1054-1077

XVI

The Cambridge Songs

1

Levis exsurgit Zephyrus,
et sol procedit tepidus,
iam terra sinus aperit,
dulcore suo diffluit.

2

Ver purpuratus exiit,
ornatus suos induit,
aspergit terram floribus,
ligna silvarum frondibus.

3

Struunt lustra quadrupedes,
et dulces nidos volucres,
inter ligna florentia
sua decantant gaudia.

4

Quod oculis dum video
et auribus dum audio,
heu, pro tantis gaudiis
tantis inflor suspiriis.

5

Cum mihi sola sedeo,
et hęc revolvans palleo,
si forte caput sublevo,
nec audio nec video.

6

Tu saltem, Veris gratia,
exaudi et considera
frondes, flores, et gramina,
nam mea languet anima.

XVII

Carmina Burana

1

Dum Dianę vitrea
sero lampas oritur,
et a fratris rosea
luce dum succenditur,
dulcis aura zephyri
spirans omnes ętheri,
nubes tollit,
sic emollit
vi chordarum pectora,
et inmutat
cor, quod nutat
ad amoris pignora.
Lętum iubar hesperi
gratiorem
dat humorem
roris soporiferi
mortalium generi.

2

O quam felix est
antidotum soporis,
quod curarum tempestates
sedat et doloris!
Dum surrepit clausis
oculorum poris,
ipsum gaudio equiparat
dulcedini amoris.

3

Morpheus in mentem
trahit inpellentem
ventum lenem
segetes maturas,
murmura rivorum
per arenas puras,
circulares ambitus
molendinorum,
qui furantur somno
lumen oculorum.

4

Post blanda Veneris
commercia
lassatur cerebri
substantia.
Hinc caligantes mira novitate
oculi nantes in palpebrarum rate!
Hei, quam felix transitus amoris ad soporem,
sed suavior regressus soporis ad amorem!

5

Fronde sub arboris amęna,
dum querens canit philomena,
suave est quiescere,
suavius ludere in gramine
cum virgine speciosa.
Si variarum odor herbarum spiraverit,
si dederit thorum rosa,
dulciter soporis alimonia
post Veneris defessa commercia
captatur,
dum lassis instillatur.

Carmina Burana, 37.

XVIII

1

Dum domus lapidea
foro sita cernitur,
et a fratris rosea
visus dum allicitur,
dulcis, ferunt socii,
locus hic est hospitii.

2

Bacchus tollat,
Venus molliat
vi bursarum pectora,
et inmutet
et computet
vestes in pignora.

3

Molles cibos edere,
inpinguari,
dilatari
studeamus ex adipe,
alacriter bibere.

Carmina Burana, 176.

XIX

1

Ęstuans intrinsecus
ira vehementi
in amaritudine
lòquar meę menti:
factus de materia,
levis elementi
similis sum folio
de quo ludunt venti.

2

Cum sit enim proprium
viro sapienti
supra petram ponere
sedem fundamenti,
stultus ego comparor
fluvio labenti,
sub eodem aere
nunquam permanenti.

3

Feror ego veluti
sine nauta navis,
ut per vias aeris
vaga fertur avis,
non me tenent vincula,
non me tenet clavis,
quęro mihi similes,
et adiungor pravis.

4

Mihi cordis gravitas
res videtur gravis;
iocus est amabilis
dulciorque favis;

quicquid Venus imperat
labor est suavis,
quę numquam in cordibus
habitat ignavis.

5

Via lata gradior
more iuventutis,
inplico me vitiis
inmemor virtutis,
voluptatis avidus
magis quam salutis,
mortuus in anima
curam gero cutis.

6

Pręsul discretissime,
veniam te precor :
morte bona morior,
nece dulci necor,
meum pectus sauciat
puellarum decor,
et quas tactu nequeo,
saltem corde męchor.

7

Res est arduissima
vincere naturam,
in aspectu virginis
mentem esse puram ;
iuvenes non possumus
legem sequi duram,
leviumque corporum
non habere curam.

8

Quis in igne positus
igne non uratur ?
Quis Papię demorans
castus habeatur,
ubi Venus digito
iuvenes venatur,
oculis inlaqueat,
facie prędatur ?

MANITIUS, *Archipoeta*, p. 24.

APPENDIX

XX

Ab ęstatis foribus
amor nos salutat.
Humus picta floribus
faciem conmutat.
Flores amoriferi
iam arrident tempori,
perit absque Venere
flos ętatis tenerę.
Omnium principium
dies est vernalis,
vere mundus celebrat
diem sui natalis.
Omnes huius temporis
dies festi Veneris.
Regna Iovis omnia
hęc agant sollemnia.

Carmina Burana, 46.

XXI

1

Salve ver optatum,
amantibus gratum,
gaudiorum
fax multorum,
florum incrementum ;
multitudo florum
et color colorum
salvetote,
et estote
iocorum augmentum !
Dulcis avium concentus
sonat, gaudeat iuventus.
Hiems seva transiit,
nam lenis spirat ventus.

2

Tellus purpurata
floribus et prata
virescunt,
umbrę crescunt,

nemus redimitur
lascivit natura
omnis creatura ;
lęto vultu,
claro cultu,
ardor investitur ;
Venus subditos titillat,
dum naturę nectar stillat.
sic ardor venereus
amantibus scintillat.

Carmina Burana, 118.

XXII

1

Dira vi amoris teror,
et venereo axe vehor,
igne ferventi suffocatus.
Deme, pia, cruciatus.

2

Ignis vivi tu scintilla,
discurrens cordis ad vexilla ;
igni incumbens non pauxillo
conclusi mentis te sigillo.

3

Męret cor, quod gaudebat ;
die, quo te cognoscebat,
singularem et pudicam
te adoptabat in amicam.

4

Profert pectoris singultus
et męstitię tumultus,
nam amoris tui vigor
urget me, et illi ligor.

5

Virginale lilium,
tuum presta subsidium ;
missus in exilium
quęrit a te consilium.

6

Nescit quid agat, moritur,
amore tui vehitur,
telo necatur Veneris,
sibi ni subveneris.

7

Iure Veneris orbata,
castitas redintegrata,
vultu decenti perornata,
veste sophię decorata.

8

Psallo tibi soli,
despicere me noli,
per me precor velis coli,
lucens ut stella poli.

Carmina Burana, 158.

XXIII

I

Si me dignetur quam desidero,
felicitate Iovem supero.
Nocte cum illa si dormiero,
si sua labra semel suxero,
mortem subire,
placenter obire,
vitamque finire
libens potero,
hei potero, hei potero, hei potero,
tanta si gaudia recepero.

Carmina Burana, 167.

APPENDIX B

EXTRACT FROM THE TRAVELLING ACCOUNTS OF BISHOP WOLFGER OF PASSAU, 1203-4

[Full text in I. Zingerle, *Reiserechnungen Wolfger's von Ellenbrechtskirchen*, 1877: re-edited in part by Höfer, *Reiserechnungen der Bischof Wolfger von Passau* (*Beiträge zur Geschichte der deutschen Sprache*, xvii. 1892.)

The MS. was found by Professor Wolf in the Archives of Cividale in Friuli, in 1874.]

BISHOP WOLFGER'S account book should stand him in stead at the Day of Judgment; it is as good a heart as Mr. Pepys. No churchman might give anything but bite and sup to a jongleur; there was good divinity against it. The *istriones* and the *ioculatores* were limbs of Satan; to share with them the funds of the church was in the same order of things as the betrayal of Judas; and above all did this apply to the apostate, the clerk turned jongleur. But the bishop's soft heart and a human hankering after vanity betray him on every page; entries such as xxx den. to a bald apostate from Einsdorf, and ij sol. to an old *joculator* in a red tunic at Ferrara, and xxx den. to a scholar *vagus*, and a talent to the jongleur Flordamor at Bologna, and worst of all, a whole talent to one who brought the bishop ivory dice, are as frequent as the legitimate xii den. for parchment, and dim. tal. for wax (the bishop used a vast quantity of wax), and vii den. to his laundress, and iii den. for a bath, and ii den. to a man who brought a puppy from Passau, and a shirt and trousers to a Bohemian, and ij sol. to a poor old man, and half a talent for the bishop's rain-coat (*pallio episcopi pluviali*), and half a talent for furs for lining his hood, and xxvii sol., this at Rome for polishing topazes for his ring, and xxviii den. at night, at Modena, to a scholar. Two entries have made the account book famous: to Walter von der Vogelweide for a fur coat,

v. sol. longos; to a certain bishop of the Eberhardini (*vide* pp. 239, 262 ff.), and another mime at Florence, half a talent; to the lord bishop, xii den. frisac. And one entry stands alone: *Sabbato apud Crugelar nihil expendimus.*

Zingerle, p. 2. 22nd Sept. *In die Sancti Mauritii* dedit magister Heinricus in monte Gotwico venatori de pattavia xxiiij den.... Nuncio regis hungarie pro tunica lxiij den. pro calceis, v den. Eidem ad redemptionem pignorum lx den. pro duabus manticis ad capellam et ad vestimenta episcopi dim. tal. et xxvii den. pro cera, dim. tal. vi den.... per percameno, xij den.

p. 3. ... Cuidam qui episcopo attulit illam eburneam aleam tal... ioculatori cuidam xii den. Gerardo... pro falconibus vi. den.... cuidam clerico xii. den. Hugoni pro redemptione pignorum lxxx den.... Calvo istrioni xxx den....

p. 4. Cuidam vetulo pauperi ii sol.... Nuncio de pattavia qui attulit catulum ij sol. Apud Wiennam... pro caligis episcopi lxij den.... Boemo pro camisia et bracis xix den.

p. 8. [Oct. 25th.] pro pallio episcopo pluviali xii sol. longos et dim. pro variis pelliculis ad furrendam cucullam. dim. tal.... pro preparandis veteris sellis et una nova v. sol. long.... cuidam vago scolari xxx den. Lotrici vii den.

p. 9. Apud Niwenburch cuidam clerico dim. tal.... xiij den. Waltero de Vogelweide pro pellicio v. sol. longos. Cuidam calvo apostate de Enstorf xxiiij den.

p. 10. Lotrici ii den. pro quibusdam minutis agendis v den.... cuidam nudo garcioni xij den.... Lotrici pro lavando et lieno vij den. Item incisori vestium iiij den.... Incisoribus pro potu iiij den.

p. 22. [At Passau. Jan. 3rd, 1204.] Pro mantica et pro camisia et bracis Ulrici garcionis xxviiij den.... pro ferramentis x den.... pro reparanda cathedra vi den.

p. 24. Equis camere iiij den. quando versus Ebbilzperch descendimus. Cuidam monacho schoto lx den.

p. 25. Aput Sonn. unum scolaribus xxiiii den. frisac.... item cuidam scolari iiii den frisac.

Aput Villacum Dietmaro . . . pro emendis asinis v marc. . . . Inter diversos histriones distribuebantur aput Paduam xxxii. sol.

Aput Ferrariam *in palmis* cuidam vetulo joculatori in rufa tunica v sol.

Aput Bononiam Flordamor ioculatori tal. bon.

p. 26. *In Pascha* aput Florentiam cuidam Ebberhardinorum episcopo et cuidam alii mimo dim. tal. ver. domino episcopo xii den. frisac.

Apud Senas . . . cuidam cantatrici et duobus ioculatoribus vij sol.

Apud Romam . . . cuidam pauperi clerico xii den. . . . ibidem *in dominica misericordia* solvi cuidam Romano de antiquo debito dim. tal.

p. 27. De parando anulo episcopi et poliendis thopazis xvii sol. . . . cuidam pauperi clerico v sol.

Illi francigene cum giga et socio suo dim. tal. . . . cuidam alii clerico in viridi tunica. ii sol.

p. 28. Apud Bononiam duobus vagis Suevis. tal. bon. . . . scolari de Aquilegia ii marc. Cuidam pingui Saxonico clerico in nigris vestibus dim. marc.

p. 29. Aput Veronam . . . ioculatori cum cultellis tal. veron. cuidam scolari pro tunica xxviiii sol. veron. Johanni Salzburgensi scolari tal. veron.

p. 34. Sabbato apud Crugelar nihil expendimus.

p. 37. Burchardo scolari Romam percurrenti pro calciis viii den. et ii tal. veron.

p. 45. . . . In nocte apud Bononiam pro gramine vi. sol. bon. pro cera xviij sol. bon . . . pro balneo iij den.

p. 50. Nocte apud Mutinam . . . Burchardo scolari Romam recurrenti tal bon. . . . Burchardo pro calceis v sol. . . . pro bursa ad piper xxv den. pro duabus servorum braccis xlij den.

APPENDIX C

INDULGENCE GIVEN BY SURIANUS, ARCH-PRIMATE OF THE WANDERING SCHOLARS, 1209

[Theodor Mayer, who edited the text, speaks of it as " this extraordinary document, copied on a loose leaf of parchment in an old Register of the Canonry of St. Pölten." *Archiv für Österreichische Geschichts-Quellen*, Bd. vi. pp. 316-18 (1851).]

In nomine summe et individue vanitatis, Surianus diutina fatuorum favente demencia per Austriam Stiriam, Bawariam et Moraviam presul et archiprimas vagorum scolarium, omnibus eiusdem secte professoribus, sociis, et successoribus universis. fame siti frigore nuditate perpetuo laborare. Quia cruda simplicitate et inerti stulticia impellente nos nostri propositi nondum piget, immo eadem mens est, ut bona summa putemus aliena vivere quadra [*Juvenal, Sat. v.*]: mobiles et instabiles instar hyrundinum victum per aëra queritantium ac et illac quocunque inconstantis mutabilis et mirabilis animi nostri levitas nos impegerit, tamquam folium quod a vento rapitur et quasi scintilla in arundineto, infatigabiliter fatigati discurrimus, et interdum iuxta rigorem inordinati nostri ordinis ludibria et verbera experti, qualia nec Sarmentis iniquas Cesaris ad mensas vel vilis Galba tulisset[1] [*lacuna in MS.*], egentes, angustiati, afflicti, fame prodigi, fame sitique tabidi, frigore tremuli, gelu rigidi, rictu tumidi, habitu miseri, vestiti lintheolo super nudo, uno semper pede nudo, a domibus laicorum expulsi, ab hostiis clericorum sepe repulsi utpote vespertiliones quibus nec inter quadrupedia nec inter volatilia locus datur, stipem tamen, tamquam in diebus rogationum nati, semper rogare cogimur alienam: dignum est ut et nos

[1] I have kept Mayer's reading, but the reference is evidently to Juvenal, *Sat.* v. ll. 3-4:

" Si potes illa pati, quae nec Sarmentus iniquas
Caesaris ad mensas, nec vilis Gabba tulisset."

quandoque iustis petencium desideriis favorabiliter annuamus. Eapropter vestre indis[crete discretioni] notum esse volumus per presentes, quod nos inclinati precibus venerabilis in Christo fratris Sighardi ecclesie sci[licet ?] . . . pti per austriam archidiaconi recognoscentes beneficia, que nobis in eadem ecclesia, pene a cunis usque ad ca[nos libera]liter sunt impensa, ipsam ecclesiam cum suis officialibus eximimus ab exactione immo potius vexatione qua eos tam in festo patroni quam dedicationis quin immo per circulum anni indebite vexabamus, de nostra . . . era liberalitate, voluntate quoque et conniventia cathedralium sociorum, contradictores ab ingressu taberne perpetuo suspendentes. Nulli ergo claustrali secularive persone, nostrum inordinatum ordinem professe, liceat hanc nostre donacionis exemtionisve paginam temerare vel ei eciam ausu temerario contraire, si nostram irracionabilem fatuam et indiscretam effugere ulcionem. Acta sunt hec anno dni. MCCIX presidente sacrosancte sedi Romane Innocencio III anno pontificatus sui XI, imperante serenissimo Romanorum imperatore Hanrico, principatum vero austrie gerente piissimo et illustrissimo duce Leopoldo, pontificatus nostri anno ultimo. Datum sub divo per manum prothonotarii nostri spiritus, sigillis nostris, proprio videlicet et universitatis appensis. Testibus quoque fideliter subnotatis.

[" *In the name of the supreme and undivided Vanity, Surianus, by grace of the continuing insanity of fools prelate and archbishop of the Wandering Scholars throughout Austria, Styria, Bavaria, and Moravia, to all members, fellows, and followers of that order, hunger, thirst, cold, nakedness, in perpetual exercise. Since, moved by crude simplicity and the inertia of folly, it does not yet repent us of our vow, yea moreover since the same mind is in us to account it the supreme good to live upon other men, swift and unstable as the swallows seeking their food through the air, hither, thither, wheresoever the levity of our inconstant, fickle and singular mind may drive us, like a leaf caught up by the wind or a spark of fire in the brushwood we wander, unweariedly weary, and withal experiencing, in accordance with the rigour of our inordinate order, mocks and blows such as neither Sarmentus at the iniquitous banquets of Caesar nor the wretch Gabba bore . . . needy, povertystricken, suffering, broken in reputation, consumed with hunger and thirst, shivering with cold, stiff with frost, swollen with wind, beggarly in habit, a linen clout on our bare backs, one foot for ever unshod, driven out from the houses of the laity, turned away from the doors of the clergy, bats that can find no place either with beast or bird, for ever driven, like those that are born in the days of Rogations, to beg a stranger's bread: fitting is it, therefore, that we should graciously receive the just desires of our petitioners. Wherefore be it known to your indiscreet discretion by these presents, that we, moved by the prayers of our venerable brother in Christ, Sighard, archdeacon of the church . . . in Austria, and recognising the benefits which, from cradle to white hair, have been bestowed on us in the aforesaid church, we release that church aforesaid with its officials from the exaction, yea rather harrying wherewith we have unrighteously harassed them at the feast of the patron, and of the dedication, yea verily, throughout the circuit of the year, of our own liberality and good pleasure, and with the connivance of our official colleagues, suspending objectors from ingress to taverns in perpetuity. To no person, therefore, religious or secular, being a member of our inordinate order, is it permitted to violate this our donation or exemption, or with rash attempt to contravene it, if he would escape our irrational absurd and indiscreet vengeance. Granted in the year of Our Lord 1209, Innocent III presiding over the most Holy Roman See, in the eleventh year of his pontificate, the most serene Henry Emperor of the Romans,*[1] *the most pious and illustrious Duke Leopold exercising the principate of Austria, in the last year of our own pontificate. Given in the open by the hand of our spiritual prothonotary, and our seals, that is to say our own proper and that of our order, appended. And thus truly witnessed by the undersigned :*]

[1] "*imperatore Hanrico*" presents a riddle. The Emperor Henry VI. died in 1198 : in 1209, Otto IV. was emperor, and was succeeded in 1211 by Frederick II., whose infant son, Henry, was crowned King of Sicily in 1212.

Dr. Coulton makes the admirable suggestion that the lacuna *ecclesie sci . . . pti* (which Mayer has supplied with sci[licet]) represents the abbreviation for *Sancti Hippolyti, i.e.* St. Pölten, from which the document derives.

Errata : *voluerit* has been omitted between *effugere* and *ultionem*, p. 240, l. 16.

APPENDIX D

THE DEPARTING OF MY BOOKS

[Méon, *Nouveau Recueil de Contes et Fabliaux*.]

He laments the loss of his " clergie " at dice

EACH man asks and each will speir
What is come of all my gear,
And how I be so desperate
To have neither cloak nor hat,
Coat ne surcote ne good tabard—
All is done and lost at hazard !
Game of hazard confoundeth me,
All is lost by mine own folie.
Dice hath cost me all my lere,
Dice hath cost me all my gear,
Turned my revel into woe.
Never a town in France, I know,
Never a château I call to mind,
Where I have not left some book behind !
At Gandalus above La Ferté,
There left I my A.B.C.,
My *Paternoster* at Soissons,
And my *Credo* at Monléon,
My *Seven Psalms* are at Tournai,
My *Fifteen Psalms* are at Cambrai,
My *Psalter* is at Besançon,
And my *Calendar* at Dijon.
Back I came through Pontarlie
And there I sold my *Litany*.
And at the town of the great salt mine
I drank my Missal down in wine.
At the spicer's in Montpellier
Left I my *Antiphonary*.

APPENDIX

My *Graduale* and *Legenda*
I left at Châteaudun behind me.
My body of Divinity
Left I at Paris, in the city.
And all my Arts and all my Physic
And all my canticles and music.
The greater part of all my authors
Left I at St. Martin at Tours.
Donatus is at Orleans,
And my *Chansons* at Amiens.
At Chartres I left *Theodulus*,
At Rouen my *Avianus*.
Ovid abideth at Namur,
Philosophy is at Saumur,
At Bouvines above Dinant
There lost I *Ovid le grant*.
My *Regimen* is at Bruyères,
And my *Glosses* at Mézières.
My *Lucan* and my *Juvenal*
I clean forgot at Bonival.
Statius the great and eke *Virgile*
I lost at dice in Abbéville.
My *Alexander* is at Guerre,
And my *Graecismus* at Auxerre.
Tobit lieth in Compiègne,
—Never handle him again—
My *Doctrinale* is at Sens,
And my most wit with it gone.
Gone is thus my whole clergie,
Even thus as I do tell ye,
Lost in all these divers ways,
All my books for all my days,
Never to be bought again,
Unless I find me some good men
Who will give me of their pelf.
It may be that God Himself
Will give some bourgeois grace and gumption
To bargain with me on presumption,
That when I come back to the cloister,
I make a prayer with all the chapter,
God of all his sins acquit him !

APPENDIX E

COUNCILS RELATING TO THE *CLERICUS VAGUS* OR *JOCULATOR*

COUNCIL AT NICAEA, 325 A.D.

xv. QUOD non oporteat ex civitate in civitatem migrare . . . neque episcopus, neque presbyter neque diaconus.

xvi. Quicunque temere . . . recesserunt ab ecclesia, sive presbyteri, sive diaconi, sive in quocumque alio ecclesiastico ordine fuerint : hi nequaquam in alia ecclesia recipi debent sed omni necessitate cogi eos par est redire in paroeceas suas : pertinaces vero excommunicari oportet.

MANSI, *Concilia*, II. 902.

COUNCIL AT LAODICAEA, *c.* 360 A.D.

liv. Quod non oporteat sacerdotes aut clericos quibuscumque spectaculis in scenis [caenis] aut in nuptiis interesse, sed antequam thymelici ingrediantur exsurgere eos convenit atque inde discedere. [*This canon is frequently repeated in later Councils.*]

MANSI, II. 582.

COUNCIL AT CARTHAGE, 398 A.D.

xv. Ut episcopi et presbyteri et diaconi vel clerici . . . neque ullo turpi vel inhonesto negotio victum quaerant.

xxvii. Ut clerici, edendi vel bibendi causa tabernas non ingrediantur, nisi peregrinationis necessitate compulsi.

MANSI, III. 883.

ST. AUGUSTINE : *De Opera Monachorum*, c. 28

Tam multos hypocritas sub habitu monachorum usque quaque dispersit hostis scilicet humani generis circumeuntes provincias, nusquam missos, nusquam fixos, nusquam stantes, nusquam sedentes. Alii membra martyrum . . . venditant . . . alii parentes aut consanguineos suos in illa vel illa regione se audisse vivere et ad eos pergere mentiuntur ; et omnes petunt, omnes exigunt aut sumptus lucrosae egestatis, aut simulatae pretium sanctitatis.

MIGNE, *P.L.* 66, c. 257.

COUNCIL AT CARTHAGE, 436 A.D.

(*Rather, a collection of statutes from various African Councils*)

lx. Clericum scurrilem et verbis turpis iocularem ab officio retrahendum.

lxi. Clericum per creaturam jurantem acerrime objurgandum : si perstiterit in vitio, excommunicandum.

lxii. Clericum inter epulas cantantem, supradictae sententiae severitate coercendum.

MANSI, III. 956.

COUNCIL OF CHALCEDON, 451 A.D.

v. De episcopo vel clericis qui a civitate in civitatem transeunt.

x. Non licere clerico in duarum civitatum ecclesiis eodem tempore in catalogum referri . . . tamquam ad majorem confugit propter inanis gloriae cupiditatem.

xiii. Externos clericos et ignotos . . . sine proprii episcopi . . . litteris nusquam ullo modo ministrare. . . .

MANSI, VII. 362.

ST. ISIDORE OF PELUSIUM TO A GYROVAGUS, PHILIP BY NAME, *c.* 450 A.D.

Loca subinde commutans pinguiorem potius ut videtur mensam quam firmioren et solidiorem eruditionem quaerens. . .

MIGNE, *P.L.* 66, c. 258.

COUNCIL AT TOURS, 461 A.D.

xii. Ut clerici non absque sacerdotum suorum commendatione ad alienas provincias vel civitates ambulare disponant.

MANSI, VII. 946.

SIXTH CENTURY

Council at Agde (Narbonne), 506 A.D.

lxx. Clericum scurrilem et verbis turpibus joculatorem ab officio detrahendum. [Cf. Toledo, c. xxiii. A.D. 694.]

Mansi, viii. 336.

Council at Orleans, 511 A.D.

xix. De Monachis vagis.

Ipsi qui fuerint pervagati, ubi inventi . . . sub custodia revocentur. [Cf. Autun, c. x. A.D. 670.]

Mansi, viii, 354.

Council at Auxerre, 578 A.D.

xl. Non licet presbytero inter epulas cantare vel saltare.

Mansi, ix. 915.

St. Benedict, Regula.

Monachorum quatuor esse genera manifestum est. . . . Quartum vero genus est monachorum quod nominatur gyro vagum qui tota vita sua per diversas provincias ternis aut quaternis diebus per diversorum cellas hospitantur, semper vagi et nunquam stabiles, et propriis voluptatibus et gulae illecebris servientes. . . .

Migne, *P.L.* 66, 246.

SEVENTH CENTURY

Council at Toledo, *c.* 684 A.D.

v. Illos autem quos tantum extrema vesania occuparit ut incertis locis vagi, atque morum depravationibus inhonesti, ullam prorsus nec stabilitatem sedis nec honestatem mentis habere extiterint cogniti, quicumque ex sacerdotibus vel ministris vagantes reperiret, aut si fas est in propriis locis cenobio suis rectoribus eos reformet : aut si difficile est, pro sola honestate, vigore suae potestatis erudiendos inclinet.

Mansi, x. 769.

APPENDIX

Council at Trullo, 692 a.d.

lxii. . . . statuentes ut nullus vir deinceps muliebri veste induatur, vel mulier veste viro conveniente. Sed neque comicas, vel satyricas, vel tragicas personas induat. . . . Si sint quidem clerici, deponi iubemus.

Mansi, xi. 971.

Council at Berghamsted, 698 a.d.

Si tonsuratus irregulariter vagetur, semel ei hospitium concedatur, et hoc non fiat, nisi licentiam habeat.

Mansi, xii. 112.

Canons from Ireland, Seventh Century

Clericus verbis turpibus iocularis degradetur.

Clericus inter epulas cantans, fidem non aedificans, sed auribus . . . pruriens, excommunis sit.

Mansi, xii. 121.

EIGHTH CENTURY

Council of Cloveshoe, 747 a.d.

xii. Ut presbyteri saecularium poetarum modo in ecclesia non garriant, ne tragico sono sacrorum verborum compositionem . . . corrumpant . . . sed simplicem sanctamque melodiam secundum morem ecclesiae sectentur.

xx. Ut provideant episcopi in suis parochiis ut sint monasteria iuxta vocabulum nominis sui, id est, honesta silentium, quietorum atque pro Deo laborantium habitacula, et non sint ludicrarum artium receptacula, hoc est poetarum, citharistarum, musicorum, scurrarum.

Mansi, xii. 399.

Regula Magistri

De generibus monachorum (see translation, p. 163 ff.). For Latin text, see Migne, *P.L.* 103, c. 735 *et seq.*

Egbert of York, 748 a.d.

xviii. Ut nullus presbyter edendi aut bibendi causa gradiatur in tabernas.

Mansi, xii. 415

Council at Verneuil, 755 a.d.

10. Ut monachi, qui veraciter regulariter vivunt, ad Romam vel aliubi vagandi non permittantur, nisi obedientiam abbatis sui exerceant.

11. De episcopis vagantibus qui parochias non habent, nec scimus ordinationem eorum qualiter fuit ; placuit . . . ut in alterius parrochia ministrare . . . non debeant, sine iussione episcopi cuius parrochia est.

M. G. H. Cap. Reg. Franc. (ed. Boretius), i. p. 35.

Admonitio Generalis, 789 a.d.

iii. Fugitivi clerici et peregrini a nullo recipiantur nec ordinentur sine commend. litt.

xiv. Monachi et clerici tabernas non ingrediantur.

xxiv. Nec episcopi nec clerici transmigrentur de civitate in civitatem.

Cap. Reg. Franc. i. 54.

Capitulary of Charlemagne, 789 a.d.

xix. Ut nulla abbatissa foras monasterio exire non praesumat sine nostra iussione, nec sibi subditas facere permittat . . . et nullatenus ibi winileodas scribere vel mittere praesumant. (See Lot, *Winileodas. Archiv. Med. Lat.* 1925, p. 102.)

Cap. Reg. Franc. i. 63.

Council at Friuli, 796-7 a.d.

vi. Nullus sub ecclesiastico canone constitutus . . . in canticis saecularibus aut in resoluta et immoderata laetitia, in liris et tibiis et his similibus lusibus . . . ob inanis laetitiae fluxum audeat . . . abuti.

M. G. H. Conc. Aev. Car. i. p. 191.

APPENDIX

Capitulary of Charlemagne, 797 a.d.

xxvii. De clericis; nequaquam de ecclesia ad aliam ecclesiam transmigrentur neque recipiantur sine conscientia episcopi et litteris commendatitiis de cuius diocesia fuerunt, ne forte discordia exinde veniat in ecclesia. Et ubi modo tales reperti fuerint, omnes ad eorum ecclesiam redeant, et nullus eum post se retinere audeat, postquam episcopus aut abbas suus eum recipere voluerit.

Cap. Reg. Franc. I. 76.

Council at Risphach, 798 a.d.

xv. Istis gyrovagis qui circumeunt mundum et seducunt multos, dicunt se esse episcopos quod non sunt, et . . . ecclesias Dei praesumunt sacrare, clericos ordinare . . . *None to be received without strict examination.*

M. G. H. Conc. Aev. Car. I. p. 200.

NINTH CENTURY

Council at Aix-la-Chapelle, 802 a.d.

xxii. Canonici . . . nequaquam foris vagari sinantur. . . . Non per vicos neque per villas ad ecclesiam vicini vel terminantes sine magisterio vel disciplina . . . luxoriando vel fornicando, vel etiam cetera iniqua operando quae consentiri absordum est.

xxiii. Presbiteri clericos quos secum habent sollicite praevideant, ut canonice vivant, non inanis lusibus vel conviviis saecularibus, vel canticis vel luxoriosis usum habeant.

Cap. Reg. Franc. I. p. 94.

Mainz, 813 a.d.

xiv. De negotio saeculari. Ministri autem altaris Domini vel monachi . . . ut a negotiis saecularibus omnino abstineant . . . turpe lucrum, munera iniusta accipere vel dare, pro aliquo saeculari conquestu pretio aliquem conducere . . . turpis verbi vel facti joculatorem esse vel iocum saeculare diligere, aleas amare, ornamentum inconveniens proposito suo querere, in deliciis vivere velle, gulam et ebrietatem sequi.

M. G. H. Conc. Aev. Car. I. p. 264.

xxii. De clericis vagis sive acephalis, id est de his qui sunt sine capite neque in servitio domini nostri neque sub episcopo neque sub abbate, sed sine canonica vel regulari vita degentes . . . praecipimus ut ubicumque inventi fuerint, episcopi sine ulla mora eos sub custodia constringant canonica et nullatenus eos amplius ita errabundos et vagos secundum desideria voluptatum suarum vivere permittant. Sin autem episcopis suis canonice obedire noluerint, excommunicentur usque ad iudicium archepiscopi regionis illius.

Conc. Aev. Car. I. p. 267.

xxxi. De fugitivis clericis.

Such to be searched for and sent back to their bishops. Each bishop to make inquiry among his priests and clerks, whence they came.

Conc. Aev. Car. I. p. 268.

Council of Châlons, 813 A.D.

ix. *General prohibition of* histriones *and obscene jesting.*

xliii. Sunt in quibusdam locis Scotti qui se dicunt episcopos esse et multos negligentes absque licentia dominorum suorum seu magistrorum presbyteros et diacones ordinant; *such ordination to be null.*

xliv. . . . Presbyteros vilicos esse non debere, in tabernis bibere, cancellarios publicos esse, nundinas insolenter peragrare, Romam sive Turonam sine licentia episcopi sui adire. . . .

Conc. Aev. Car. I. 276, 282.

Council of Tours, 813 A.D.

viii. Ab omnibus quaecumque ad aurium et ad oculorum pertinent illecebras, unde vigor animi emolliri posse credatur, quod de aliquibus generibus musicorum, aliisque nonnullis rebus sentiri potest Dei sacerdotes abstinere debent. . . .

Mansi, XIV. 84.

Council at Aix-la-Chapelle, 816 A.D.

De clericis et monachis non manentibus in suo proposito.

[*This council is a complete corpus of divinity and discipline.*]

M.G.H. Conc. Aev. Car. I. 368.

APPENDIX

Council at Rome, 826 a.d.

xxviii. *Monks who are such in habit only . . . to be returned to their own monasteries, or to another,* prospectu congruo.

Conc. Aev. Car. i. 579.

Capitulary, 827 a.d., collected for Louis the Pious by Benedict and Ansegisus

i. 3. Fugitivi clerici et peregrini . . . *not to be received.*

Mansi, *Concil.* xv. Appendix, p. 475.

xxii. Nec monachi nec clerici nec presbyteri in saecularia negotia transeant.

xxiv. Nec episcopus nec clerici transmigrent de civitate in civitatem.

Ib. p. 477.

vi. 127. Ne passim episcopus multitudinem clericorum faciat, sed secundum meritum vel reditum ecclesiarum numerus moderetur.

Ib. p. 631.

Council at Paris, 829 a.d.

xxxvi. *An unhappy custom has arisen in our time, that many subject to ecclesiastical rule, deserting their vow and their place, . . . make their way wherever their desire persuadeth them. They are received not only by bishops and abbots, but by counts and nobles. It is entreated, and the imperial power appealed to, that no layman shall receive a clerk of this kind. And especially that no Italian bishop, abbot, count, or noble shall presume to receive clerks fleeing thither from Germany and from Gaul.*

M.G.H. Conc. Aev. Car. i. 635.

xiii. *The king is besought* "ut sacerdotes et levitae et sequentis ordinis clerici qui in diversas imperii partes maximeque in Italiae regionem fuga lapsi sunt . . . per missos vestros diligenter perquirantur et in praesentiam vestram venire compellantur et . . . unicuique ecclesiae a qua per contumaciam defecerunt restituantur."

xiv. *That monks, priests, and clerks be discouraged from coming about the palace.*

Conc. Aev. Car. i. 675.

Council at Aix-la-Chapelle, 836 a.d.

viii. *Against priests disgracing their order in taverns* inhoneste et impudice, *in drinking bouts and feasting*. . . .

xxii., xxiii. *Against priests who hang about the palace, fearing canonical penalty for a crime committed in their parish.*

Monks forbidden in publicis locis . . . discurrere. Fieri potest ut quidam . . . perpetrato scelere in monasterio causam vagandi potius eligat quam regularibus disciplinis subiacere.

Conc. Aev. Car. i. 712.

Council at Mainz, 847 a.d.

xiii. Canonici et monachi *forbidden* verbi vel facti joculatorem esse, vel iocum saecularem diligere.

Mansi, xiv. 907.

Synod held at Pavia, 849 a.d.

Let there be removed from the episcopal table . . . cuncta argumenta turpitudinis . . . fatuorum stultiloquia.

Mansi, xiv. 930.

Synod at Rome, 853 a.d.

ix. *Ordain no more clerks than can be provided for.*

Mansi, xiv. 1004.

Capitula of Walter of Orleans, *c.* 858 a.d.

xvi. Ut presbyteri, vel reliqui ordinis ecclesiastici . . . in tabernis non bibant nec scurrilitatibus cachinnum moventibus consuescant.

xvii. *At banquets* " rusticis cantilenis caveant nec saltatrices in modum filiae Heriodiadis coram se turpes facere ludos permittant."

Mansi, xv. 507.

Capitula of Hincmar of Rheims, *c.* 859 a.d.

xiv. Ut nullus presbytorum . . . nec plausus et risus inconditos et fabulas inanes ibi ferre aut cantare praesumat, nec turpia joca cum urso vel tornatricibus ante se fieri permittat.

Mansi, xv. 478.

APPENDIX

Council at Tours, 860 a.d.

v. Quia . . . plurima loca Deo sacrata incensa vel vastata sunt a perfidiis Christianis et a crudeli etiam gente Northmannorum, aut hac occasione multi lascivi clerici et monachi relicto religionis habitu retro abierunt, et absque ulla canonica licentia et reverentia vagabundi feruntur, ab ovile gregis Dei errantes . . . *let them return to their bishops and abbots and remain under their discipline.*

Mansi, xv. 560.

Council at Worms, 868 a.d.

xviii. *Priests, deacons, or clerks found without licence of* ambulandi *shall not assist in celebration.*

Mansi, xv. 872.

Council at Tribur, 895 a.d.

xxvi. Monachus fuga regularis disciplinae elapsus . . . *to be discountenanced on every side, that shamefaced and poverty-stricken he may return.* Si autem tam irreverens et pertinax est . . . ergastulo decoqui possit poenitudinis igne purgatorio.

xxvii. Clerici qui semel in clericatu deputati sunt, neque ad militiam neque ad aliam veniant dignitatem mundanam; et hoc tentantes et penitentiam non agentes quo minus redeant ad hoc quod propter Deum primitus eligere, anathematizari. Nos autem statuimus ut clericus ecclesiastice nutritus, in ecclesia coram populo legens vel cantans, si post modum relicto clericatus habitu, a castris dominicis quibus adscriptus est, profugus et apostata elabitur, et ad saeculum egreditur, ab episcopo canonice coerceatur, ut ad sinum matris ecclesiae revertatur. Quod si in hac indisciplinatione perdurat, ut comam nutriat, constringatur ut iterum detondeatur et postea nec uxorem accipiat, nec sacrum ordinem attingat.

Mansi, xviii. 146.

TENTH CENTURY

The Deposition of Pope John XII

Diaboli in amorem vinum bibisse omnes tam clerici quam laici acclamarunt. In ludo aleae Jovis, Veneris, ceterorumque daemonum auxilium poposcisse dixerunt.

Mansi, xviii. 466.

COUNCIL AT TROSLEY, 909 A.D.

(*Inaugurates the reform of Cluny*)

iii. De monasteriorum vero non statu sed lapsu.

The pillage and spoiling of the heathen have left the monasteries under alien heads. Some driven by poverty abandon the septa, *and take to worldly trades not only indistinguishable* a vulgo, sed propter infima quae sectantur opera, despectionis expositi sunt ludibrio.

Let there be no occasion evagandi.

MANSI, XVIII. 270, 272.

[*Spurious*]

COUNCIL UNDER WALTER, ARCHBISHOP OF SENS, A.D. 913.

xiii. Statuimus quod clerici ribaldi, maxime qui vulgo dicuntur de familia Goliae per episcopos, archdiaconos, officiales et decanos Christianitatis tonderi praecipiantur vel etiam radi, ita quod eis non remaneat tonsura clericalis; ita tamen quod sine periculo et scandalo ita fiant.

MANSI, XVIII. 324.

["*Il ne faut pas aller chercher trop haut mention des goliards. . . . En tout état de cause on ne saurait faire état du texte cité par M. Faral, d'après Labbé et Mansi, comme un concile de Sens de* 913. *Le c.* 9. *mentionne les dispositions d'un concile général sur le costume des clercs. Ce ne peut être que le concile de Latran de* 1215. *Le c.* 13 *cite, parmi les autorités écclésiastiques chargées de sévir contre les goliards, les officiaux. Il ne saurait être question d'officiaux au X*[e] *siècle. D'ailleurs, le même texte est reproduit par Mansi lui-même comme un concile de Sens de* 1239."] (Génestal, *Privilegium Fori*, p. 165.)

COUNCIL AT ALTHEIM, 916 A.D.

xxvii. *Fugitive clerks to be excommunicated unless they returned to their church.*

MANSI, XVIII. 329.

CANONS UNDER KING EDGAR, *c.* A.D. 967

lviii. Docemus etiam ut nullus sacerdos fit cerevisiarius, nec aliquo modo scurram agat secum ipso vel aliis; sed sit, sicut ordinem eius decet, prudens et venerandus.

lxiv. . . . ut sacerdos non sit venator . . . nec potator sed incumbat libris suis.

MANSI, XVIII. 517.

EDGAR TO DUNSTAN, 967 A.D.

Iam domus clericorum putentur prostibula meretricum, conciliabulum histrionum. Ibi aleae, ibi saltus et cantus, ibi usque ad medium noctis spatium protractae in clamore et horrore vigiliae.

MANSI, XVIII. 527.

EDGAR'S CHARTER TO MALMESBURY, 974 A.D.

. . . monasteria quae velut muscivis scindulis, cariosis tabulis tigno tenus visibiliter diruta. . . . Idiotis nempe clericis ejectis, nullis regularis religionis disciplinae subjectis . . .

MANSI, XIX. 47.

LEGES PRESBYTERUM NORTHUMBRENSIUM

Si presbyter ebrietati deditus sit, vel scurrilis aut cerevisarius fuerit, hoc compenset.

MANSI, XIX. 69.

CAPITULA OF ATTO, BISHOP OF VERCELLI

xliv. Clericum scurrilem et verbis turpibus jocularem ab officio retrahendum.

xlvi. Clericum inter epulas cantantem supradictae sententiae severitate coercendum [*i.e.* degradetur ab officio].

MANSI, XIX. 253.

SYNOD AT MONT NOTRE DAME, UNDER ADALBERO OF RHEIMS, *c.* 970 A.D.

Complaint against monkish disorder, desertion of monasteries, wearing of orange, and shoes with beaks and ears.

RICHER, *Hist.* III. 45 (MIGNE, 138, c. 98).

ELEVENTH CENTURY

Letter of Licence for a Clerk

Alberic of Monte Cassino

[Rockinger, *Briefstellen und Formelbücher* in *Quellen zur Bayerischen und Deutschen Geschichte*, Munich, 1863]

Quoniam clericorum plerique diabolice fraudis suggestione decepti, cum longius a propria civitate destiterant instabiles et vagabundi, nec urbis sua statione contenti ab antistite proprio licentiam ad alia loca conmigrandi accepisse se verbis litterisque mendacibus confiteri non metuunt. . . .

Laws of Edward the Confessor

1. Omnis clericus et etiam scholaris et omnes eorum res et possessiones ubicumque fuerit, pacem Dei et sanctae ecclesiae habeant.

Mansi, xix. 715.

Letter of Nicholas II. to the Bishops of Gaul, Aquitaine, and Gascony, 1059 A.D.

Against those clerks who reject the tonsure and depart from the order . . . Julianistas apostatas.

Mansi, xix. 873.

Council at Rouen, 1072 A.D.

xii. Ut monachi vagi ad monasteria sua redire compellantur.

xv. De clericis uxoratis (*priests, deacons, subdeacons*), ut ecclesiis non ministrent nec fructus percipiant.

Mansi, xx. 35, 38.

Council at Rome, 1074 A.D.

Ne hi qui culpis urgentibus ab ordine sunt depositi quasi ab omni clericatu liberi, militent saeculo more laicali.

Mansi, xx. 399.

Council at Malfi (Apulia), 1090 A.D.

ix. Quia novum hoc tempore clericorum Acephalorum genus emersit, qui morantur in curiis, et viris et feminis ad sui ordinis dedecus subditi . . . *Let no one maintain such without the bishop's leave, or should he be a bishop, without leave of his metropolitan.*

MANSI, XX. 723.

COUNCIL AT SZABOLCH (HUNGARY)

xvii. Contra clericos et religiosos vagabundos.

MANSI, XX. 769.

Marbod on the wandering monks, who can only endure three or four years of the monastic tedium.

" Effectique vagi, currunt per devia pagi,
Iam mundo viles propter causas monachiles
Iam monachi viles, ut regi transfuga miles."

MIGNE, *P.L.* 171, 1669.

TWELFTH CENTURY

HISTORY OF FARFA, 1122 A.D.

After the peace between pope and emperor, the monks return as men spoiled and robbed ; they sing in black cowls and everyday garb in the choir. Adolescentes quoque vel iuniores fratres cantuum neumas et organa solita respuebant, et non spirituali honestate et gravitate sed istrionum more canere studebant, et multas nenias extraneasque cantilenas satagebant, nec huius loci consuetudinem sed diversarium partium levitates et extollentias quas in exteris locis quebus degebant audierant vel viderant, exercere curabant.[1]

M. G. H. Script. XI. 583.

[1] Cf. Ælred of Rievaulx, *Speculum Charitatis*, II. 23 (Migne, *P.L.* CXCV. 571). Gerhoh of Augsburg describes the laxity of church and cloister at Augsburg when he was *magister scholarum* there in 1122 ; how the refectory was empty unless a Herod play was toward, or *ludis aliis aut spectaculis quasi-theatralibus* : and he laments his own share in these follies—*non solum interfui sed praefui* (*P.L.* CXCIV. 890). Cf. the chapter *De spectaculis theatricis* in his *De Investigatione Antichristi*, written *c.* 1161. (Scheibelberger, *Gerhohi Opera Inedita*, I. 25).

COUNCIL AT CLERMONT, 1130 A.D.

v. Prava consuetudi et detestabilis . . . *monks and regular canons study temporal law and medicine.*

x. Si quis . . . in clericos vel monachos manus iniecerit, anathemati subjaceat.

MANSI, XXI. 438.

The canon against the study of medicine and civil law by regulars is repeated at Rheims, 1131 *: Lateran Council,* 1139 *: Tours,* 1163*. The canon against striking clerks, at Rheims,* 1131 *: London,* 1138 *: Lateran,* 1139*. Canons against clerical truancy appear in Toulouse,* 1119 *: Lateran,* 1179 *: Rouen,* 1189 *: and Toul,* 1192.

THIRTEENTH CENTURY

COUNCIL AT LONDON, 1200 A.D.

x. *Clerks must not go to taverns. Hence arise contentions and quarrels ; and laymen striking clerks* incident in canonem. *These are sent to the pope, but the clerks remain unpunished, which is not fair.*

MANSI, XXII. 718.

DECRETAL OF INNOCENT III, 1207.

(*Issued to the Archbishop of Gnesen in Poland.*)

Cum decorem domus Domini . . . diligere vos oporteat . . . [*follows a complaint against the sons of canons being admitted* ad ministerium altaris], interdum ludi fiunt in eisdem ecclesiis theatrales, et non solum ad ludibriorum spectacula introducuntur in eas monstra larvarum, verum etiam in tribus anni festivitatibus quae continue Natalem Christi sequuntur, diaconi, presbiteri et subdiaconi vicissim insaniae suae ludibria exercentes, per gesticulationum suarum debacchationes obscenas in conspectu populi decus faciunt clericale vilescere . . . mandamus quatenus . . . ludibriorum consuetudinem . . . curetis e vestris ecclesiis . . . exstirpare.

MIGNE, *P.L.* CCXV. 1070.

CONSTITUTIONS OF CARDINAL GUALO AT PARIS, 1208 A.D.

1. *Excommunications of priests and clerks, who, after admonition, have women in keeping : married clerks in minor orders excepted, but these may hold no benefice.*

viii. Ut cum magistris et scholaribus agatur indulgentius. *As much as may be* "cum Deo et honeste," *this rigour is tempered to masters and scholars: a general admonition precedes, then a particular*, nominatim et in scholis, *finally excommunication.*

MANSI, XXII. 763.

COUNCIL AT PARIS, 1212 A.D.

iv. *No one having the pastoral care shall learn the secular sciences. . . . If he has a licence from his bishop to go to the schools, it shall be to learn* veram litteram aut sacram paginam.

MANSI, XXII. 845.

xvi. Ne in domibus clericorum . . . inhonestas commessationes vel ludos talorum fieri permittant, vel conventionem ribaldorum ibi recipiant.

MANSI, XXII. 823.

COUNCIL AT ROUEN, 1214 A.D.

ii. *Prelates are not to hear matins in bed.*

MANSI, XXII. 917.

LATERAN COUNCIL (IV), 1215 A.D.

xvi. Clerici officia vel commercia saecularia non exerceant, maxime inhonesta. Mimis, ioculatoribus et histrionibus non intendant et tabernas prorsus evitent, nisi in itinere, . . . ad aleas vel taxillos non ludant.

xiii. *Prelates as well as minor clergy spend half the night in superfluous feasting and illicit confabulation, not to mention other things, then sleep in a syncope, hardly to be wakened even* ad diurnum concentum avium.

MANSI, XXII. 1003, 1006.

PROVINCIAL COUNCIL AT TREVES, 1227 A.D.

ix. Item praecipimus ut omnes sacerdotes non permittant trutannos et alios vagos scholares aut goliardos cantare versus super *Sanctus* et *Agnus Dei* aut alias in missis vel in divinis officiis.

MANSI, XXIII. 33.

COUNCIL AT ROUEN, 1231 A.D.

viii. Statuimus quod clerici ribaudi, maxime qui dicuntur de familia Goliae, per episcopos, archdiaconos, officiales et decanos Christianitatis tonderi praecipiantur, vel etiam radi, ita quod eis tonsura non remaneat clericalis ; ita tamen quod sine scandalo et periculo ista fiant.

MANSI, XXIII. 215.

COUNCIL AT CHÂTEAU GONTHIER, 1231 A.D.

xxi. De Goliardis.

Item in concilio provinciali statuimus quod clerici ribaldi, maxime qui Goliardi nuncupantur, per episcopos et alios prelatos praecipiantur . . . *etc.*

MANSI, XXIII. 237.

CONSTITUTIONS OF BONFILIUS, BISHOP OF SENS, 1232 A.D.

No clerk to play at dice . . . to go into a tavern, or suspicious place . . . or to allow joculatores *to perform in church at the time of the Office, or to eat at table with clerks.*

MANSI, XXIII. 244.

DECRETALES GREGORII IX, *c.* 1234.

Lib. iii. tit. I, cap. XII. Cum decorem . . . [*repeats the Decretal of Innocent III of* 1207, *with the alteration of* tribus festivitatibus *to* aliquibus . . .].

Corpus Iuris Canonici, ed. Freidberg, ii. 452.

COUNCIL AT SENS, 1239 A.D.

xii. Statuimus quod clerici ribaldi . . . de familia Goliae . . . *etc.*

MANSI, XXIII. 512.

INNOCENT IV, *Apparatus super Decretalibus* [*Gregorii IX*], *c.* 1245

De vita et honestate clericorum . . . [cap. xii] Cum decorem (Theatrales) Mimi et histriones nullo tempore post poenitentiam sunt promovendi nisi per dispensationem pape . . . hoc intelligo de his qui publice coram populis faciunt gesticulationes sui corporis . . . si enim in occulto etiam coram pluribus aliis saltaret vel corizaret, non prohiberetur a promotione post poenitentiam. Idem etiam videtur si semel tantum vel etiam pluries fecisset coram populo dummodo non assuefecisset nec esset infamis. Infamia enim et vilitas personarum est causa quare promoveri prohibentur, et non peccatum, quia sine peccato hoc fieri posset, quia David et plures alii saltaverunt sine peccato. Qui etiam hoc faceret ad consolationem alicuius infirmi vel ex alia iusta causa non peccaret, sed assuescere in his non posset esse sine infamia et nota vilitatis et maxime in his qui querunt inde lucrum. Illud autem certum est quod si habet beneficium alias officium histrionis in aliqua curia quod ille promoveri non potest. . . .

(Theatrales) sic dicti quia fiunt in theatro, id est loco ad theorandum sive ad speculandum apto.

(Larvarum) larvae dicuntur deformitates hominum, sive per appositiones pellium sive colorum.

(Ludibria) nedum quod monachi vel alii clerici exerceant ludibria, sed etiam in eorum habitu exercere prohibentur. . . . Aliqua autem ad compunctionem fieri non prohibentur, puta presepe Domini et sepultura et consimilia. . . .

Ed. Lyons, 1525, *lib.* III. *f.* 133v.

HOSTIENSIS, *Lectura in Decretales Gregorii IX*

[I have only seen this passage in its skeleton form in numerous editions of the *Summa* of Hostiensis, under the titulus *De Sententia Excommunicationis*: it is here quoted from Génestal, *Privilegium Fori*, p. 165. Henry of Segusio was a canonist in Paris before 1244, and died Cardinal-Bishop of Ostia (hence his name) in 1271.]

Quid de goliardis, numquid qui tales percutit est excommunicatus? Videtur quod sic, nam clerici sunt et tonsuram deferunt patentem et latam, unde non licet ignorantiam allegare. Nec obstat lascivia sive vanitas, quia etiam tales semper privilegium retinent nisi trina monitione premissa incorrigibiles sint. Sed contra, quia vilitas vitae tales gaudere non patitur privilegio clericali . . . Solve: si de novo incipiant, et spes correctionis sit, quousque trina monitio praecesserit, privilegium retinent . . . si vero notorii sint, puta nudi incedunt, in furnis iacent, tabernas ludos et meretrices frequentant et in errore iam inveterati sunt, ita quod nec spes correctionis est, reatus huius modi omne privilegium excludit. . . . Sed quando dicentur inveterati? Hoc arbitrabitur bonus iudex, cum non sit iure cautum . . . tutius tamen esset si papa illud determinaret et tempus hoc limitaret et videretur annus sufficere.

COUNCIL AT BÉZIERS, 1255 A.D.

xxiv. Nullus omnino ad taxillos ludat, sive aleis, sive scacis. Scolas etiam deciorum prohibemus.

MANSI, XXIII. 882.

COUNCIL AT GERONA (CATALONIA), 1274 A.D.

xxv. *Beneficed clerks unable to speak Latin, unless their age forbids hope, to be sent for the triennium to the schools, and may hold their benefices.*

MANSI, XXIII. 935.

COUNCIL AT MONTPELLIER, 1258 A.D.

iii. Clerici mercimonia publice exercentes, operatorium sive mensam . . . pro vendendis mercibus . . . vel scholares . . . qui tonsuram dimiserint . . . qui mechanicas artes exerceant aut qui operas suas aliis locaverint vilia exercendo quamdiu notabiles se reddiderint . . . *these are in no way defended by the church from taxation ; but the privilege of canon remains.*

MANSI, XXIII. 992.

PROVINCIAL COUNCIL AT MAINZ, 1259 A.D.

De clericis vagabundis est statutum et prohibetur quod nullis a clericis vel personis ecclesiasticis recipi nec dari quidquam debeat eisdem, cum vitam ducant reprobam et infamem.

MANSI, XXIII. 997.

SYNOD AT VALENTIA, 1261 A.D.

Against clerks who dice, drink, wear green and yellow garments, and carry arms.

MANSI, XXIII. 1055-6-7.

COUNCIL AT MAINZ, 1261 A.D.

xvii. Clerici et vagabundi quos vulgus Eberhardinos vocat quorum vita Deo odibilis etiam laicos scandalizat . . . a clericis vel personis Ecclesiasticis recipi prohibemus, firmiter statuentes ne aliquid dent iisdem ; nolumus tamen ut huiusmodi occasione statuti Concilii, vel Scholares pauperes, quos quando justa eos necessitas peregrinari compellit, a caritatis operibus excludantur. *The aforesaid Eberhardini, who live a reprobate and infamous life, are to be admitted neither to Holy Orders nor to a benefice, lest our ministry be made a scandal, unless by long emendation of morals and worthy conversation the Diocesan is satisfied that their previous infamy is expiated.*

MANSI, XXIII. 1086.

COUNCIL AT AVIGNON, 1270 A.D.

viii. *No clerk who* verbis vel factis graviter dehonestaverit *a dignitary of the Church shall be admitted to any benefice without satisfaction given.*

MANSI, XXIV. 18.

COUNCIL AT SALZBURG, 1274 A.D.

xii. *The clerk in holy orders, monk or regular canon, not a traveller, who goes into a tavern, without evident, reasonable and worthy cause, and there eats and drinks . . . to be suspended from office, until he has fasted for a day ; if he has played there at dice, fast for two days. At the third offence, the bishop deprives him of his benefice ; if not beneficed, he is punished at the bishop's pleasure.*

xv. *Let no prelate give the tonsure to man or woman, unless they profess a recognised Rule and are going to a definite place, for otherwise the habit gives* materiam vagandi et opportunitatem deliquendi.

xvi. De vagis scholaribus.

Sub vagorum scholarium nomine quidam per Salzburgensem provinciam discurrentes, monasteriis et ecclesiis se exhibent adeo onerosos, quod per eorum importunitatis audaciam nonnunquam clerici illud eis erogare coguntur de quo fuit necessitatibus pauperum providendum : denegantibus sibi suffragia, per quae occasionem nutriunt malae vitae, calumnias inferunt ; conferentibus sibi quod postulant vituperium existunt ; reverentia clericali utique multum detrahitur dum blasphemia huiusmodi se personas ecclesiasticas profitentur. Ut autem viri huiusmodi per subtractionem nostri et nobis subditorum suffragii resipiscere compellantur, auctoritate sacri concilii prohibemus, ne quis prelatorum, plebanorum, aut vicariorum, seu quaecumque persona ecclesiastica, post spatium duorum mensium, infra quem terminum de ordinata sibi vita provideant, ipsis aliquid beneficii, vel juvaminis erogare praesumat. Qui contrarium fecerit, tamdiu ab ingressu ecclesiae sit suspensus, donec in subsidium terrae sanctae usualis monetae conferat unam libram. Hanc tamen constitutionem extendi nolumus ad pauperes advenas, et pro necessitatibus suis publice mendicantes.

MANSI, XXIV. 140, 141.

PENITENTIAL OF THOMAS OF CABHAM

(*on the three kinds of* histriones. *The* vagi *are not described as clerks, but the description tallies*)

Sunt etiam alii qui nihil operantur, sed criminose agunt, non habentes certum domicilium, sed sequuntur curias magnatum et dicunt opprobria et ignominias de absentibus ut placeant aliis. Tales etiam damnabiles sunt, quia prohibet Apostolus cum talibus cibum sumere, et dicuntur tales scurrae vagi, quia ad nihil utiles sunt, nisi ad devorandum et maledicendum.

CHAMBERS'S *Mediaeval Stage*, II. 262.

COUNCIL AT TRÈVES, 1277 A.D.

94. Item praecipimus ut omnes sacerdotes non permittant trutannos et alios vagos scholares aut goliardos cantare versus super Sanctus et Agnus Dei in missis vel in divinis officiis.

MANSI, XXIV. 201.

COUNCIL AT PONT-AUDÉMAR, 1279 A.D.

xx. Ut clerici . . . a saecularibus negotiis abstineant, maxime inhonestis, quodque tonsuram deferant et habitum clerico congruentes. *After three monitions, the Church will no longer protect them from the secular authority.*

MANSI, XXIV. 224.

COUNCIL AT BUDA, 1279 A.D.

74. *Monks and canons regular are wont* tam patenter quam latenter, tam turpiter quam damnabiliter, per terram saepius evagari.

76. *Excommunication of monks going without licence to the schools*, vel aliud quam grammaticam, theologiam aut logicam in scholis audire.

MANSI. XXIV. 302, 303.

APPENDIX

Council at Munster, 1279 A.D.

ii. Ne clerici vagentur nocturno tempore per plateas, et si quos ex justa et legitima causa transire contingat, hoc decenter faciant sine clamore, sine fistulis, sine tympanis, et quolibet strepitu et chorea.

v. Item propter apostatas discursores, vagos et ignotos clericos *none to be admitted to celebrate mass or exercise the priestly function unless attested.*

Mansi, xxiv. 312, 313.

Council at Cologne, 1280

i. *Repetition of the foregoing, against nightly divagation, with drums, flutes and singing. Also of canon v.*

Mansi, xxiv. 346.

Council at Salzburg, 1281 A.D.

vi. De discursu religiosorum.

Item inhonestos et indecentes religiosorum discursus amputare volentes . . . mancipare carceribus penitus incorrigibiliter obstinatos.

Mansi, xxiv. 399.

Council at St. Hippolyte (Pölten), 1284 A.D.

Item de vagis scholaribus duximus statuendum, districte praecipientes, ut cultellos longos et gladios ac arma deferentes non recipiantur omnino, nec aliquales eisdem exhibeantur consolationes. Aliis autem humanitatis causa uni vel duobus tantum modo venientibus, et non pluribus, detur modicus pastus in caritate ; et si importuni vel infesti fuerint, vel alia dona petiverint, puta denarios vel vestes, penitus repellantur. *The pastor so doing to be fined* 60 *d. and failing that, suspended from his church for a month.*

Admittimus tamen, si quis necessitate suadente, ex liberalitate vestem aliquam scholari pauperi dare voluerit propter Deum. Vagos autem Scholares detrahentes clericis nullus omnino clericorum modo aliquo recipiat, vel ad panem admittat, cui hoc constiterit, quod qui non fecerit, poenae subjaceat praedictae. De vagis vero sacerdotibus idem.

Mansi, xxiv. 511.

COUNCIL AT RAVENNA, 1286 A.D.

i. *An injunction against giving entertainment to* joculatores *sent to them for that purpose by laymen, on the occasion of a marriage or a knighting, whereby the substance of the church is squandered to the detriment of the poor.*

MANSI, XXIV. 615.

COUNCIL AT EXETER, 1287 A.D.

xvii. Ut inter clericos et histriones, sicut est, ita appareat in omnibus dispar professio. . . .

xxix. Beneficia aquae benedictae, *as of old, to be the perquisite of poor clerks in the schools.*

MANSI, XXIV. 806, 816.

STATUTES OF SYNOD AT LIEGE, 1287 A.D.

xii. 5. Item prohibemus, ne clerici exerceant negotia turpia, et officia inhonesta, quae non decent clericos, qualia sunt haec . . . officium cambitoris, carnificis, tabernarii, procenetae, fullonis, sutoris, textoris, nec sint histriones, joculatores, ballivi, forestarii saeculares, goliardi, thelonarii, unguentarii, triparii, molendinarii. Si vero clerici aliqui officia talia exercuerint, a suo prelato super hoc puniantur.

xii. 8 Statuimus propter apostatas, desertores et vagos et ignotos clericos . . . *warning against allowing unauthorised priests to celebrate.*

MANSI, XXIV. 910, 911.

STATUTES: CAHORS, RODEZ, AND TOUL, 1289 A.D.

Item praecipimus quod clerici non sint joculatores, goliardi, seu bufones, declarantes quod si per annum illam artem diffamatoriam exercuerint omni privilegio ecclesiastico sunt nudati, et etiam temporaliter graviori si moniti non destiterint. Clerici conjugati . . . volentes gaudere privilegio clericali tonsuram et vestes deferant clericales; et tunc duo privilegia sibi retinent, quia puniri non possunt pro criminibus pecuniariter nec corporaliter per judicem saecularem; et si quis manus suas in eos temere violentas injecerit, erit excommunicatus; alias vero nullum retinent privilegium clericale.

Item, clerici qui ex levitate, vel lascivia, vel negligentia, tonsura demissa et habitu clericali, arma deferunt vel saecularibus negotiationibus prohibitis se immiscent, et tertio moniti desistere nolunt quousque se corrigant. Item si in goliardia, vel histrionatu per annum fuerint vel breviori tempore, et ter moniti non desistunt. Item bigami a foro ecclesiastico omni clericali privilegio sunt exclusi. Clerici qui etiam non demisso habitu clericali ut laici mercaturas et negotiationes clericis prohibitas exercent, privilegium de non praestandis talliis, muneribus laicalibus, post trinam monitionem amittunt.

MANSI, XXIV. 1017, 1019.

COUNCIL AT SALZBURG, 1291 A.D.

De secta vagorum scholarium.

Licet contra quosdam sub vagorum scholarium nomine discurrentes, scurriles, maledicos, blasphemos, adulationibus importune vacantes, qui se clericos in vituperium clericalis ordinis profitentur, nonnulla pio zelo pro salubri eorum correctione emanaverint instituta: ex his tamen nullus fructus aut modicus iam provenit. Publice nudi incedunt, in furnis jacent, tabernas, ludos, et meretrices frequentant, peccatis suis victum sibi emunt, inveterati sectam suam non deserunt sicut de eorum correctione nullus remaneat locus spei. Ideoque prioribus statutis pro salute animarum suarum, quam quaerimus, salvis: adjicimus et denunciamus in hac sacra synodo, sub poena privilegii clericalis publice prohibentes, ne quis sectam vagorum scholarium reprobatam assumat, seu in ea permaneat, vel iam exercere praesumat. Alioquin eos qui huiusmodi sectam ante hanc nostram constitutionem temere assumptam, infra mensem, a tempore promulgationis eiusdem constitutionis numerandum, penitus non dimiserit, et illos qui nunc assumere praesumpserint, ipso facto statim omni privilegio clericali exui praecipimus et nudari: volentes, ut quandocumque a monasteriis, ecclesiis, vel clericis, cuiuscumque rei importuni vel violenti fuerint exactores, ipsis eosdem liceat nostra auctoritate capere, invocato ad hoc, si opus fuerit, brachio saeculari. Et eos captos nobis vel archidiaconis nostris assignari volumus nostro carceri, ut nobis videbitur, includendos; ut sic reatus, omne excludat privilegium in his, quos vilitas vitae eo nec frui patitur, nec gaudere.

MANSI, XXIV. 1077.

BONIFACE VIII., *c.* 1298 A.D.

Clerici qui, clericalis ordinis dignitati non modicum detrahentes, se joculatores seu goliardos faciunt aut bufones, si per annum artem illam ignominiosam exercuerint, ipso iure, si autem tempore breviori, et tertio moniti non resipuerint, careant omni privilegio clericali.

SEXT. DECRET. III. i. I.

FOURTEENTH CENTURY

COUNCIL AT COLOGNE, 1300 A.D.

iii. Aliqui clerici utpote apostatae, discursores et vagi de aliis provinciis et diocesibus . . . qui ab aliis diocesibus tamquam irregulares et indigni pro eorum culpis et excessibus sunt remoti *are forbidden the* regimen animarum. *Any ecclesiastic admitting them thereto to be excommunicated.*

MANSI, XXV. 17.

COUNCIL AT SALZBURG, 1310 A.D.

iii. De clericis ioculatoribus.

Item iuxta constitutionem domini Bonifacii, quae est talis "Clerici qui clericali ordini non modicum detrahentes se ioculatores seu goliardos faciunt, aut buffones, si per annum artem illam ignominiosam exercuerint ipso jure; si autem tempore breviori et tertio admoniti non resipuerint, careant omni privilegio clericali; monemus huius approbatione concilii, omnes et singulos tales, ut talem habitum et vitam non assumant, et assumptam deponant infra tres menses, quorum unum pro primo, alterum pro secundo, et tertium pro tertio termino peremptorio assignamus; si poenam praedictam, quam ipso facto incidunt, voluerint evitare."

i. De clericis tabernariis.

A kindly canon moderating the rigors of the earlier clericus non viator. *If the* clericus, *in orders or religion, entered the tavern to the honouring of some friend, lord, or distinguished person, or entered it without premeditation, forgetful of the prohibition, or for some necessary and useful cause, not voluptuous, and there drank or ate, he shall not incur the statutory penalty. But this moderation does not extend to* lusores, *players.*

MANSI, XXV. 226.

APPENDIX

Council at Trèves, 1310 a.d.

xxviii. Contra monachos qui vadunt per civitates.

Mansi, xxv. 257.

Council at Mainz, 1310 a.d.

De clericis vagabundis.

Clerici vagabundi quos vulgus Eberhardinos vocat, quorum vita est odibilis, et laicos scandalizat ; priori inhaerentes concilio a clericis et personis ecclesiasticis recipi prohibemus, firmiter statuentes, ne aliquid eisdem detur. Nolumus tamen ut huius occasione statuti clerici vel saeculares pauperes quos quamquam iusta necessitas peregrinari compellit, a caritatis operibus excludantur. . . . *The necessitous may have alms* sine personarum differentia. Qui Eberhardini privati vitam ducunt reprobam et infamem, ne ad sacros ordines, vel ecclesiastica beneficia aliquatenus admittantur, ut nostrum non vituperetur ministerium . . . *unless a long course of discretion commends them to the diocesan.*

De eisdem clericis vagabundis, qui praesumant aliquando celebrare.

Ad huc quia clerici vagabundi qui Eberhardini vocantur quorum vita Deo odibilis, clericos et ipsos laicos scandalizat, discurrendo per terras in villas quae carent propriis sacerdotibus aliquando celebrare praesumunt, seu quod verius est, divina officia profanare, statuimus ut tales ad mandatum diocesani, seu loci archidiaconi teneantur in custodia carcerali, ad hoc si necesse fuerit, invocando auxilium brachii saecularis.

Mansi, xxv. 311.

Council of Tarragon, 1317 a.d.

Because of frequent disputes between the secular and ecclesiastical judges, all clerks wishing to enjoy privilege are to present themselves within three months to the bishop or official to be enrolled ; and are to be enjoined by name to wear habit and tonsure, and abstain a negotiationibus . . . inhonestis . . . Mimi, histriones, vel lenones . . . cursarii seu piratae, nisi contra infideles . . . non existant.

Mansi, xxv. 630.

Council at Paris, 1323 a.d.

Against clerks wearing red, green, yellow, and white hose.

Mansi, xxv. 730.

Constitutions at Ferrara, 1332 a.d.

Ne clericus aliquis aut persona ecclesiastica habitans in civitate Ferrariensi . . . tabernas intret ut bibat in eis. Ne cum mulieribus vel aliis . . . in choreis cantare, saltare vel balare . . . seu . . . lascivire vel obscenitates aut ludibria sui corporis exercere . . . Ne ad azardium . . . aut aliquem alium ludum inhonestum . . . nisi forte ad schacos absque taxillis . . . ludere praesumant.

Mansi, xxv. 920.

Synod at Arezzo, 1350 a.d.

43. De poena Clericorum choreizantium vel sonantium Instrumenta.

Mansi, xxvi. 214.

Provincial Council at Padua, 1350 a.d.

Revokes the severe penalties against the clerks in taverns instituted by the Archbishop of Salzburg.

Mansi, xxvi. 227.

Synod at Prague, 1355 a.d.

xxvi. Clerici insuper, maxime beneficati, tabardis rubeis aut viridibus uti non debent, nec joculatores se faciant, et si post unam aut trinam admonitionem artem illam ignominiosam exerceant, eo ipso privati sint omni beneficio clericali. . . . Clericos qui vagi communiter nuncupantur in domibus suis non recolligant, nec eis aliquid munus nec parvum nec magnum tribuant.

Concil. xxvi. 390.

Provincial Council at Magdeburg, 1370 a.d.

xix. Quia clerici vagabundi qui eberhardini dicuntur . . . *Against celebration by such* . . . teneantur in custodia carcerali

Mansi, xxvi. 579.

TABLE OF BIOGRAPHICAL DATES

Abelard, 1079–1142.
Absolon of St. Victor, *ob.* 1203.
Adam du Petit Pont, 1105–1181, *ob.* Bp. of St. Asaph.
Adam of St. Victor, *fl.* 1130–1192.
Adelard of Bath, *fl.* 1109–1142.
Adelmann of Liege, *ob.* Bp. of Brescia, *c.* 1062.
Adhemar of Chavannes, *c.* 988–*post* 1028.
Alanus ab Insulis (Alain de Lille), *ob.* 1202.
Alberic of Monte Cassino, Cardinal Deacon, *fl.* 1079.
Albero, Bp. of Liege, *ob.* 1145.
Albert of Morra (Gregory VIII), *fl.* 1157–1188.
Alcuin, *c.* 735–*c.* 804.
Aldhelm, St., *c.* 650–709.
Alexander III, Pope from 1159–1181.
Alexander of Hales, *c.* 1175–1245.
Alexandre de Ville-Dieu, *c.* 1160–*post* 1203.
Alphanus, Abp. of Salerno, *fl.* 1058–1085.
Ambrose, St., *c.* 340–397.
André le Chapelain, *fl.* 1174.
Angilbert, Abbot of St. Riquier, *ob.* 814.
Anselm of Bisate, *fl.* 1049.
Arator, *fl.* 544.
Archpoet, 1130 ?–1165 ?
Arnold of Brescia, *ob.* 1155.
Arnulfus Rufus, *fl. c.* 1140.
Augustine, St., 354–430.
Ausonius, *c.* 310–*c.* 395.
Aymon of Fleury, *c.* 970–*post* 1005.

Bacon, Roger, *c.* 1214–1294.
Barbarossa (Frederick I), *c.* 1123–1190.
Baudri de Bourgeuil, 1046–1130.
Becket, St. Thomas, 1118–1170.
Bede, *c.* 673–735.
Benedict, St., 480–543.
Benedict of Aniane, *c.* 751–821.
Benedict Biscop, *ob.* 690.
Benoît de Sainte-More, *fl. c.* 1175.
Berengarius of Tours, *c.* 1010–1088.
Berengarius, disciple of Abelard, *fl.* 1140.
Bernard, St., of Clairvaux, 1090–1153.
Bernard of Chartres, *ob. c.* 1126.
Bernard of Meung, *fl. c.* 1180.
Bernard of Morlas, *fl.* 1140.
Bernard Sylvestris of Tours, *fl. c.* 1140.
Boethius, *c.* 470–525.
Boniface, St., *c.* 680–755.
Boniface VIII, Pope 1294–1303.
Breakspere, Nicholas (Adrian IV), *c.* 1100–1159.
Bruno, St., Abp. of Cologne, 925–965.
Bruno, Giordano, *c.* 1548–1600.
Buoncompagno, *fl.* 1198–1235.

Caesarius of Heisterbach, *c.* 1170–*c.* 1240.
Cassian (founded St. Victor at Marseilles), 360–435.
Cassiodorus, *c.* 490–585.
Charlemagne, *c.* 742–814.
Charles the Bald, 823–877.
Chilperic, *ob.* 584.
Chrétien de Troyes, *fl. c.* 1164.
Clement the Irishman, *fl. c.* 800–826.
Coelcu of Clonmacnoise, *ob.* 794.
Columba, St., 521–597.
Columbanus, St., 543–615.

Damiani, St. Peter, 1007–1072.
Dicuil, *fl.* 825.
Dungal, *fl.* 810, at Pavia, 825.
Dunstan, St., 909–988.

Eberhard of Bethune, *fl.* 1210.
Eberhard the German (unknown: his *Laborintus* later than 1213, earlier than 1280).
Eginhard, *c.* 770–840.
Ekkehard I of St. Gall, *c.* 900–973.
Ekkehard IV of St. Gall, *c.* 980–1060.
Eleanor of Aquitaine, *c.* 1122–1204.
Ennodius of Arles, Bp. of Pavia, 474–521.
Ermenric of Ellwangen, *ob.* 874.

Faba, Guido, *fl.* 1226–1243.
Flodoard of Reims, 894–966.
Fortunatus, Venantius, *c.* 530–600 ?
Foulques of Toulouse, *fl.* 1180–1231.
Frederick II, 1194–1250.
Froumund of Tegernsee, *c.* 960–*c.* 1008.
Fulbert, St., of Chartres, *c.* 975–1029.
Fursa, St., *fl.* 644.

Garnier de Pont-Sainte-Maxence, *fl. c.* 1170.
Gautier de Château Thierry, Chancellor, *ob.* Bp. of Paris, 1249.
Gautier de Châtillon, born not later than 1135, died not before 1184.
Geoffrey de Vinesauf, *fl.* 1194.
Gerbert (Silvester II), *post* 940–1003.
Gilles de Corbeil, 1140–1224 ?
Gilles d'Orval, *fl.* 1251.
Giraldus Cambrensis, 1147–1223.
Gosvin, prior of St. Médard, abbot of Anchin, *fl.* 1113–1166.
Gottschalk, *c.* 805–870.
Gratian, *fl.* 1139–1151.
Gregorius, Magister, *fl. c.* 1200 ?
Gregory the Great, *c.* 540–604.
Gregory IX, Pope 1227–1241.
Gregory of Tours, 538–594.
Grimold, Abbot of St. Gall 841–872.
Grossetête, Robert, Bp. of Lincoln, *c.* 1175–1253.
Guibert de Nogent, 1053–1121.
Guido de Bazoches, *ante* 1146–1203.
Guillaume IX, 1071–1127.
Guillaume le Breton, *ob. c.* 1250.
Guillaume de Lorris, *fl.* 1230.
Guillaume, Abbot of St. Thierry, *ob. c.* 1148.
Gunzo of Novara, *fl.* 965.

Hadrian, Abbot of SS. Peter and Paul at Canterbury, *fl.* 671.
Heiric of Auxerre, 841–*c.* 876.
Helgaldus, *fl. c.* 1040.
Helinand, *fl.* 1229.
Heloise, *ob.* 1164.
Henri d'Andeli, *fl.* 1236.
Henry II, 1133–1189.
Henry IV, Emperor, 1050–1106.
Henry of Blois, Bp. of Winchester, *fl.* 1126–1171.
Hermann of Dalmatia, *fl.* 1143.
Herrad von Landsberg, *ob.* 1195.
Hilarius the Goliard, *fl.* 1125.
Hildebert of Le Mans, 1056–1133.
Hildebrand (Gregory VII), *c.* 1023–1085.
Hincmar of Rheims, *c.* 805–882.
Honorius d'Autun, *fl. c.* 1120.
Hrabanus, Maurus, 776–856.
Hroswitha, *c.* 935–*post* 973.
Hucbald of St. Amand, *c.* 840–930.
Hugh of Nunant, Bp. of Coventry, *fl.* 1186–1199.

Innocent III, Pope 1198–1216.
Innocent IV, Pope 1243–1254.
Isidore of Pelusium, *fl. c.* 440.
Isidore of Seville, *c.* 570–636.
Iso of St. Gall, *fl.* 852–868.
Ivo of Chartres, 1040–1116.

Jacques de Lausanne, *ob. ante* 1322.
Jacques de Vitry, *c.* 1160–1240.
Jean de Meung, 1250 ?–1305 ?
Jean de St. Gilles, *fl.* 1235.

BIOGRAPHICAL DATES

Jerome, St., *c.* 340–420.
Jocelin of Brakelonde, *fl.* 1173–1211.
John, King, 1167–1216.
John XII, Pope 955–964.
John of Garland, *c.* 1180–*post* 1252.
John of Ravenna, *fl.* 1364.
John of Salisbury, *c.* 1115–1180.
John Scotus Erigena, *fl.* 851.
Josephus Scotus, *ob. c.* 791.

Lambert of Ardres, *fl.* 1194.
Lanfranc, 1003–1089.
Lothair I, Emperor, 795–855.
Louis the Pious, 778–840.
Liutprand of Cremona, *c.* 920–*c.* 972.
Lupus, Servatus, Abt. of Ferrières, *c.* 805–862.

Maelbrigde, Abt. of Armagh, *ob.* 927.
Mainerius, Magister, *fl. c.* 1160.
Maiolus of Cluny, professed *c.* 943, *ob.* abbot, 994.
Map, Walter, 1140–1208 ?
Marbod of Angers, 1035–1123.
Marcellus *see* Moengal.
Marcus, Irish bishop, *ob. c.* 875.
Martianus Capella, *fl. c.* 410–427.
Martin of Laon, *ob.* 875.
Martin, St., of Tours, *c.* 316–400.
Matthew Paris, of St. Albans, *ob.* 1259.
Matthew of Vendôme, *fl.* 1140–1185.
Maurice de Sully, Bp. of Paris 1160–1196.
Maximian, *fl. c.* 525.
Moengal, *fl.* 853–865.

Neckam, Alexander, 1157–1217.
Nicholas, Chancellor of Paris, *fl.* 1284.
Notker Balbulus, *c.* 840–912.
Notker, Bp. of Liege, *ob.* 1008.

Odilo, St., of Cluny, *ob.* 1049.
Odo, St., of Cluny, 879–942.
Odo, Bp. of Paris 1196–1208.
Orderic Vitalis, 1075–*post* 1143.
Otto I, 912–973.
Otto II, 955–983.
Otto III, 980–1002.
Otto von Freisingen, *c.* 1114–1159.

Paul the Deacon, *c.* 720–*c.* 800.
Paulinus of Nola, 353–431.
Paulus Albarus of Cordova, *fl.* 851.
Peter of Blois, 1153–*post* 1204.
Peter of Pisa, *fl. c.* 760–790 ?
Peter Riga, *fl.* 1165–*c.* 1209.
Peter the Venerable, Abbot of Cluny, *c.* 1094–1155.
Petrus Pictor, Canon of St. Omer, *fl.* 1110.
Philip, Abp. of Ravenna, *fl.* 1250–1270.
Philippe Auguste, 1165–1223.
Philippe le Bel, 1268–1314.
Philippe de Grêve, Chancellor of Notre Dame, *fl.* 1211–1236.
Philippe of Harvengt, *ob.* 1182.
Piero della Vigna, *fl.* 1221–1249.
Ponce de Provence, *fl.* 1249 ?
Primas, Hugh of Orleans, 1094 ?–1160 ?
Priscian, *fl. c.* 518.
Prudentius, 348–*c.* 405.

Radegunde, St. *ob.* 587.
Radulfus of Beauvais, *fl. c.* 1155.
Radulfus Glaber, *ante* 1000–*post* 1046.
Rahingus of Flavigny, *fl. c.* 900.
Ratherius of Liege, *c.* 887–974.
Ratpert of St. Gall, *ob. c.* 890.
Reginald von Dassel, *ob.* 1167.
Richard de Bury, 1287–1345.
Richard, St., of Chichester, *c.* 1197–1253.
Richer, *fl.* 987.
Robert II, King of France, *c.* 970–1031.
Robert of Brunne, *fl.* 1288–1338.
Robert of Melun, 1100–1167.
Robert de Sorbon, 1201–1274.
Rudel, Jaufré, *fl.* 1147.

Salimbene, 1121–*post* 1287.
Salomo, Abt. of St. Gall, Bp. of Constance, *c.* 860–920.

BIBLIOGRAPHY[1]

Books containing valuable bibliographies have been marked with an asterisk. The reader is also referred to the bibliographies at the end of each chapter in the *Cambridge Medieval History*, and to the revised bibliographies to the first volume of the *Cambridge History of English Literature*, now in the press. New publications are recorded in the admirable yearly Bulletin of the *Revue Bénédictine* and the *Bulletin of Historical Studies*.

The following abbreviations have been used :

A.H.R. - - -	*American Historical Review*. New York.
Archiv. Med. Aev. Lat.	*Archivum Medii Aevi Latinitatis*. Paris.
Corp. SS. Ecc. Lat. -	*Corpus Scriptorum Ecclesiasticorum Latinorum*. Vienna.
E.H.R. - - -	*English Historical Review*. London.
G.R.M. - - -	*Germanisch-Romanische Monatsschrift*. Heidelberg.
Migne, *P.L.* - -	*Patrologiae Cursus Completus . . . J. P. Migne. Series Latina*. Paris.
M.G.H.SS. - -	*Monumenta Germaniae Historica : Scriptores*. Hanover and Berlin.
M.G.H. Auct. Ant. -	*Auctores Antiquissimi*. Berlin.
P.L.C. - - -	*Poetae Latini Carolini Aevi*. Berlin.
Script. Rer. Germ. -	*Scriptores Rerum Germanicarum*. Hanover and Leipsig.
Z.F.D.A. - - -	*Zeitschrift für deutsches Alterthum*, Leipsig.

GENERAL

Acta Sanctorum, ed. J. Bollandus. Paris. 1863 ff.

Allen, P. S. *The Romanesque Lyric : Studies in its Background and Development from Petronius to the Cambridge Songs*, 50-1050. Chapel Hill. 1928.

—— *Medieval Latin Lyrics*. Chicago. 1931.

Beddie, J. S. " The Ancient Classics in the Medieval Libraries " [Appendix of Catalogues, A.D. 1050-1250, already in print]. *Speculum*, v. Camb. Mass. 1930.

—— " Libraries in the Twelfth Century : their Catalogues and Contents." *Haskins Anniversary Essays*. Boston. 1929.

[1] The word is too ambitious for what is merely a personal selection from the material most used in working out the present volume : from works and articles published since 1927, and a few older monographs which would have profited me if I had come to the knowledge of them earlier.

BRINKMANN, H. *Geschichte der lateinische Liebesdichtung im Mittelalter.* Halle. 1925.

—— " Zu Wesen und Form mittelalterlicher Dichtung." *G.R.M.* xv. Heidelberg. 1927.

BUTLER, E. C. *Benedictine Monachism : studies in Benedictine Life and Rule.* 2nd ed. London. 1924.

COMPARETTI, D. *Virgilio nel medio aevo.* Livorno. 1872.

COULTON, G. G. *Five Centuries of Religion,* vols. I, II. Cambridge. 1923-27.

COUSSEMAKER, C. DE. *Histoire de l'harmonie au moyen âge.* Paris. 1852.

CRUMP, C. J., and JACOB, E. F. *The Legacy of the Middle Ages.* Oxford. 1926.

DELISLE, L. V. *Cabinet des MSS. de la Bibliothèque Nationale.* Paris. 1868-81.

DRANE, F. R. *Christian Schools and Scholars . . . to the Council of Trent.* 3rd ed. London. 1924.

DRÈVES, G. M., and BLUME, C. *Analecta Hymnica Medii Aevi.* Leipsig. 1886-1922.

EBERT, A. *Allgemeine Geschichte der Literatur des Mittelalters im Abendlande.* Leipsig. 1874-87.

GASELEE, STEPHEN. *Oxford Book of Medieval Latin Verse.* Oxford. 1928.

—— *The Transition from the Late Latin Lyric to the Medieval Love Poem.* Cambridge. 1931.

GENESTAL, R. *Le Privilegium Fori en France du Décret de Gratien à la fin du* XIVe *siècle.* (Bibliothèque de l'École des Hautes Études : Sciences religieuses. 35.) Paris. 1921.

GILSON, É. *La philosophie au moyen âge.* 2 vols. Paris. 1922.

GOTTLIEB, T. *Mittelalterliche Bibliothekskataloge Österreichs.* Vienna. 1915.

GOURMONT, RÉMY DE. *Le Latin mystique.* 2nd ed. Paris. 1922.

HASKINS, C. H. *Studies in the History of Medieval Science.* Camb. Mass. 1924. 2nd ed. 1927.

HAURÉAU, J. B. *Notices et Extraits de quelques MSS. de la Bibliothèque Nationale.* 6 vols. Paris. 1890-3.

—— *Histoire de la philosophie scholastique.* 2 vols. Paris. 1872-80.

Histoire littéraire de la France par les religieux Bénédictins de la congrégation de S. Maur. Paris. 1753 ff.

KER, W. P. *The Dark Ages.* Edinburgh. 1904.

LEHMANN, P. *Mittelalterliche Bibliothekskataloge Deutschlands und der Schweiz. I. Die Bistümer Konstanz und Chur. II. Erfurt.* Munich. 1918.

LEYSER, P. *Historia poetarum et poematum medii aevi.* Halle. 1721.

MÂLE, É. *L'Art religieux du* XIIe *siècle en France.* Paris. 1922.

—— *L'Art religieux du* XIIIe *siècle en France.* Paris. 1923.

BIBLIOGRAPHY

*Manitius, M. *Geschichte der lateinischen Literatur des Mittelalters.* 3 vols. Munich. 1911, 1923, 1931.

—— "Beiträge zur Geschichte römischer Prosaiker im Mittelalter." *Philologus,* XLVII, XLVIII. Göttingen. 1889-90.

—— "Beiträge zur Geschichte römischer Dichter im Mittelalter." *Philologus.* 1889-97. [Persius, 1889. Claudian: Martial, 1890. Juvenal: Ilias Latina, 1891. Anthologia Latina: Disticha Catonis: Aemilius Macer: Tibullus: Serenus Sammonicus; Avianus: Lucan: 1892. Lucretius: Statius: Aemilius Macer: Terence, 1893. Ausonius: Petronius: Seneca: Nux elegia: Calpurnius: Nemesianus: 1897.]

—— "Beiträge zur Geschichte des Ovidius und andrer römischer Schriftsteller im Mittelalter." *Philologus, Supplement* VII. Leipsig. 1899.

Mansi, J.D. *Sacrorum Conciliorum Amplissima Collectio.* Florence. 1759 ff.

Meyer, W. *Gesammelte Abhandlungen zur mittellateinischen Rythmik.* 2 vols. Berlin. 1905.

*Molinier, A. *Les Sources de l'histoire de France.* (Origines-1494.) Paris. 1901-6.

Notices et Extraits des MSS. de la Bibliothèque Nationale. Publiés par l'Académie des Inscriptions et Belles-Lettres. Paris. 1787 ff.

*Paetow, L. J. *Guide to the Study of Medieval History, with Bibliographies.* (Revised edition prepared under the auspices of the Medieval Academy of America.) New York. 1931.

Poole, R. L. *Illustrations of the History of Medieval Thought and Learning.* 2nd ed. London. 1920.

*Raby, F. J. E. *A History of Christian Latin Poetry from the Beginnings to the Close of the Middle Ages.* Oxford. 1927.

—— * *A History of Secular Latin Poetry in the Middle Ages.* Oxford. [*In the press.*]

*Rand, E. K. *Ovid and his Influence.* London. 1925.

Richter and Friedberg. *Corpus Iuris Canonicus.* 2 vols. 2nd ed. Leipsig. 1879.

Saintsbury, George. *The Flourishing of Romance and Rise of Allegory.* Edinburgh. 1907.

Sandys, J. E. *History of Classical Scholarship.* I. 3rd ed. Cambridge. 1920.

Sedgwick, W. B. "The Origin of Rhyme." *Revue Bénédictine.* Maredsous. 1924.

Strecker, Karl. *Einführung in das Mittellatein.* Berlin. 1928.

—— *Studien zür lateinische Dichtung des Mittelalters. Ehrengabe für K. Strecker.* Dresden. 1931.

Stubbs, W. *Councils and Ecclesiastical Documents relating to Great Britain and Ireland.* Oxford. 1869-71.

—— *Germany in the Early Middle Ages, 476-1250.* London. 1908.

STUBBS, W. *Historical Introductions to the Rolls Series*, ed. by A. Hassall. London. 1902.

TAYLOR, H. O. *The Medieval Mind.* 2nd ed. 2 vols. London. 1914.

TRENCH, R. C. *Sacred Latin Poetry.* 3rd ed. London. 1874.

WADDELL, H. *Medieval Latin Lyrics.* 3rd ed. London. 1930.

WALPOLE, A. S. *Early Latin Hymns.* Cambridge. 1922.

WRIGHT, F. A., and SINCLAIR, T. A. *History of Later Latin Literature from the Middle of the Fourth to the end of the Seventeenth Century.* London. 1931

CHAPTER I

THE BREAK WITH THE PAGAN TRADITION

Anthologia Latina, ed. Buecheler, F., and Riese, A. (Teubner). Leipsig. 1887-1906.

ARATOR. *Opera.* Migne, *P.L.* 68. Paris. 1847.

AUSONIUS. *Epistolae et Carmina*, ed. R. Peiper (Teubner). 1886.

AVITUS. *Opera*, ed. R. Peiper. [*M.G.H. Auct. Ant.*) Berlin. 1883.

BERNARD and ATKINSON. *The Irish Liber Hymnorum.* 2 vols. Henry Bradshaw Society. London. 1898.

BOETHIUS. *De Consolatione Philosophiae*, ed. G. D. Smith. London. 1925.

[For his complete works, see Migne, *P.L.* 64 (1883). The definitive text is in preparation for the *Corpus Scriptorum Ecclesiasticorum Latinorum.*]

BOISSIER, GASTON. *La Fin du Paganisme.* Paris. 1891.

—— " Le Carmen Paschale de Sedulius." *Revue de philologie, de littérature, et d'histoire anciennes.* Paris. 1882.

CAPELLA, MARTIANUS. *De Nuptiis Philologiae et Mercurii*, ed. A. Dick (Teubner). Leipsig. 1925.

CASSIODORUS. *Variae*, ed. T. Mommsen. (*M.G.H. Auct. Ant.*) Berlin. 1894.

—— *Opera.* (Migne, *P.L.* 69-70.) Paris. 1848.

COMMODIANUS. *Carmina*, ed. E. Ludwig (Teubner). Leipsig. 1878.

—— SCHILS, L. " Commodien Poéte Rythmique ? " *Neophilologus.* Groningen. 1929.

DRACONTIUS. *Carmina*, ed. E. Baehrens. (*Poetae Latini Minores*, v.) Leipsig. 1910.

ENNODIUS. *Opera*, ed. W. Hartel. (*Corp. SS. Ecc. Lat.* VI.) Vienna. 1882.

Also in Migne, *P.L.* 63. Paris. 1847.

EUGENIUS OF TOLEDO. *Carmina*, ed. F. Vollmer. (*M.G.H. Auct. Ant.*) Berlin. 1905.

Also in Migne, *P.L.* 87. Paris. 1851.

GREGORY THE GREAT. *Opera.* (Migne, *P.L.* 77-79.) Paris. 1849-50.

HODGKIN, T. *Italy and her Invaders.* 8 vols. Oxford. 1892-99.

IUVENCUS. *Opera*, ed. C. Marold (Teubner). Leipsig. 1886.

*LABRIOLLE, P. DE. *Histoire de la littérature chrétienne latine.* 2nd ed. Paris. 1924.

*LOT, FERDINAND. *La fin du monde antique et les débuts du moyen âge.* Paris. 1927.

MAXIMIAN. *Elegiae*, ed. E. Baehrens. (*Poet. Lat. Min.* III.)

PAULINUS OF NOLA. *Epistolae et Carmina*, ed. G. Hartel. (*Corp. SS. Ecc. Lat.* XXIX, XXX.) Vienna. 1893-4.

PRUDENTIUS. *Opera*, ed. Bergman. (*Corp. SS. Ecc. Lat.* LXI.) Vienna. 1926.

RAND, E. K. *Founders of the Middle Ages.* Harvard. 1928.

SEDULIUS. *Opera*, ed. J. Huemer. (*Corp. SS. Ecc. Lat.* X.) Vienna. 1885.
Also in Migne, *P.L.* 19. Paris. 1848.

SEECK, O. *Geschichte des Untergangs der antiken Welt.* 6 vols. Berlin. 1895-1909.

SIDONIUS APOLLINARIS. *Epistolae et Carmina*, ed. P. Mohr (Teubner). 1895.

SULPICIUS SEVERUS. *Dialogi*, ed. C. Halm. (*Corp. SS. Ecc. Lat.* I.) Vienna. 1866.
Also in Migne, *P.L.* 20. Paris. 1849.

URANIUS PRESBYTER. *De obitu S. Paulini.* Migne, *P.L.* 53. 1847.

VIRGILIUS MARO GRAMMATICUS. *Opera*, ed. J. Huemer (Teubner). Leipsig. 1886.

CHAPTER II

FORTUNATUS TO SEDULIUS OF LIEGE

ADAMNAN. *Vita S. Columbae*, ed. J. T. Fowler. Oxford. 1920.

ALCUIN. *Carmina*, ed. E. Dümmler. *Poetae Latini Aevi Carolini*, I. Berlin. 1881.

—— *Epistolae*, ed. E. Dümmler. *M.G.H. Epistolae Aevi Carolini*, II. Berlin. 1895.

—— *Opera.* Migne, *P.L.* 100, 101. Paris. 1851.

—— *Monumenta Alcuiniana*, ed. W. Wattenbach and E. Dümmler. (Jaffé, *Bibliotheca Rerum Germanicarum*, VI.) Berlin. 1873.

—— Gaskoin, C. J. B. *Alcuin: his Life and his Work.* Camb. 1904.

—— Dümmler, E. "Alchvinstudien." *Sitszungsberichte der Kgl. Akad.* Berlin. 1891.

—— Dümmler. "Zur Lebensgeschichte Alchvins." *Neues Archiv.* 1893.
See Rand, E. K., *infra.*

ALDHELM. *Opera*, ed. R. Ehwald. *M.G.H. Auct. Ant.* XV. Berlin. 1919.

ANGILBERT. *Carmina*, ed. E. Dümmler. *P.L.C.* I. 1881.

ANGILBERT. Tardi, D. "Fortunat et Angilbert." *Arch. Med. Aev. Lat.* Paris. 1925.

Annals of the Kingdom of Ireland by the Four Masters, ed. J. O'Donovan. 7 vols. Dublin. 1851.

BALUZE, E. *Capitularia Regum Francorum.* 2 vols. Paris. 1780.

BEDE. *Historia ecclesiastica gentis Anglorum*, ed. C. Plummer. 2 vols. Oxford. 1896.

—— *Opera.* 6 vols. Migne, *P.L.* 90-95. Paris. 1850.

BEESON, C. H. *See* Lupus of Ferrières *infra.*

BETT, J. H. *See* John Scotus Erigena *infra.*

BONIFACE, ST. *Carmina*, ed. E. Dümmler. *P.L.C.* I. 1881.

—— *Epistolae*, ed. E. Dümmler. *M.G.H. Epist. Mer. et Car.* I. 1892.

BURY, J. B. *Life of St. Patrick.* London. 1905.

Capitularia Regum Francorum, ed. A. Boretius. 2 vols. *M.G.H.* Hanover. 1891-7.

CLARK, J. M. *The Abbey of St. Gall as a Centre of Literature and Art.* Camb. 1926.

COLGAN, J. *Acta Sanctorum Hiberniae.* 2 vols. Louvain. 1645.

COLUMBANUS, ST. *Epistolae et Carmina*, ed. W. Grundlach. *M.G.H. Epist. Mer. et Car.* 1892.

Concilia Aevi Carolini, ed. A. Werminghoff. 2 vols. *M.G.H.* 1906-8.

DELISLE, L. V. *L'École calligraphique de Tours au* IXe *siècle.* Paris. 1885. [*See* Rand, E. K., *infra.*]

—— *Les Bibles de Théodulfe.* Paris. 1879.

DICUIL. *De Mensura orbis terrae*, ed. G. Parthey. Paris. 1870.

—— "An unpublished astronomical treatise by Dicuil," ed. Mario Esposito. *Proceedings of the Royal Irish Academy*, XXVI. Dublin. 1907.

—— Dümmler, E. "Dicuil." *Neues Archiv.* 1879.

DILL, SAMUEL. *Roman Society in Gaul in the Merovingian Age.* London. 1926.

DÜMMLER, E. *Epistola Ermenrici ad Grimoldum.* Halle. 1873.

—— *Epistolae Carolini Aevi.* *M.G.H.* 2 vols. Berlin. 1892-5.

—— *Poetae Latini Carolini Aevi*, I, II. *M.G.H.* Berlin. 1881-4.

EGINHARD. *Vita Caroli Magni*, ed. G. H. Pertz. *M.G.H. SS.* II. Hanover. 1829.

—— *Editée et traduite par* L. Halphen. Paris. 1923.

EKKEHARD IV. *Casus Sancti Galli*, ed. G. H. Pertz. *M.G.H. SS.* II. Hanover. 1829.

ESPOSITO, MARIO. "Hiberno-Latin MSS. in the Libraries of Switzerland." *Proceedings of the Royal Irish Academy*, XXVIII, XXX. Dublin. 1909-11.

FLOWER, ROBIN. "Ireland and Medieval Europe." *Proceedings of the British Academy.* London. 1927.

BIBLIOGRAPHY

FORTUNATUS, VENANTIUS. *Opera*, ed. F. Leo. *M.G.H. Auct. Ant.* Berlin. 1881.

—— Meyer, W. "Der Gelegenheitsdichter Venantius Fortunatus." *Abhandlungen der Kgl. Akad. der Wiss. zu Göttingen. Phil.-Hist. Klasse.* Göttingen. 1901.

—— Tardi, D. *Fortunat:* Paris. 1927.

—— Nisard, M. L. C. *Le Poète Fortunat.* Paris. 1890.

GASKOIN, C. J. B. *See* Alcuin *supra.*

GOTTSCHALK. *Carmina*, ed. L. Traube. *Poet. Lat. Car.* III.

GOUGAUD, L. *Les chrétientés celtiques.* Paris. 1911.
[A new edition, in English, is in preparation.]

GREGORY OF TOURS. *Historia Francorum*, ed. B. Krusch. *M.G.H. SS. Mer.* II. Berlin. 1889.

—— *Historia Francorum*, ed. H. Omont and G. Collon. (*Coll. de Textes.*) Paris. 1913.

HADDAN, A. W. "The Scots on the Continent." *Remains of A. W. Haddan*, ed. A. P. Forbes. London. 1876.

HALPHEN, L. *Études critiques sur l'histoire de Charlemagne.* Paris. 1921.

HARIULF. *Chronicon Centulense*, ed. F. Lot. Paris. 1894.

HAURÉAU, J. B. *Charlemagne et sa cour.* Paris. 1888.

—— *Les Écoles d'Irlande: Théodulfe, etc.*, in *Singularités historiques et littéraires.* Paris. 1861.

HAVET, L. "Que doivent à Charlemagne les classiques latins?" *Revue bleue.* Paris. 1906.

HELLMANN, S. *See* Sedulius Scottus *infra.*

HIBERNICUS EXUL. *Carmina*, ed. E. Dümmler. *P.L.C.* I. 1881.

Hisperica Famina, ed. F. J. H. Jenkinson. Cambridge. 1908.

—— Rand, E. K. "The Irish Flavour of *Hisperica Famina.*" *Studien zur Lateinischen Dichtung des Mittelalters*, ed. W. Stach and H. Walther. Dresden. 1931.

HRABANUS MAURUS. *Carmina*, ed. E. Dümmler. *P.L.C.* I. 1881.

—— *Opera.* Migne, *P.L.* 107-112.

JARCHO, B. I. *See* Sedulius Scottus *infra.*

JOHN SCOTUS ERIGENA. *Opera.* Migne, *P.L.* 122. Paris. 1853.

—— Bett, J. H. *John Scotus Erigena.* Cambridge. 1925.

—— Webb, C. C. J. "Scotus Erigena *De Divisione Natura.*" *Proceedings of the Aristotelian Society*, II. 1892-4.

*KENNEY, J. F. *Sources for the Early History of Ireland*, I. New York. 1929.

*LAISTNER, M. L. *Thought and Letters in Western Europe*, A.D. 500-900. London. 1931.

—— "Notes on Greek from Lectures by Martin of Laon." *Bulletin of John Rylands Library.* Manchester. 1923.

LINDSAY, W. M. *Early Irish Minuscule Script.* (*St. Andrews University Publications*, VI.) Oxford. 1910.

LINDSAY, W. M. *The Bobbio Scriptorium.* Leipsig. 1909.

LOT, FERDINAND. "*Winileodas.*" *Archiv. med. aev. lat.* Paris. 1925.

LUPUS, SERVATUS, OF FERRIÈRES. *Lettres : Texte, notes et introduction,* ed. G. Desdevises du Dezert. (*Bibl. de l'École des Hautes Études. Sc. phil. et hist.* 77.) Paris. 1888.

—— Beeson, C. H. *Lupus of Ferrières as Scribe and Text Critic.* Camb. Mass. 1930.

MEYER, KUNO. *A Primer of Irish Metrics.* Dublin. 1909.

—— *Instructions of King Cormac mac Airt.* (Royal Irish Academy. Todd Lecture Series, xv.) Dublin. 1909.

—— *King and Hermit : a Colloquy between King Guaire of Aidne and his brother Marban.* London. 1901.

—— *Selections from Ancient Irish Poetry.* London. 1913.

—— *Four Old Irish Songs of Summer and Winter.* London. 1903.

—— *La Vision de Tondal.* Paris. 1907.

MEYER, WILHELM. "Ein merowinger Rythmus über Fortunat und altdeutsche Rythmik in lateinischen Versen." *Göttingen Nachrichten.* 1908.

MULLINGER, J. B. *The Schools of Charles the Great.* London. 1877.

NIGRA, C. *Reliquie Celtiche : il manoscritto irlandese di S. Gallo.* Florence. 1872.

NOTKER BALBULUS. *Gesta Caroli Magni.* *M.G.H. SS.* II. Hanover. 1829.

See Chapter III *infra.*

OZANAM, F. *La civilisation chrétienne chez les Francs.* Paris. 1849.

—— *Documents inédits pour servir à l'histoire d'Italie depuis le* VIIIe *jusqu'au* XIIIe *siècle.* Paris. 1850.

PIRENNE, H. *See* Sedulius Scottus *infra.*

PLUMMER, C. *Vitae Sanctorum Hiberniae partim hactenus ineditae.* 2 vols. Oxford. 1910.

Poetae Latini Carolini Aevi, vols. I. II., ed. E. Dümmler. Berlin. 1881-4. III., ed. L. Traube. 1896. IV. (1), ed. Paul von Winterfeld. 1899. IV. (2, 3), ed. K. Strecker. 1923.

RAND, E. K. *Studies in the Script of Tours. I. A Survey of the MSS. of Tours.* Camb. Mass. 1929.

—— *A Preliminary Study of Alcuin's Bible.* Camb. Mass. 1931.

ROGER, M. *L'Enseignement des lettres classiques d'Ausone à Alcuin.* Paris. 1905.

SEDULIUS SCOTUS. *Carmina,* ed. L. Traube. *P.L.C.* III.

—— Hellmann, S. *Sedulius Scottus.* (Traube, *Quellen und Untersuchungen zur lateinischen Philologie des Mittelalters,* I.) Munich. 1906.

—— Jarcho, B. I. "Die Vorlaufer des Golias." *Speculum.* Camb. Mass. 1928.

—— Pirenne, H. *Sedulius of Liege.* (*Mémoires couronnés par l'Académie Royal de Bruxelles,* XXXIII.) Brussels. 1882.

SEDULIUS SCOTUS, Traube, L. "Sedulius Scotus." (*Abhandlungen der Kgl. bay. Akad. der Wiss. Philos.-philol. Klasse*, IX.) Munich. 1892.

STOKES, WHITLEY. *Thesaurus Paleohibernicus: a collection of Old Irish scholia, prose and verse.* 3 vols. Camb. 1901-10.

—— *Lives of Saints from the Book of Lismore.* Oxford. 1890.

STRECKER, K. "Studien zu Karolingischen Dichtern." *Neues Archiv.* XLIII, XLIV, XLV. Hanover. 1920-24.

THEODULFUS. *Carmina*, ed. E. Dümmler. *P.L.C.* I.

THURNEYSEN, J. N. A. *Mittelirische Verslehren.* (Stokes and Windisch, *Irische Texte*, III.) Leipsig. 1891.

TODD, J. H. *St. Patrick.* Dublin. 1863.

TRAUBE, L. "O Roma Nobilis." "Dungal." "Sedulius Scotus." } *Abhandlungen der Kgl. bay. Akad. der Wiss. Philos.-philol. Klasse* IX. Munich. 1892.

USSHER, J. *Veterum Epistolarum Hibernicarum Sylloge.* Dublin. 1632.

WALAFRID STRABO. *Carmina*, ed. E. Dümmler. *P.L.C.* II.

WATTENBACH, W. "Die Kongregation der Schotten Klöster." Translated by Reeves in *Ulster Journal of Archaeology*, VII. Belfast. 1859.

ZIMMER, H. *Glossae Hibernicae.* Berlin. 1881.

—— *The Irish Element in Medieval Culture.* (Translation.) New York. 1891.

CHAPTER III

THE TENTH CENTURY

AELFRIC BATA. *See* Stevenson, W. H., *infra.*

AYMON, MONK OF FLEURY. *Opera.* Migne, *P.L.* 139. Paris. 1853.

Chronica S. Bertini. Bouquet, *Recueil des Historiens des Gaules et de la France*, X. Paris. 1760.

DELISLE, L. V. *Deux MSS. de l'Abbaye de Flavigny au* xe *siècle.* Dijon. 1887.

—— *Un Virgile copié au* xe *siècle par le moine Rahingus.* Rome. 1886.

DÜMMLER, E. *Auxilius und Vulgarius.* Leipsig. 1866.

Ecbasis Captivi, ed. Grimm and Schmeller. *Lateinische Gedichte des X und XI Jahrhunderts.* Göttingen. 1838.

—— ed. F. A. E. Voigt. *Quellen und Forschungen zur Sprache . . . der germanischen Völker*, VIII. Strasburg. 1875.

EKKEHARD I. *Waltharius*, ed. K. Strecker. Berlin. 1907.

EKKEHARD IV. *Casus S. Galli.* *M.G.H. SS.* II. 1829.

EUGENIUS VULGARIUS. *Carmina*, ed. P. v. Winterfeld. *P.L.C.* IV (1). *See* Dümmler *supra.*

FRERE, W. H. *The Winchester Troper.* Henry Bradshaw Society. London. 1894.

FLODOARD OF RHEIMS. *Opera.* Migne, *P.L.* 135. Paris. 1853.

GAUTIER, LÉON. *Histoire de la poésie liturgique au moyen âge*, I. Paris. 1886.

GRIMM and SCHMELLER. *Lateinische Gedichte des X und XI Jahrhunderts.* Göttingen. 1838.

GUNZO OF NOVARO. *Epistola ad Fratres Augienses.* Migne, *P.L.* 141. Paris. 1853.

HASKINS, C. H. *The Normans in European History.* London. 1915.

HAVET, L. *Les Lettres de Gerbert.* Paris. 1889.

HELGALDUS. *Vita Roberti Regis Francorum.* Migne, *P.L.* 141. Paris. 1853.

HROTSWITHA. *Opera*, ed. Paul von Winterfeld. *Script. Rer. Germ.* 1902.

—— *Opera*, ed. K. Strecker (Teubner). Leipsig. 1906.

HUCBALD OF ST. AMAND. *Opera.* Migne, *P.L.* 132. Paris. 1853.

—— Coussemaker, C. H. de. *Mémoire sur Hucbald et ses traités de musique.* Paris. 1841.

KURTH, G. *Notger de Liege et la civilisation au xe siècle.* Paris. 1905.

*LOT, FERDINAND. *Les Derniers Carolingiens.* Paris. 1891.

*—— *Études sur le règne de Hugues Capet et la fin de xe siècle.* Paris. 1903.

LIUTPRAND OF CREMONA. *Opera*, ed. J. Becker. 3rd ed. *Script. Rer. Germ.* Hanover. 1915.

NOTKER BALBULUS. *De Interpretatione Divini Scripti.* Migne, *P.L.* 131.

—— *Carmina*, ed. P. v. Winterfeld. *P.L.C.* IV (I).

—— Blume and Bannister. *Liturgische Prosen erster Epoche aus den Sequenzen-Schulen des Abendlandes in besondere die dem Notkerus Balbulus zugeschreibenen. Analecta Hymnica* 53. Leipsig. 1911.

Odilonis, Vita S. Migne, *P.L.* 132. Paris. 1853.

Odonis, Vita S. Migne, *P.L.* 133. Paris. 1853.

RADBOD. *Carmina*, ed. P. v. Winterfeld. *P.L.C.* IV. (I).

RADULFUS GLABER. *Historiarum sui temporis libri V.*, ed. M. Prou. (*Coll. de Textes.*) Paris. 1886.

RATHERIUS OF LIEGE. *Opera.* Migne, *P.L.* 136. Paris. 1853.

RICHER. *Historiae*, ed. G. Waitz. *Script. Rev. Germ.* Hanover. 1877.

ROBINSON, J. ARMITAGE. *The Times of S. Dunstan.* Oxford. 1923.

SALOMO, ABBOT OF ST. GALL. *Carmina*, ed. P. v. Winterfeld. *P.L.C.* IV. (I).

STEVENSON, W. H. *Early Scholastic Colloquies.* Oxford. 1929.

STUBBS, W. *Memorials of St. Dunstan. Archbishop of Canterbury.* (Rolls Series.) London. 1874.

CHAPTER IV

THE REVIVAL OF LEARNING IN FRANCE

ADHEMAR DE CHABANNES. *Opera*, ed. G. Waitz. *M.G.H. Scriptores*, IV. Hanover. 1841.

ADELMANN. *De viris illustribus. Epistola ad Berengarium.* Migne, *P.L.* 143. Paris. 1853.

BIBLIOGRAPHY

BAUDRI DE BOURGEUIL. *Œuvres Poétiques : édition critique d'après le MS. du Vatican :* par P. Abrahams. Paris. 1926.

—— edited in part by Delisle in *Romania*. Paris. 1872.

—— *Poème à Adèle, fille de Guillaume le Conquérant*, ed. L. V. Delisle. Caen. 1871.

—— *Opera*. Migne, *P.L.* 171. Paris. 1854.

—— Pasquier, H. *Un poète latin du* XIe *siècle : Baudri, abbé de Bourgeuil*. Paris. 1878.

BREUL, K. *The Cambridge Songs : a Goliard's Songbook of the XIth Century*. Cambridge. 1913.

CLERVAL, J. A. *Les Écoles de Chartres au moyen âge, du* Vme *au* XVIme *siècle*. Chartres. 1895.

—— *Une correspondance d'écolâtres du* XIe *siècle. Notices et Extraits*, XXXVI. Paris. 1900.

DAMIANI, S. PETER. *Opera*. Migne, *P.L.* 145. Paris. 1853.

—— *See* A. Wilmart.

DELISLE, L.V. *Rouleaux des Morts du* IXe *au* XVe *siècle*. Paris. 1886.

FROUMUND OF TEGERNSEE. *Epistolae*. Migne, *P.L.* 141. Paris. 1853.

FULBERT OF CHARTRES. *Epistolae et Carmina*. Migne, *P.L.* 141. Paris. 1853.

GUIBERT DE NOGENT. *De vita sua*, ed. G. Bourgin. *Coll. de Textes*. Paris. 1907.
Also in Migne, *P.L.* 156.

HAURÉAU, J. B. *Notice sur un MS. de Cambrai. Notices et Extraits*, XXXI. 2. Paris. 1884.

—— *Mélanges poétiques d'Hildebert de Lavardin*. Paris. 1882.

—— *Notice sur les sermons attribués à Hildebert de Lavardin. Notices et Extraits*, XXXII. (2). Paris. 1886.

HILDEBERT OF LE MANS *or* DE LAVARDIN. *Epistolae et carmina*. Migne, *P.L.* 171. Paris. 1854.
See Hauréau, J. B.

IVO OF CHARTRES. *Epistolae et Decreta*. Migne, *P.L.* 162. Paris. 1854.

MARBOD. *Carmina*. Migne, *P.L.* 171. Paris. 1854.

—— *Marbode, Évêque de Rennes*, 1035-1153, by L. V. E. Ernault. Rennes. 1889.

PARIS, GASTON. *La vie de S. Alexis*. Paris. 1903.

RADULFUS GLABER. *See* Chapter III. *supra*.

RONÇA, U. *Cultura medievale e poesia latina d'Italia nei secoli* XIe *e* XIIe. 2 vols. Rome. 1892.

SIGEBERT OF LIEGE. *Carmina*, ed. E. Dümmler. *Abhandlungen der Kgl. Akad. der Wiss. zu Berlin*. 1893.

STRECKER, KARL. *Die Cambridger Lieder*. Berlin. 1926.

WILLARD, H. M. " The Use of Classics in the *Flores Rhetorici* of Alberic of Monte Casino." *Haskins Anniversary Essays*. Boston. 1929.

WILMART, A. " Le Recueil des Poèmes et des Prières de S. Pierre Damien." *Revue Bénédictine*, XLI. 1929.

THE WANDERING SCHOLARS

CHAPTERS V AND VI

HUMANISM IN THE FIRST HALF OF THE TWELFTH CENTURY: PARIS AND ORLEANS

ABELARD, PETER. *Ouvrages Inédits*, ed. V. Cousin. Paris. 1836.

—— *Opera*, ed. V. Cousin. 2 vols. Paris. 1849-59.

—— *Opera*. Migne, *P.L.* 178. Paris. 1885.

—— *Planctus*, ed. W. Meyer. *Romanische Forschungen*. Erlangen. 1890.

—— *Planctus virginum Israel super Filia leptae*, ed. W. Meyer and W. Brambach. Munich. 1885.

—— *P. Abaelardi hymnarius Paraclitensis*, ed. G. M. Drèves. Paris. 1891.

—— Carnandet, J. *Notice sur le bréviaire d'Abailard conservé à la bibliothèque de Chaumont*. Paris. 1855.

—— Hauréau, J. B. " Le Poème addressé par Abelard à son fils Astrolabe." *Notices et Extraits*, XXXIV. (2). Paris. 1891.

—— Poole, R. L. " Abailard as a Theological Teacher." *Church Quarterly Review*. London. 1896.

—— Rémusat, C. *Abélard*. 2 vols. Paris. 1845.

—— Schmeidler, B. " Der Briefwechsel zwischen Abälard und Heloise eine Falschung ? " *Archiv für Kulturgeschichte*, XI. 1913.

—— Webb, C. C. J. *Studies in the History of Natural Theology* (pp. 199-232). Oxford. 1915.

—— Sikes, J. G. *Peter Abailard*. Camb. 1932.

ALEXANDRE DE VILLE-DIEU. *Doctrinale*, ed. D. Reichling. *Mon. Germ. Ped.* XII. Berlin. 1893.

—— Delisle, L. V. " Alexandre de Ville Dieu." *Bibliothèque de l'École des Chartes*, 55. Paris. 1894.

BACON, ROGER. *Opus Tertium: Compendium Studii*, ed. J. S. Brewer London. 1859.

BÄRNSTEIN, A. P. VON. *Beiträge zur Geschichte und Literatur des deutschen Studententhums*. Würzburg. 1882.

BERENGAR. *Apologeticus contra beatum Bernardum*. Migne, *P.L.* 178. Paris. 1885.

BERNARD OF CLAIRVAUX, ST. *Epistolae*. Migne, *P.L.* 182. Paris. 1855.

—— Vacaudard, E. *Vie de S. Bernard*. 2 vols. 4th ed. Paris. 1910.

—— Morrison, J. C. *Life and Times of St. Bernard*. London. 1868.

—— Hauréau, B. *Poèmes latins attribués à S. Bernard*. Paris. 1890.

—— Gilson, É. " Sur le *Jesu Dulcis Memoria*." *Speculum*. 1928.

BERNARD OF MEUNG. *Summa Dictaminis*.

—— Bib. Nat. MS. Lat. 1093, f. 55 ff. (written *c*. 1200).

—— *ib*. 994, f. 30 ff. (*c*. 1187-98).

—— *ib*. 14193, f. 20 thirteenth cent. (see Hauréau, *Not. et Ext.* II. 356).

BIBLIOGRAPHY

BERNARD OF MEUNG. *ib.* 8635, f. 23, thirteenth cent.

—— Brit. Mus., Add. MS. 18382, f. 65.

—— *ib.* Cott. MS. Vit. c. VIII., f. 128.

—— *ib.* Add. MS. 8167, f. 169.

(*See* Hauréau, *Mémoires de l'Académie des Inscriptions*, XXXI, (2). C. V. Langlois, *Maître Bernard. Bibliothèque de l'École des Chartes*, 54.)

—— See *Romania*, IX. p. 496.

BERNARD SYLVESTRIS. *De Mundi Universitate*, ed. C. S. Barach. Innsbruck. 1876.

—— *Mathematicus*, ed. Hauréau, B. Paris. 1895.

See Hauréau, J. B., and Poole, R. L., *infra*.

BOUTARIC. "Vincent de Beauvais et la connaissance de l'antiquité classique au XIIIe siècle." *Revue des questions historiques*, XVII. Paris. 1875.

BUONCOMPAGNO. *Antiqua Rhetorica*. B.N. MS. 8654 : 7732 : 7731. (Edited in part by Rockinger, *q.v.*)

CAESARIUS VON HEISTERBACH. *Dialogus Miraculorum*, ed. K. Drescher. Berlin. 1929.

—— *Dialogus Miraculorum*, ed. J. Strange. Cologne. Bonn. Brussels. 1851.

CAVAZZA, F. G. *Le Scuole dell' antico studio bolognese*. Milan. 1896.

CLARK, A. C. *The Cursus in Medieval and Vulgar Latin*. Oxford. 1910.

CLERVAL, J. A. *L'ancienne Maîtrise de Notre Dame de Chartres*. Paris. 1899.

—— *L'Enseignement des Arts libéraux à Paris et à Chartres, après l'Heptateuchon de Thierry de Chartres*. Paris. 1889.

—— *Hermann le Dalmate et les premiers traductions latines des traités arabes d'astronomie au moyen âge*. Paris. 1891.

DELÈGUE, R. *L'Université de Paris*. 1220-1224. Paris. 1902.

DELISLE, L. V. *Les Écoles d'Orléans au* XIIe *et au* XIIIe *siècle*. Paris. 1869.

—— *Le Formulaire de Tréguier et les écoliers bretons des écoles d'Orléans au commencement du* XIVe *siècle*. Orleans. 1890.

—— *Notice sur une Summa Dictaminis conservée à Beauvais*. Paris. 1909.

—— *Rouleau mortuaire du B. Vital* [facsimile with a possible autograph by Héloïse]. Paris. 1909.

DENIFLE et CHATELAIN. *Chartularium Universitatis Parisiensis*. Paris. 1889.

—— *Auctuarium Universitatis Parisiensis*. Paris. 1894.

EBERHARD OF BETHUNE. *Graecismus*, ed. J. Wrobel. Wratislau. 1887.

—— "Eberhardi Bethunensis Graecismus." Comte rendu par J. B. Hauréau, *Journal des Savants*. Paris. 1889.

EBERHARD THE GERMAN. *Laborintus*, ed. Faral (*vide infra*).

FABA, GUIDO. *Dictamina Rhetorica*. B.N. MS. Latin 8653, edited by A. Gaudenzi in *Il Propugnatore*. Bologna. 1892.

FARAL, E. *Les Arts poétiques du* XIIe *et du* XIIIe *siècle.* Paris. 1923.

FOURNIER, M. *Les Statuts et privilèges des universités françaises.* Paris. 1890.

—— *Histoire de la science du droit en France*, vol. III. Paris. 1892.

—— *La Nation allemande à l'université d'Orléans au* XIVe *siècle.* Paris. 1888.

—— "Les Bibliothèques des collèges de l'Université de Toulouse." *Bibl. de l'École des Chartes*, 51. 1890.

GAUDENZI, A. "Sulle opere dei dettatori bolognesi." *Bulletino dell'Istituto Storico Italiano.* Rome. 1895.

GIRALDUS CAMBRENSIS. *Opera*, ed. J. B. Brewer. London. 1861.

Gosvini, Vita S., ed. R. Gibbon. Douai. 1620.

GREENAWAY, G. W. *Arnold of Brescia.* Camb. 1932.

HASKINS, C. H. "The Life of Medieval Students as illustrated by their Letters." *A.H.R.* III., 1898, reprinted in *Studies in Medieval Culture.* Oxford. 1929.

—— "The University of Paris in Thirteenth Century Sermons." *A.H.R.* x, 1905, reprinted as above.

—— "Manuals for Students." *Studies in Medieval Culture.*

—— "The Early Artes Dictandi in Italy." *Studies in Medieval Culture.*

—— *The Rise of Universities.* New York. 1923.

—— *Studies in the History of Medieval Science.* Camb. Mass. 1924. 2nd ed. 1927.

—— *The Renaissance in the Twelfth Century.* Camb. Mass. 1927.

—— *Studies in Medieval Culture.* Oxford. 1929.

—— "Albericus Casinensis." Monte Cassino Anniversary *Miscellanea.* 1929.

—— "Orleanese Formularies in a MS. at Tarragona." *Speculum*, v. Camb. Mass. 1930.

—— "An early Bolognese Formulary." *Mélanges d'histoire offerts à Henri Pirenne.* Brussels. 1926.

—— "A list of Textbooks from the Close of the Twelfth Century." *Harvard Studies in Classical Philology*, XX. 75-94. 1909. Reprinted in *Studies in the History of Medieval Science.*

—— "Adelard of Bath." *E.H.R.* XXVI. 1911. "Adelard of Bath and Henry Plantagenet." *E.H.R.* XXVIII. 1913.

—— "The Greek Element in the Renaissance of the Twelfth Century." *A.H.R.* XXV. 1920.

—— "Henry II as a Patron of Literature." *Essays in Medieval History presented to T. F. Tout.* Manchester. 1925.

—— "An Italian Master Bernard." *Essays in History presented to R. L. Poole.* Oxford. 1927.

HAURÉAU, J. B. "Bernard et Thierry de Chartres." *Comtes rendus de l'Académie des Inscriptions.* Paris. 1872.

—— "Mémoires sur quelques maîtres du XIIe siècle." *Mém. de l'Acad. des Insc.* XXVIII. (2). Paris. 1876.

BIBLIOGRAPHY

HAURÉAU, J. B. "Mémoires sur quelques chanceliers de l'église de Chartres." *Mém. de l'Acad. des Insc.* XXXI. (2). 1884.

—— Les Propos de Maître Robert de Sorbon. *Mém. de l'Acad. des Insc.* XXXI. (2). 1884.

—— *See* John of Garland.

HENRI D'ANDELI. *Œuvres*, ed. A. Héron. Rouen. 1881.
See Paetow, *infra*.

HERRAD VON LANDSBERG. *Hortus Deliciarum.* [Facsimile with explanatory text.] La Société pour la préservation des monuments historiques d'Alsace. Strasburg. 1901.

JACQUES DE VITRY. *Exempla*, ed. T. F. Crane. London. 1890.

JOCELIN OF BRAKELOND. *Cronica*, ed. J. G. Rokewode. Camden Society, 13. London. 1840.

JOHN OF GARLAND. *Poetria magistri Johannis Anglici de arte prosaica.* Mari, G., *Romanische Forschungen*, XIII. Erlangen. 1902.

—— *Morale Scholarium*, ed. with introduction by L. J. Paetow. *Memoirs of the Univ. of California*, IV. (2). Berkeley. 1927.

—— Hauréau, J. B. "Notice sur les œuvres authentiques ou supposés de Jean de Garlande." *Notices et Extraits*, XXVII. (2). Paris. 1879.

JOHN OF SALISBURY. *Policraticus*, ed. C. C. J. Webb. Oxford. 1909.

—— *Metalogicon*, ed. C. C. J. Webb. Oxford. 1929.

—— *Historia Pontificalis*, ed. R. L. Poole. Oxford. 1927.

—— *Opera* (including *Epistolae*). Migne, *P.L.* 199.

—— Poole, R. L. *The Early Correspondence of John of Salisbury.* Proceedings of the British Academy, XI. London. 1924.

—— Poole, R. L. "John of Salisbury at the Papal Court." *E.H.R.* XXXVIII. 1923.

—— Webb, C. C. J. "The Policraticus of John of Salisbury." *Church Quarterly Review*, 71. London. 1910.

—— Webb, C. C. J. "John of Salisbury." *Proceedings of the Aristotelian Society*, II. London. 1893.

—— Waddell, H. "John of Salisbury." *Essays and Studies . . . of the English Association*, XIII. Oxford. 1928.

—— Webb, C. C. J. *John of Salisbury.* London. 1932.

—— Demimuid, M. *Jean de Salisbury.* Paris. 1873.

—— Schaarschmidt, C. *Johannes Saresberiensis nach Leben und Studien, Schriften und Philosophie.* Leipsig. 1862.

LANGLOIS, C. V. "Formulaires des lettres du XIIe, XIIIe, et XIVe siècle." *Notices et Extraits*, XXXIV, XXXV.

—— "Maître Bernard." *Bibliothèque de l'École des Chartres*, 54. Paris. 1893.

LECOY DE LA MARCHE. *La chaire française au moyen âge.* Paris. 1886.

MANDONNET, P. F. *Siger de Brabant et l'averroisme latin au* XIIIe *siècle.* 2nd ed. Louvain. 1911.

MAP, WALTER. *Latin Poems attributed to Walter Mapes*, ed. T. Wright. Camden Society, XVI. London. 1850.

MAP, WALTER. *De Nugis Curialium*, ed. M. R. James. Oxford. 1914.

MATTHEW PARIS. *Chronica Maiora*, ed. H. R. Luard. 7 vols. Rolls Series. London. 1872-80.

OTTO VON FREISINGEN. *Gesta Frederici I*, ed. G. Waitz. 3rd ed. *Script. Rer. Germ.* Hanover and Leipsig. 1912.

—— *Chronica sive Historia de duabus civitatibus*, ed. A. Hofmeister. *Script. Rer. Germ.* 19c2.

PAETOW, L. J. *The Arts Course at Medieval Universities.* University of Illinois Studies, III. Urbana. 1910.

—— *The Battle of the Seven Arts* (text and translation). Memoirs of the Univ. of California, IV. (1). Berkeley. 1914.
See John of Garland *supra*.

PETER OF BLOIS. *Epistolae.* Migne, *P.L.* 207. Paris. 1855.

—— Cohn, E. S. "The MS. Evidence for the Letters of Peter of Blois." *E.H.R.* 41. 1926.

PETER THE VENERABLE. *Epistolae.* Migne, *P.L.* 189. Paris. 1854.

—— Demimuid, M. *Pierre le Vénérable.* 2nd ed. Paris. 1895.

PONCE DE PROVENCE. *Summa de Dictamine.* B.N. MS. Lat. 8653.

POOLE, R. L. "The Masters of the Schools at Paris and Chartres." *E.H.R.* 35. London. 1920.

—— *Lectures on the History of the Papal Chancery to the time of Innocent III.* Cambridge. 1915.

RAND, E. K. "The Classics in the Thirteenth Century." *Speculum.* 1929.

RASHDALL, H. *The Universities of Europe in the Middle Ages.* 3 vols. Oxford. 1925.

ROBERT, M. G. *Les Écoles et l'enseignement de la théologie pendant la première moitié du* XIIe *siècle.* Paris. 1909.

ROCKINGER. *Briefsteller und Formelbücher* [with texts]. *Quellen zur bayerischen und deutschen Geschichte.* Munich. 1863.

SALIMBENE. *Cronica*, ed. O. Holder-Egger. *M.G.H. SS.* XXXII. Hanover. 1905-13.

SANDYS, J. "English Scholars in Paris." *Camb. Hist. of Lit.* I. 1907.

SERLON OF WILTON. *See* Chaps. VII.-IX. *infra.*

STUBBS, W. *Learning and Literature in England under Henry II.* in *Seventeen Lectures.* 3rd ed. Oxford. 1900.

THUROT, C. "Notices et extraits des divers MSS. latins pour servir à l'histoire des doctrines grammaticales au moyen âge." *Notices et Extraits*, XXII. (2). Paris. 1868.

WATTENBACH, W. *Der poetische Briefsteller des Matthaeus von Vendôme. Sitzungsberichte . . . München . . . phil.-phil. Klasse.* Munich. 1872.

—— "Über Briefsteller des Mittelalters." *Archiv. für Kunde österreichischer Geschichts-Quellen*, XIV. Vienna. 1855.

BIBLIOGRAPHY

CHAPTERS VII, VIII, AND IX

THE ARCH POET : THE *Ordo Vagorum* : THE SCHOLAR'S LYRIC

ABELARD. *Vide supra*, Chapter VI.

ALAIN DE LILLE (Alanus de Insulis). *Anticlaudianus : De Contemptu Naturae*, ed. T. Wright. *Anglo-Norman Satirical Poets of the Twelfth Century*. 2 vols. London. 1872.

—— Hauréau, J. B. " Mémoires sur la vie et quelques œuvres d'Alain de Lille." *Mém. de l'Acad. des Insc.* XXXII. (1). Paris. 1886.

ALLEN, P. S. " Medieval Lyrics." *Modern Philology*. Chicago. 1908-9.

See under General *supra*.

ANDREAS CAPELLANUS. *De Amore*, ed. E. Trojel. Hauniae. 1892.

ARCHIPOETA. *Die Gedichte des Archipoeta*, ed. M. Manitius. Munich. 1913. 2nd ed. 1929.

—— *Die Gedichte des Archipoeta* (transl. and notes). B. Schmeidler. Leipsig. 1911.

—— Grimm, J. *Gedichte des Mittelalters auf König Friedrich den Staufer*. 1844. Reprinted in *Kleinere Schriften*, III. Berlin. 1866.

—— Brinkmann, H. " Die Dichterpersönlichkeit des Archipoeta." *G.R.M.* XIII. Heidelberg. 1925.

—— Strecker, K. " Die zweite Beichte des Archipoeta." *Mittelalterliche Handschriften*. 1926. (*Festschrift Degering.*) Leipsig. 1926.

ARUNDEL MS. *See* Meyer, W.

BARBAZON ET NÉON. *Fabliaux et contes des poètes français des* XI, XII, XIII, XIV *et* XV *siècles*. 4 vols. Paris. 1808.

BAUDOUIN, A. *Lettres inédites de Philippe le Bel*. Paris. 1887.

BÉDIER, J. *Les Fabliaux : études de littérature populaire et d'histoire littéraire du moyen âge*. 4th ed. Paris. 1925.

BERNARD OF MORLAS. *De contemptu mundi*, ed. H. C. Hoskier. London. 1929.

BEUGNOT, A. *Les " Olim " : Registre des arrêts par la Cour du Roi, sous les règnes de St. Louis . . . et de Philippe le Long*. 4 vols. Paris. 1839.

BOCCACCIO. *Il Decamerone*, I. 7 [on Primas of Orleans].

BÖMER, A. " Eine Vagantenlieder Sammlung des 14 Jahrhunderts " [Herdringer]. *Z.F.D.A.* XLIX. 8.

BRINKMANN, H. " Das Vagantenlied von Phyllis und Flora." *Z.F.D.A.* LVI. 1919.

—— " Die *Metamorphosis Goliae* und das Streitgedicht Phyllis und Flora." *Z.F.D.A.* LXII. 1925.

—— " Die Goliarden." *G.R.M.* XII. 1924.

—— *Die Entstehungsgeschichte des Minnesangs*. Halle. 1926.

CARMINA BURANA. *Carmina Burana : lateinische und deutsche Lieder und Gedichte einer Handschrift des* XIII *Jahrhunderts aus Benedictbeuern*, ed. J. A. Schmeller. Stuttgart. 1847.

*CARMINA BURANA. *Mit Benutzung der Vorarbeiten Wilhelm Meyers Kritisch herausgegeben von Alfons Hilka und Otto Schumann.* [General introduction: critical text, with commentary, of the first 55 poems: remainder in progress.] 2 vols. Heidelberg. 1930.

—— Strecker, K. Über Hilka und Schumann *Carmina Burana*, I. *Z.F.D.A.* 1931.

—— Meyer, W. *Fragmenta Burana.* Festschrift der Kgl. Gesellsch. der Wissensch. zu Göttingen. Abhandlungen philo-hist. Klasse. Göttingen. 1901.

—— Meyer, W. *Die erste Gedicht der Carmina Burana.* Göttingen. 1908.

—— Schumann, O. " Die deutschen Strophen der Carmina Burana." *G.R.M.* XIV. Heidelberg. 1926.

—— Schumann, O. " Über enige Carmina Burana." *Z.F.D.A.* LXIII. 1926.

—— Herkenrath, E. " Tempus instat floridum." *Neophilologus.* Groningen. 1930.

—— Luers, F. *Die deutsche Lieder der Carmina Burana.* Bonn. 1922.

—— Lundius, B. " Deutsche Vagantenlieder in den Carmina Burana." *Zeitschrift für deutsche Philologie*, 39. Halle. 1907.

—— Schreiber, J. *Die Vagantenstrophe der mittellateinischen Dichtung und das Verhältnis derselben zu mittelhochdeutschen Strophenformen. Ein Beitrag zur Carmina Burana Frage.* Strasburg. 1894.

—— Wustmann, R. " Zum Text der Carmina Burana." *Z.F.D.A.* 35. 1891.

—— Patsig, H. " Zur Handschrift und zum Text der Carmina Burana." *Z.F.D.A.* 36. 1892.

CRESCINI, V. " Appunti sur l'etimologia di Goliardo." *Atti del Reale Instituto Veneto.* Venice. 1920.

DELISLE, L. V. *Le Poète Primat.* Paris. 1870. (Extract from *Bibliothèque de l'École des Chartes*, XXX.)

—— *Notice sur quelques MSS. de la Bibliothèque de Tours* [also on Primas of Orleans]. Paris. 1868. (*Bib. de l'École des Chartes*, XXIX.) *See* Meyer, W., *infra.*

*DOBIACHE-ROJDESVENSKY, O. *Les Poésies des Goliardes.* Paris. 1931.

ERMINI, G. " Il Golia dei Goliardi." *La Cultura.* Rome. 1922.

FARAL, É. *Les Jongleurs en France au moyen âge.* [Appendix I: " Golias."] Paris. 1910.

—— *Mimes françaises du* XIIIe *siècle.* Paris. 1910.

—— *Recherches sur les sources latines des contes et romans courtois du moyen âge.* Paris. 1913.

FRANTZEN, J. J. A. " Zur Vagantendichtung." *Neophilologus*, V. Groningen. 1920.

GARNIER DE PONT-SAINTE-MAXENCE. *La vie de S. Thomas Martyr*, ed E. Étienne. Paris. 1883.

—— ed. E. Walberg. Lund. 1922.

BIBLIOGRAPHY

GAUTIER DE CHATILLON. *Die Lieder Walthers von Chatillon in der Handschrift* 351 *von St. Omer*. ed. K. Strecker. Berlin. 1925.

—— *Moralisch-satirische Gedichte Walthers von Chatillon aus deutschen, englischen, französischen und italienischen Handschriften*, ed. K. Strecker. Heidelberg. 1929.

—— Strecker, K. " Walther von Chatillon der Dichter des Lieder von S. Omer." *Z.F.D.A.* LXI. 1924.

—— Strecker, K. " Walther von Chatillon und seine Schule." *Z.F.D.A.* LXIV. 1927.

—— Müldener, W. *Die zehn Gedichte des Walther von Lille*. Hanover. 1859.

—— Novati, F. " L' ultima poesia di Gualterio di Chatillon." *Romania*, XVIII. Paris. 1889.

—— Hauréau, J. B. " Notice sur un MS. de la reine Christine . . . Vatican." *Notices et Extraits*, XXIX. (2). 1880.

GENESTAL, R. *Le Privilegium Fori . . . See under* General *supra*.

GIESEBRECHT, W. *Die Vaganten oder Goliardi. Allgemeine Monatschrift für Wissenschaft und Litteratur*. Halle. 1853.

HANFORD, J. H. " The Progenitors of Golias." *Speculum*. 1926.

HASKINS, C. H. " Latin literature under Frederick II." *Speculum*. 1928. Reprinted in *Studies in Medieval Culture*.

HÄSSNER, M. *Die Goliarden Dichtung und die Satire im* 13 *Jahrhundert in England*. Leipsig. 1905.

HAURÉAU, J. B. *Notice sur un MS. de le reine Christine à la Bibliothèque du Vatican. Notices et Extraits*, XXIX. (2). 1880.

—— *Les œuvres de Hugues de S. Victor : essai critique*. Paris. 1886.

—— " Poésies latines du MS. Add. 44 de la Bodléienne." *Bibliothèque de l'École des Chartes*, XLVII. Paris. 1886.

HELINAND, MONK OF FROIDMONT. *Opera*. Migne, *P.L.* 212.
See Walberg and Wulf. *Vers de la Mort, infra*.

HILARIUS. *Versus et Ludi*, ed. J. J. Champollion-Figeac. Paris. 1838.

—— *Versus et Ludi : edited from the Paris MS. :* J. B. Fuller. New York. 1929.

HILKA, A. " Eine mittellateinische Dichterfehde: Versus Michaelis Cornubiensis contra Henricum Abringensum." *Mittelalterliche Handschrift* (*Festschrift Degering*). Leipsig. 1926.
See Carmina Burana *supra*.

HÖFER, A. *Die Reiserechnungen der Bischop Wolfger von Passau. Beiträge zur Geschichte der deutschen Sprache und Litteratur*, XVII. Halle. 1893.
See Zingerle *infra*.

HUBATSCH, O. *Die lateinische Vagantenlieder des Mittelalters*. Görlitz. 1870.

INNOCENT IV. *Apparatus super Decretalium v. libris*. Lyons. 1525.

JAFFÉ, S. *Die Vaganten und ihre Lieder*. Berlin. 1908.

JEANROY, A. *Les origines de la poésie lyrique en France au moyen âge* 3rd ed. Paris. 1925.

JEANROY, A., and LANGFORS. *Chansons satiriques et bacchiques du* XIIIe *siècle.* Paris. 1921.

JUBINAL, M. L. A. *Jongleurs et trouvères.* Paris. 1835.

—— *Nouveau recueil des contes, dits, fabliaux* . . . 2 vols. Paris. 1839-42.

LANGLOIS, C. V. *La vie en France au moyen âge de la fin du* XIIe *au milieu du* XIVe *siècle.* Paris. 1924.

—— " La littérature goliardique." *Revue bleue,* L, LI. Paris. 1892-3.

LANGLOIS, ERNEST. *Les origines et sources du Roman de la Rose.* Paris. 1891.

—— *Le Roman de la Rose d'après les MSS.* (*Anciens Textes français.*) 5 vols. Paris. 1914-20.

LAPÔTRE, A. " Le Souper de Jean Diacre " [*Cena Cypriani*]. *Mélanges d'Archéologie et d'Histoire de l'école française de Rome.* 1901.

LEHMANN, P. *Die Parodie im Mittelalter.* Munich. 1922.

—— *Parodistische Texte : Beispiele zur lateinischen Parodie im Mittelalter.* Munich. 1923.

LUCHAIRE, A. *La Société française au temps de Philippe Auguste.* Paris. 1909.

LUDWIG, F. *Repertorium organorum recentioris et motetorum vetustissimi stili.* Halle. 1910.

LUERS, F. *See* Carmina Burana *supra.*

MANITIUS, M. and ÜLICH, R. *Vagantenlieder.* [Text by Manitius.] Jena. 1927.
See Archpoet *supra.*

MANLY, J. M. " The *Familia Goliae.*" *Modern Philology.* Chicago. 1907.

MAP, WALTER. *Latin Poems attributed to Walter Mapes,* ed. T. Wright. London. 1850.

MÉON, D. *Nouveau recueil de fabliaux et contes inédits* . . . Paris. 1823.

MEYER, KUNO. *The Vision of MacConglinne.* London. 1892.

MEYER, R. M. " Alte deutsche Volksliedchen." *Z.F.D.A.* XXIX. Berlin. 1885.

MEYER, WILHELM. *Die Arundel Sammlung mittellateinischer Lieder.* (*Abhandlungen der Kgl. Akad. der Wiss. zu Göttingen. Phil.-hist. Klasse,* XI. (2).) Göttingen. 1909.

—— *Zu dem Tiresias-Gedicht des Primas.* Göttingen. 1907.

—— *Die Oxforder Gedichte des Primas, Magister Hugo von Orleans.* 2 vols. Göttingen. 1907.

—— *Die moderne Leda : ein lateinische Gedicht des* 12 *Jahrhunderts.* Leipsig. 1908.

—— *Das Liebesconcil im Remiremont.* Göttingen. 1914.

—— *Quondum fuit factus festus : ein Gedicht in Spot latein.* Göttingen. 1908.

—— *Zwei Gedichte zur Geschichte des Cistercienser Ordens.* Göttingen Nachrichten. 1908.

MONTAIGLON-REYNAUD. *Recueil général des fabliaux des* XIIIe *et* XIVe *siècles.* 6 vols. Paris. 1872-90.

MOZLEY, J. H. *See* Wireker, Nigel, *infra*.

NERI, F. "La Famiglia di Golia." *Atti della Reale Accademia delle Scienze di Torino*, L. Turin. 1914-15.

NICHOLAS DE BIBERA. *Carmen satiricum*, ed. Fischer. *Geschichts-Quellen der Provinz Sachsen*. 1870.

NIEDHART VON REUENTHAL. *Lieder*, ed. F. Keinz. Leipsig. 1910.

NOVATI, F. "La Parodia sacra nella Letteratura moderna." *Studi critici e letterari*. Turin. 1889.

—— *Carmina medii aevi*. Florence. 1883.

Pamphilus. De Amore, ed. A. Baudouin. Paris. 1874.

—— *Una commedia latina di siglo* XII, ed. Bonilla y San Martin. Madrid. 1917.

PHILIPPE DE GRÈVE. *Dicta magistri Philippi* (*Egerton MS*. 274), ed. P. Meyer. *Documents MSS. de l'ancienne littérature de France conservée dans les Bibliothèques de Grande Bretagne*. Paris. 1871.

—— Meyer, P. "Henri d'Andeli et le Chancelier Philippe." *Romania*, I. Paris. 1872.

—— Hauréau, J. B. *Notices et Extraits*, XXI. (2), pp. 183-194.

—— Salimbene de Adam. *Chronica*, pp. 182-3, 442-4, ed. Holder-Egger. *M.G.H. SS*. XXXII.

PRIMAS, HUGH OF ORLEANS. *See* Meyer, W.; Delisle, L. V.; Hanford, J. H.; Hauréau, J. B.

REIMAR DER ALTE. *Lieder*, ed. C. v. Kraus. (*Abhandlungen bay. Akad. Phil. philol.-hist. Klasse*. XXX.) Munich. 1919.

—— Burdach, K. *Reinmar der Alte und Walther von der Vogelweide*. Leipsig. 1880.

RICHARD DE BURY. *Philobiblon*, ed. E. C. Thomas. London. 1888.

ROGER, J. E. T. *Oxford City Documents*, 1268-1665. Oxford. 1891.

RUSSELL, J. C. "Master Henry of Avranches." *Speculum*, III. 1928. *See* Hilka, A.

SALIMBENE. *Cronica* [on Primas and Philippe de Grève]. *M.G.H. Script*. 32.

SCHUMANN, O. *See* Carmina Burana *supra*.

SCHREIBER, J. *See* Carmina Burana *supra*.

SEDGWICK, W. B. "The Textual Criticism of Medieval Latin Poets." *Speculum*, V. 1930.

SERLON OF WILTON. Meyer, Paul. *Versus magistri Serlonis*. (MS. Digby, Bodl. 53.) *Documents MSS. . . . Grande Bretagne*. Paris. 1871.

—— Hauréau, J. B. Notice on B.N. MS. 6765 in *Notices et Extraits*, I. 302-324 ff. Paris. 1890.

—— Hauréau, J. B. "Un MS. de la reine Christine." *Notices et Extraits*, XXIX. (2), 234 ff. Paris. 1880.

SPANKE, H. "Klangspielerein im mittelalterliche Liede." *Studien zur lateinische Dichtung des Mittelalters*. Dresden. 1931.

SPIEGEL, N. *Die Vaganten und ihr Orden.* Spires. 1892.

—— *Die Grundlägen der Vagantenpoesie.* Würzburg. 1908.

STRACCALI, A. *I Goliardi.* Florence. 1880.

STRECKER, K. *Die Apokalypse des Golias.* (Texte zur Kulturgeschichte des Mittelalters," ed. F. Schneider.) Rome. 1928.

—— *See* Gautier de Chatillon *supra.*

—— " Kritisches zu mittellateinischen Dichtern." *Z.F.D.A.* LXIII. 1926.

SÜSSMILCH, H. *Die lateinische Vagantenpoesie der* 12 *und* 13 *Jahrhunderts.* Leipsig. 1917.

SYMONDS, J. A. *Wine, Women, and Song : medieval Latin student songs, now first translated into English verse.* London. 1884.

THOMPSON, J. W. " The Origin of the word *Goliardi.*" *Studies in Philology,* XX. Chapel Hill. 1923.

WAITZ, G. " *Concilium in Monte Romarici.*" *Z.F.D.A.* VII. Berlin. 1849.

WALBERG, E., and WULFF, F. *Vers de la Mort* [attributed to Helinand, *q.v.*]. *Anciens Textes français.* Paris. 1905.

WALTHER VON DER VOGELWEIDE. *Gedichte,* ed. E. K. Lachmann, revised by C. v. Kraus. 7th ed. Berlin. 1907.

WALTER OF CHATILLON. *See* Gautier de Chatillon *supra.*

WATTENBACH, W. " Die Anfänge lateinischer profaner Rythmen des Mittelalters." *Z.F.D.A.* 1872.

WERNER, J. " Handschrift C. 58/275 der Stadtbibliothek, Zürich." *Beiträge zur Kunde der lateinischen litteratur des Mittelalters.* Aarau. 1905.

—— " Poetische Versuche und Sammlungen eines Basler Klerikers aus dem Ende des 13 Jahrhunderts." *Göttingen Nachrichten.* 1908.

WIREKER, NIGELLUS. *Speculum Stultorum* in *Anglo-Latin Satirical Poets of the XIIth Century,* W. T. Wright. London. 1872.

—— Mozley, J. H. " On the Text and MSS. of the *Speculum Stultorum.*" *Speculum.* 1929-30.

—— Mozley, J. H. " The Unprinted Poems of Nigel Wireker." *Speculum.* 1932.

—— Mozley, J. H. " Nigel Wireker or Wetekre ? " *Modern Language Review.* xxvii. 1932.

WRIGHT, THOMAS. *Anecdota Literaria.* London. 1844.

—— *Anglo-Latin Satirical Poets of the Twelfth Century.* 2 vols. London. 1872.
See Sedgwick, W. B., *supra.*

—— *Reliquiae Antiquae.* London. 1841.

—— *Early Mysteries and other Latin Poems of the XIIth and XIIIth Centuries.* London. 1838.
See Map, Walter.

ZINGERLE, I. V. *Reiserechnungen Wolfgers von Ellenbrechts-Kirchen.* Heilbronn. 1877.

INDEX

INDEX